POWER

This is the story of
how we came to be.
Of what happened to us,
and to those we knew,
and loved, and fought.
Where it went right...
and where it went wrong.

Sixty years.

One-hundred and thirteen people,
born with the **power**.

The story of the
world we touched.
And all places where
the world touched us.

And the terror
and the beauty
and the death
that happened in
the spaces in-between

Our kind has never been seen before.
And when the last of us are gone,
will never be seen again.
Because there is a secret behind our creation,
and secrets like this only come around once.

Also available from Top Cow Productions & Image Comics:

Cyberforce: Assault with a Deadly Woman (ISBN: 1-887279-04-0)

Cyberforce: Tin Men of War (ISBN: 1-58240-190-x)

The Darkness Deluxe Collected Edition (ISBN: 1-58240-032-6)

The Darkness: Spear of Destiny (ISBN: 1-58240-147-0)

The Darkness: Heart of Darkness (ISBN: 1-58240-205-1)

Delicate Creatures (ISBN: 1-58240-225-6)

Kin: Descent of Man (ISBN: 1-58240-224-8)

Magdalena: Blood Divine (ISBN: 1-58240-215-9)

Medieval Spawn/Witchblade (ISBN: 1-887279-44-x)

Michael Turner's Fathom Hard Cover (ISBN: 1-58240-158-6)

Michael Turner's Fathom Hard Cover Limited Edition (ISBN: 1-58240-159-4)

Rising Stars: Born in Fire (ISBN: 1-58240-172-1)

Tomb Raider: Saga of the Medusa Mask (ISBN: 1-58240-164-0)

Tomb Raider: Mystic Artifacts (ISBN: 1-58240-202-7)

Witchblade: Origins (ISBN: 1-887279-65-2)

Witchblade: Revelations (ISBN: 1-58240-161-6)

Witchblade: Prevailing (ISBN: 1-58240-175-6)

Witchblade: Distinctions (ISBN: 1-58240-199-3)

Witchblade/Darkness: Family Ties (ISBN: 1-58240-030-x)

ISBN: 1-58240-226-4

Published by Image Comics®
RISING STARS: POWER, Vol. 2, 2002. FIRST PRINTING.
Office of Publication: 1071 North Batavia Street Suite A Orange, California 92867.
RISING STARS™ it's logo, all related characters and their likenesses are ™ & © 2002 J. Michael Straczynski
and Top Cow Productions Inc. ALL RIGHTS RESERVED. The entire contents of this book are © 2002 Top
Cow Productions Inc. Any similarities to persons living or dead is purely coincidental. With the exception of
artwork used for review purposes, none of the contents of this book may be reprinted in any form without
the express written consent of J. Michael Straczynski, Marc Silvestri or Top Cow Productions Inc.

PRINTED IN CANADA

To order by telephone call **1-888-TOPCOW1** (1-888-867-2691) or go to a comics shop near you.
To find the comics shop nearest you call **1-888-COMICBOOK** (1-888-266-4226)

What did you think of this book? We love to hear from our readers.
Please email us at: **risingstars@topcow.com.**

or write to us at:
RISING STARS c/o Top Cow Productions Inc.
10390 Santa Monica Blvd. Suite 110
Los Angeles, CA. 90025

for this edition
Book Design/Collected Editions Editor—Peter Steigerwald
Cover Art—Brent Anderson and John Starr
Cover Design—Peter Steigerwald
Managing Editor—Renae Geerlings
Editor In Chief—David Wohl
Editorial Assistants—Sina Grace and CJ Wilson
Production—Alvin Coats

for Top Cow Productions Inc.
Marc Silvestri—chief executive officer
Matt Hawkins—president / chief operating officer
David Wohl—president of creative affairs / editor in chief
Peter Steigerwald—vp of publishing and design / art director
Renae Geerlings—managing editor
Frank Mastromauro—director of sales and marketing
Alvin Coats—special projects coordinator

for Image Comics
Jim Valentino—publisher
Brent Braun—director of production

Rising Stars Created by: **J Michael Straczynski**

Written by: J Michael Straczynski

i   *Title*

iii   *Table of Contents/Credits*

p1   CHAPTER 1—*"Choices Made"*
Penciler: Christian Zanier *w/layouts by Ken Lashley*, Inker: Livesay *w/assists by Steve Nelson*, Colorist: Brett Evans.

p27   CHAPTER 2—*"Reversals of Fortune"*
Penciler: Christian Zanier *w/layouts by Ken Lashley*, Inker: Livesay,
Colorist: Brett Evans.

p51   CHAPTER 3—*"What Goes Around..."*
Penciler: Christian Zanier *w/layouts by Ken Lashley*,
Inker: Marlo Alquiza and Livesay,
Colorist: Avalon Studio's Matt Milla and Justin Ponsor.

p74   CHAPTER 4—*"A, B, C and D"*
Penciler: Christian Zanier *w/layouts by Ken Lashley*, Inker: Marlo Alquiza
and Alp Altiner, Colorist: Avalon Studio's Dan Kemp

p96   CHAPTER 5—*"Stalingrad"*
Penciler: Christian Zanier, Inker: Marlo Alquiza and Danny Miki,
Colorist: Avalon Studio's Dan Kemp.

p119   CHAPTER 6—*"Things Change"*
Penciler: Stuart Immonen, Inker: Marlo Alquiza,
Colorist: Avalon Studio's Dan Kemp with Peter Steigerwald.

p142   CHAPTER 7—*"Power"*
Penciler: Brent Anderson, Inker: Marlo Alquiza, Colorist: John Starr.

p165   CHAPTER 8—*"Selah"*
Penciler: Brent Anderson, Inker: Marlo Alquiza, Colorist: John Starr.

Lettered by: Dreamer Design's Robin Spehar and Dennis Heisler

Cover Plates———————————————————————

p1   Penciler: Christian Zanier, Inker: Livesay, Colorist: Matt Nelson.

p26   Penciler: Gary Frank, Inker: Livesay, Colorist: Matt Nelson.

p27   Penciler: Gary Frank, Inker: Livesay, Colorist: Peter Steigerwald.

p50   Penciler/Inker: Dave Gibbons, Colorist: Brett Evans.

p51   Penciler: Christian Zanier, Inker: Livesay, Colorist: Brett Evans.

p74   Penciler: Ken Lashley, Inker: Kevin Conrad, Colorist: Dan Kemp.

p96   Penciler: Christian Zanier, Inker: Marlo Alquiza, Colorist: Dan Kemp.

p119   Penciler: Stuart Immonen, Inker: Marlo Alquiza, Colorist: Dan Kemp.

p142   Penciler/Inker: Brent Anderson, Colorist: John Starr.

p165   Penciler/Inker: Brent Anderson, Colorist: John Starr.

p189   Penciler: Gary Frank, Inker: Jason Gorder, Colorist: Peter Steigerwald.

“Choices Made”

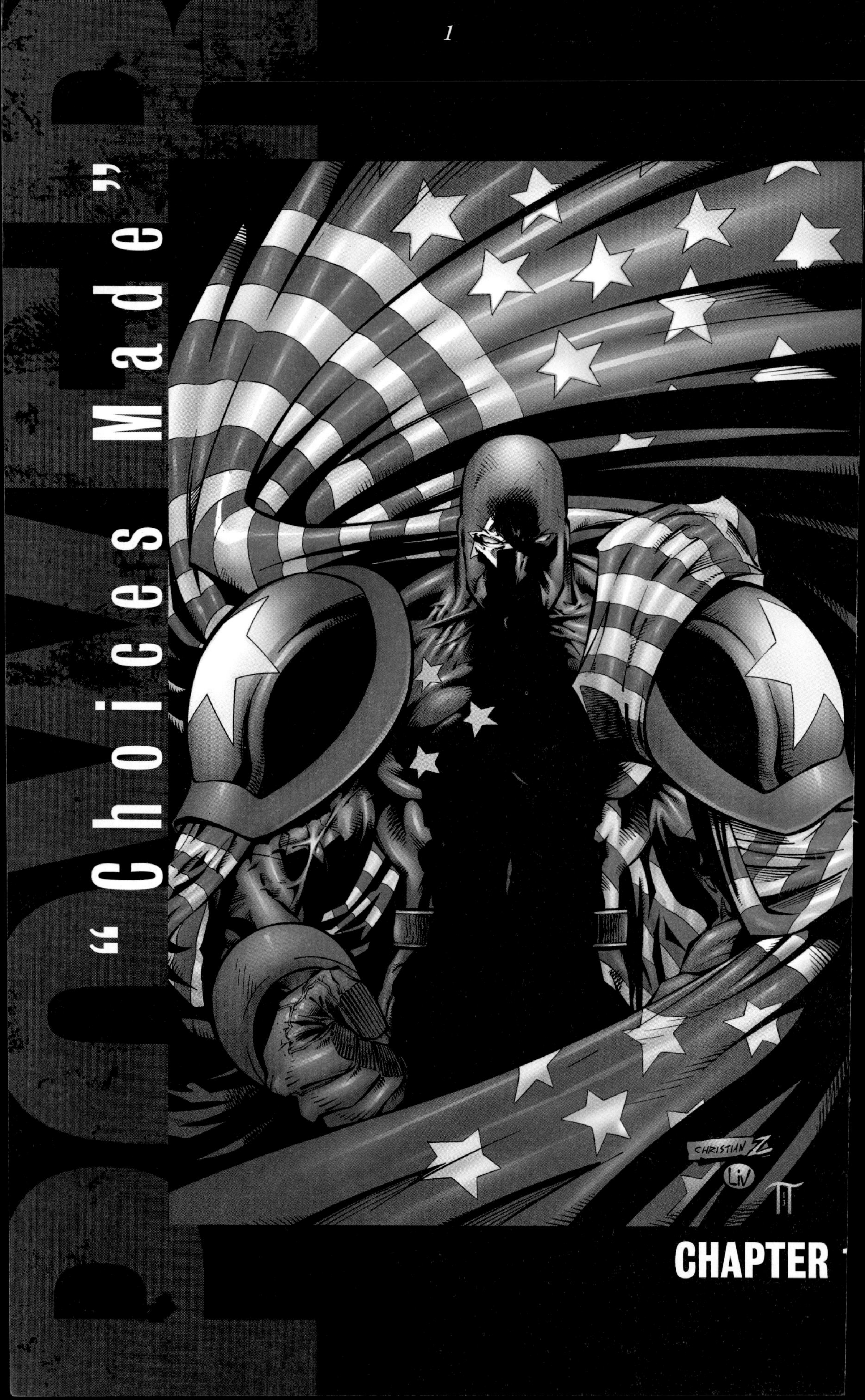
CHRISTIAN Z
LiV

CHAPTER

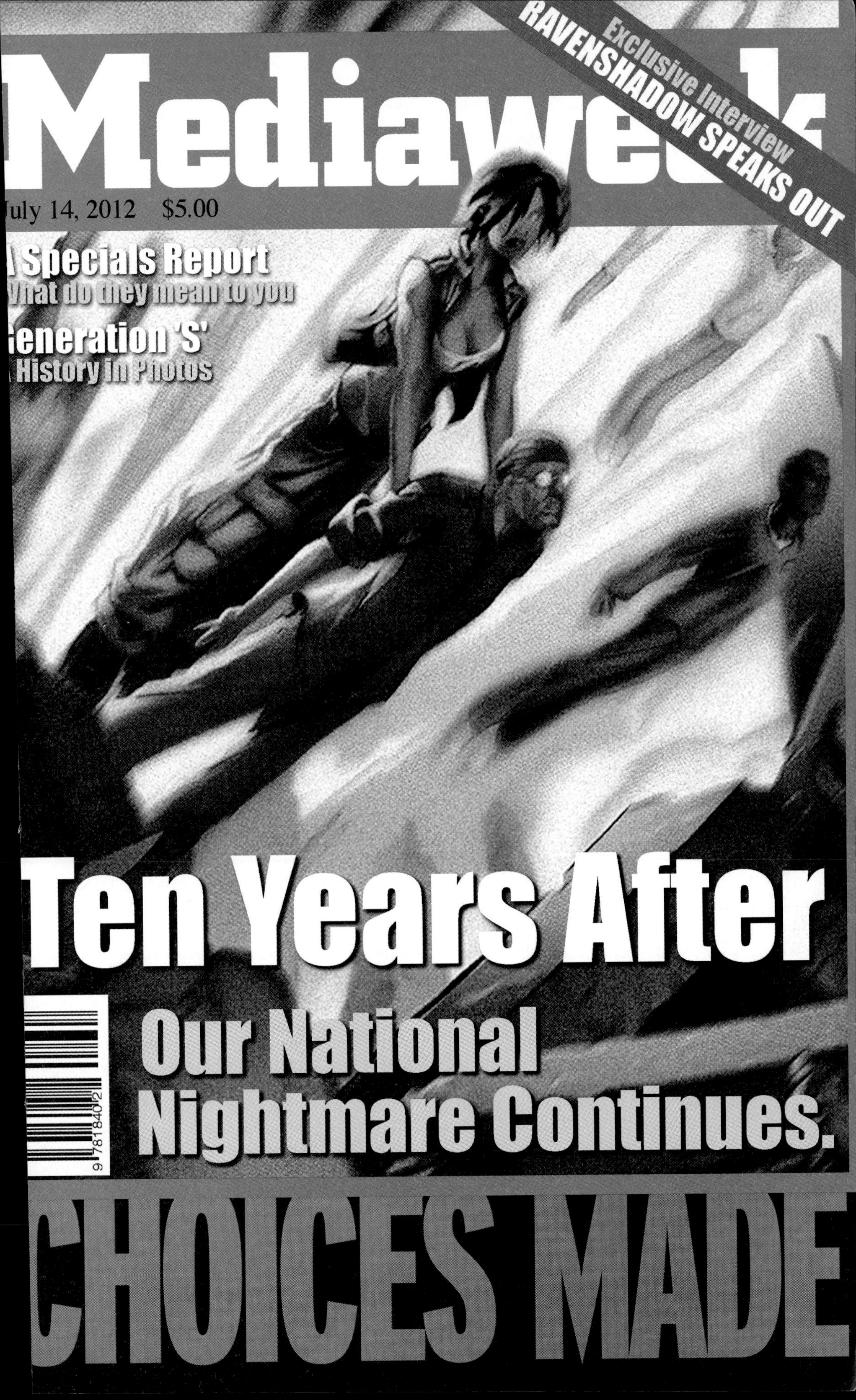

Mediaweek
Exclusive Interview
RAVENSHADOW SPEAKS OUT
uly 14, 2012 $5.00
Specials Report
hat do they mean to you
eneration 'S'
History in Photos
Ten Years After
Our National
Nightmare Continues.
CHOICES MADE

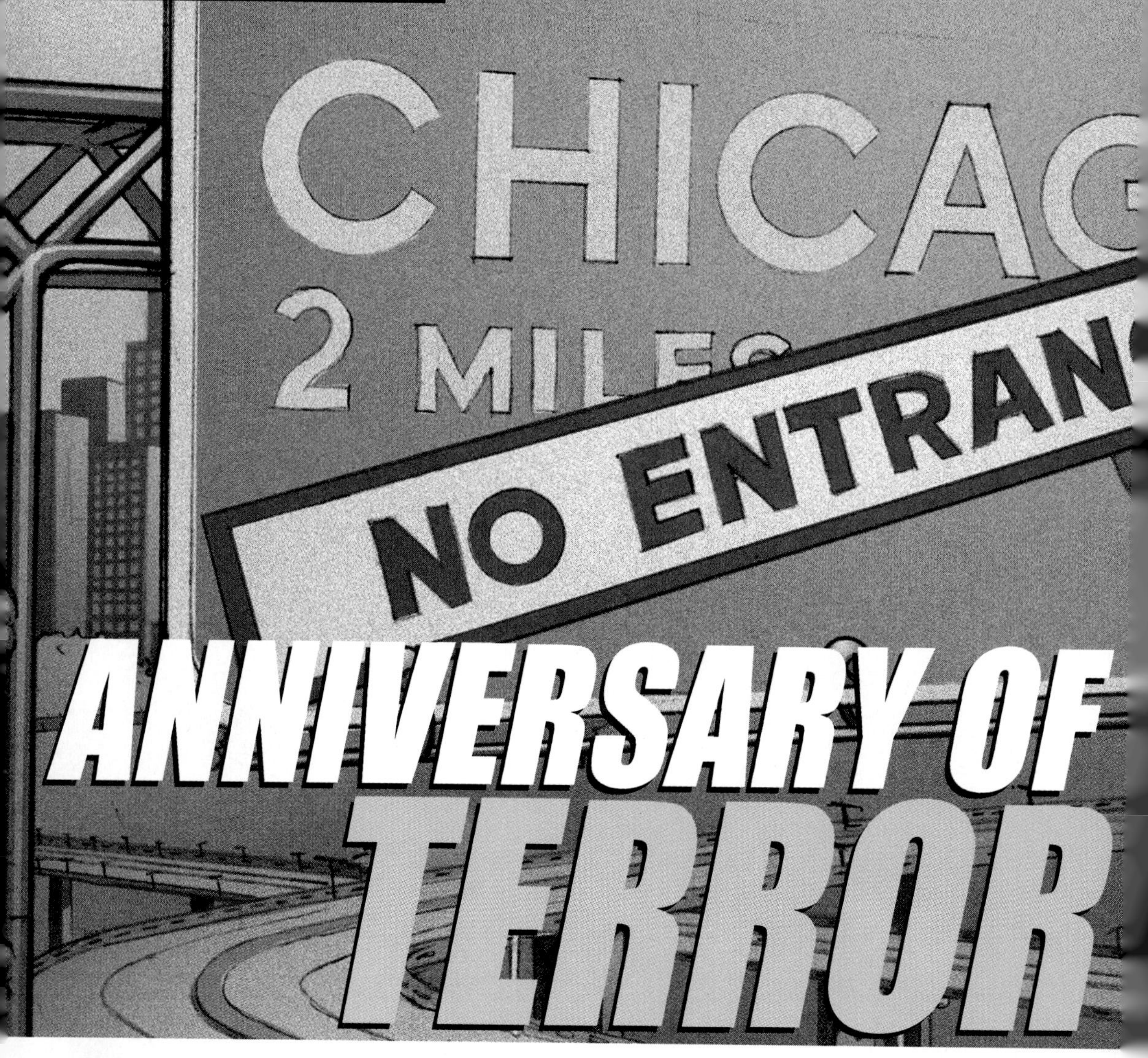
CHICAG
2 MIL
NO ENTRAN

ANNIVERSARY OF TERROR

IT'S A TYPICALLY HOT LAS VEGAS AFTERNOON. THE SLOT MACHINES IN Caesar's Palace are jammed with tourists jamming quarters into the machines with machine-like efficiency. Slightly after one p.m., Jerry Montrose (aka Pyre) steps out of a casino elevator and makes his way to the buffet. Heads turn and patrons gently nudging each other as he passes. Some are clearly pleased to see him, while others seem nervous. But the slot machines continue to be fed.

"I'd rather have him for us than against us," explained convention attendee Tyler Frontiere. It's a sentiment shared by many casino employees and visitors. "Starting ten years ago, things went a little nuts," commented casino floor manager Fred Casey. "It's dangerous out there. We needed protection. Jerry provided it."

Others, however, aren't so sure. "He scares me," said one hotel guest who declined to be identified. "If he loses his temper and decides to torch the place and everyone in it, who's going to stop him?"

It's an uneasy alliance shared by 23 other recreational and corporate locations that have hired Specials for protection after the events ten years ago that made a national concern into a worldwide problem.

"It's better than what happened in Chicago," a hotel employee commented. "I mean, we still got jobs, we still work, people still come around. I've got friends and relatives in Chicago, and I'm worried sick about them. Nobody's heard a word. Nobody goes in, nobody comes out. Who knows what's going on there with Maas in charge?"

Such questions require a look back before we can look forward to what the future might bring. ●

TEN YEARS AFTER THE fact, despite the best efforts of Special Prosecutor Hamilton Sinclair, two congressional hearings and a Senate investigation, contradictions continue to thwart any attempt to form a full understanding of the events that changed the American landscape forever.

Some events, however, are indisputable. It is known that concerns were raised by some members of the Senate that a group of Specials were allegedly planning to use their enhanced abilities to overthrow the Government. This, in turn, led to several closed Senate hearings, at which time still-sealed evidence and testimony were given to the Senate Judiciary Committee.

Following those hearings, a decision was made to invoke the Stanwick Powers Act, enacted when the existence of the Specials was detected, which authorized the Senate to locate, detain and question the Specials to determine which these charges could be substantiated.

What is less certain is the sequence of events that took place in the days and weeks after subpoenas and warrants were issued by the Senate.

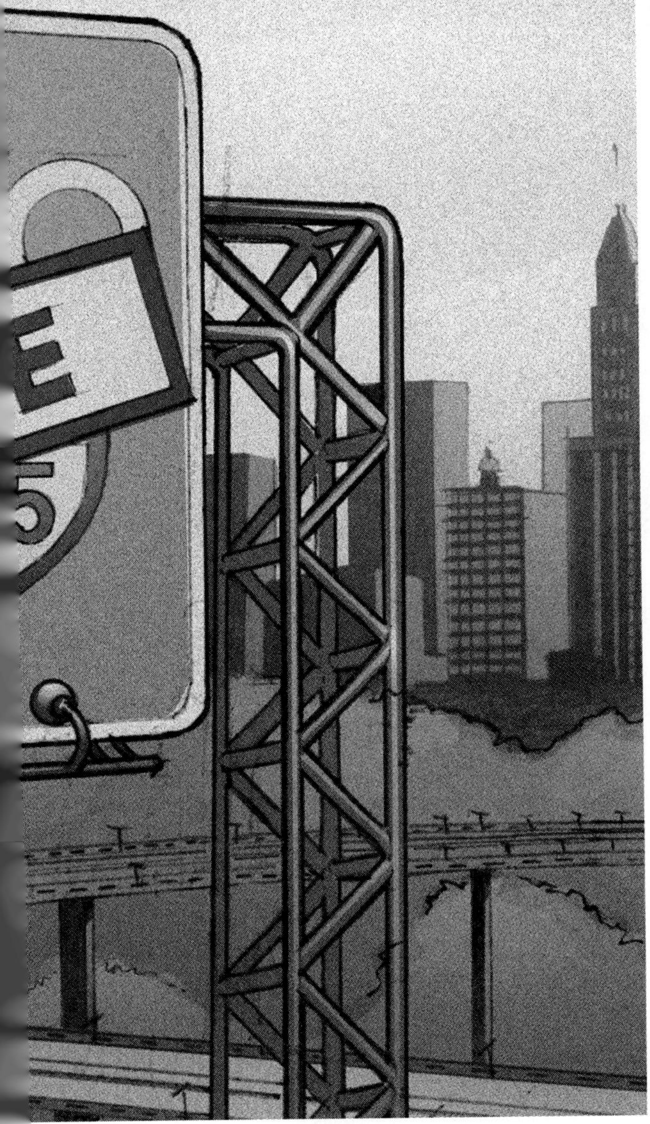

Chicago: *No one gets out, or in.*

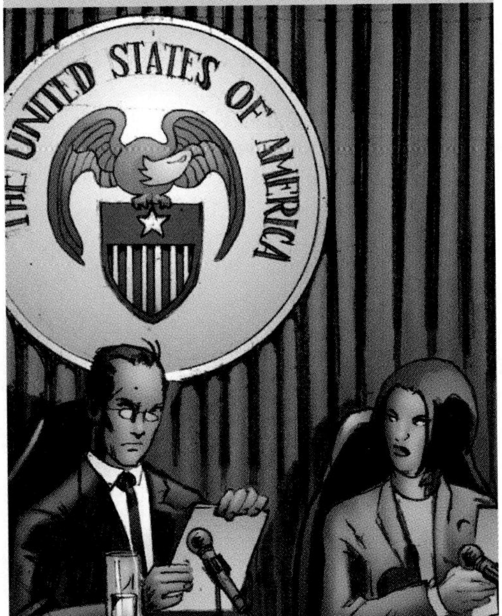
THE UNITED STATES OF AMERICA

The Senate Select Committee on Specials invokes the Stanwick powers Act.

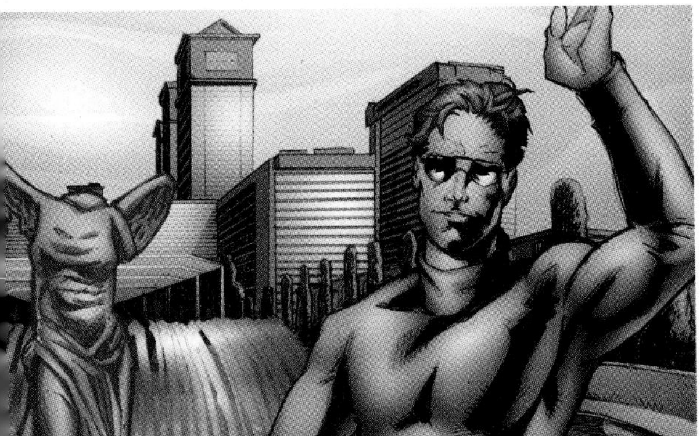

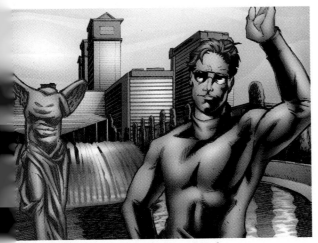

Jerry Montrose waves outside Caesar's Palace.

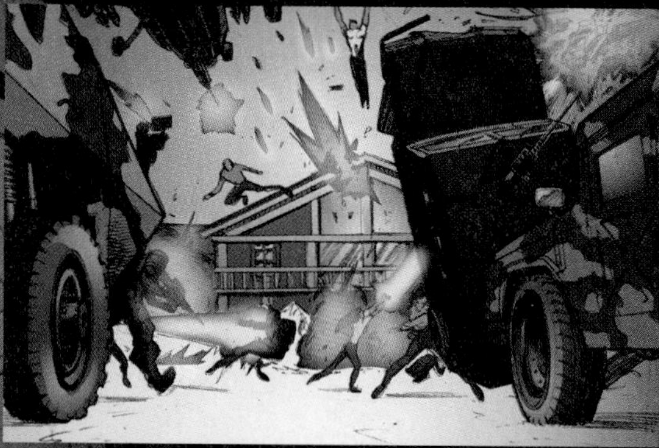

The raid on the Specials compound in Colorado. (UPI)

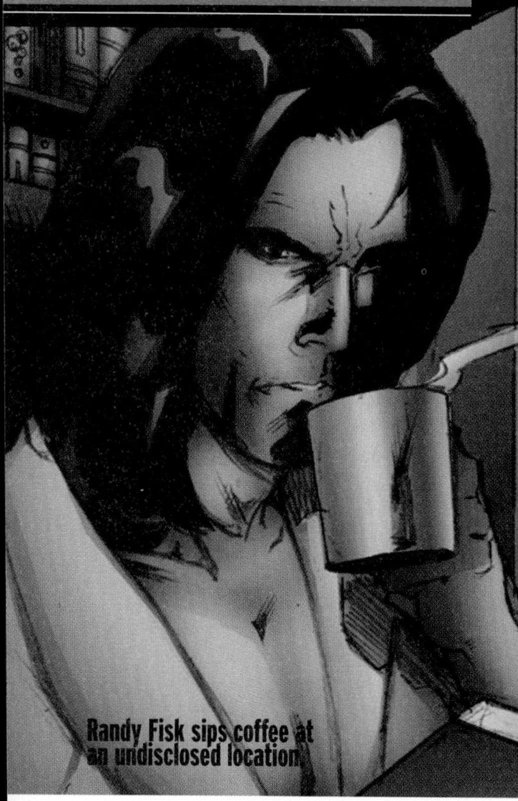

Randy Fisk sips coffee at an undisclosed location

"THEY CAME AFTER US GUNS BLAZING," said commercial artist and Special Randy Fisk, aka "Ravenshadow." Speaking on behalf of many of the Specials, Fisk agreed to an exclusive Mediaweek interview on the condition that his location not be revealed. "There was no negotiation, no warning, just heavily armed soldiers with tanks suddenly showing up at your door. It was Waco all over again. Given that several of us had recently been murdered, we had every right to protect ourselves."

"The charge that certain individuals associated with the government's actions were also responsible for the death of several of the Specials is hardly new," one anonymous source in the Senate Judiciary panel snapped back. "They've been making that claim for ten years and haven't produced a shred of proof. For all we know, some of them may have killed their own kind to provoke just this kind of situation. Remember, they're not human in the way we understand that word to mean. Seeing what they've done to the rest of the world since then, who knows what they're capable of doing to each other?"

In her first public comment on the subject in over a year, United States Attorney General Luanne Michaels told Mediaweek "There's no question that, in the attempt to detain these individuals for questioning, mistakes were made. On the other hand, it must be remembered that these were duly appointed officers of the court serving legally obtained warrants and subpoenas. They were met with resistance, and given the power of the opposition, had no choice but to defend themselves."

To the charge that infrared reconnaissance video footage of the raid on the Specials compound in Colorado shows armed soldiers firing on fleeing Specials — who despite their unique abilities were still civilians — Michaels responded, "The FBI computer labs have demonstrated repeatedly that the hot-spots in question are not gunshots, they are reflections of sunlight."

Another Justice source com-

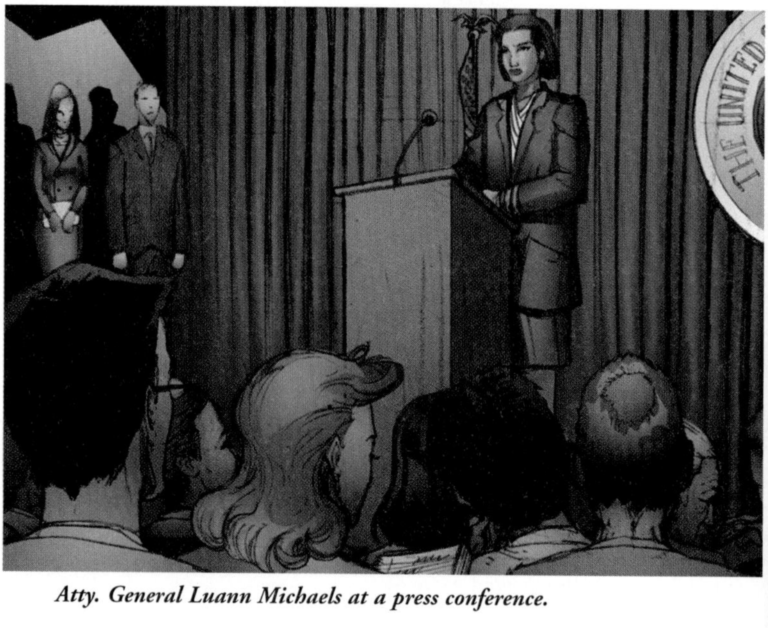
THE UNITED

Atty. General Luann Michaels at a press conference.

mented, "It's unfair to accuse us of over-reacting because we came armed with guns when these people are guns, walking, living weapons. It looks worse for us in the pictures, but the real danger was always on the other side."

While there's no question that a half dozen soldiers and a still-undetermined number of Specials were killed during the siege at their Colorado compound, the facts blur again when it comes to the details of the conflict.

"They [the Specials] always told us there were high powers and low powers and medium powers among them, but that day in Colorado we found out that was a lie," said a Justice Department source. "They were all high-powers. Which proves we were right to believe they were withholding information about the extent of their abilities. If they were conspiring in one area, then it makes it that much easier to believe they were conspiring in another."

But according to Randy Fisk, the situation is more complicated than the administration portrays. "Whenever one of us dies, his latent energy is transferred back to the rest of us as a group. The surge happened after a number of us died. At some point, the energy transfer hit critical mass.

The aftermath of the Colorado siege.

❚❚It's unfair to accuse us of over-reacting... these people are guns, walking, living weapons. ❚❚

— ATTY. GEN. MICHAELS

Suddenly we all found our abilities multiplied ten-fold, or several hundred fold, depending on where each of us was on the power scale when the surge hit."

Dismissed by the administration as improbable, some scientists, such as Dr. Lowell Francis of Harvard's High Technology Research Lab, have suggested that this scenario is possible. "Energy cannot be created or destroyed," Francis said told Mediaweek. "It can only be transformed from one state or condition to another. So yes, such a transfer of energy could theoretically take place among the Specials."

Because many scientists have taken opposing sides in this debate, it is doubtful that there will ever be any conclusive proof demonstrating that either there really was a so-called "surge" in power, or that the Specials were withholding information concerning the extent of their abilities may never be known.

What is certain is that the events of that day have had far reaching and enduring consequences for all Americans. ●

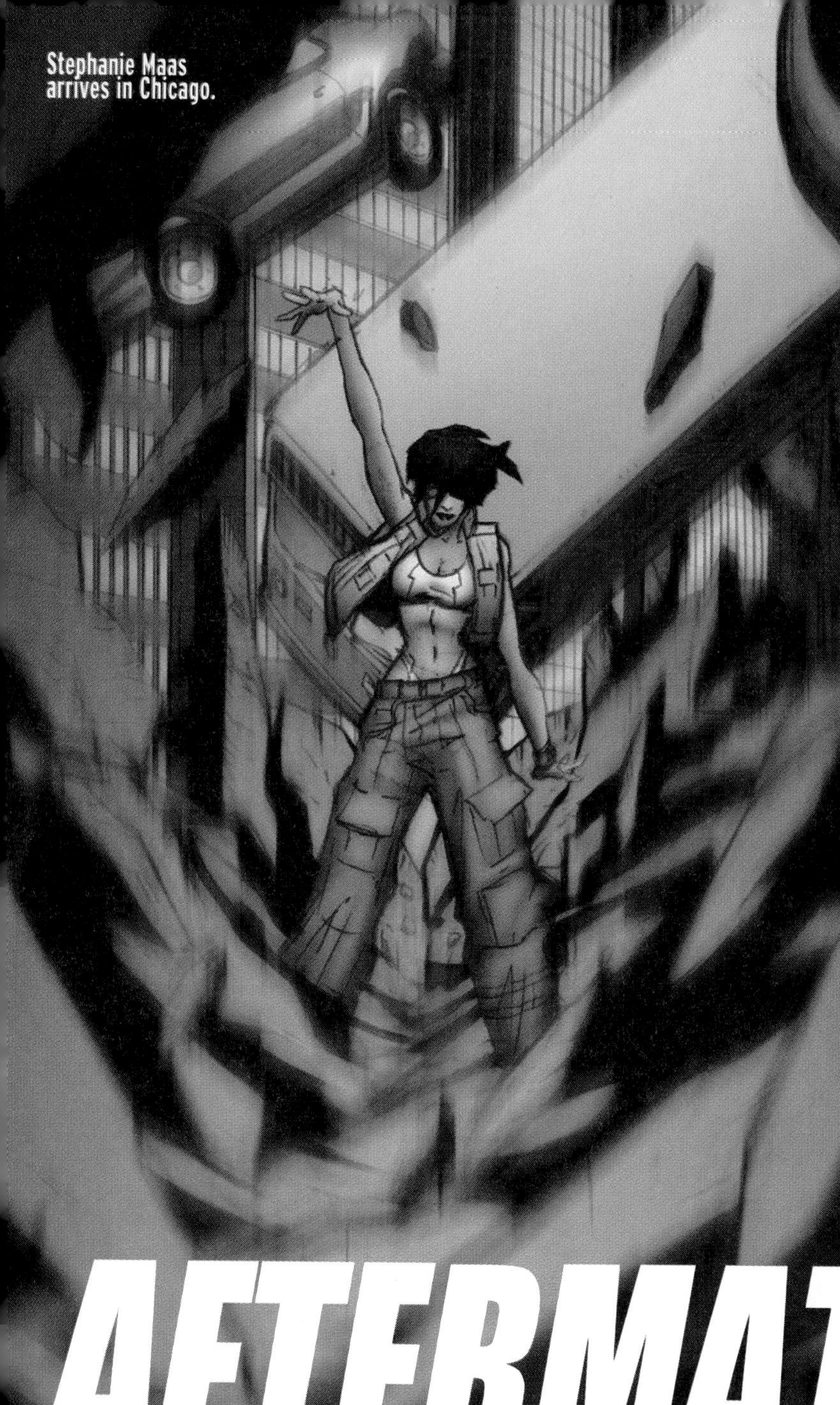

Stephanie Maas arrives in Chicago.

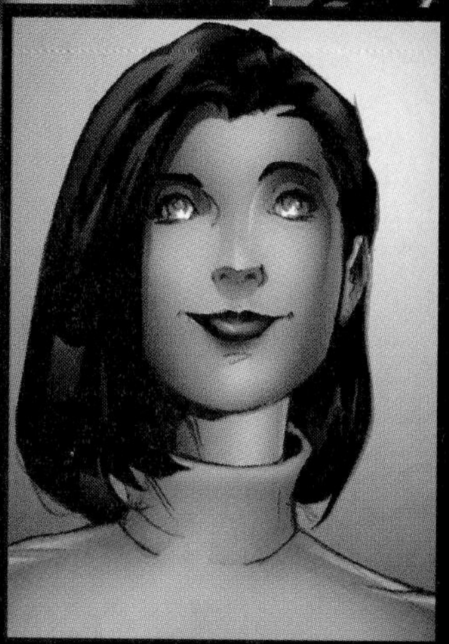

Before and After Photos of Stephanie Maas and Critical Maas.

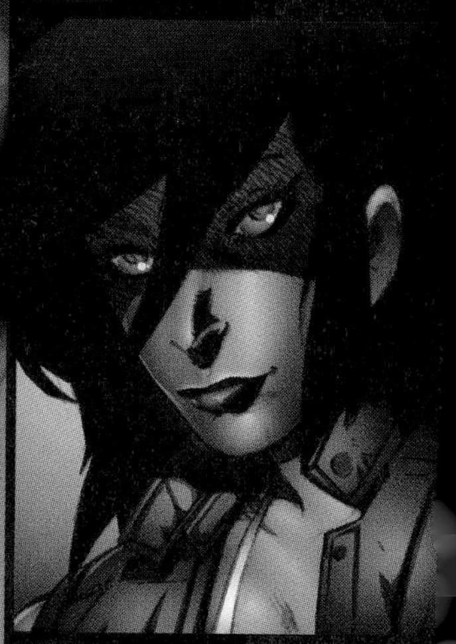

AFTERMATH

"I THINK IT WAS AROUND SUPPER TIME — six, maybe six-fifteen — when we saw this young woman come down out of the sky in the middle of the street," remembers Henry Ducet, an unemployed cab driver, previously of Chicago. "She stood there, looking around for a while, like she'd just moved in and was deciding where to put the furniture.

"NEXT THING WE KNEW, THERE WAS THIS BLUR, and the streets began to pull up all around us. Sidewalks, streets, concrete...it all just started coming down around us. Was she upset? Yeah, I'd say so."

MEDIAWEEK JULY 14, 2012

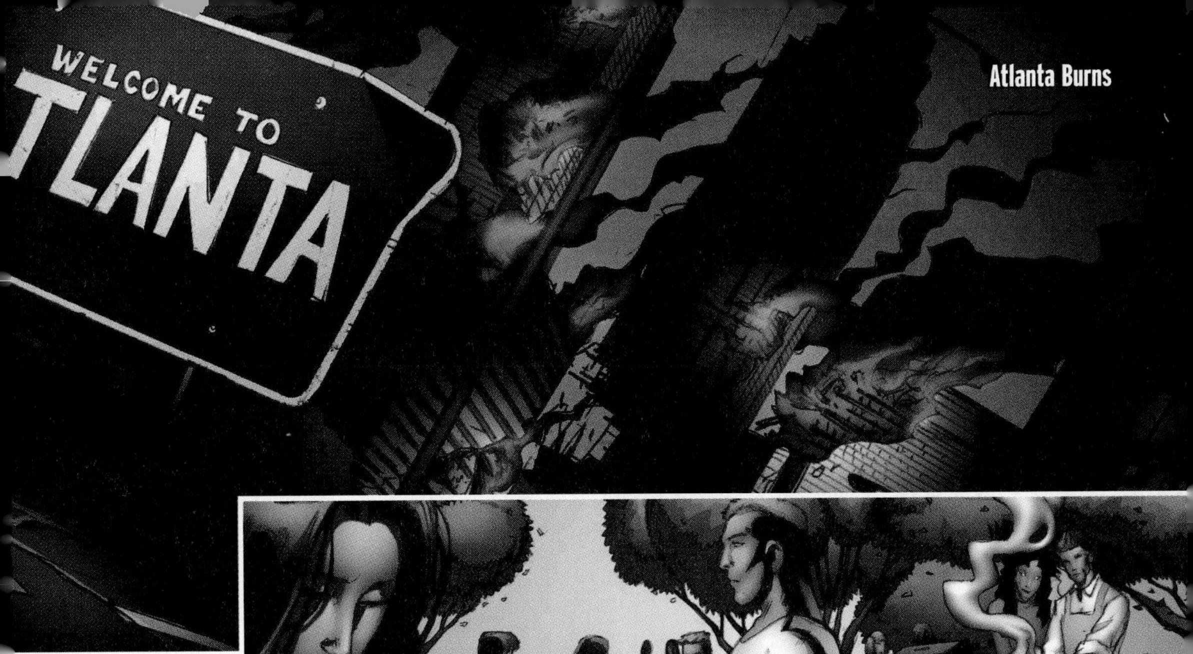
WELCOME TO
TLANTA

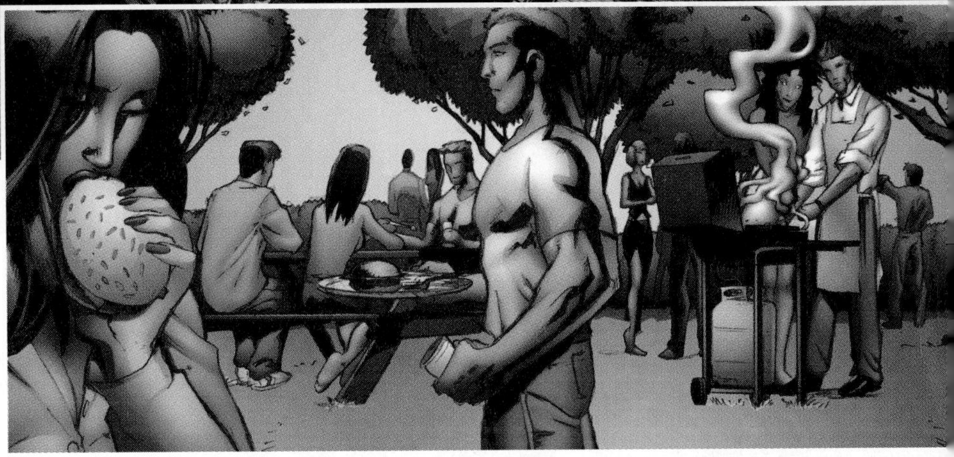

Specials gather for barbeque outside Griffith Park Observatory.

As is now generally known, the "young woman" in question was Stephanie Maas, aka Critical Maas, described by court psychiatrists as "emotionally disturbed and extremely dangerous, erratic and definitely pathological."

Maas declared that Chicago, located roughly one hour from the Specials' hometown of Pederson, Illinois, was her own private domain. Within an hour of her arrival, every major highway, bridge and roadway out of Chicago had been destroyed. The destruction of all local telephone and microwave transmission towers and cell phone repeaters guaranteed that no inside information would escape to the outside world.

From time to time, some have escaped Chicago on foot, carrying tales of destruction and excess, but none of them have ever been independently verified. Several attempts by military forces to take Chicago have met with swift and deadly reprisals.

Chicago was not the only city to be affected by the arrival of escaping Specials, though few suffered as severely.

According to the best data available to the administration (see sidebar), the highest concentration of Specials at present is in California. A dozen or so have taken up residence in and around Griffith Park and the Observatory, closing off the grounds to all "normals" under threat of retaliation. Democratic Mayor Julius Cohn has worked closely with the refugee Specials to guarantee their safety, and the safety of the community.

Over the last ten years, other Specials, alone or in smaller groups, have taken up residence or been sighted in San Francisco, Seattle, Austin, Denver, Tulsa, Boston and Portland, Oregon. New York remains clear of Specials due to the continued presence of Police Officer Matthew Bright, himself a Special. In several celebrated encounters with rogue Specials, Bright has continued to win a place in the hearts of even hardened New Yorkers.

"We're very glad to have him here," explained New York's newly elected Mayor Simon St. Claire. "We're pretty sure he's the only thing that's kept us from becoming another Atlanta."

The second burning of Atlanta took place only a few months after the Surge, when a dozen rogue Specials landed in Fulton County Stadium during the fourth game of the Braves/Dodgers World Series. The conflict that followed began when Atlanta police forces attempted to seize the Specials upon arrival.

There is no archival or photographic footage of what ensued. The ferocity of the destruction can only be seen in photos taken in the aftermath of the conflict, which leveled most of downtown Atlanta, causing billions of dollars of damage and destroying the corporate headquarters of Ted Turner's TNT and CNN operations.

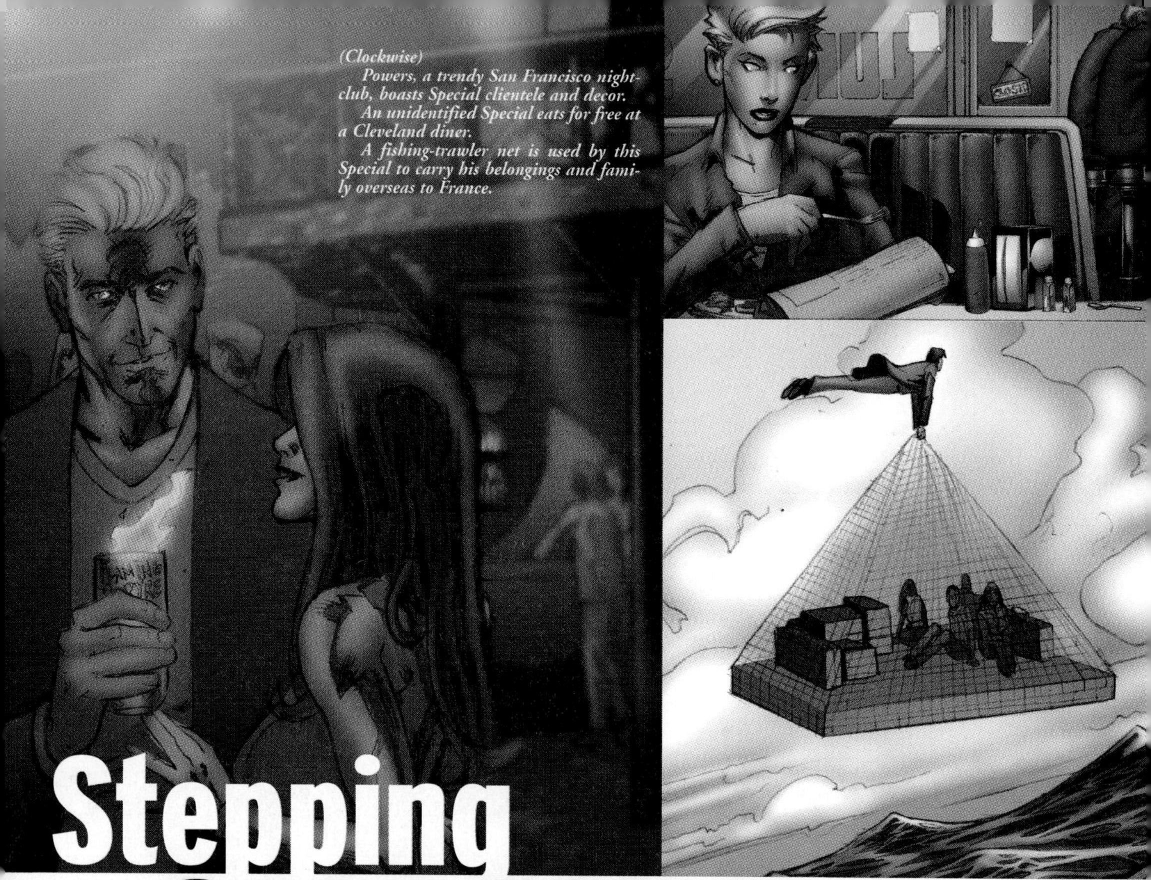

(Clockwise)
Powers, a trendy San Francisco nightclub, boasts Special clientele and decor.
An unidentified Special eats for free at a Cleveland diner.
A fishing-trawler net is used by this Special to carry his belongings and family overseas to France.

Stepping OUTSIDE

“T that the loss of life and property damage in Chicago, Atlanta and other major cities was terrible,” says Dr. Quentin Mallone, head of the Department of Psychology at San Diego State University. “But there's also no question that it could have been profoundly worse.

“You're dealing with a group of extremely powerful people who feel, rightly or wrongly, that they have been oppressed,” Mallone said. “The natural reaction, when handed the opportunity, especially after friends or loved ones have been killed, is to lash out at your perceived enemies. The extent of the damage makes us lose perspective: this damage was done by only 25-30 of the Specials, who still number nearly one hundred.”

What about the rest? According to State Department files, some of the Specials fled the United States after the Surge, taking up residence overseas, often under assumed names. “Most people, even Specials, want to live normal lives. They want to have families, good jobs, and raise their children. They didn't ask for these abilities, and in many cases don't want them. They find their powers as much of a burden as a blessing.”

The rest, Mallone says, “stepped outside.” He explains: “Imagine it: one day, you wake up, and you're invulnerable. You can fly, you're impossibly strong, with who knows what other additional powers, like flight or pyrokinetics. No one can stop you from doing whatever you want to do; there is

> “They go where they want, and do pretty much whatever they want.”
>
> — Dr. Quentin Mallone

(left) Special uniforms and costumes are the Special-ty of the day at these youth gatherings.

(below) Randy Fisk meets with town officials.

no weapon that can hurt you short of a tactical nuke, no cell that can hold you. For a lot of the Specials, that realization meant stepping outside the system."

Mallone feels his observations have been borne out by the facts. "Many Specials no longer hold a job. They do not use money. They don't have to. If they are hungry, they walk into a restaurant or grocery store, and quietly take whatever they want. They don't have to make a scene; the threat implicit in who and what they are is usually sufficient motivation for most people to stand aside. If they're tired, they go into a hotel and sleep. Who's going to evict them? They go where they want, and do pretty much whatever they want.

"Most of it's fairly benign. There are even some clubs — mainly in San Francisco and Seattle — that compete for Specials as clientele."

This competition has extended into other cities and major corporations eager to ensure that their interests are protected from rogue Specials. Jason Miller, aka Patriot, remains the corporate

Rev. William Kane at the Cathedral of Light.

symbol of NexusCorp, and has been loaned out to other cities and states as needed. Despite threats of Federal prosecution, Randy (Ravenshadow) Fisk operates pro bono to help small cities that cannot afford the NexusCorp fees to deal effectively with Special incursions. Other corporations rumored to have Specials on the payroll do so with a minimum of publicity.

Among some young people who spent their formative years after the Surge, and who have never known a world in which there were no Specials, the enhanced few have become the equivalent of rock stars. For many alienated young people, who consider themselves outside "normal" society, the Specials represent the ultimate in non-comformity and rebellion against authority. Others are drawn by the lure of power and danger. Entire subgroups of youthful underground

society have dedicated themselves to emulating the Specials in attitude and dress.

Many find this trend troubling, including the Reverend William Kane, founder and head of the Cathedral of Light in Urbana, Illinois, who is also the father of a Special, Joshua Kane. "Young people are not being warned sufficiently about the danger of holding these individuals up as role models. Some of these people have murdered law enforcement officials, and pose a threat to our very way of life. Much of the blame for this must rest with the media, which has glorified these people and given them cult status."

Whatever one's feelings might be concerning the Specials, the reality is that they are still here, among us. They are a force that must be contended with. So the question becomes, what is being

For a live virtual Townhall meeting on the influence of the Specials on today's youth go to jqpublic.mediaweek.com, July 17 at 3:00 EDT.

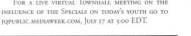

done now to deal with the situation, and where are things headed for the next few years?

PRESENT TENSE

Following the Atlanta and Chicago incidents, most cities quickly adopted a "don't start trouble" stance in response to visiting or resident Specials. "We don't bother them, and in most cases, they don't bother us," one local city government source noted.

In some cases, however, that approach falls short. At last count, nearly twenty Specials have adopted criminal lifestyles, based either on previous run-ins with the law that have now become daily routine, or in response to their perception that the government is responsible for their situation, tried to have them killed or imprisoned, and is thus deserving of retribution.

The litany of their crimes fills an FBI task book that is only slightly smaller than the New York Yellow Pages: Bank and armored car robbery, assault, grand larceny, manslaughter, murder and attempted murder comprise only a fraction of the charges made against them.

"It's a frustrating situation for us," said FBI agent Ned Carstairs, lead agent on the Specials Crime Task Force. "We've got a few Specials on our side we can call in when we hear about one of them in action, but usually by the time our side can get there, the bad guys are gone.

"We've managed to apprehend a few of them from time to time, mainly the ones who can't fly, but once you've got them, the question becomes where do you put them? What do you do with them? There isn't a prison in existence that's been built capable of holding these people. Jason or Matthew or some of the others can hold onto them, but even they have to go to the bathroom sometime, you know?"

The result so far has been an imperfect solution. Criminal

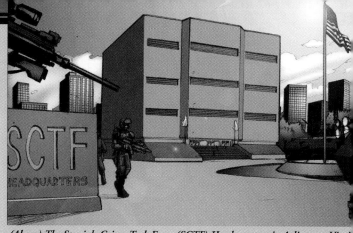

(Above) The Specials Crime Task Force (SCTF) Headquarters in Arlington, Virgi
(Below) An unidentified Special clashes with local police in Cavenaugh, Montan

Specials — those who can't fly — are dropped into barren environments, usually the North or South Poles, or parts of equatorial Africa or the Sudanese desert. The climate has no affect on them, but walking out again can take weeks or even months. Once they reach civilization, however, they can quickly find passage back to the United States.

"And when they get here, they're just that much more angry and dangerous," said Carstairs. "It gets them out of the system for a while, but in the end it doesn't solve the problem, it only makes it worse."

Despite public demands for intervention, the military option has also proven useless, much to the dismay of Administration officials who, early in the crisis, promised to contain the situation. "We didn't understand that the situation had changed," said Attorney General Michaels. "Our data was based on an understanding of their abilities pre-Surge. At

that time, early on, they cou have been contained. Not so lat Which, I think, gives some cr dence to the idea that perhaps should have been more aggressi early on in containing these ind viduals.

"Based on the revised figur we're reasonably sure that a tac cal field nuke could take some them out," Michaels added, "b who wants to pursue that option downtown Austin or S Francisco?"

Many, however, refuse accept that logic. "The admin tration is asking us to accept th we have, in essence, lc Chicago," remarked Senat Edward Farrell (R-MD). "I' sorry, but that's just insane. If foreign power had invaded a conquered a major American ci there is no recourse we would r pursue, no effort we would r make, no pain we would r endure to push them from o shores. This is the policy of cap ulation, not leadership. If v

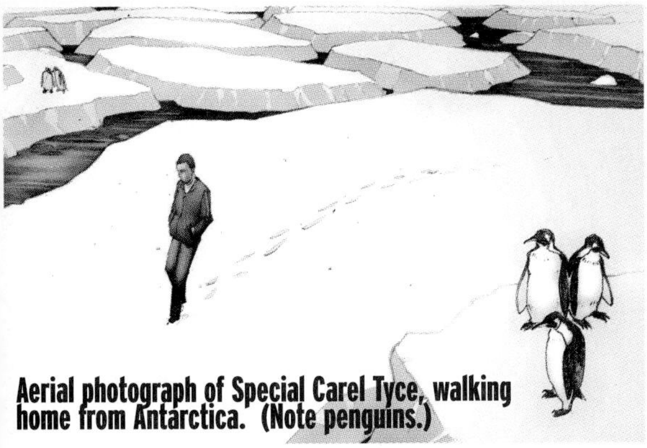

Aerial photograph of Special Carel Tyce, walking home from Antarctica. (Note penguins.)

don't know a way to deal with these people then we have to find one. If the current administration is incapable of finding one, then they should step aside and let our party try it, because I can tell you right now, we'd get the job done."

Reached for comment, a senior White House aide would only say, "Senator Farrell should spend less time making speeches and more time attending to the business of government. If he has any ideas, he should say them now, rather than waiting to retake the Oval Office. Otherwise it sounds to us like he's putting his political agendas ahead of the public good."

And what of the Specials themselves, who have paid a price of their own? At least eleven of them, one-tenth of their total number, are dead. In any group of childhood friends, how rare is it that one or two of them are murdered? Here, however, the Specials can point to all eleven dead Specials, and know that they were murdered, most by the soci-

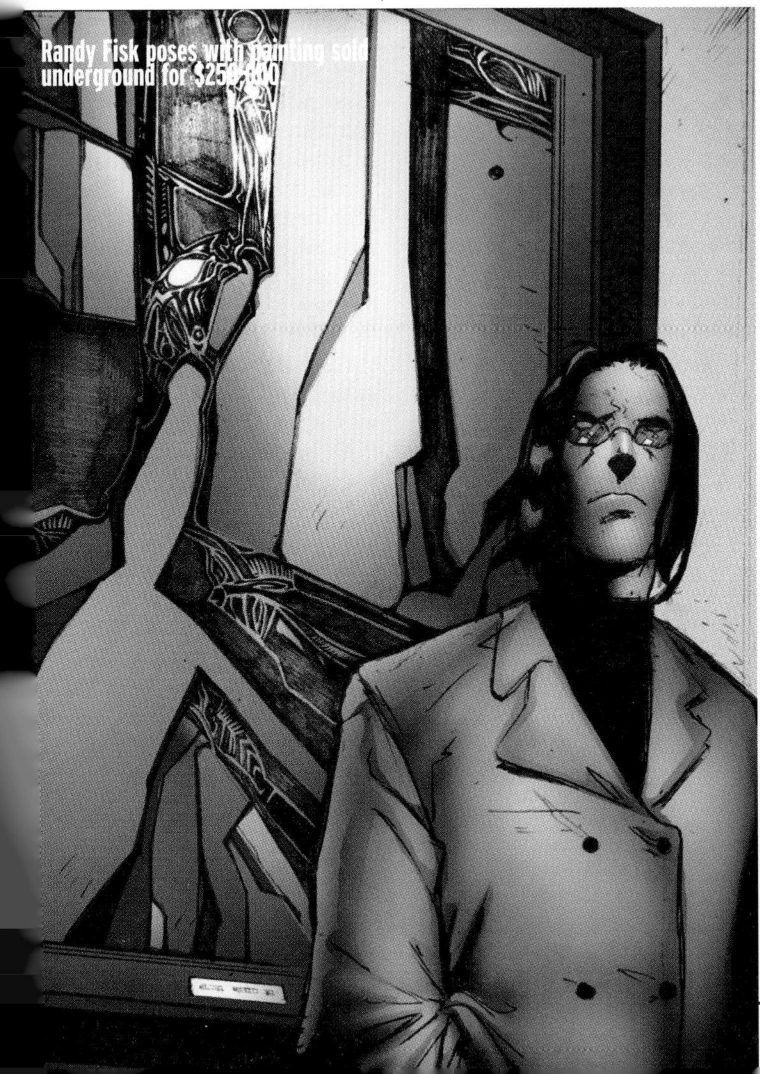

Randy Fisk poses with painting sold underground for $250,000.

THE SPECIALS: WHERE ARE THEY?

Mediaweek Adds Up the Figures

(Estimates Only)

CALIFORNIA:	19
TEXAS:	8
COLORADO:	10
ILLINOIS:	2
VIRGINIA:	3
OKLAHOMA:	7
MASSACHUSETTS:	4
OREGON:	16
MONTANA:	4
ARIZONA:	6
NEVADA:	2
NEW YORK:	1
"STEPPED OUTSIDE":	20
UNACCOUNTED FOR:	5
TOTAL:	102

Reconnaissance telephoto of Chicago skyline. (Note shattered highrise apartments.

ety around them.

Eleven of the most powerful, potentially gifted humans ever to walk on the planet, dead. One can only wonder at the sheer loss and waste of potential.

There has also been a price for the survivors, beyond having to carry the pain for those already dead.

Chandra, once the most popular and highly-paid model in history, has lost every contract, her homes, and every source of income.

Randy Fisk, once a millionaire several times over, can only sell his artwork on the underground art circuit. Each time the government discovers one of his hidden accounts, the money is seized.

And Singer Paula Ramirez, once the darling of the concert circuit, is said to be on the run in Montana, living on the streets.

THINGS TO COME

What, then, of the future?

"We have, grudgingly, come to accept that the Specials are now a part of everyday life," Psychiatrist Dr. Mallone suggests. "They represent a crisis, and as humans we have a remarkable capacity to accept the changes wrought by crises. How many people die each year of AIDS? At another time, the idea of millions of people dying as the result of a

sexually transmitted disease was terrifying. Now, sadly, we look at the figures in the newspaper and move on to the sports pages.

"People at the time have been able to accept the death of millions and the transformation of the map of Europe caused by the Black Plague, and two World Wars. It is hardly a leap in logic to say that we have, in time, learned to accept the current situation as the status quo."

But even Mallone agrees that it will not remain the status quo indefinitely. Several Specials have married and had children, some even before the Surge, and there is no question that their unique abilities are not genetically transferred, their children show no sign of having inherited their enhancements.

Time is the inexorable force that shapes all our lives, and for all their powers and abilities, the Specials are no different than the rest of us. They age, as we do, and though they may be impervious to bullets and bazookas, they

have shown no evidence of being immune to the passage of time. Their faces show wrinkles where there once were none, others are turning prematurely gray, and some of them have begun to show early traces of male pattern baldness. Some scientists have begun to speculate that the energy they use may burn up their bodies even sooner than a normal human lifespan.

Sooner or later, one at a time, they will leave us. Once, their existence would have been unthinkable. Now they are here, and we can hardly imagine a world without them. Twenty, fifty or a hundred years from now, when they are gone, it will be hard for our inheritors to imagine what it was like to have them.

The question that we, and they, must one day face is this: what was done in their presence? What have we, and they, brought to the table of human existence to justify our time on Earth? Has the mishandling of the Specials crisis turned this into something worse than a national nightmare: has it been a catalog of missed opportunities?

Only time will tell. ●

(The following correspondents contributed to this report: Suzanne Milch, New York; Harrison Frank, California; Melissa Turstone, Washington DC; Samuel Kincaid, Los Angeles.)

Dr. Mallone speaks at a recent symposium, "Specials vs. Everyone: A Dynamic for Failure."

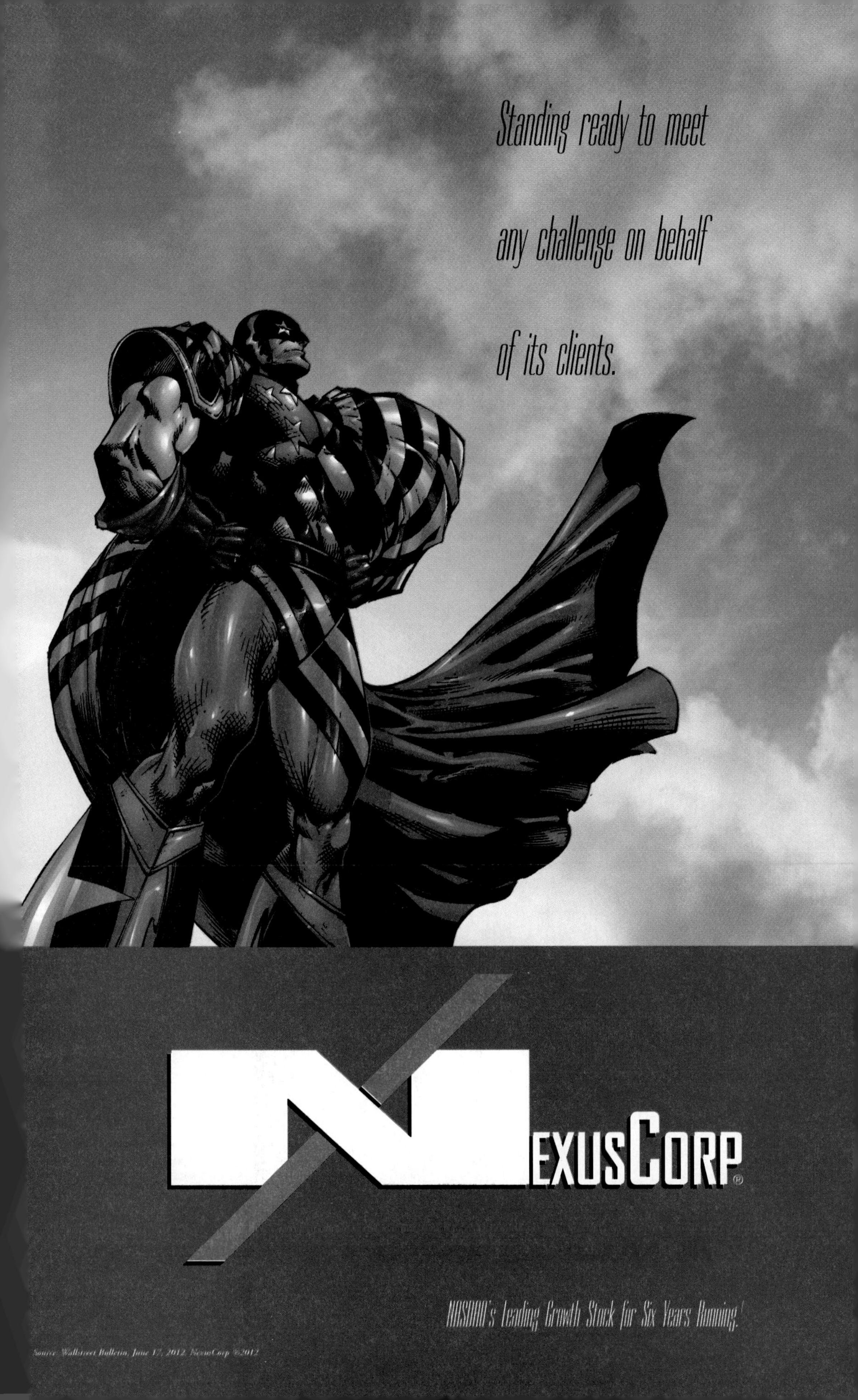

Standing ready to meet
any challenge on behalf
of its clients.
NexusCorp®
NASDAQ's leading Growth Stock for Six Years Running!
Source: Wallstreet Bulletin, June 17, 2012. NexusCorp ©2012

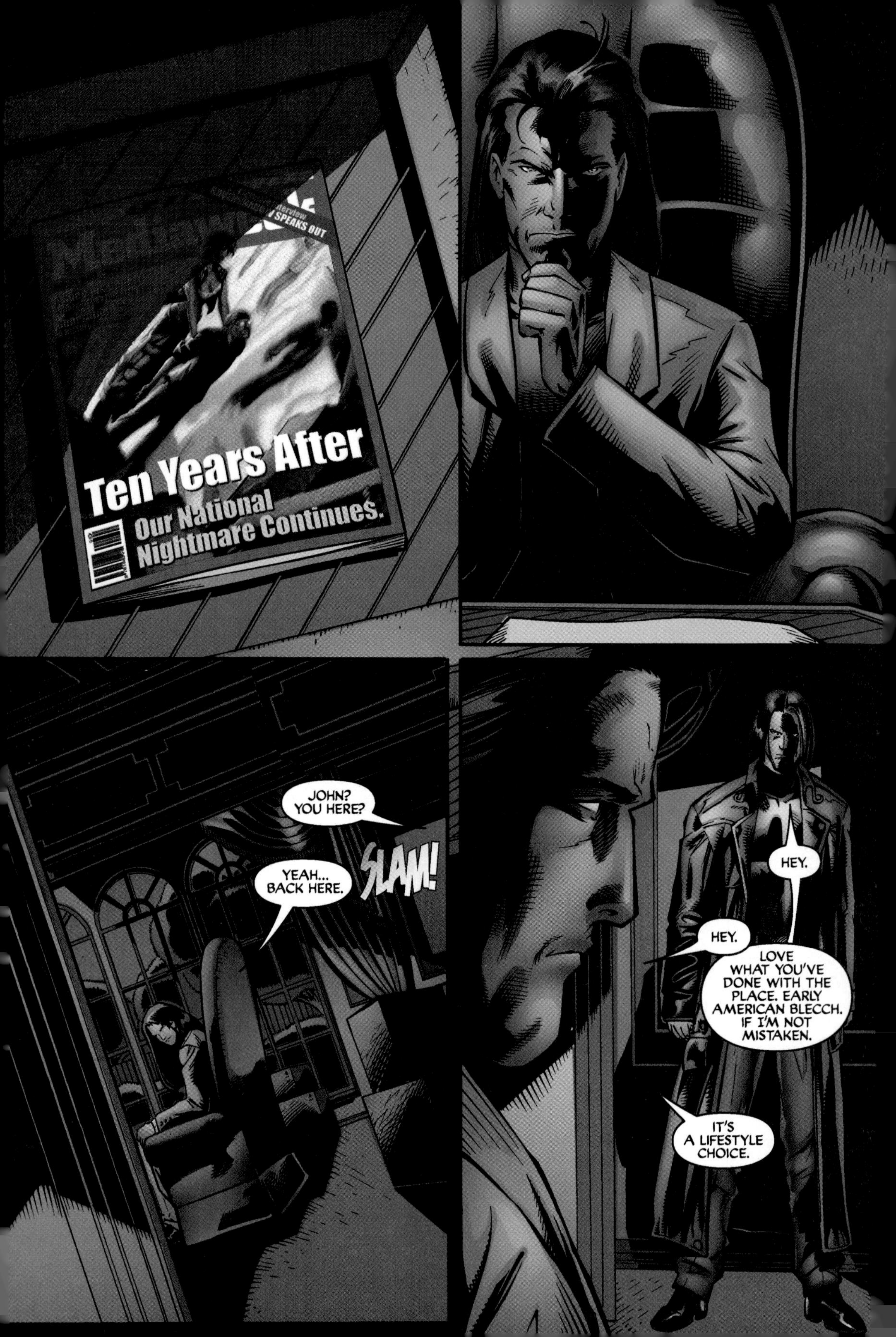
Ten Years After
Our National Nightmare Continues.
JOHN? YOU HERE?
SLAM!
YEAH... BACK HERE.
HEY.
HEY.
LOVE WHAT YOU'VE DONE WITH THE PLACE. EARLY AMERICAN BLECCH. IF I'M NOT MISTAKEN.
IT'S A LIFESTYLE CHOICE.

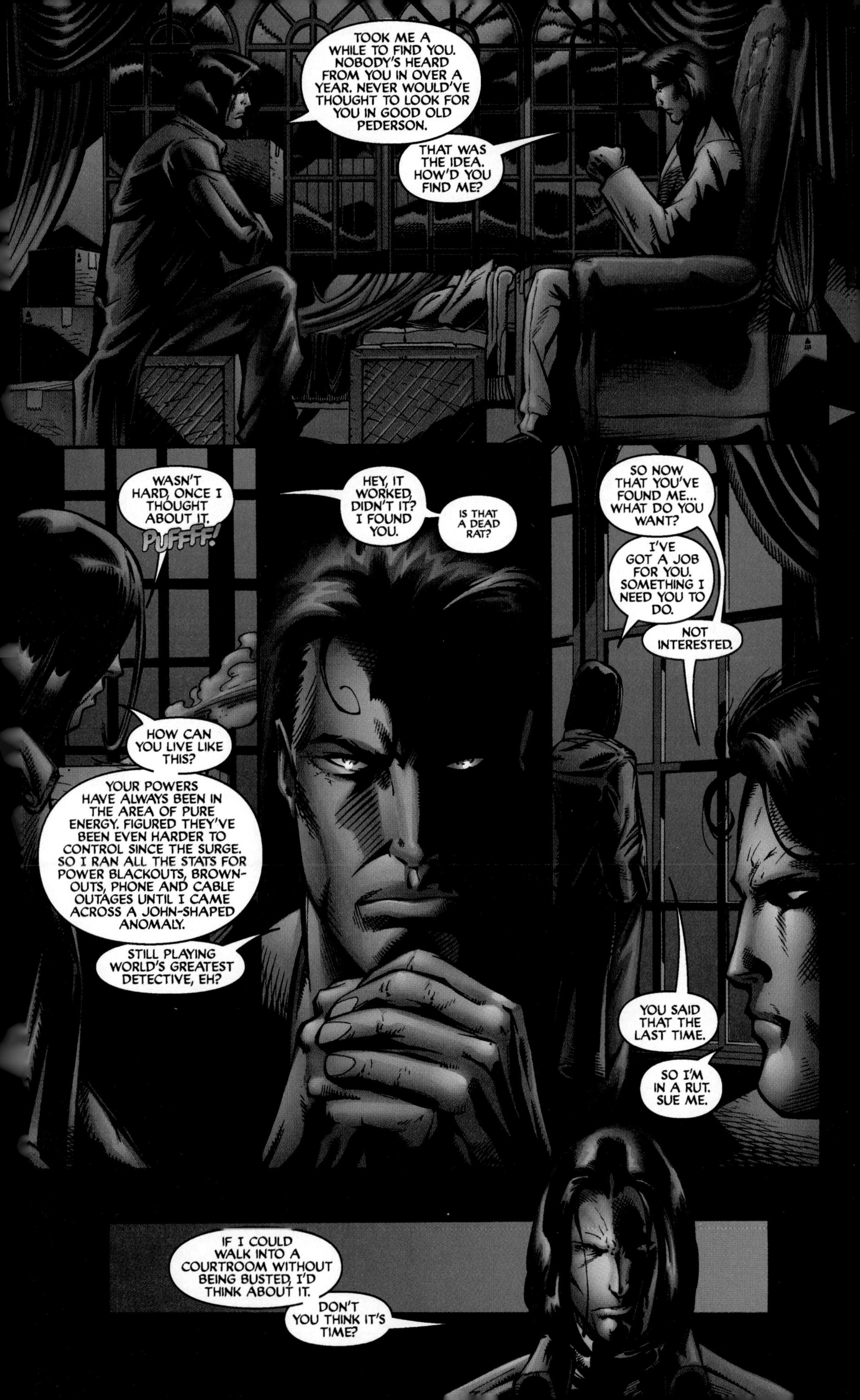
TOOK ME A WHILE TO FIND YOU. NOBODY'S HEARD FROM YOU IN OVER A YEAR. NEVER WOULD'VE THOUGHT TO LOOK FOR YOU IN GOOD OLD PEDERSON.
THAT WAS THE IDEA. HOW'D YOU FIND ME?
WASN'T HARD, ONCE I THOUGHT ABOUT IT.
PUFFFF!
HEY, IT WORKED, DIDN'T IT? I FOUND YOU.
IS THAT A DEAD RAT?
SO NOW THAT YOU'VE FOUND ME... WHAT DO YOU WANT?
I'VE GOT A JOB FOR YOU. SOMETHING I NEED YOU TO DO.
NOT INTERESTED.
HOW CAN YOU LIVE LIKE THIS?
YOUR POWERS HAVE ALWAYS BEEN IN THE AREA OF PURE ENERGY. FIGURED THEY'VE BEEN EVEN HARDER TO CONTROL SINCE THE SURGE. SO I RAN ALL THE STATS FOR POWER BLACKOUTS, BROWN-OUTS, PHONE AND CABLE OUTAGES UNTIL I CAME ACROSS A JOHN-SHAPED ANOMALY.
STILL PLAYING WORLD'S GREATEST DETECTIVE, EH?
YOU SAID THAT THE LAST TIME.
SO I'M IN A RUT. SUE ME.
IF I COULD WALK INTO A COURTROOM WITHOUT BEING BUSTED, I'D THINK ABOUT IT.
DON'T YOU THINK IT'S TIME?

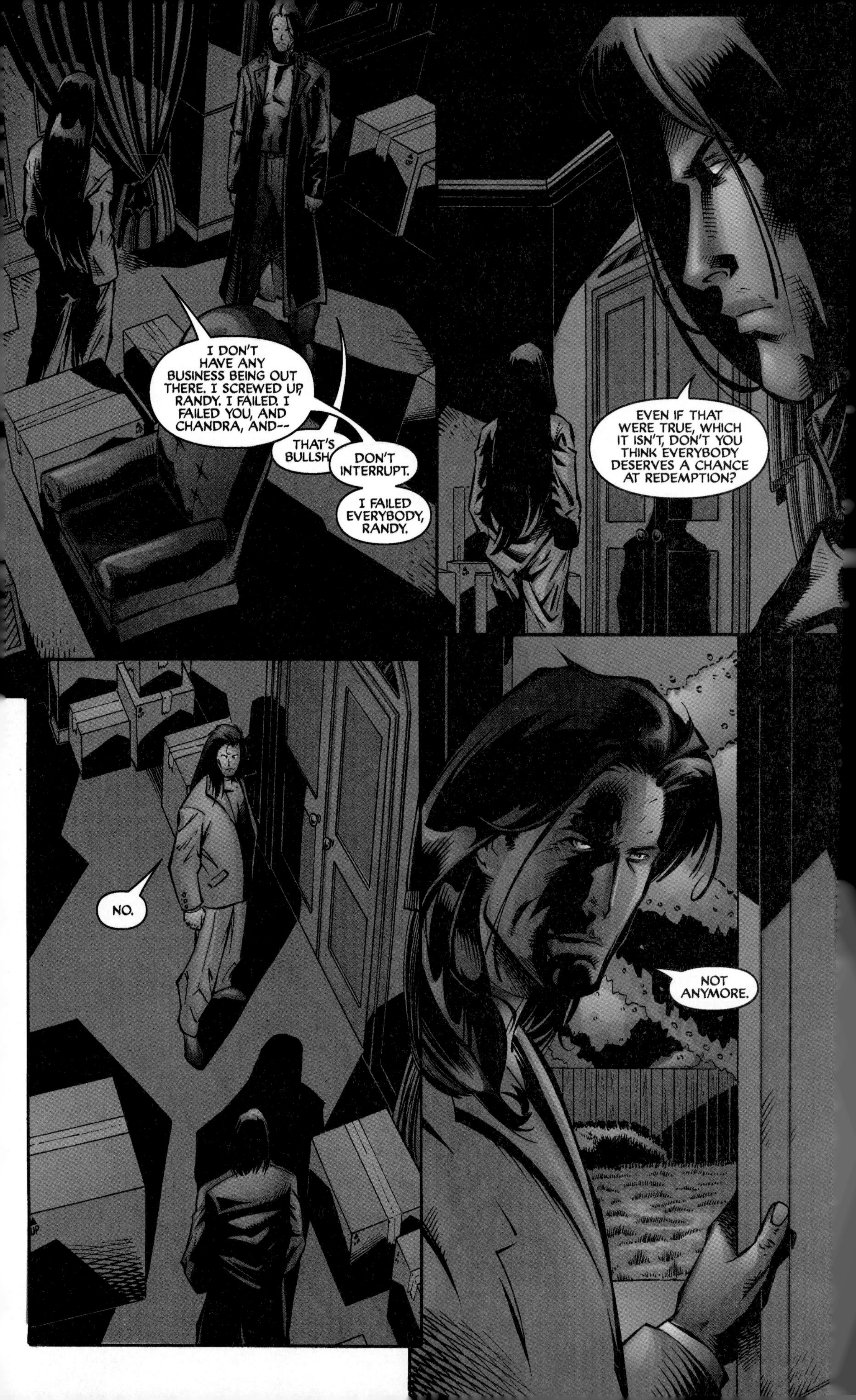
I DON'T HAVE ANY BUSINESS BEING OUT THERE. I SCREWED UP, RANDY. I FAILED. I FAILED YOU, AND CHANDRA, AND--
THAT'S BULLSH
DON'T INTERRUPT.
I FAILED EVERYBODY, RANDY.
EVEN IF THAT WERE TRUE, WHICH IT ISN'T, DON'T YOU THINK EVERYBODY DESERVES A CHANCE AT REDEMPTION?
NO.
NOT ANYMORE.

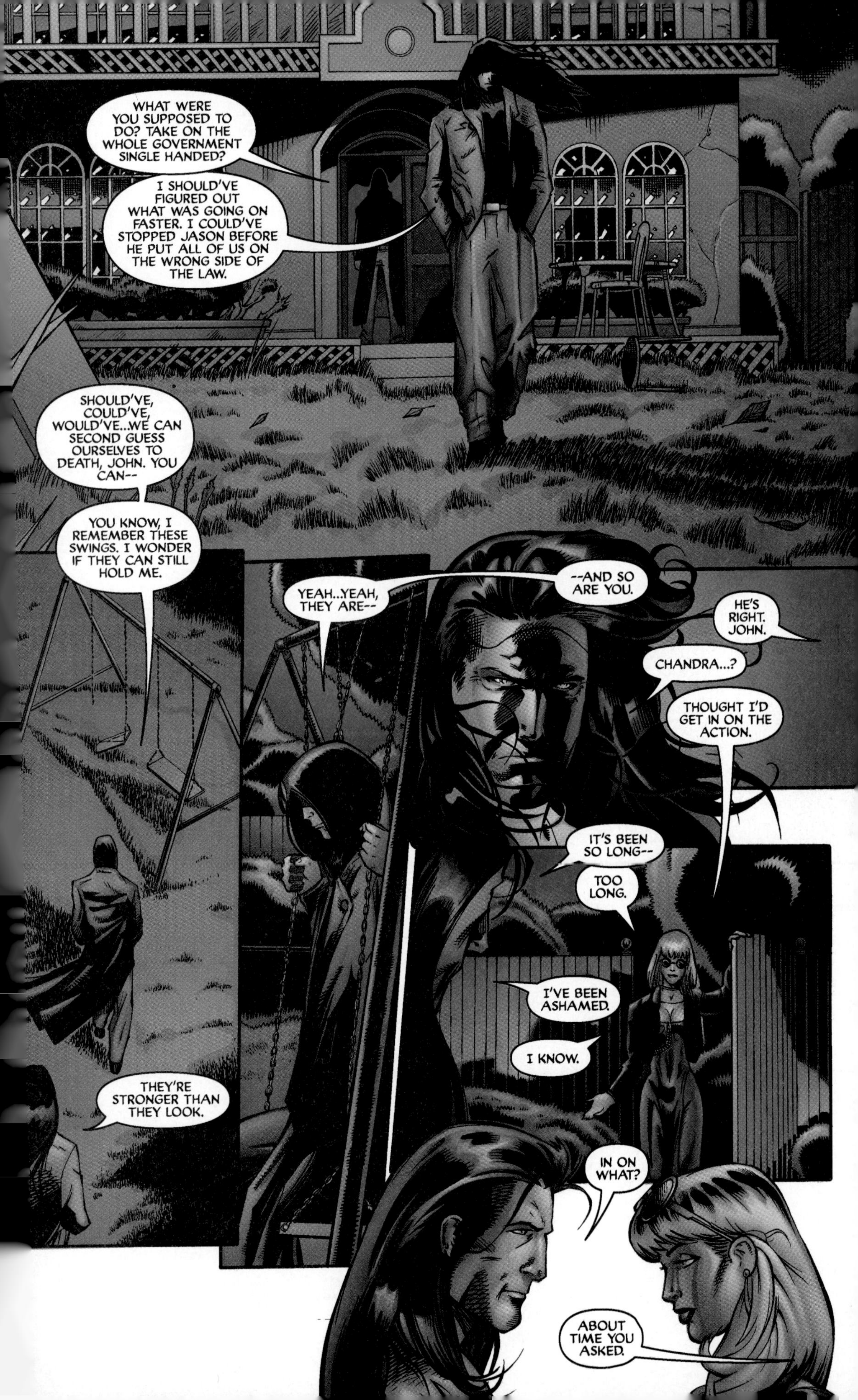
WHAT WERE YOU SUPPOSED TO DO? TAKE ON THE WHOLE GOVERNMENT SINGLE HANDED?
I SHOULD'VE FIGURED OUT WHAT WAS GOING ON FASTER. I COULD'VE STOPPED JASON BEFORE HE PUT ALL OF US ON THE WRONG SIDE OF THE LAW.
SHOULD'VE, COULD'VE, WOULD'VE...WE CAN SECOND GUESS OURSELVES TO DEATH, JOHN. YOU CAN--
YOU KNOW, I REMEMBER THESE SWINGS. I WONDER IF THEY CAN STILL HOLD ME.
THEY'RE STRONGER THAN THEY LOOK.
YEAH...YEAH, THEY ARE--
--AND SO ARE YOU.
HE'S RIGHT. JOHN.
CHANDRA...?
THOUGHT I'D GET IN ON THE ACTION.
IT'S BEEN SO LONG--
TOO LONG.
I'VE BEEN ASHAMED.
I KNOW.
IN ON WHAT?
ABOUT TIME YOU ASKED.

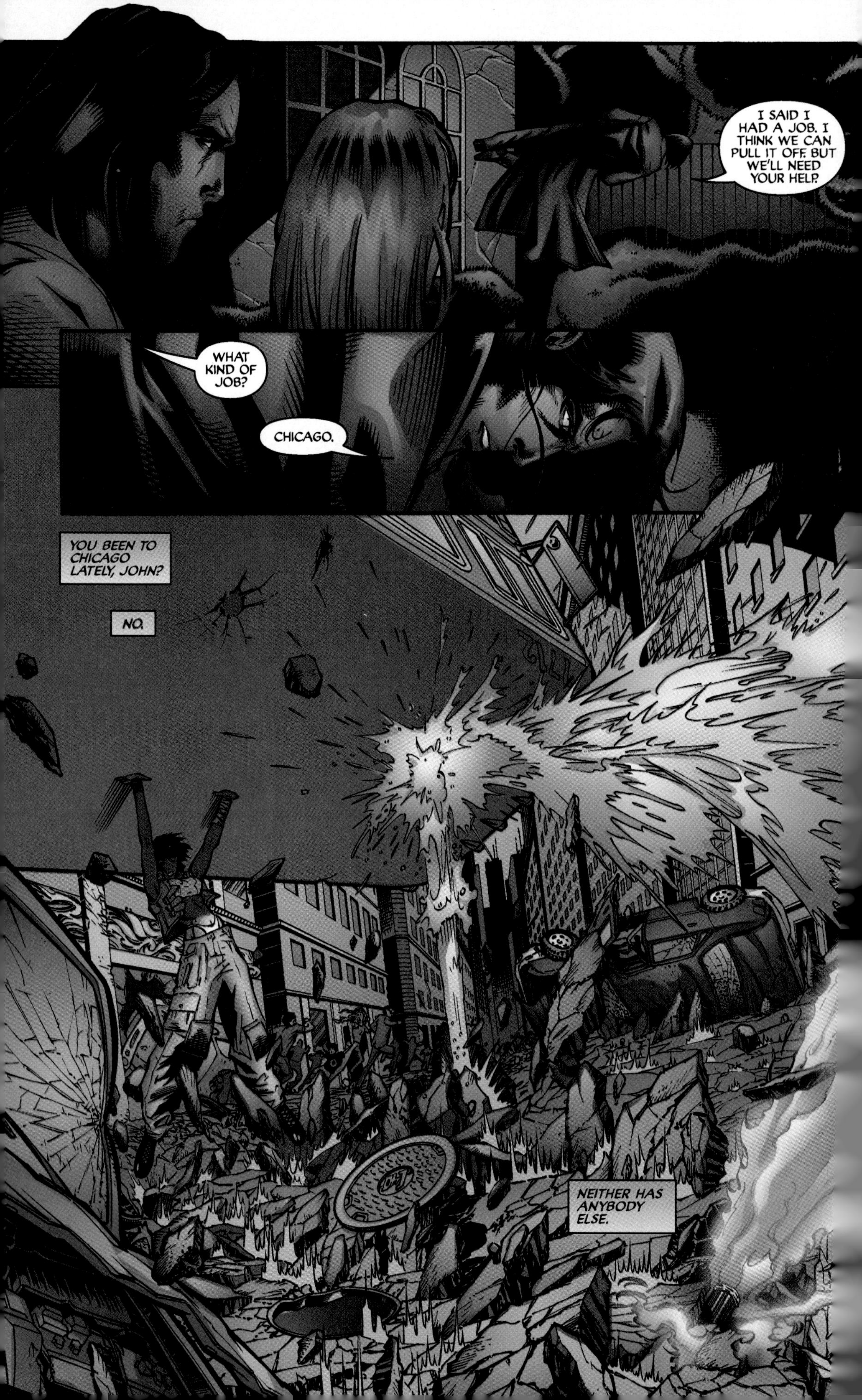
I SAID I HAD A JOB. I THINK WE CAN PULL IT OFF. BUT WE'LL NEED YOUR HELP.
WHAT KIND OF JOB?
CHICAGO.
YOU BEEN TO CHICAGO LATELY, JOHN?
NO.
NEITHER HAS ANYBODY ELSE.

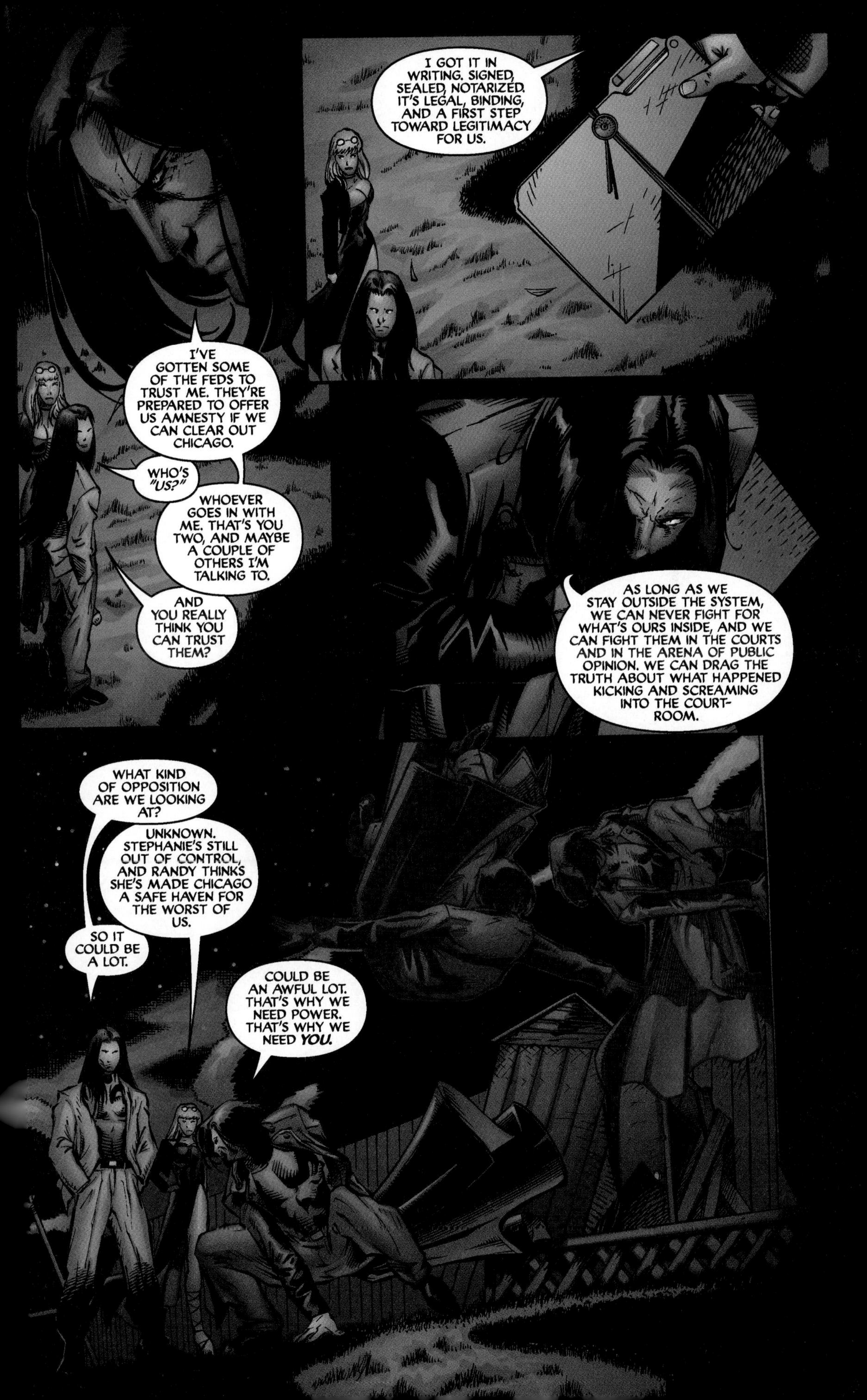
I GOT IT IN WRITING. SIGNED, SEALED, NOTARIZED. IT'S LEGAL, BINDING, AND A FIRST STEP TOWARD LEGITIMACY FOR US.
I'VE GOTTEN SOME OF THE FEDS TO TRUST ME. THEY'RE PREPARED TO OFFER US AMNESTY IF WE CAN CLEAR OUT CHICAGO.
WHO'S "US?"
WHOEVER GOES IN WITH ME. THAT'S YOU TWO, AND MAYBE A COUPLE OF OTHERS I'M TALKING TO.
AND YOU REALLY THINK YOU CAN TRUST THEM?
AS LONG AS WE STAY OUTSIDE THE SYSTEM, WE CAN NEVER FIGHT FOR WHAT'S OURS INSIDE, AND WE CAN FIGHT THEM IN THE COURTS AND IN THE ARENA OF PUBLIC OPINION. WE CAN DRAG THE TRUTH ABOUT WHAT HAPPENED KICKING AND SCREAMING INTO THE COURT-ROOM.
WHAT KIND OF OPPOSITION ARE WE LOOKING AT?
UNKNOWN. STEPHANIE'S STILL OUT OF CONTROL, AND RANDY THINKS SHE'S MADE CHICAGO A SAFE HAVEN FOR THE WORST OF US.
SO IT COULD BE A LOT.
COULD BE AN AWFUL LOT. THAT'S WHY WE NEED POWER. THAT'S WHY WE NEED *YOU.*

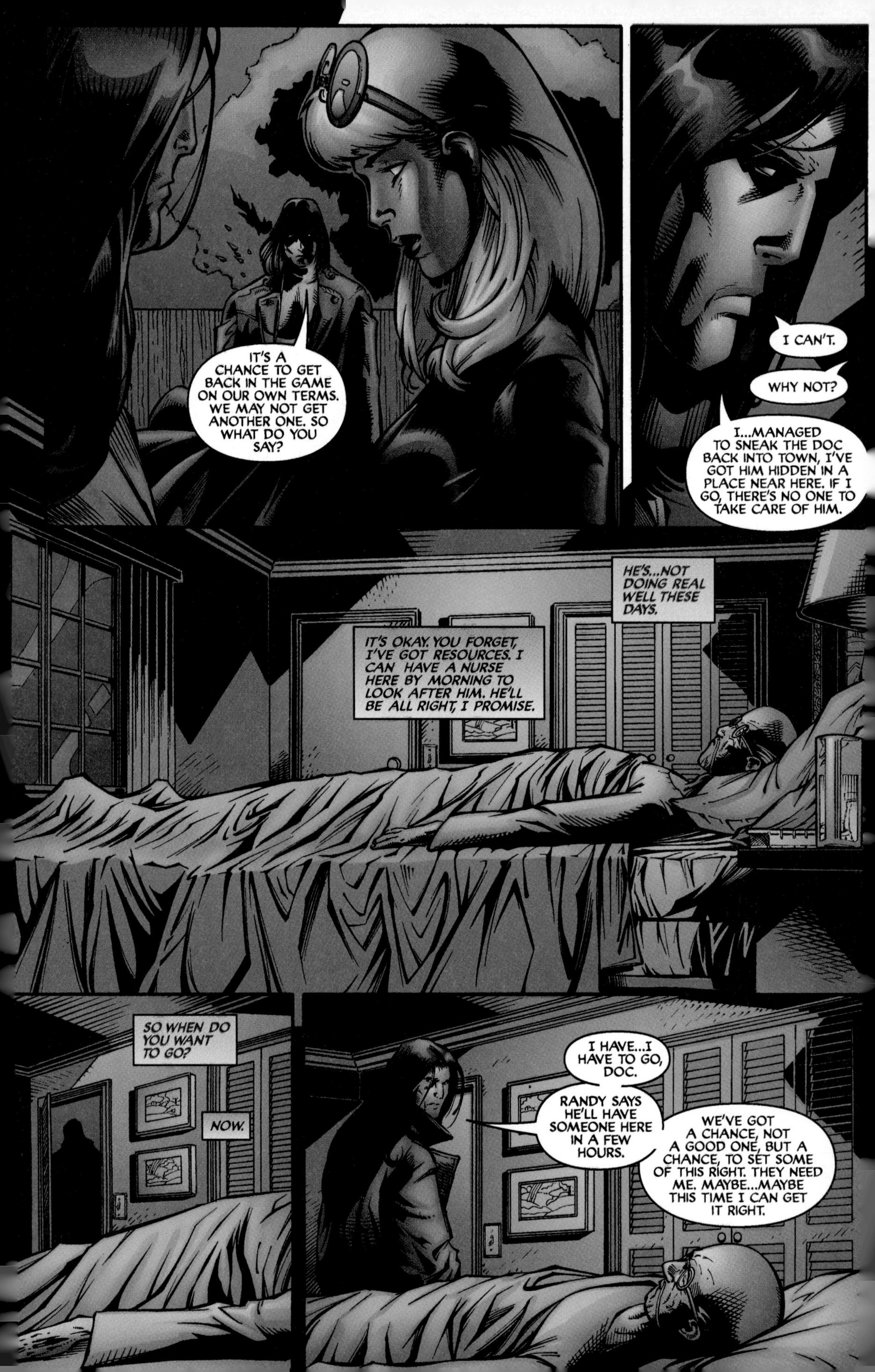
IT'S A CHANCE TO GET BACK IN THE GAME ON OUR OWN TERMS. WE MAY NOT GET ANOTHER ONE. SO WHAT DO YOU SAY?
I CAN'T.
WHY NOT?
I...MANAGED TO SNEAK THE DOC BACK INTO TOWN, I'VE GOT HIM HIDDEN IN A PLACE NEAR HERE. IF I GO, THERE'S NO ONE TO TAKE CARE OF HIM.
HE'S...NOT DOING REAL WELL THESE DAYS.
IT'S OKAY. YOU FORGET, I'VE GOT RESOURCES. I CAN HAVE A NURSE HERE BY MORNING TO LOOK AFTER HIM. HE'LL BE ALL RIGHT, I PROMISE.
SO WHEN DO YOU WANT TO GO?
NOW.
I HAVE...I HAVE TO GO, DOC.
RANDY SAYS HE'LL HAVE SOMEONE HERE IN A FEW HOURS.
WE'VE GOT A CHANCE, NOT A GOOD ONE, BUT A CHANCE, TO SET SOME OF THIS RIGHT. THEY NEED ME. MAYBE...MAYBE THIS TIME I CAN GET IT RIGHT.

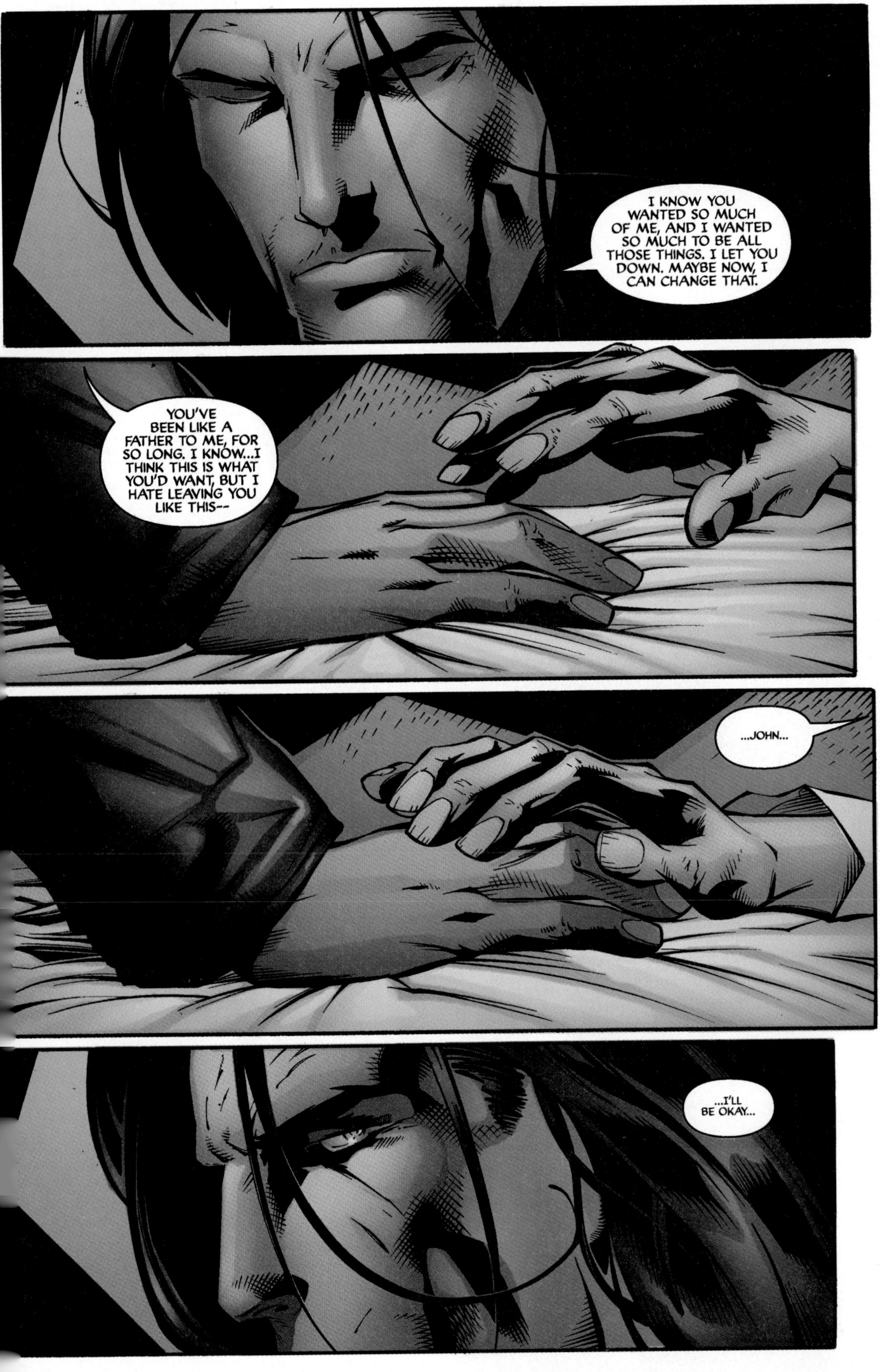
I KNOW YOU WANTED SO MUCH OF ME, AND I WANTED SO MUCH TO BE ALL THOSE THINGS. I LET YOU DOWN. MAYBE NOW, I CAN CHANGE THAT.
YOU'VE BEEN LIKE A FATHER TO ME, FOR SO LONG. I KNOW...I THINK THIS IS WHAT YOU'D WANT, BUT I HATE LEAVING YOU LIKE THIS--
...JOHN...
...I'LL BE OKAY...

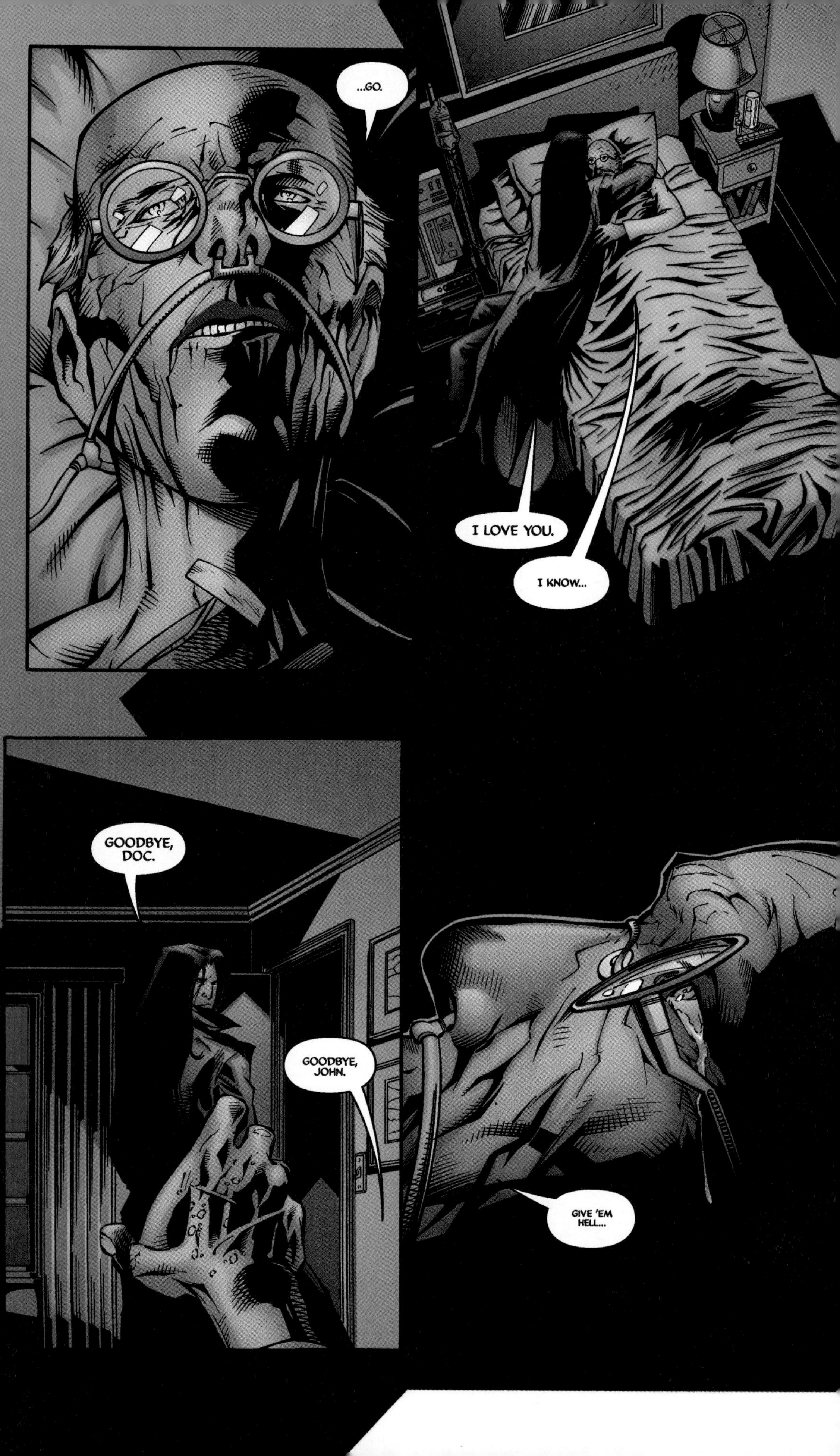
...GO.
I LOVE YOU.
I KNOW...
GOODBYE, DOC.
GOODBYE, JOHN.
GIVE 'EM HELL...

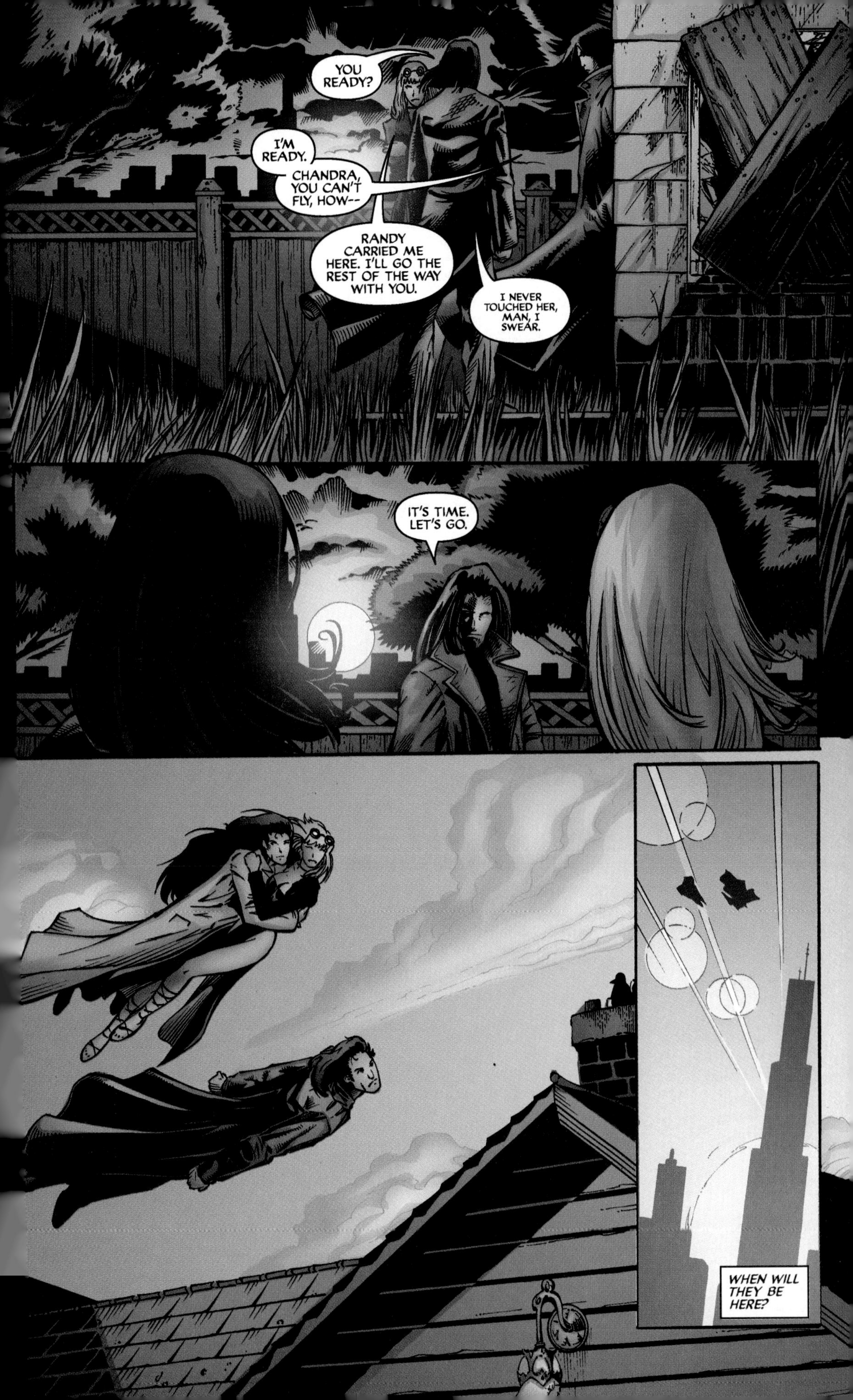
YOU READY?
I'M READY.
CHANDRA, YOU CAN'T FLY, HOW--
RANDY CARRIED ME HERE. I'LL GO THE REST OF THE WAY WITH YOU.
I NEVER TOUCHED HER, MAN, I SWEAR.
IT'S TIME. LET'S GO.
WHEN WILL THEY BE HERE?

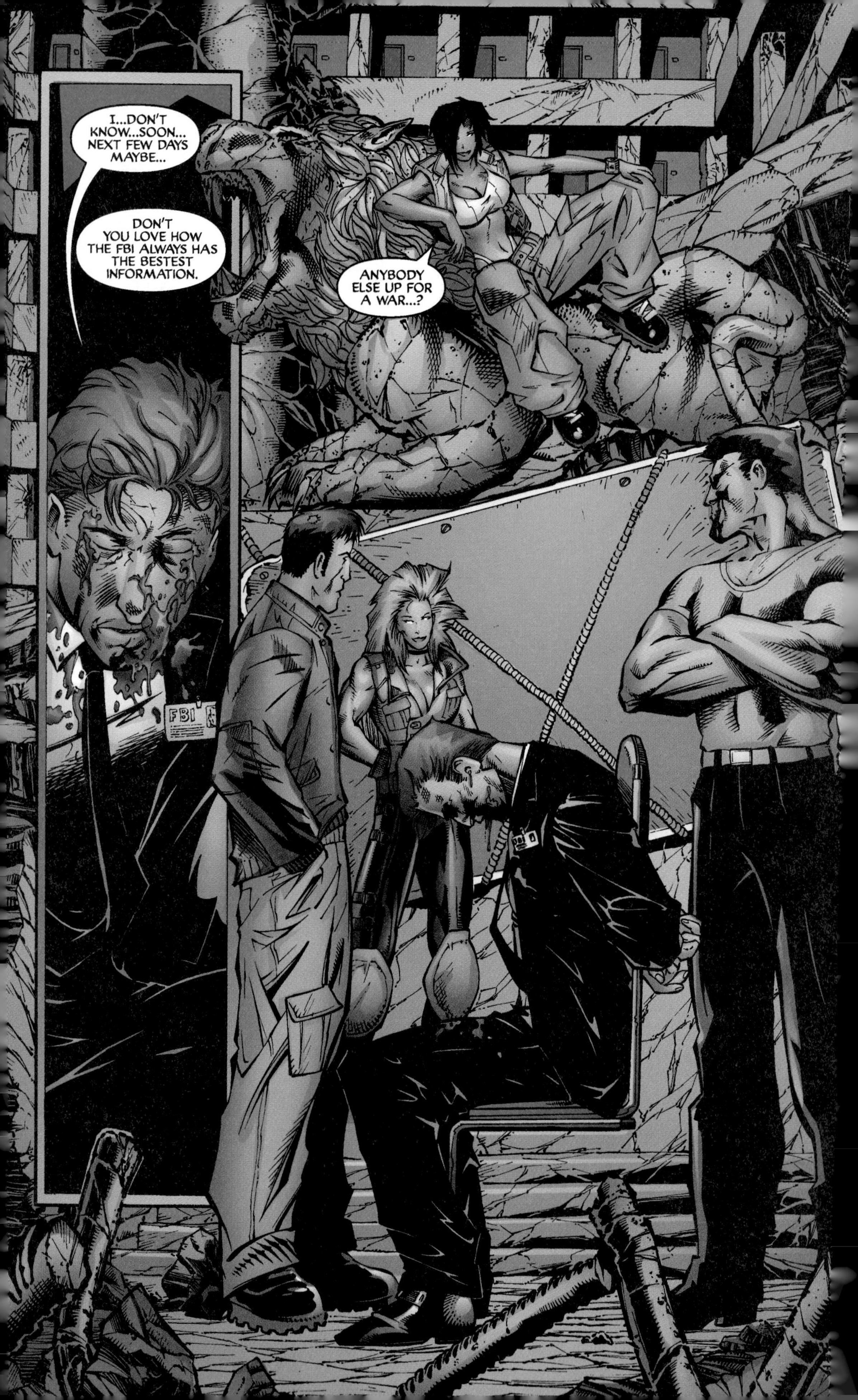
I...DON'T KNOW...SOON... NEXT FEW DAYS MAYBE...
DON'T YOU LOVE HOW THE FBI ALWAYS HAS THE BESTEST INFORMATION.
ANYBODY ELSE UP FOR A WAR...?
FBI

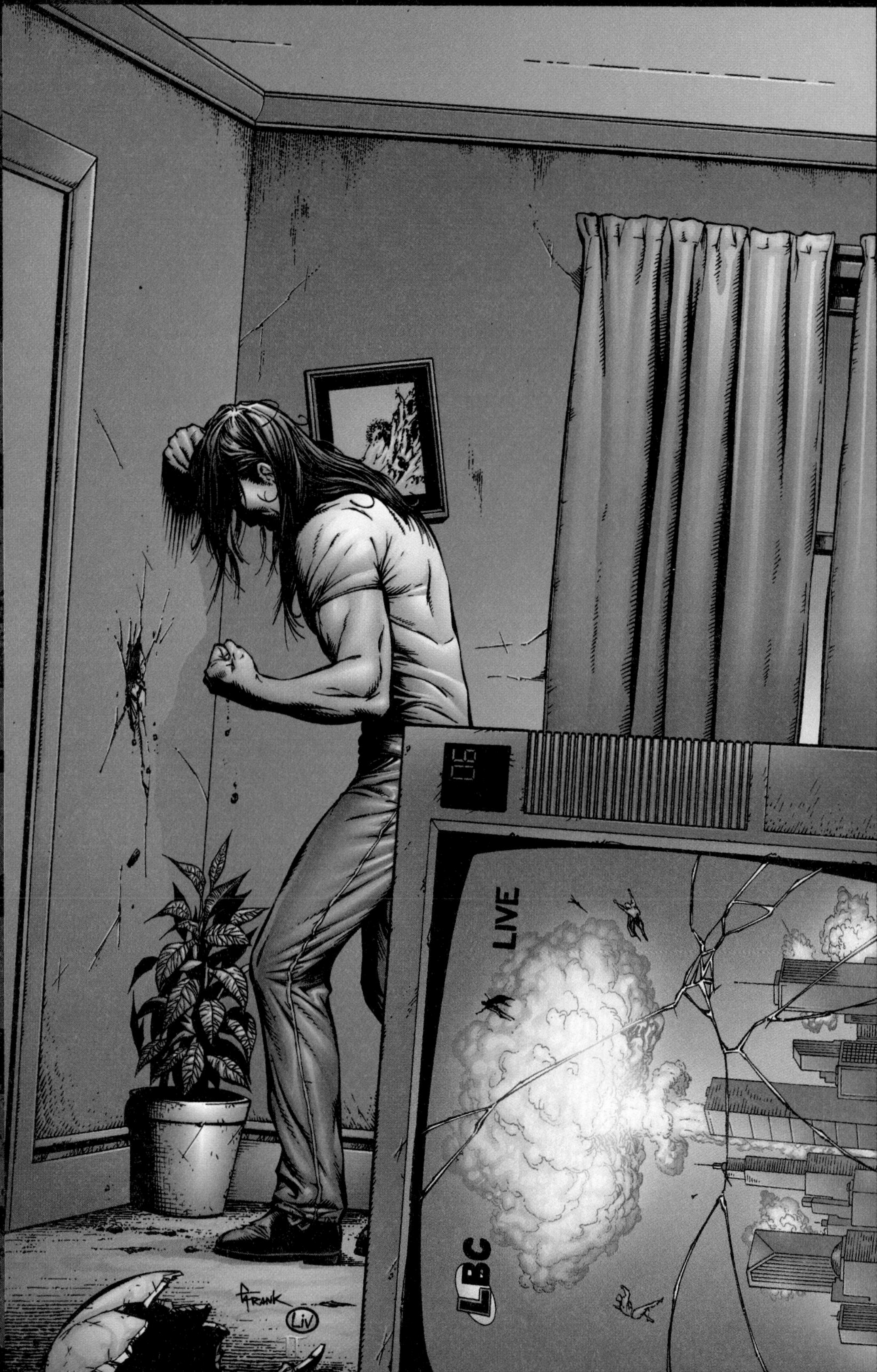
LIVE
LBC

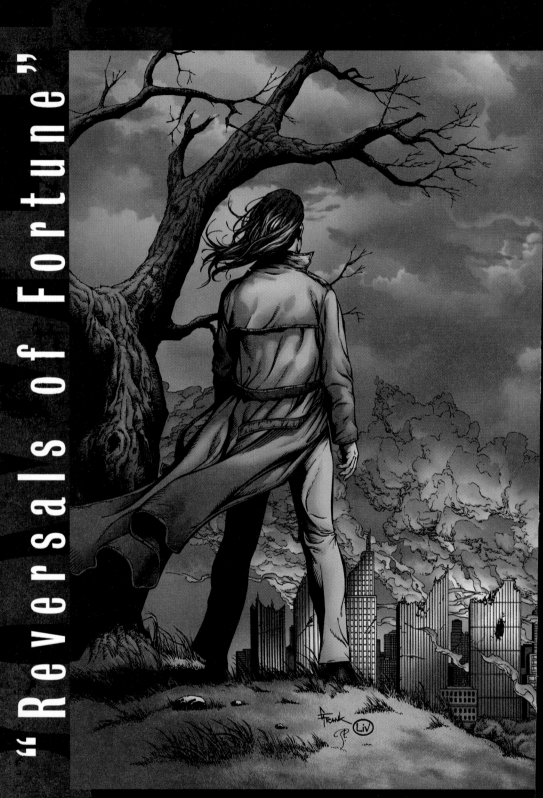

"Reversals of Fortune"

CHAPTER

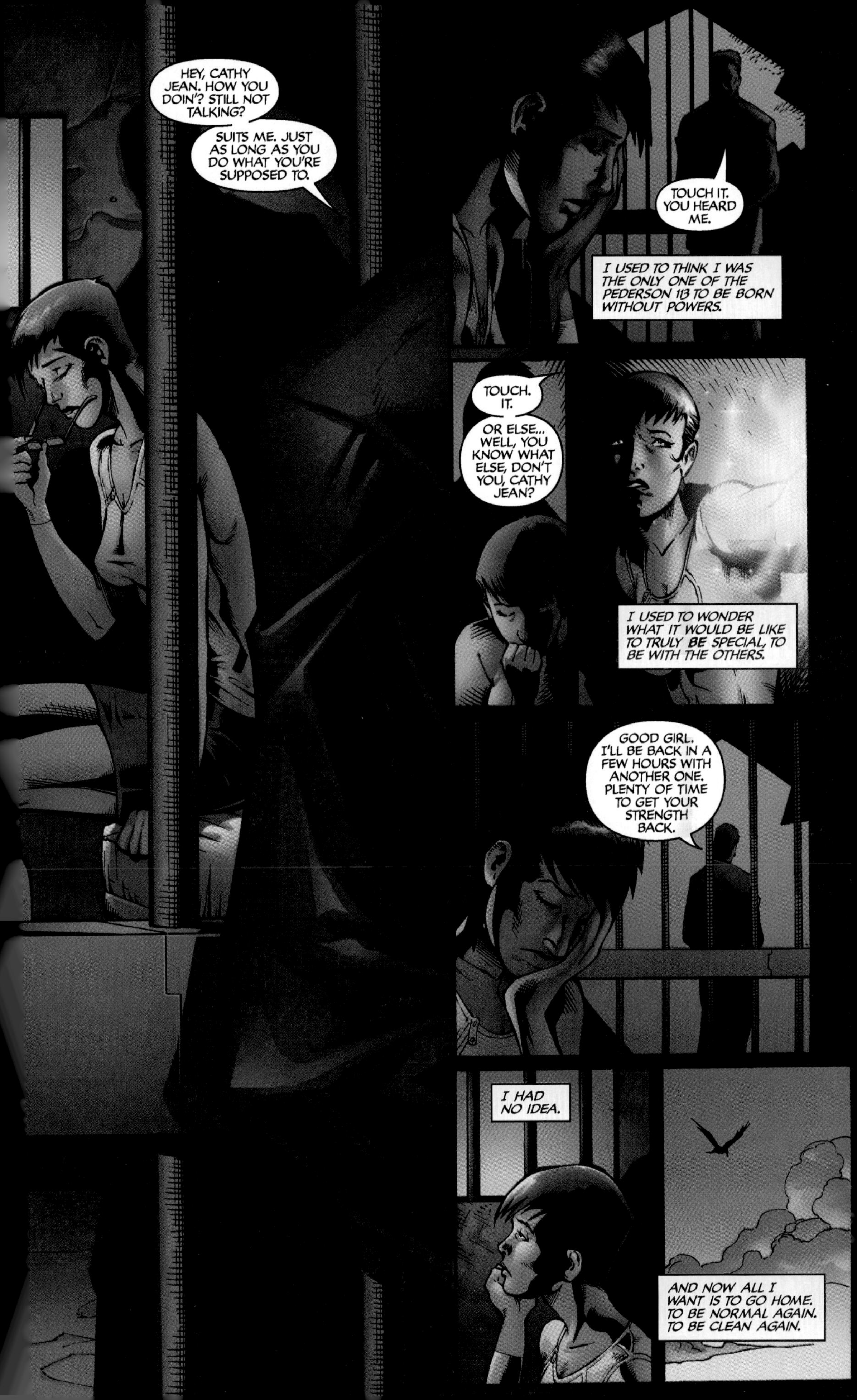
HEY, CATHY JEAN. HOW YOU DOIN'? STILL NOT TALKING?
SUITS ME. JUST AS LONG AS YOU DO WHAT YOU'RE SUPPOSED TO.
TOUCH IT. YOU HEARD ME.
I USED TO THINK I WAS THE ONLY ONE OF THE PEDERSON 113 TO BE BORN WITHOUT POWERS.
TOUCH. IT.
OR ELSE... WELL, YOU KNOW WHAT ELSE, DON'T YOU, CATHY JEAN?
I USED TO WONDER WHAT IT WOULD BE LIKE TO TRULY BE SPECIAL, TO BE WITH THE OTHERS.
GOOD GIRL. I'LL BE BACK IN A FEW HOURS WITH ANOTHER ONE. PLENTY OF TIME TO GET YOUR STRENGTH BACK.
I HAD NO IDEA.
AND NOW ALL I WANT IS TO GO HOME. TO BE NORMAL AGAIN. TO BE CLEAN AGAIN.

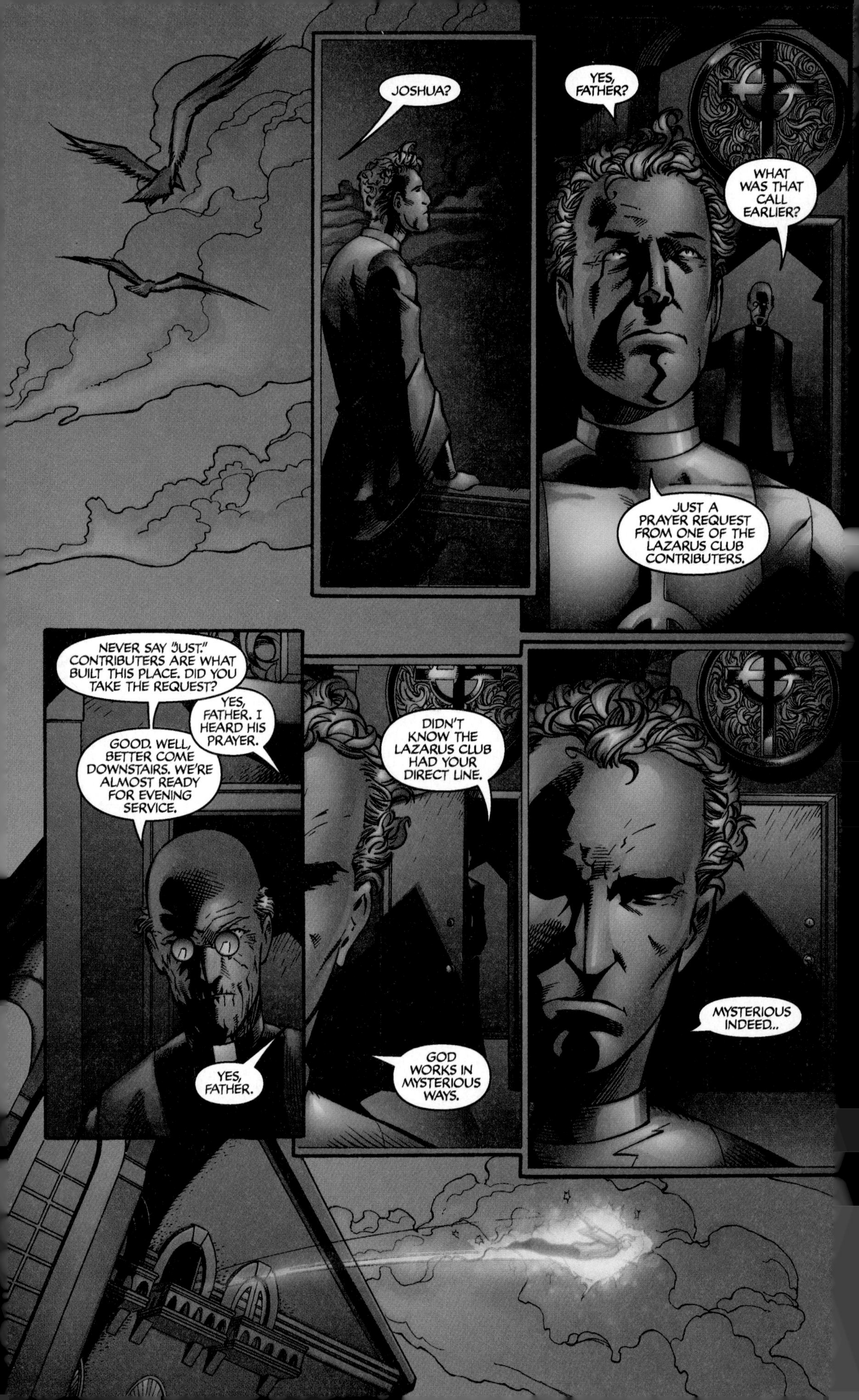
JOSHUA?
YES, FATHER?
WHAT WAS THAT CALL EARLIER?
JUST A PRAYER REQUEST FROM ONE OF THE LAZARUS CLUB CONTRIBUTERS.
NEVER SAY "JUST." CONTRIBUTERS ARE WHAT BUILT THIS PLACE. DID YOU TAKE THE REQUEST?
YES, FATHER. I HEARD HIS PRAYER.
GOOD. WELL, BETTER COME DOWNSTAIRS. WE'RE ALMOST READY FOR EVENING SERVICE.
YES, FATHER.
DIDN'T KNOW THE LAZARUS CLUB HAD YOUR DIRECT LINE.
GOD WORKS IN MYSTERIOUS WAYS.
MYSTERIOUS INDEED...

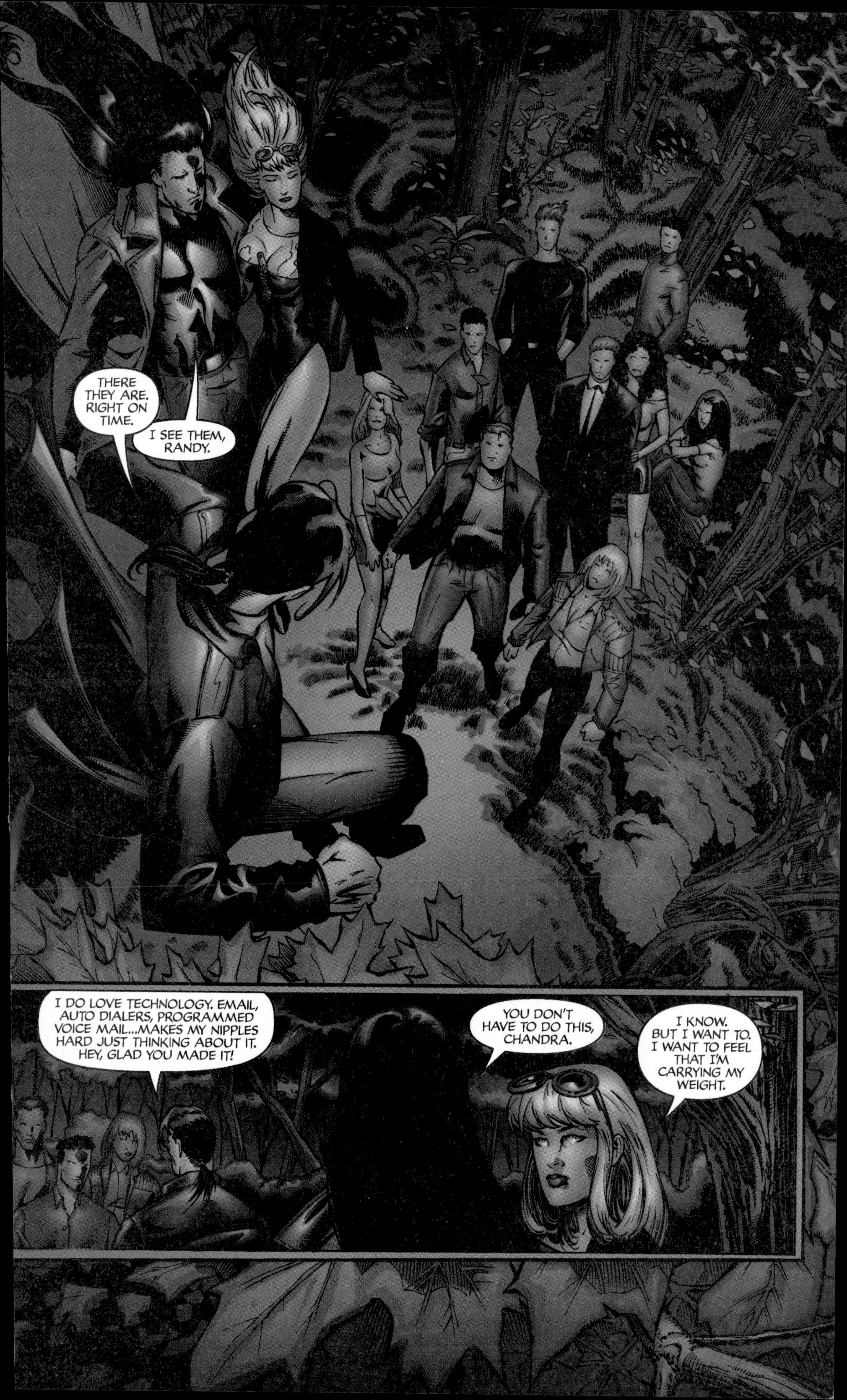
THERE THEY ARE. RIGHT ON TIME.
I SEE THEM, RANDY.
I DO LOVE TECHNOLOGY. EMAIL, AUTO DIALERS, PROGRAMMED VOICE MAIL...MAKES MY NIPPLES HARD JUST THINKING ABOUT IT. HEY, GLAD YOU MADE IT!
YOU DON'T HAVE TO DO THIS, CHANDRA.
I KNOW. BUT I WANT TO. I WANT TO FEEL THAT I'M CARRYING MY WEIGHT.

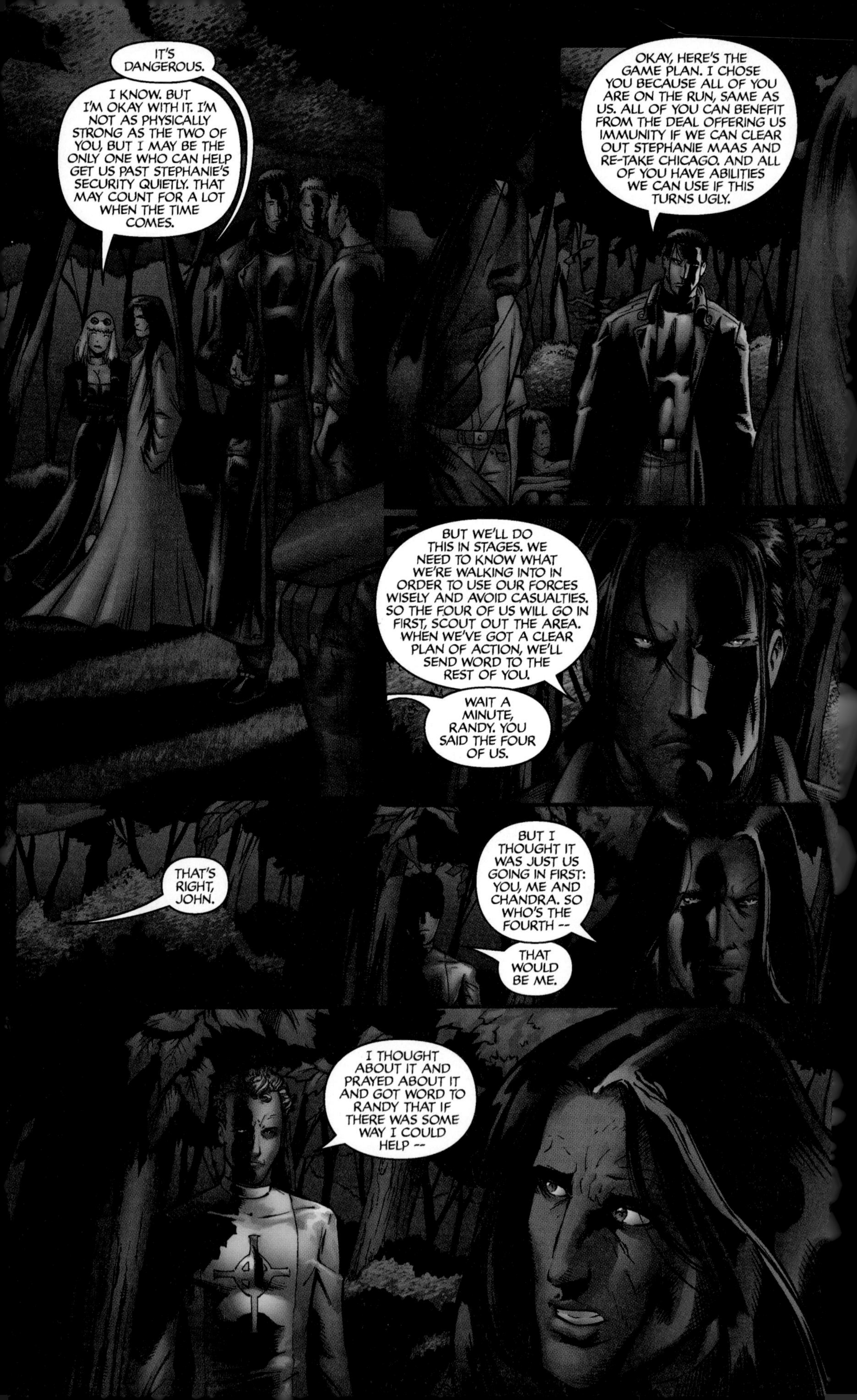
IT'S DANGEROUS.
I KNOW. BUT I'M OKAY WITH IT. I'M NOT AS PHYSICALLY STRONG AS THE TWO OF YOU, BUT I MAY BE THE ONLY ONE WHO CAN HELP GET US PAST STEPHANIE'S SECURITY QUIETLY. THAT MAY COUNT FOR A LOT WHEN THE TIME COMES.
OKAY, HERE'S THE GAME PLAN. I CHOSE YOU BECAUSE ALL OF YOU ARE ON THE RUN, SAME AS US. ALL OF YOU CAN BENEFIT FROM THE DEAL OFFERING US IMMUNITY IF WE CAN CLEAR OUT STEPHANIE MAAS AND RE-TAKE CHICAGO. AND ALL OF YOU HAVE ABILITIES WE CAN USE IF THIS TURNS UGLY.
BUT WE'LL DO THIS IN STAGES. WE NEED TO KNOW WHAT WE'RE WALKING INTO IN ORDER TO USE OUR FORCES WISELY AND AVOID CASUALTIES. SO THE FOUR OF US WILL GO IN FIRST, SCOUT OUT THE AREA. WHEN WE'VE GOT A CLEAR PLAN OF ACTION, WE'LL SEND WORD TO THE REST OF YOU.
WAIT A MINUTE, RANDY. YOU SAID THE FOUR OF US.
THAT'S RIGHT, JOHN.
BUT I THOUGHT IT WAS JUST US GOING IN FIRST: YOU, ME AND CHANDRA. SO WHO'S THE FOURTH --
THAT WOULD BE ME.
I THOUGHT ABOUT IT AND PRAYED ABOUT IT AND GOT WORD TO RANDY THAT IF THERE WAS SOME WAY I COULD HELP --

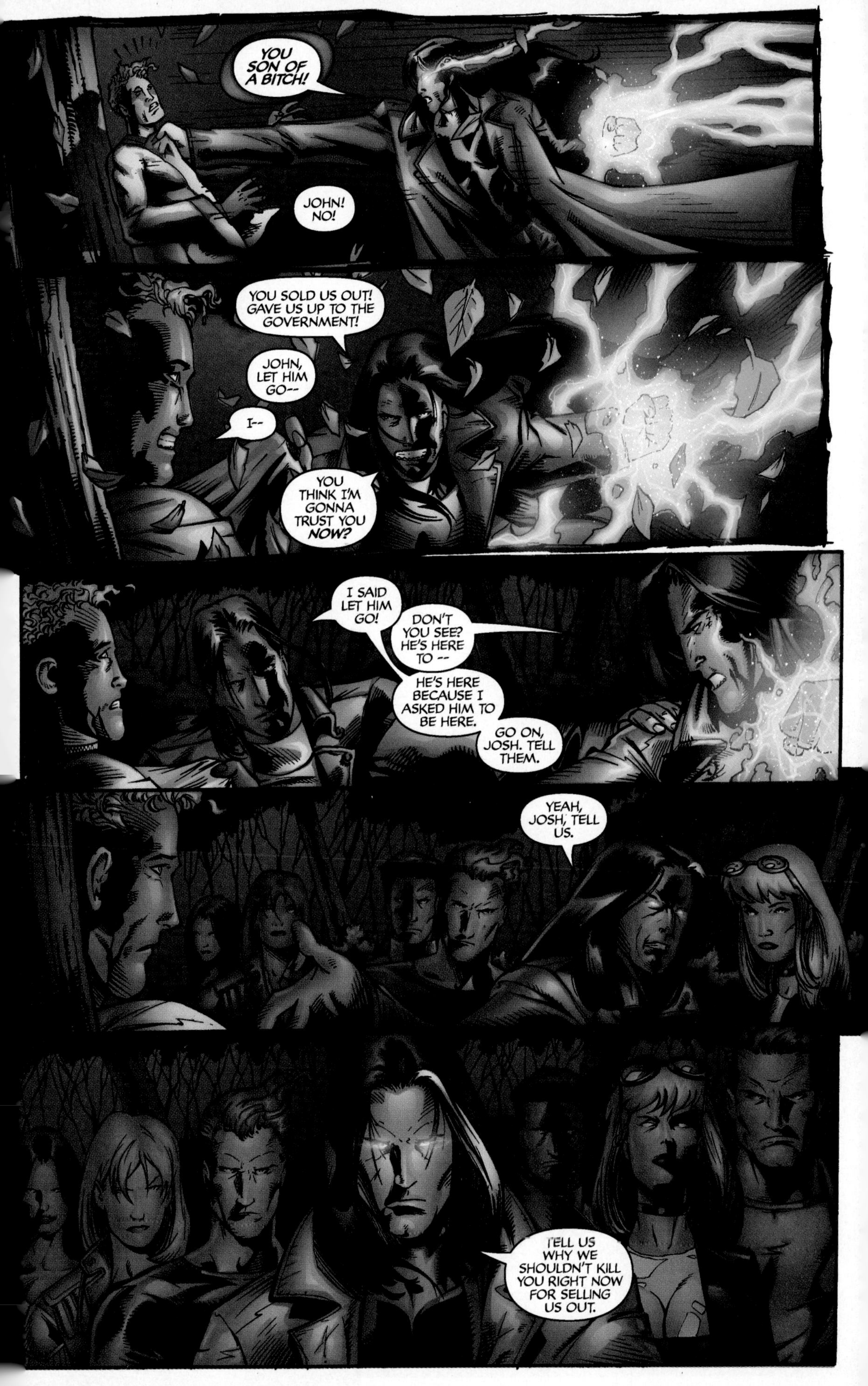
YOU SON OF A BITCH!
JOHN! NO!
YOU SOLD US OUT! GAVE US UP TO THE GOVERNMENT!
JOHN, LET HIM GO--
I--
YOU THINK I'M GONNA TRUST YOU *NOW?*
I SAID LET HIM GO!
DON'T YOU SEE? HE'S HERE TO --
HE'S HERE BECAUSE I ASKED HIM TO BE HERE.
GO ON, JOSH. TELL THEM.
YEAH, JOSH, TELL US.
TELL US WHY WE SHOULDN'T KILL YOU RIGHT NOW FOR SELLING US OUT.

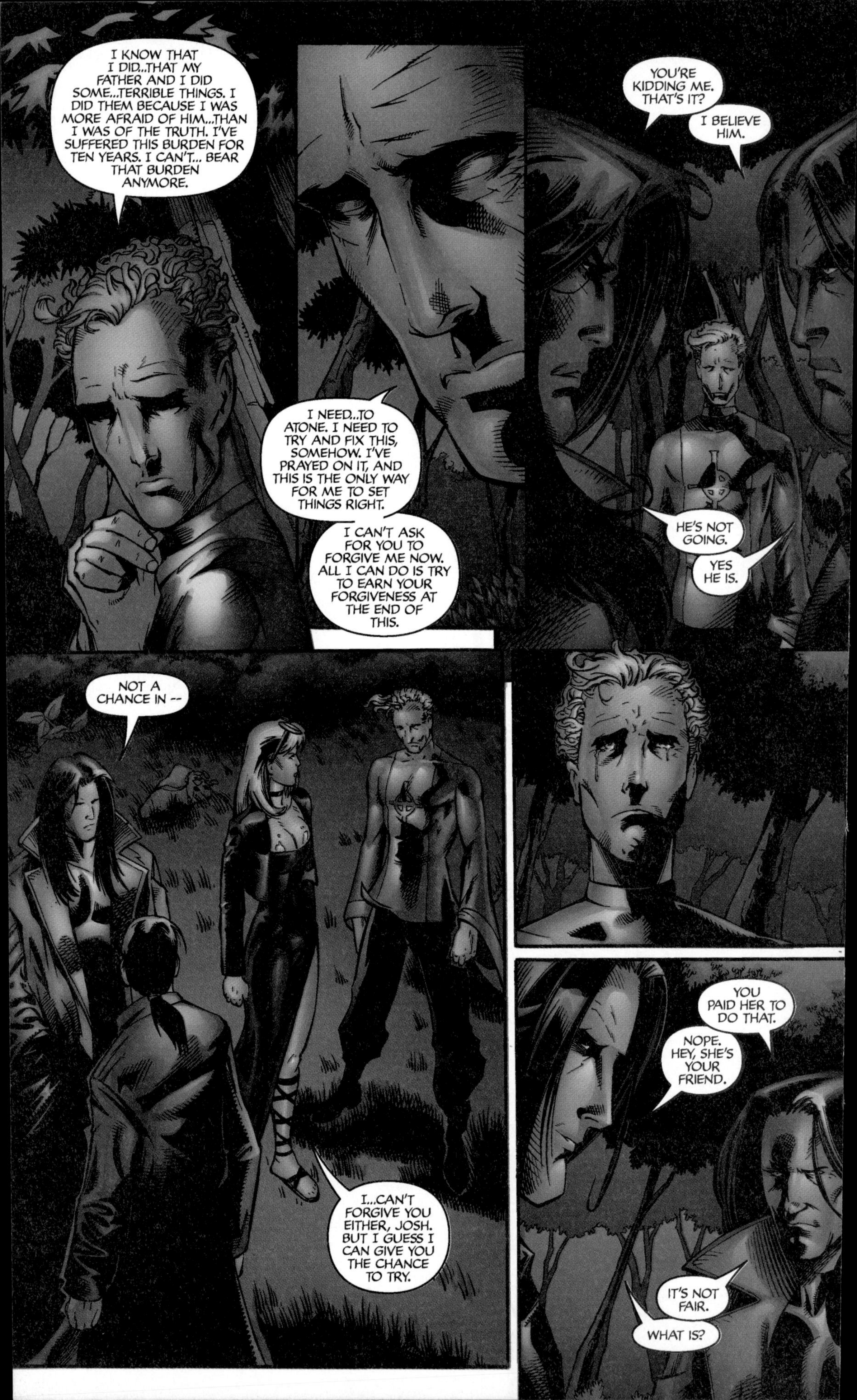

I KNOW THAT I DID...THAT MY FATHER AND I DID SOME...TERRIBLE THINGS. I DID THEM BECAUSE I WAS MORE AFRAID OF HIM...THAN I WAS OF THE TRUTH. I'VE SUFFERED THIS BURDEN FOR TEN YEARS. I CAN'T... BEAR THAT BURDEN ANYMORE.
I NEED...TO ATONE. I NEED TO TRY AND FIX THIS, SOMEHOW. I'VE PRAYED ON IT, AND THIS IS THE ONLY WAY FOR ME TO SET THINGS RIGHT.
I CAN'T ASK FOR YOU TO FORGIVE ME NOW. ALL I CAN DO IS TRY TO EARN YOUR FORGIVENESS AT THE END OF THIS.
YOU'RE KIDDING ME. THAT'S IT?
I BELIEVE HIM.
HE'S NOT GOING.
YES HE IS.
NOT A CHANCE IN --
I...CAN'T FORGIVE YOU EITHER, JOSH. BUT I GUESS I CAN GIVE YOU THE CHANCE TO TRY.
YOU PAID HER TO DO THAT.
NOPE. HEY, SHE'S YOUR FRIEND.
IT'S NOT FAIR.
WHAT IS?

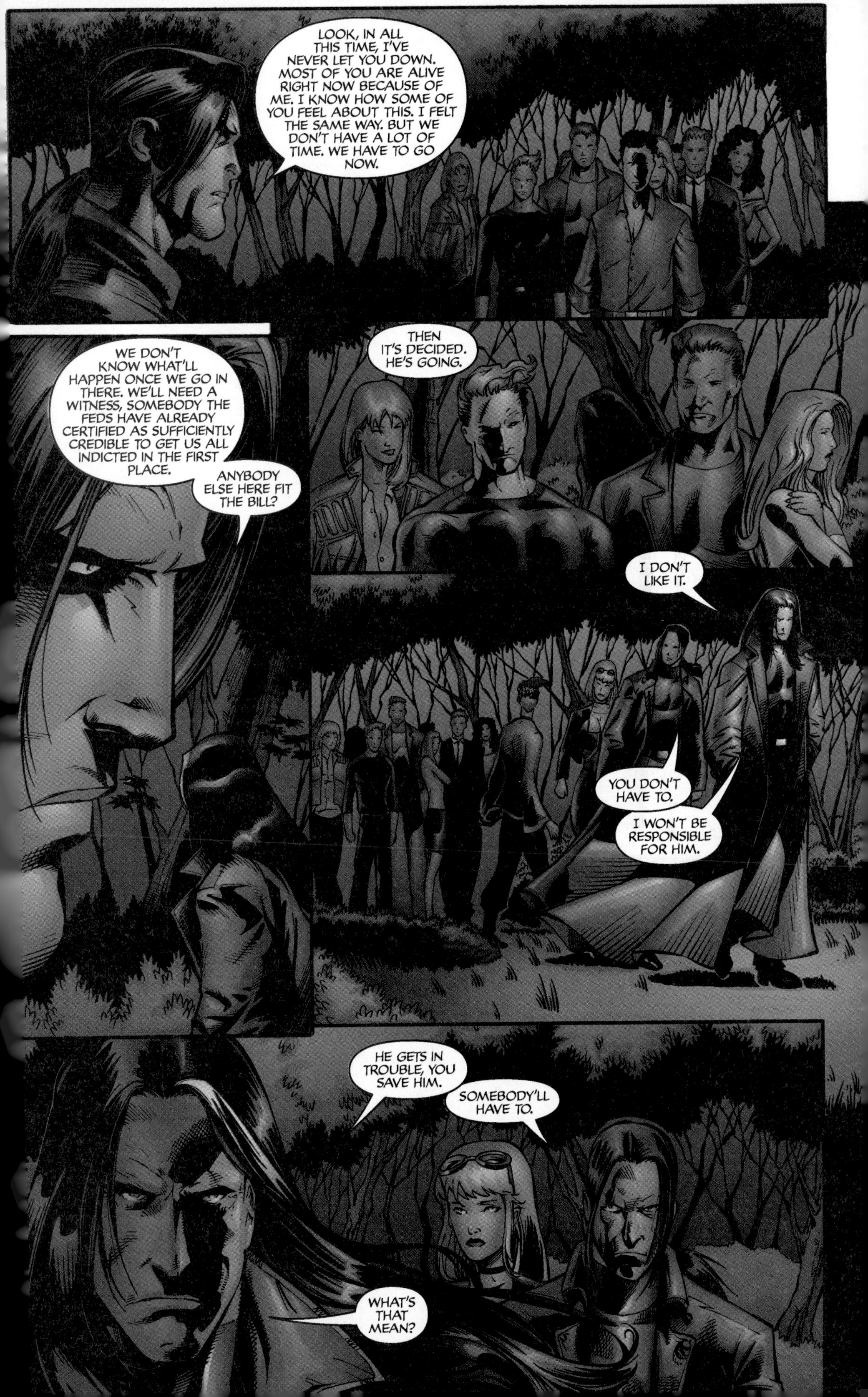
LOOK, IN ALL THIS TIME, I'VE NEVER LET YOU DOWN. MOST OF YOU ARE ALIVE RIGHT NOW BECAUSE OF ME. I KNOW HOW SOME OF YOU FEEL ABOUT THIS. I FELT THE SAME WAY. BUT WE DON'T HAVE A LOT OF TIME. WE HAVE TO GO NOW.
WE DON'T KNOW WHAT'LL HAPPEN ONCE WE GO IN THERE. WE'LL NEED A WITNESS, SOMEBODY THE FEDS HAVE ALREADY CERTIFIED AS SUFFICIENTLY CREDIBLE TO GET US ALL INDICTED IN THE FIRST PLACE.
ANYBODY ELSE HERE FIT THE BILL?
THEN IT'S DECIDED. HE'S GOING.
I DON'T LIKE IT.
YOU DON'T HAVE TO.
I WON'T BE RESPONSIBLE FOR HIM.
HE GETS IN TROUBLE, YOU SAVE HIM.
SOMEBODY'LL HAVE TO.
WHAT'S THAT MEAN?

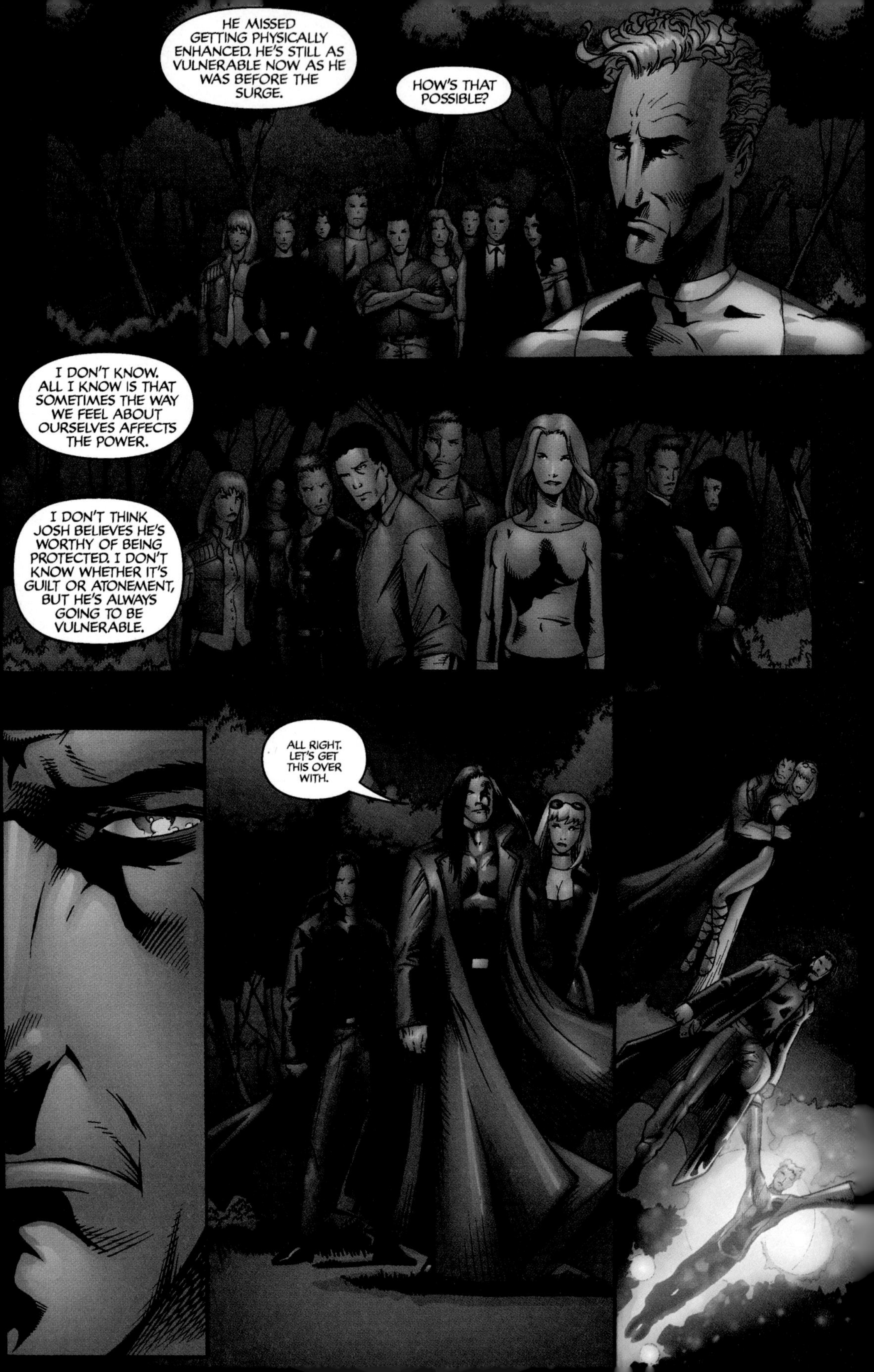
HE MISSED GETTING PHYSICALLY ENHANCED. HE'S STILL AS VULNERABLE NOW AS HE WAS BEFORE THE SURGE.
HOW'S THAT POSSIBLE?
I DON'T KNOW. ALL I KNOW IS THAT SOMETIMES THE WAY WE FEEL ABOUT OURSELVES AFFECTS THE POWER.
I DON'T THINK JOSH BELIEVES HE'S WORTHY OF BEING PROTECTED. I DON'T KNOW WHETHER IT'S GUILT OR ATONEMENT, BUT HE'S ALWAYS GOING TO BE VULNERABLE.
ALL RIGHT. LET'S GET THIS OVER WITH.

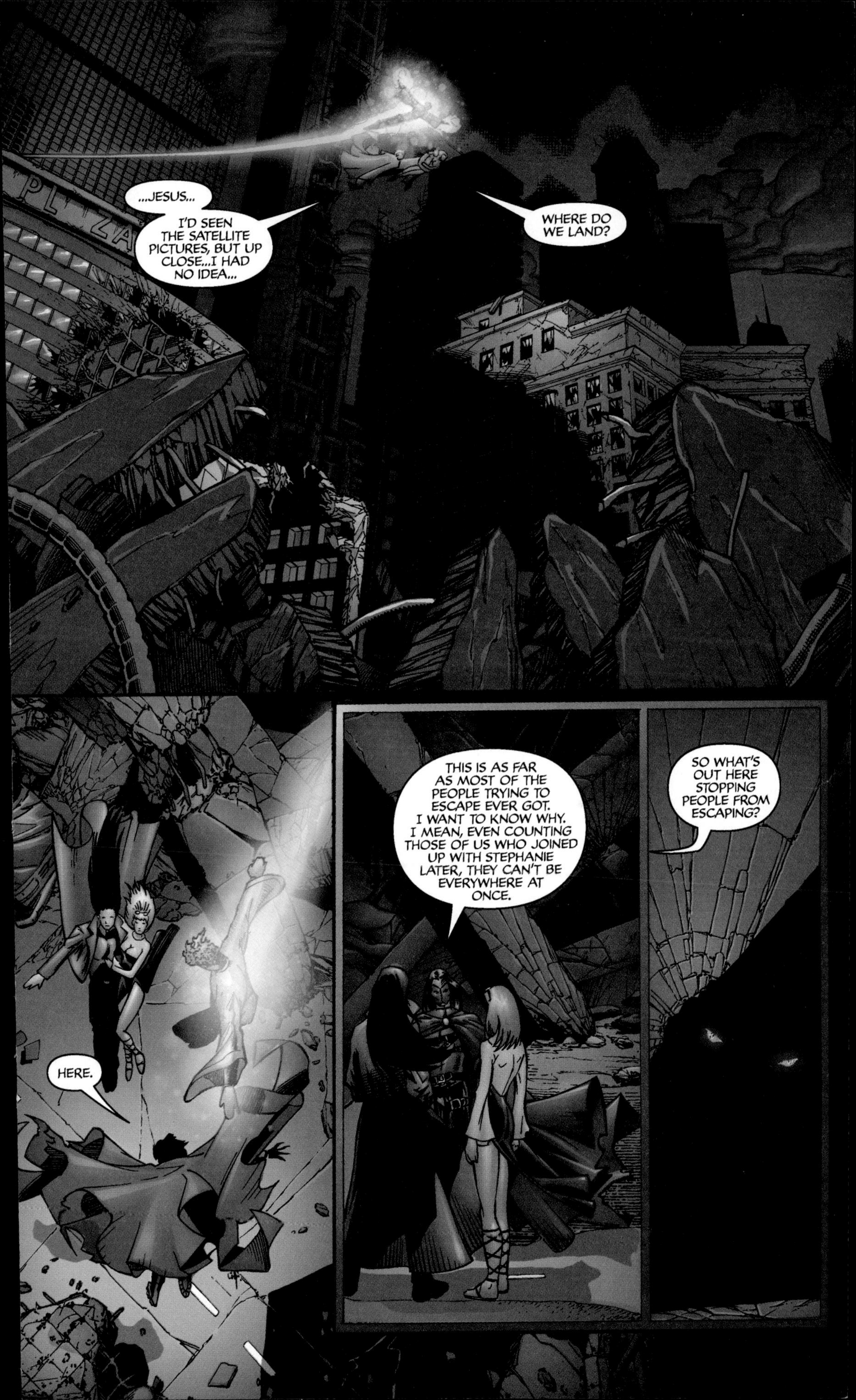
...JESUS...
I'D SEEN THE SATELLITE PICTURES, BUT UP CLOSE...I HAD NO IDEA...
WHERE DO WE LAND?
HERE.
THIS IS AS FAR AS MOST OF THE PEOPLE TRYING TO ESCAPE EVER GOT. I WANT TO KNOW WHY. I MEAN, EVEN COUNTING THOSE OF US WHO JOINED UP WITH STEPHANIE LATER, THEY CAN'T BE EVERYWHERE AT ONCE.
SO WHAT'S OUT HERE STOPPING PEOPLE FROM ESCAPING?

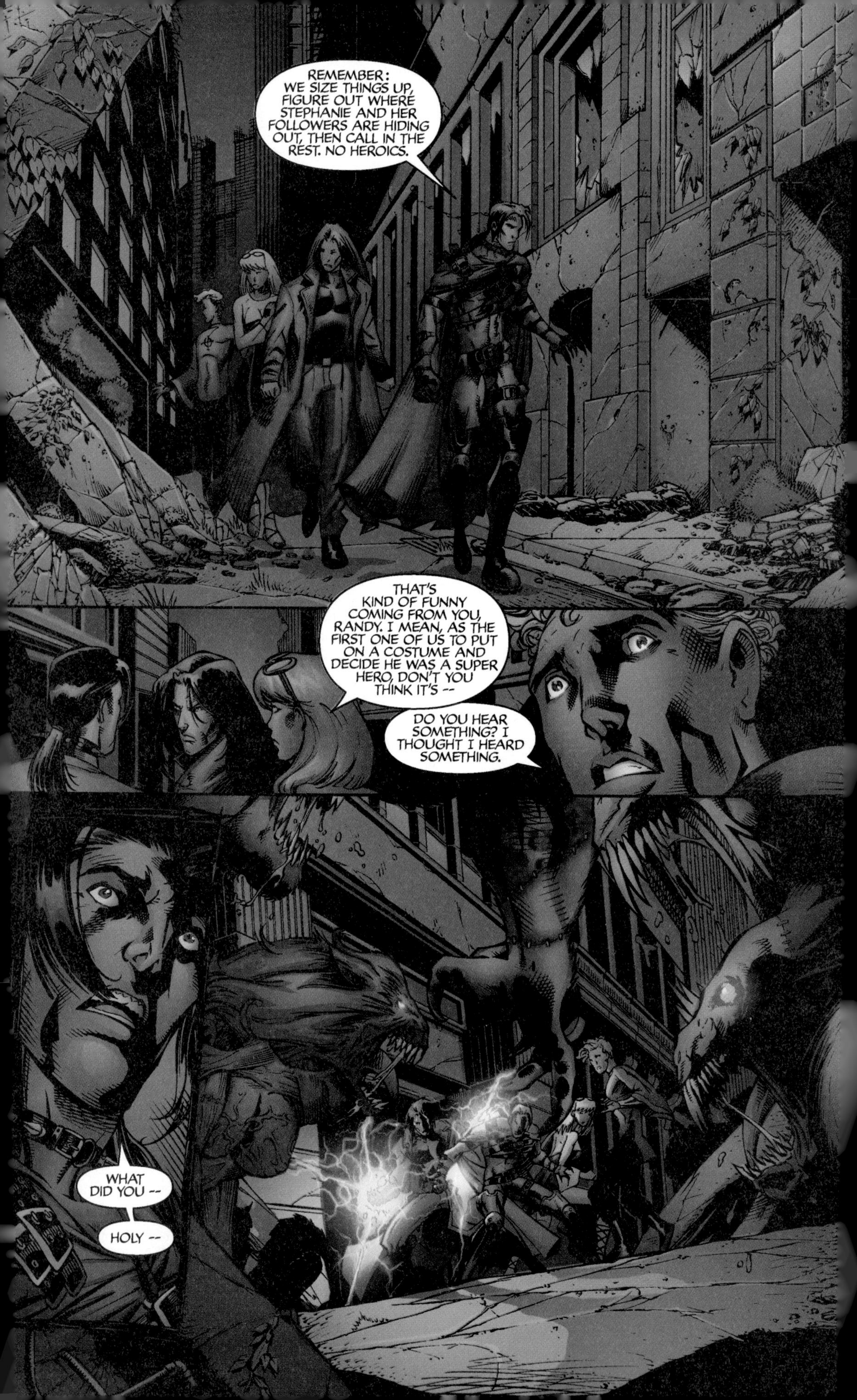
REMEMBER: WE SIZE THINGS UP, FIGURE OUT WHERE STEPHANIE AND HER FOLLOWERS ARE HIDING OUT, THEN CALL IN THE REST. NO HEROICS.
THAT'S KIND OF FUNNY COMING FROM YOU, RANDY. I MEAN, AS THE FIRST ONE OF US TO PUT ON A COSTUME AND DECIDE HE WAS A SUPER HERO, DON'T YOU THINK IT'S --
DO YOU HEAR SOMETHING? I THOUGHT I HEARD SOMETHING.
WHAT DID YOU --
HOLY --

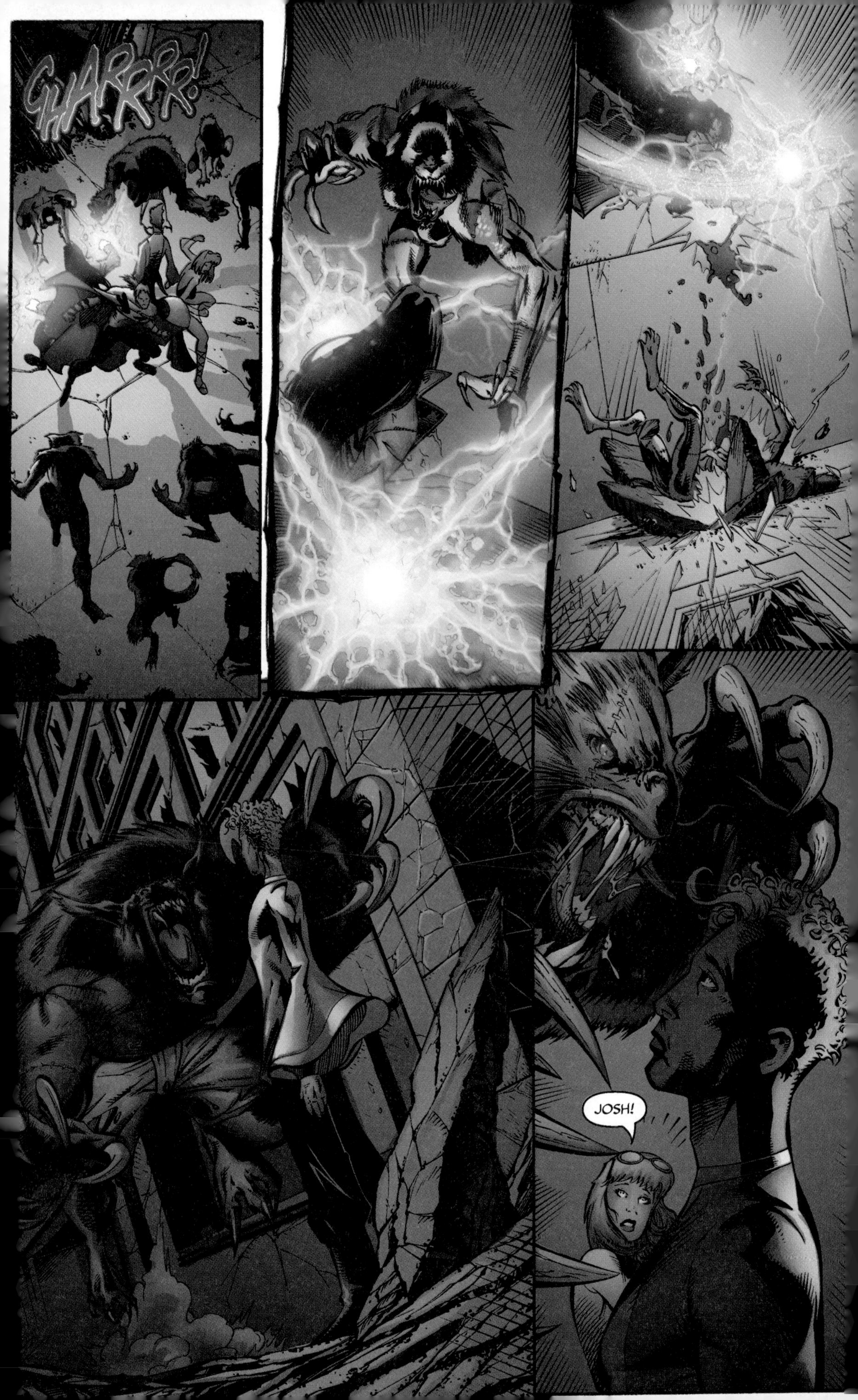
GHARRRR!
JOSH!

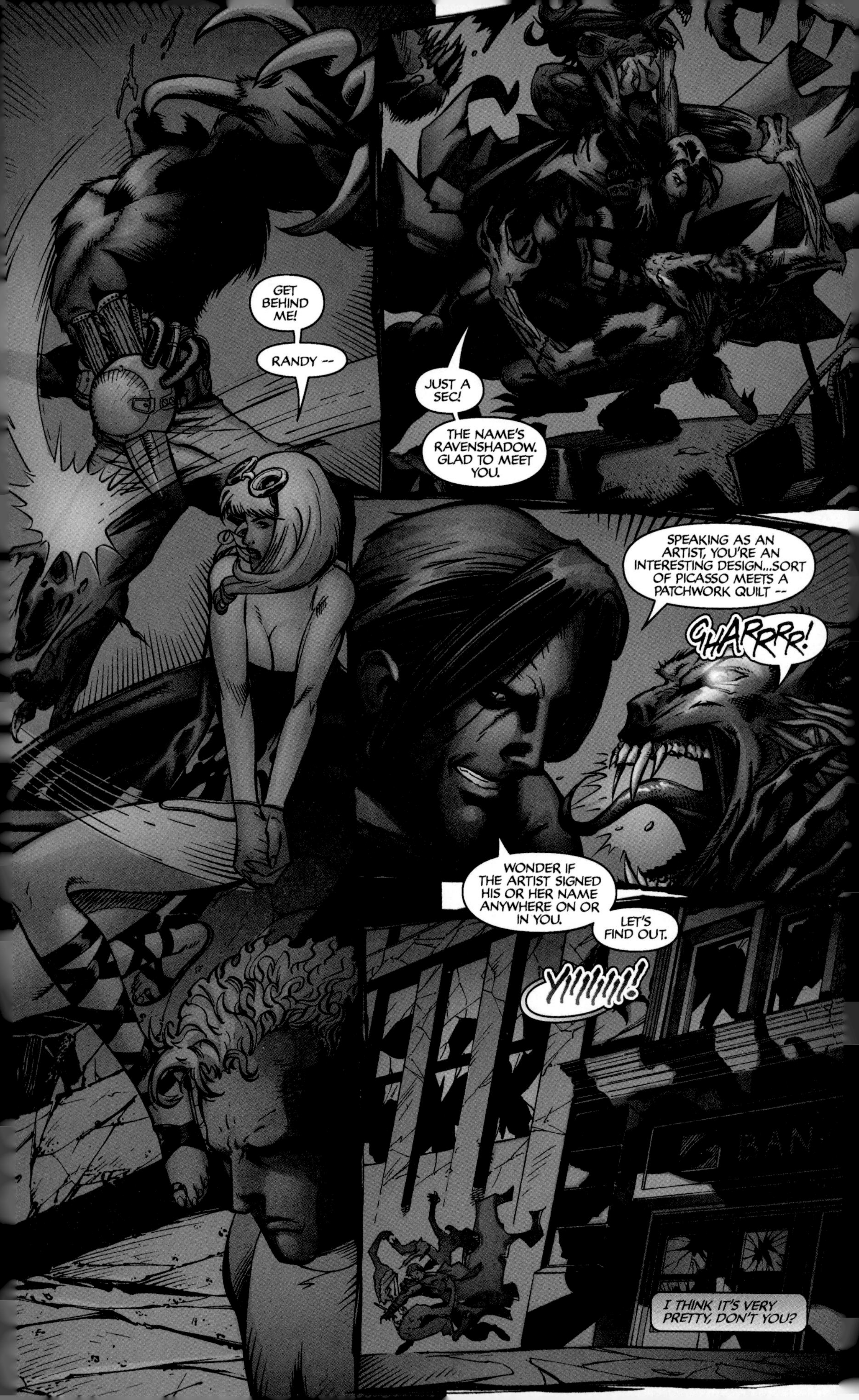
GET BEHIND ME!
RANDY --
JUST A SEC!
THE NAME'S RAVENSHADOW. GLAD TO MEET YOU.
SPEAKING AS AN ARTIST, YOU'RE AN INTERESTING DESIGN...SORT OF PICASSO MEETS A PATCHWORK QUILT --
GHARRRR!
WONDER IF THE ARTIST SIGNED HIS OR HER NAME ANYWHERE ON OR IN YOU.
LET'S FIND OUT.
YIIIIII!
BAN
I THINK IT'S VERY PRETTY, DON'T YOU?

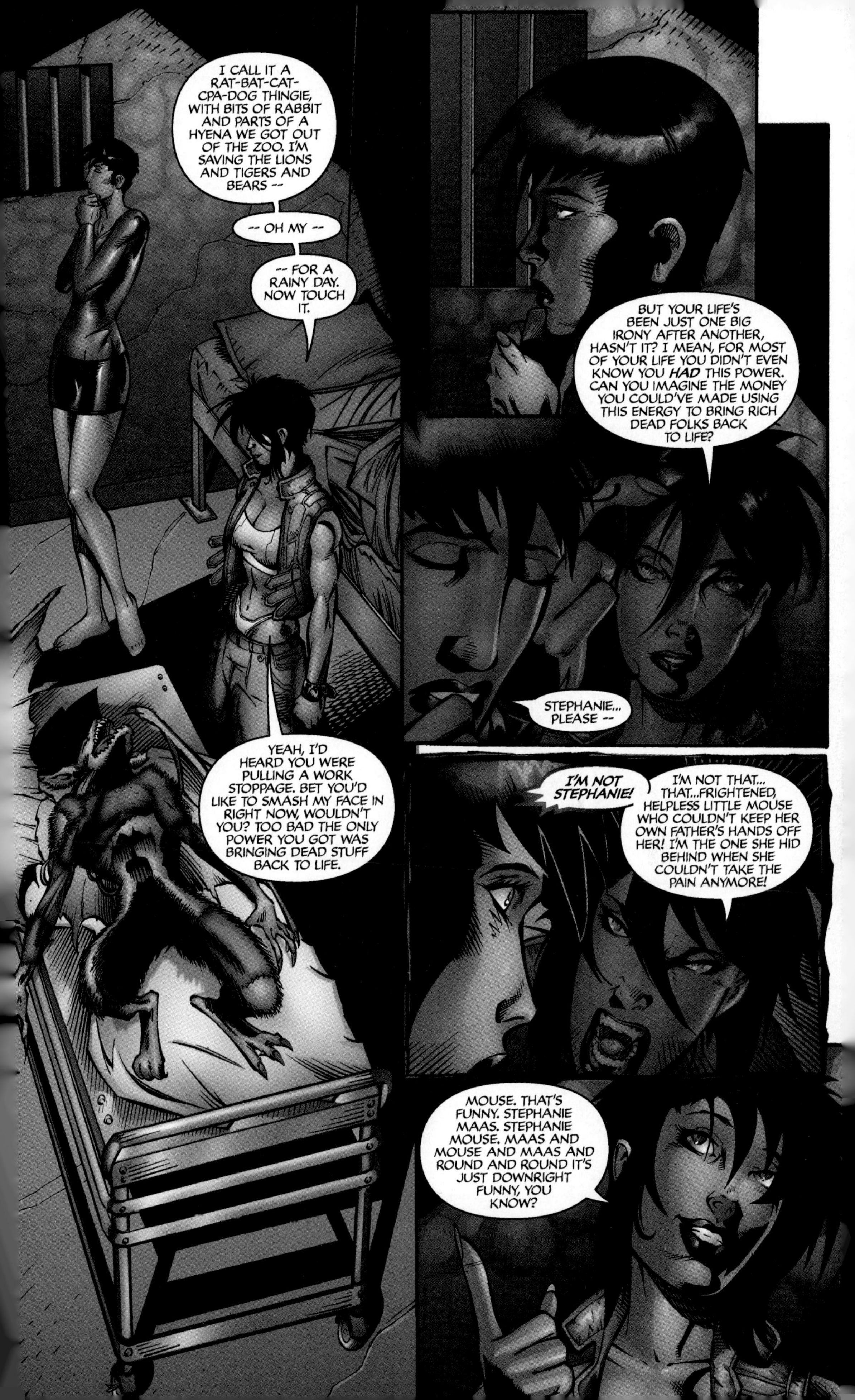
I CALL IT A RAT-BAT-CAT-CPA-DOG THINGIE, WITH BITS OF RABBIT AND PARTS OF A HYENA WE GOT OUT OF THE ZOO. I'M SAVING THE LIONS AND TIGERS AND BEARS --
-- OH MY --
-- FOR A RAINY DAY. NOW TOUCH IT.
YEAH, I'D HEARD YOU WERE PULLING A WORK STOPPAGE. BET YOU'D LIKE TO SMASH MY FACE IN RIGHT NOW, WOULDN'T YOU? TOO BAD THE ONLY POWER YOU GOT WAS BRINGING DEAD STUFF BACK TO LIFE.
BUT YOUR LIFE'S BEEN JUST ONE BIG IRONY AFTER ANOTHER, HASN'T IT? I MEAN, FOR MOST OF YOUR LIFE YOU DIDN'T EVEN KNOW YOU HAD THIS POWER. CAN YOU IMAGINE THE MONEY YOU COULD'VE MADE USING THIS ENERGY TO BRING RICH DEAD FOLKS BACK TO LIFE?
STEPHANIE... PLEASE --
I'M NOT STEPHANIE!
I'M NOT THAT... THAT...FRIGHTENED, HELPLESS LITTLE MOUSE WHO COULDN'T KEEP HER OWN FATHER'S HANDS OFF HER! I'M THE ONE SHE HID BEHIND WHEN SHE COULDN'T TAKE THE PAIN ANYMORE!
MOUSE. THAT'S FUNNY. STEPHANIE MAAS. STEPHANIE MOUSE. MAAS AND MOUSE AND MAAS AND ROUND AND ROUND IT'S JUST DOWNRIGHT FUNNY, YOU KNOW?

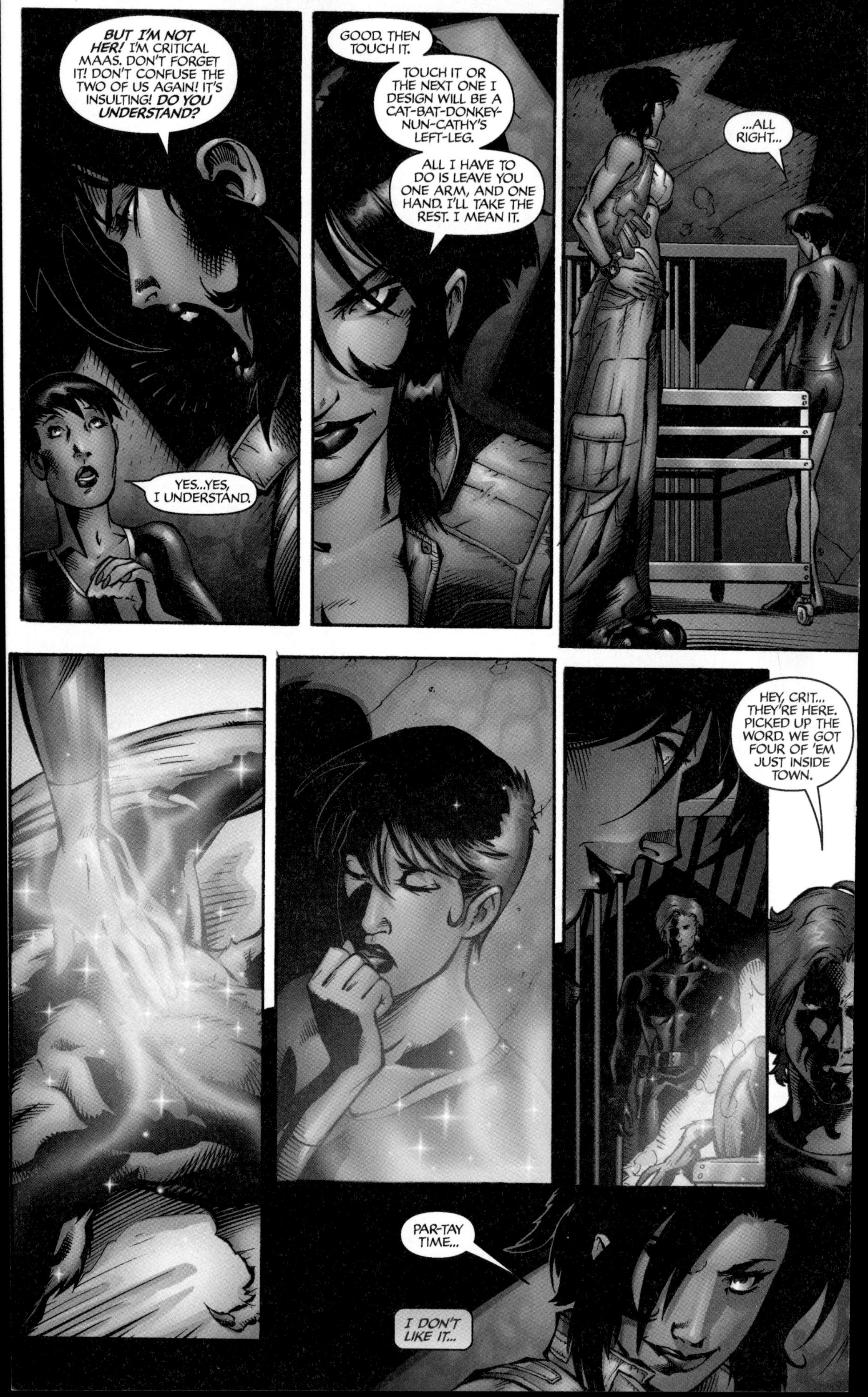

BUT I'M NOT HER! I'M CRITICAL MAAS. DON'T FORGET IT! DON'T CONFUSE THE TWO OF US AGAIN! IT'S INSULTING! DO YOU UNDERSTAND?
YES...YES, I UNDERSTAND.
GOOD. THEN TOUCH IT.
TOUCH IT OR THE NEXT ONE I DESIGN WILL BE A CAT-BAT-DONKEY-NUN-CATHY'S LEFT-LEG.
ALL I HAVE TO DO IS LEAVE YOU ONE ARM, AND ONE HAND. I'LL TAKE THE REST. I MEAN IT.
...ALL RIGHT...
HEY, CRIT... THEY'RE HERE. PICKED UP THE WORD. WE GOT FOUR OF 'EM JUST INSIDE TOWN.
PAR-TAY TIME...
I DON'T LIKE IT...

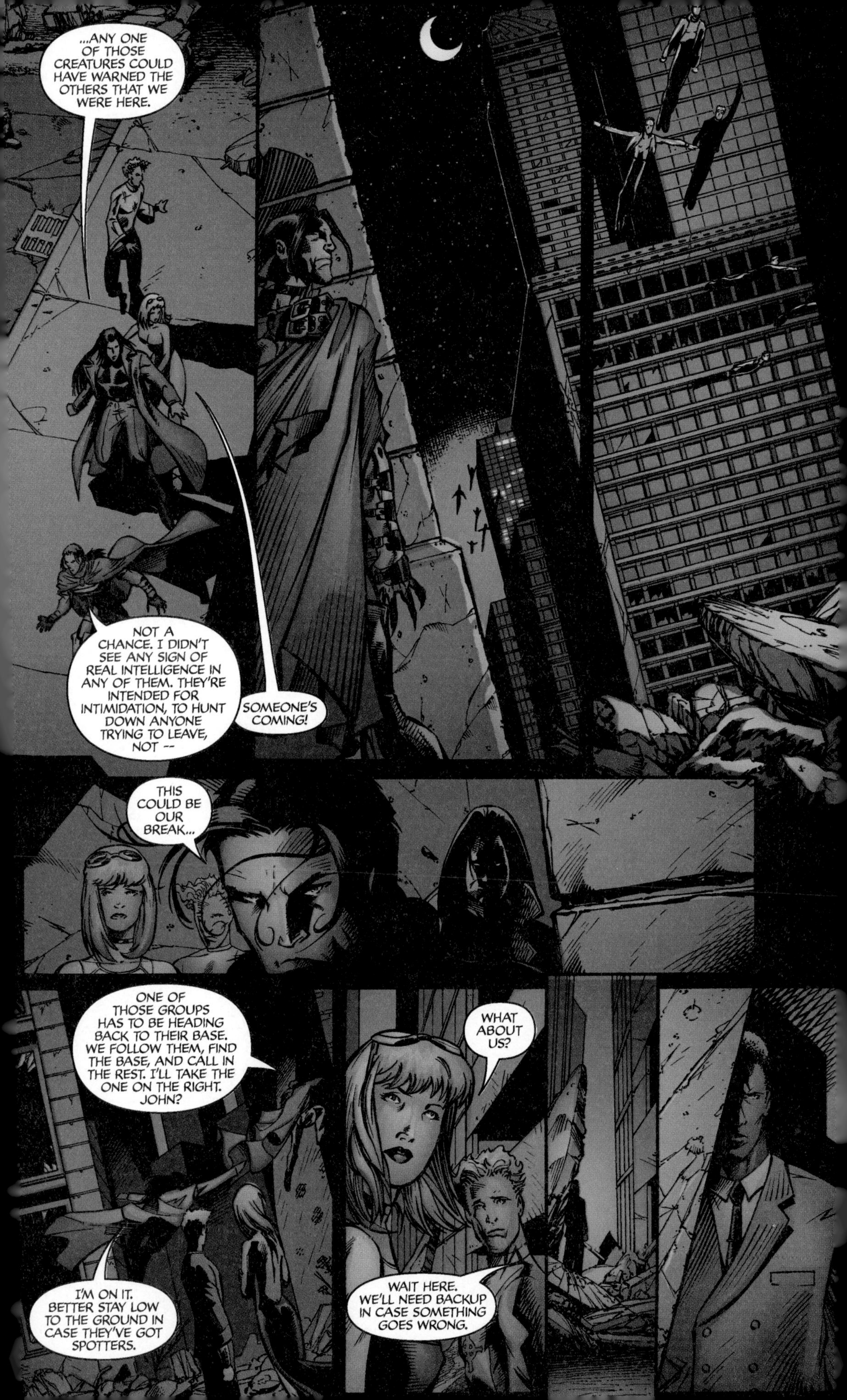
...ANY ONE OF THOSE CREATURES COULD HAVE WARNED THE OTHERS THAT WE WERE HERE.
NOT A CHANCE. I DIDN'T SEE ANY SIGN OF REAL INTELLIGENCE IN ANY OF THEM. THEY'RE INTENDED FOR INTIMIDATION, TO HUNT DOWN ANYONE TRYING TO LEAVE, NOT --
SOMEONE'S COMING!
THIS COULD BE OUR BREAK...
ONE OF THOSE GROUPS HAS TO BE HEADING BACK TO THEIR BASE. WE FOLLOW THEM, FIND THE BASE, AND CALL IN THE REST. I'LL TAKE THE ONE ON THE RIGHT. JOHN?
I'M ON IT. BETTER STAY LOW TO THE GROUND IN CASE THEY'VE GOT SPOTTERS.
WHAT ABOUT US?
WAIT HERE. WE'LL NEED BACKUP IN CASE SOMETHING GOES WRONG.

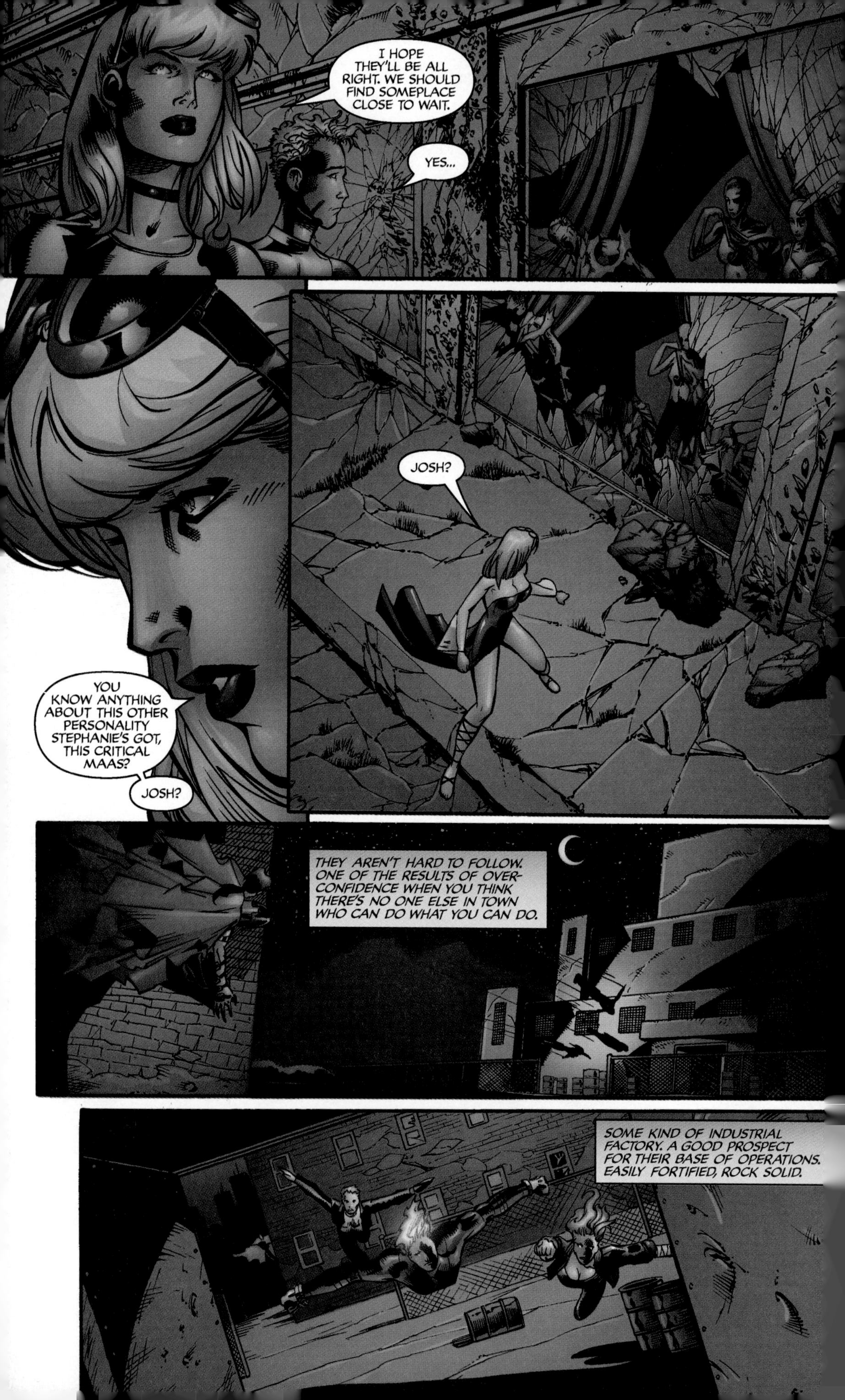
I HOPE THEY'LL BE ALL RIGHT. WE SHOULD FIND SOMEPLACE CLOSE TO WAIT.
YES...
YOU KNOW ANYTHING ABOUT THIS OTHER PERSONALITY STEPHANIE'S GOT, THIS CRITICAL MAAS?
JOSH?
JOSH?
THEY AREN'T HARD TO FOLLOW. ONE OF THE RESULTS OF OVER-CONFIDENCE WHEN YOU THINK THERE'S NO ONE ELSE IN TOWN WHO CAN DO WHAT YOU CAN DO.
SOME KIND OF INDUSTRIAL FACTORY. A GOOD PROSPECT FOR THEIR BASE OF OPERATIONS. EASILY FORTIFIED, ROCK SOLID.

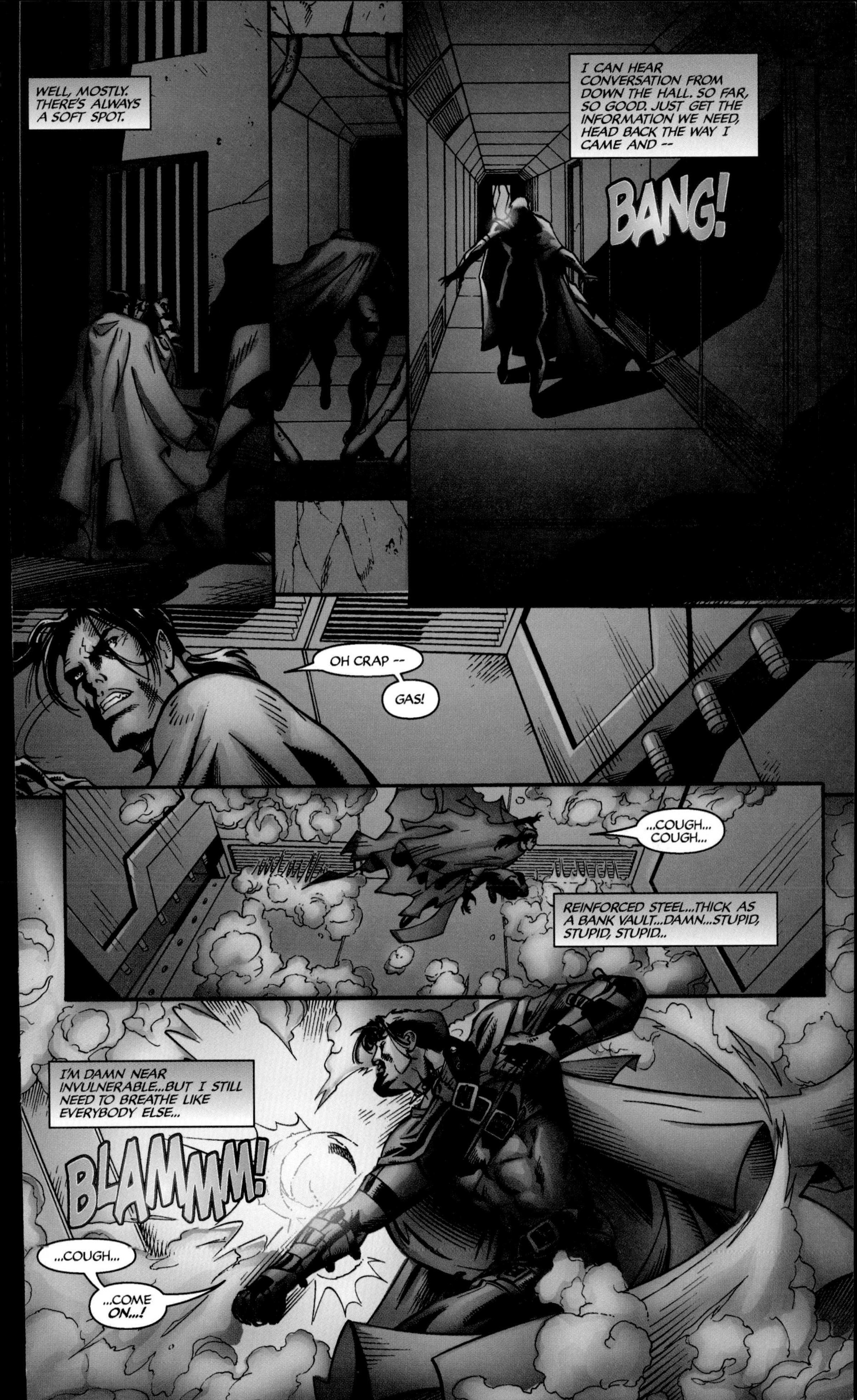
WELL, MOSTLY. THERE'S ALWAYS A SOFT SPOT.
I CAN HEAR CONVERSATION FROM DOWN THE HALL. SO FAR, SO GOOD. JUST GET THE INFORMATION WE NEED, HEAD BACK THE WAY I CAME AND --
BANG!
OH CRAP --
GAS!
...COUGH... COUGH...
REINFORCED STEEL...THICK AS A BANK VAULT...DAMN...STUPID, STUPID, STUPID...
I'M DAMN NEAR INVULNERABLE...BUT I STILL NEED TO BREATHE LIKE EVERYBODY ELSE...
BLAMMM!
...COUGH...
...COME ON...!

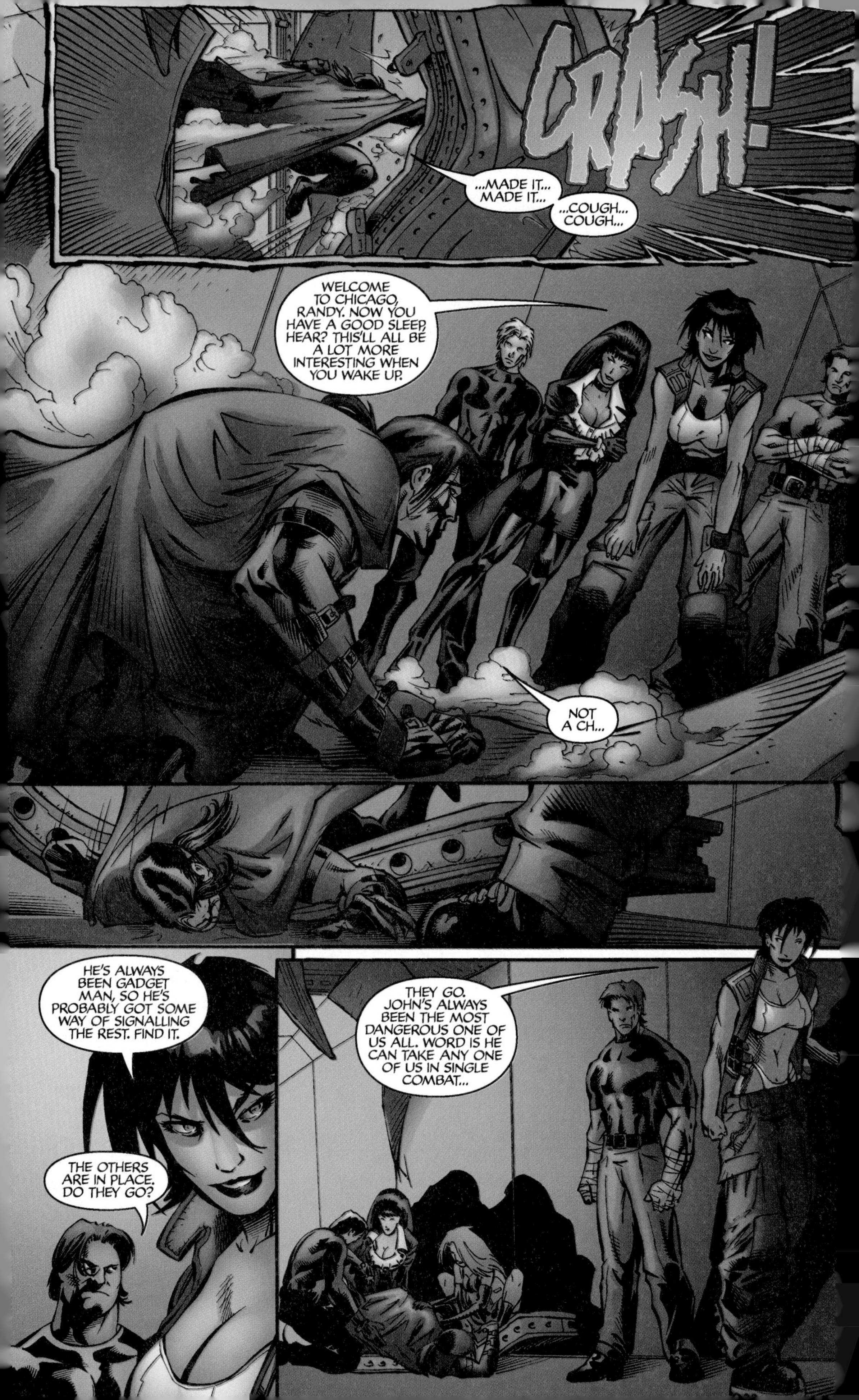
CRASH!
...MADE IT... MADE IT...
...COUGH... COUGH...
WELCOME TO CHICAGO, RANDY. NOW YOU HAVE A GOOD SLEEP, HEAR? THIS'LL ALL BE A LOT MORE INTERESTING WHEN YOU WAKE UP.
NOT A CH...
HE'S ALWAYS BEEN GADGET MAN, SO HE'S PROBABLY GOT SOME WAY OF SIGNALLING THE REST. FIND IT.
THE OTHERS ARE IN PLACE. DO THEY GO?
THEY GO. JOHN'S ALWAYS BEEN THE MOST DANGEROUS ONE OF US ALL. WORD IS HE CAN TAKE ANY ONE OF US IN SINGLE COMBAT...

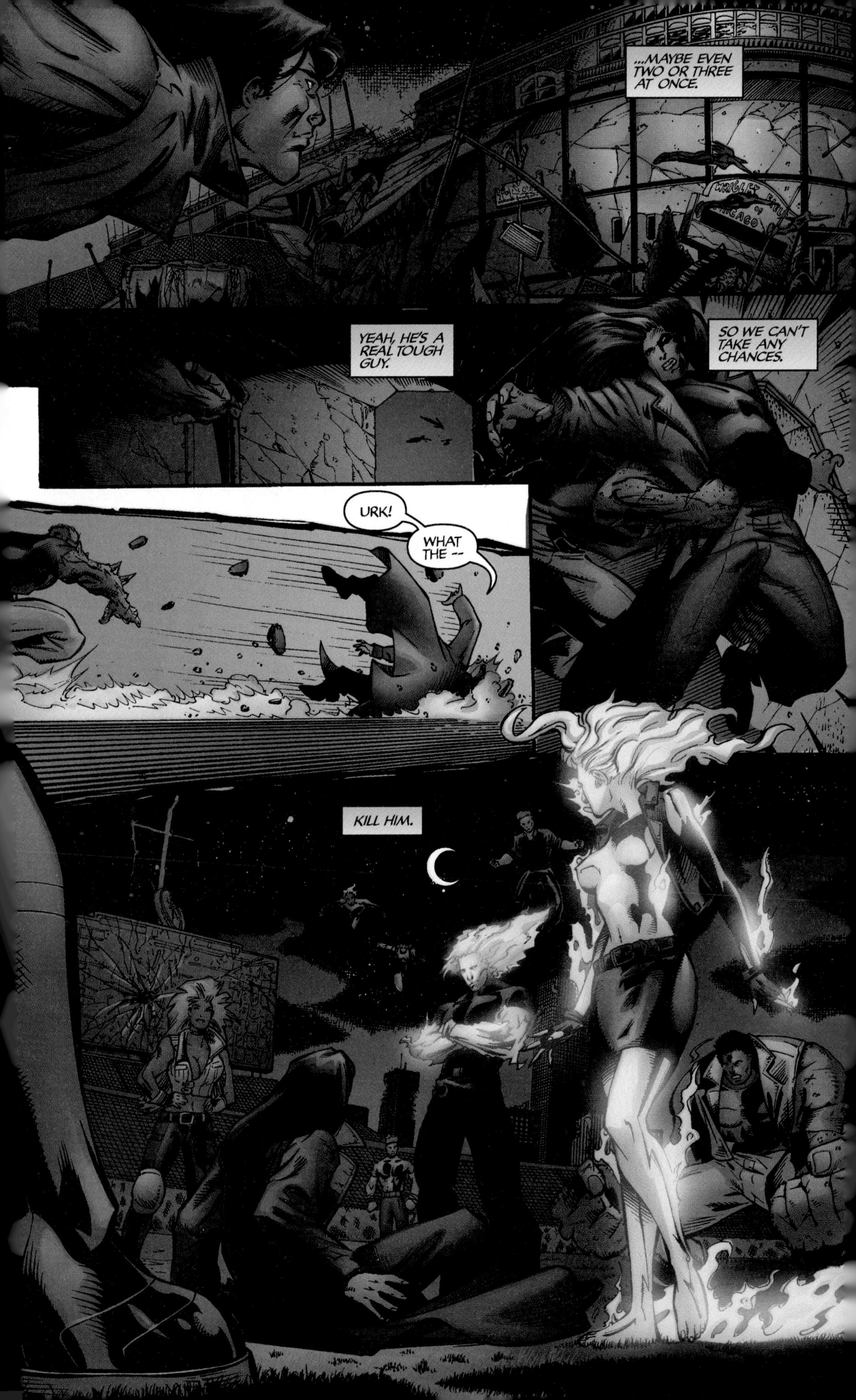
...MAYBE EVEN TWO OR THREE AT ONCE.
YEAH, HE'S A REAL TOUGH GUY.
SO WE CAN'T TAKE ANY CHANCES.
URK!
WHAT THE --
KILL HIM.

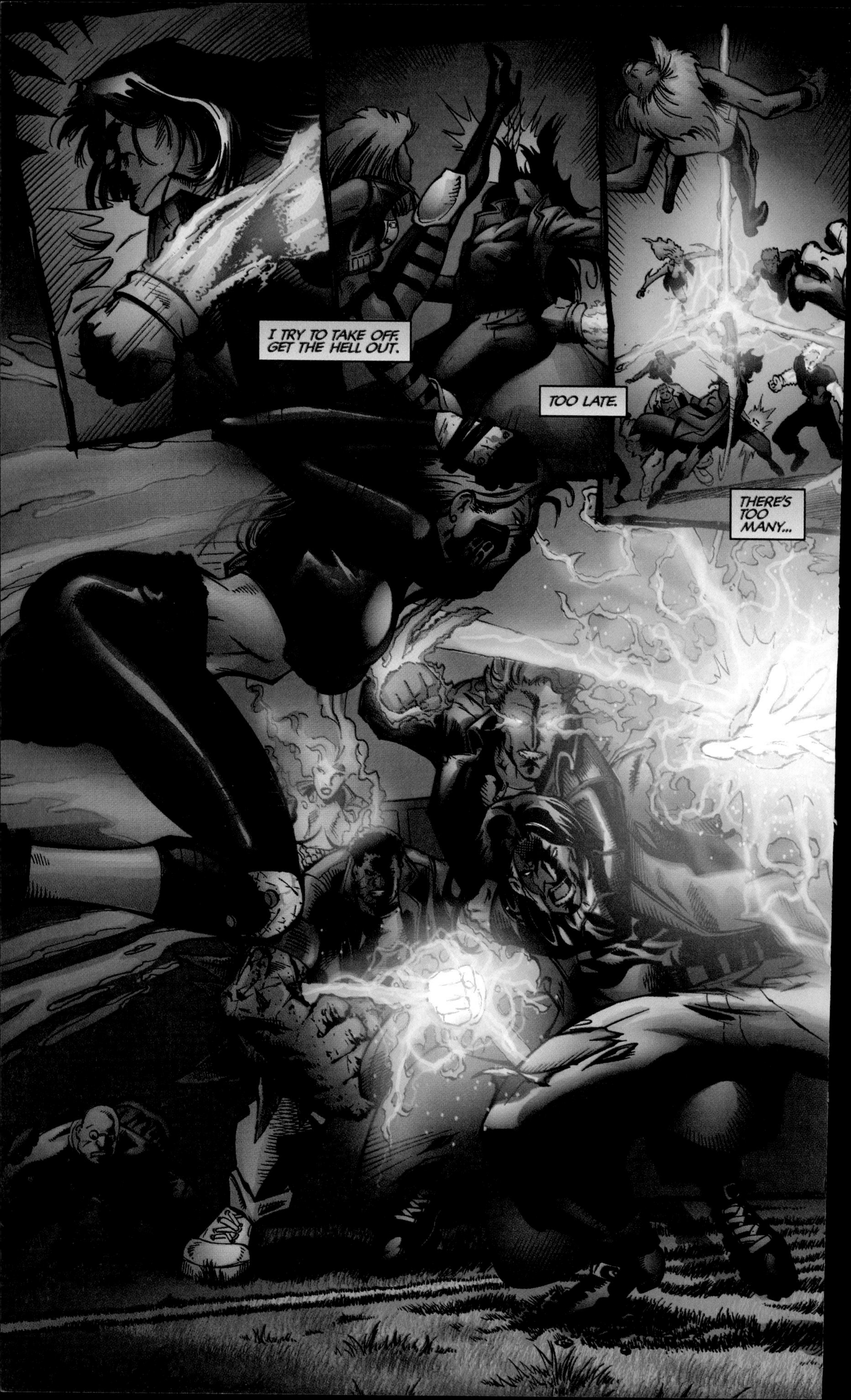
I TRY TO TAKE OFF. GET THE HELL OUT.
TOO LATE.
THERE'S TOO MANY...

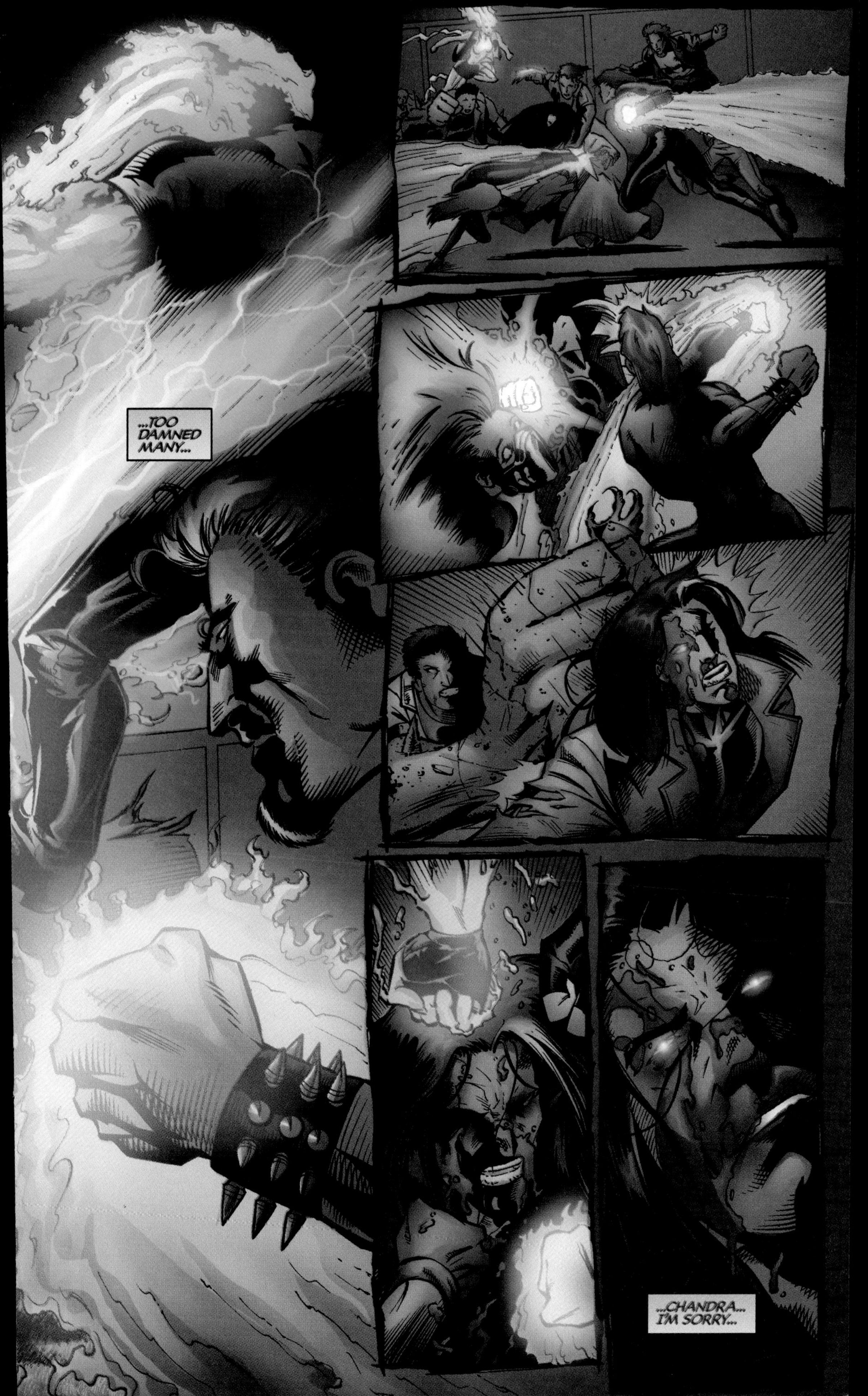
...TOO DAMNED MANY...
...CHANDRA... I'M SORRY...

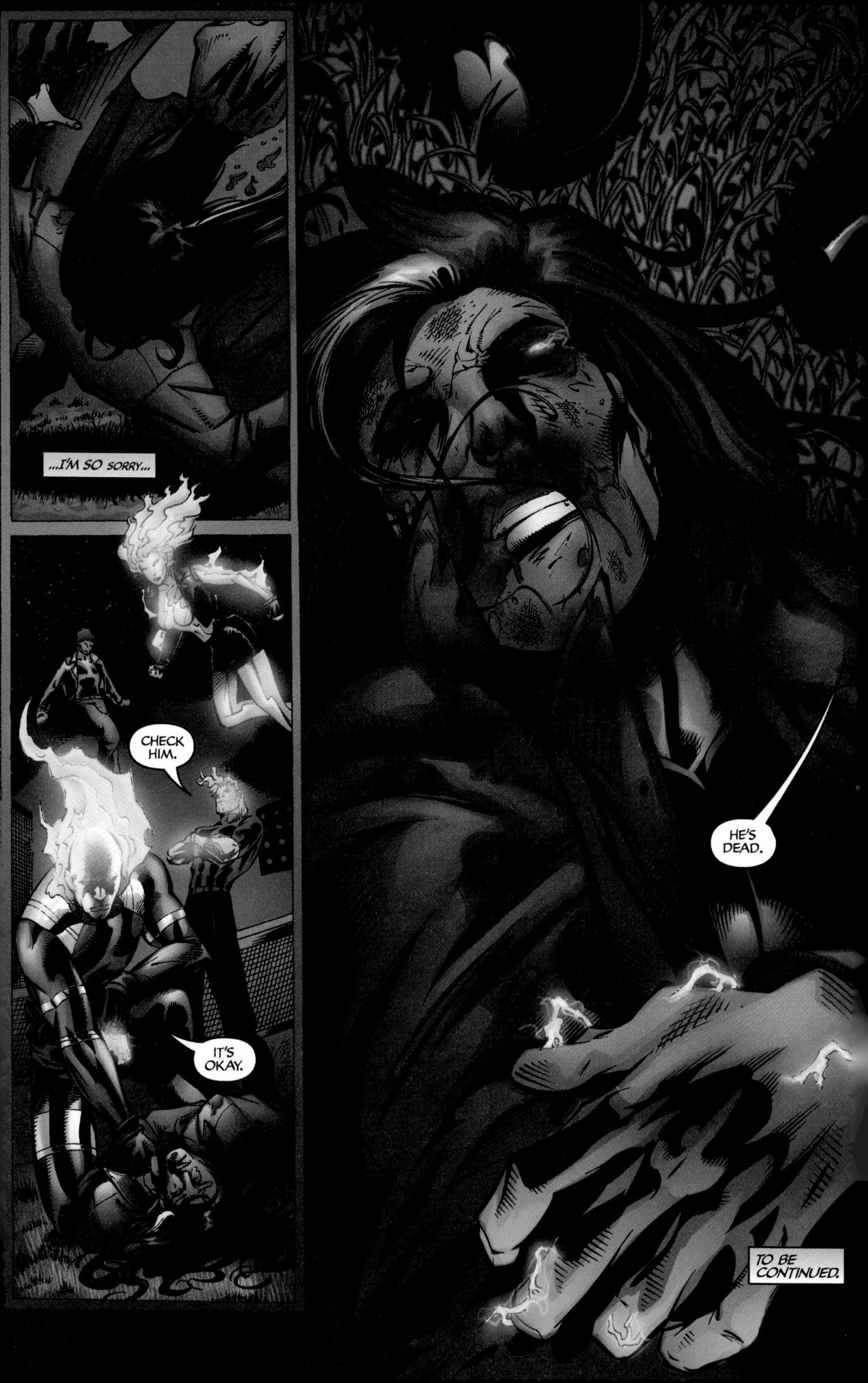
...I'M SO SORRY...
CHECK HIM.
IT'S OKAY.
HE'S DEAD.
TO BE CONTINUED.

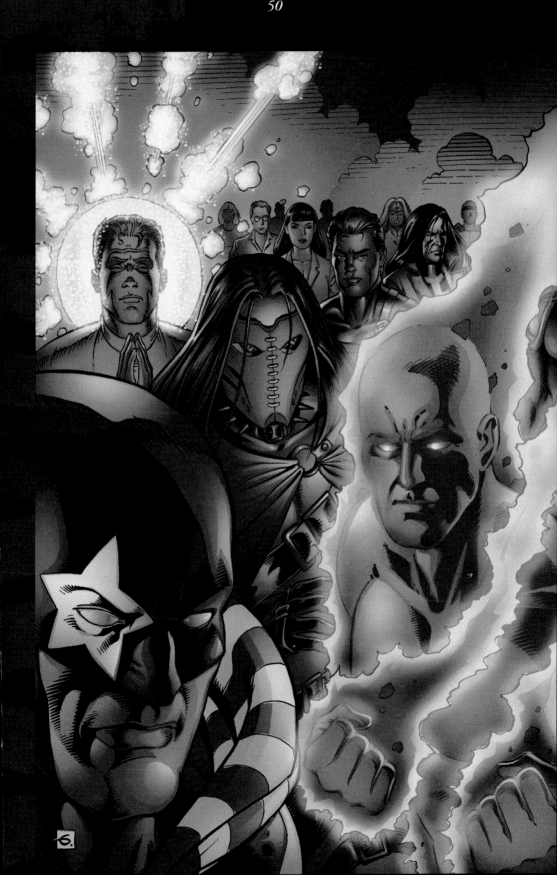

"What Goes Around..."

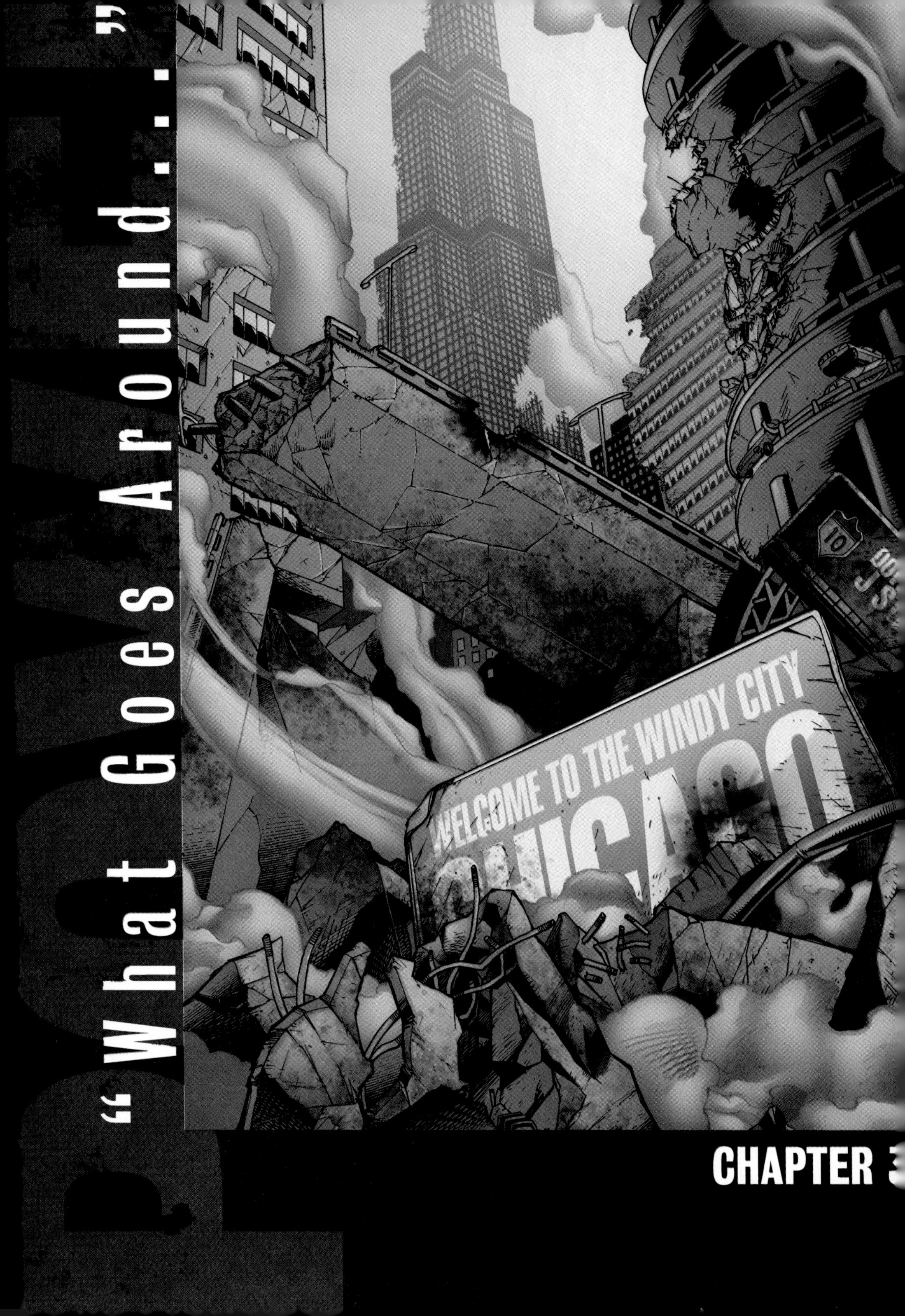

WELCOME TO THE WINDY CITY

CHAPTER 3

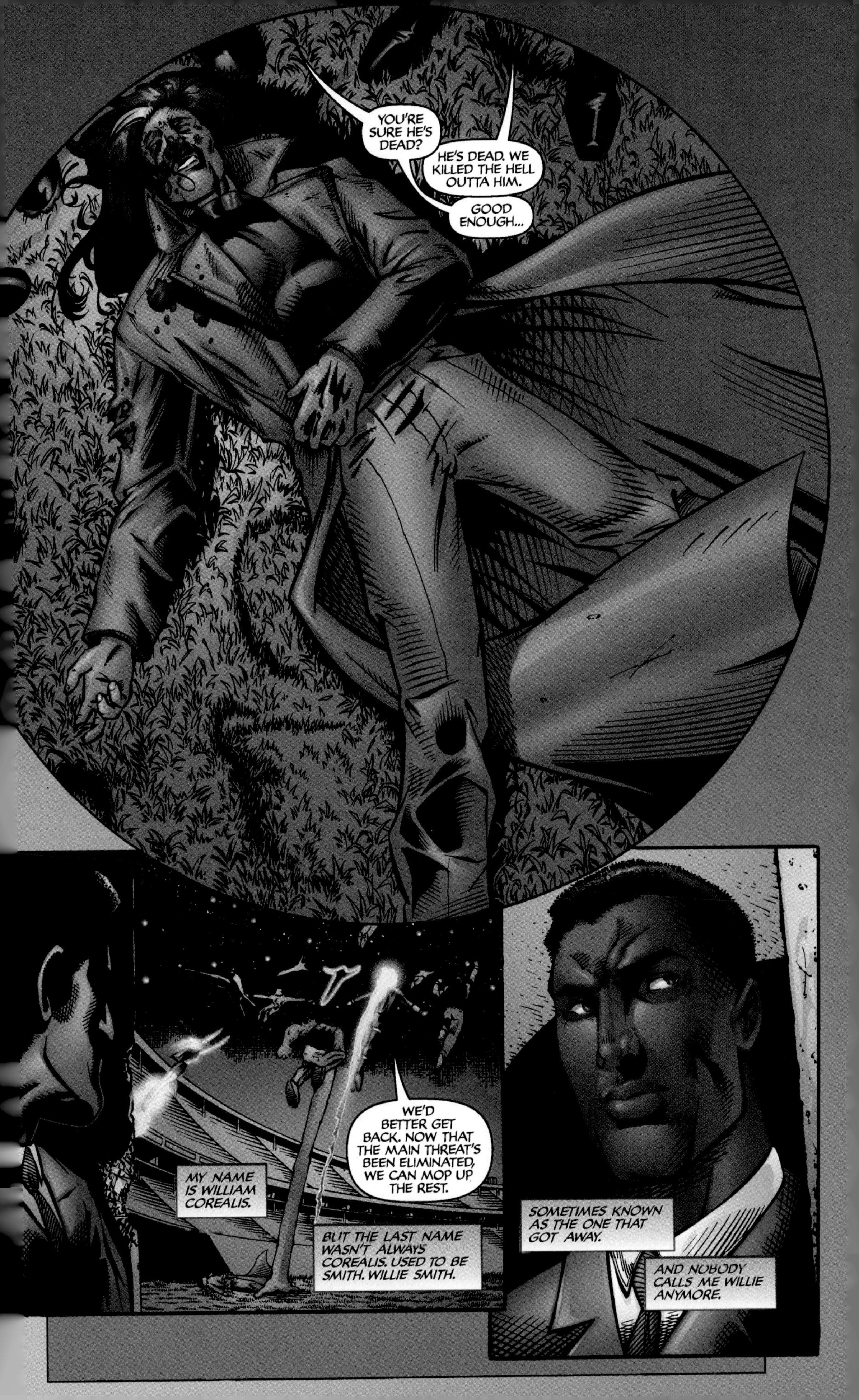
YOU'RE SURE HE'S DEAD?
HE'S DEAD. WE KILLED THE HELL OUTTA HIM.
GOOD ENOUGH...
MY NAME IS WILLIAM COREALIS.
WE'D BETTER GET BACK. NOW THAT THE MAIN THREAT'S BEEN ELIMINATED, WE CAN MOP UP THE REST.
BUT THE LAST NAME WASN'T ALWAYS COREALIS. USED TO BE SMITH. WILLIE SMITH.
SOMETIMES KNOWN AS THE ONE THAT GOT AWAY.
AND NOBODY CALLS ME WILLIE ANYMORE.

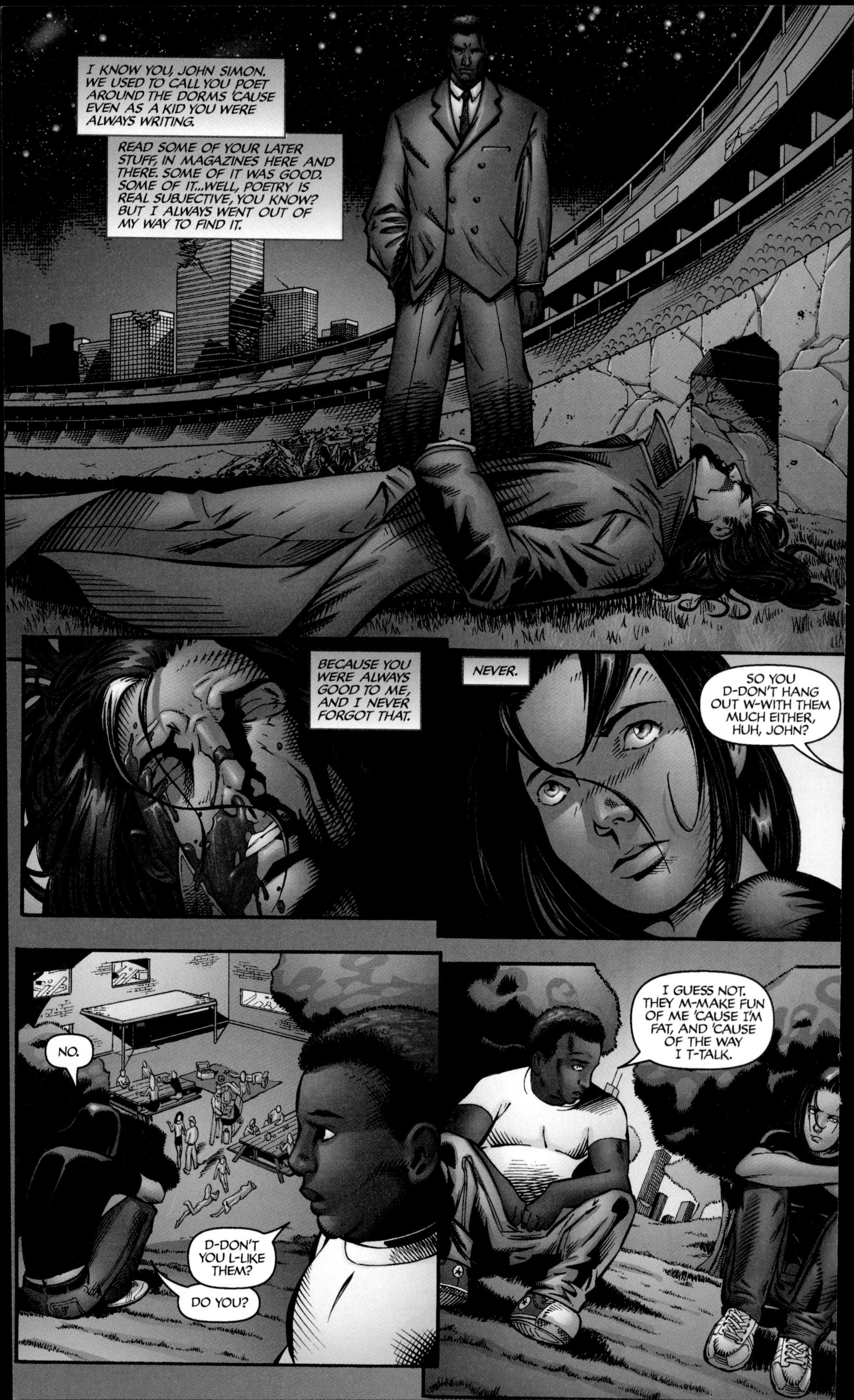

I KNOW YOU, JOHN SIMON. WE USED TO CALL YOU POET AROUND THE DORMS 'CAUSE EVEN AS A KID YOU WERE ALWAYS WRITING.
READ SOME OF YOUR LATER STUFF, IN MAGAZINES HERE AND THERE. SOME OF IT WAS GOOD. SOME OF IT...WELL, POETRY IS REAL SUBJECTIVE, YOU KNOW? BUT I ALWAYS WENT OUT OF MY WAY TO FIND IT.
BECAUSE YOU WERE ALWAYS GOOD TO ME, AND I NEVER FORGOT THAT.
NEVER.
SO YOU D-DON'T HANG OUT W-WITH THEM MUCH EITHER, HUH, JOHN?
NO.
D-DON'T YOU L-LIKE THEM?
DO YOU?
I GUESS NOT. THEY M-MAKE FUN OF ME 'CAUSE I'M FAT, AND 'CAUSE OF THE WAY I T-TALK.

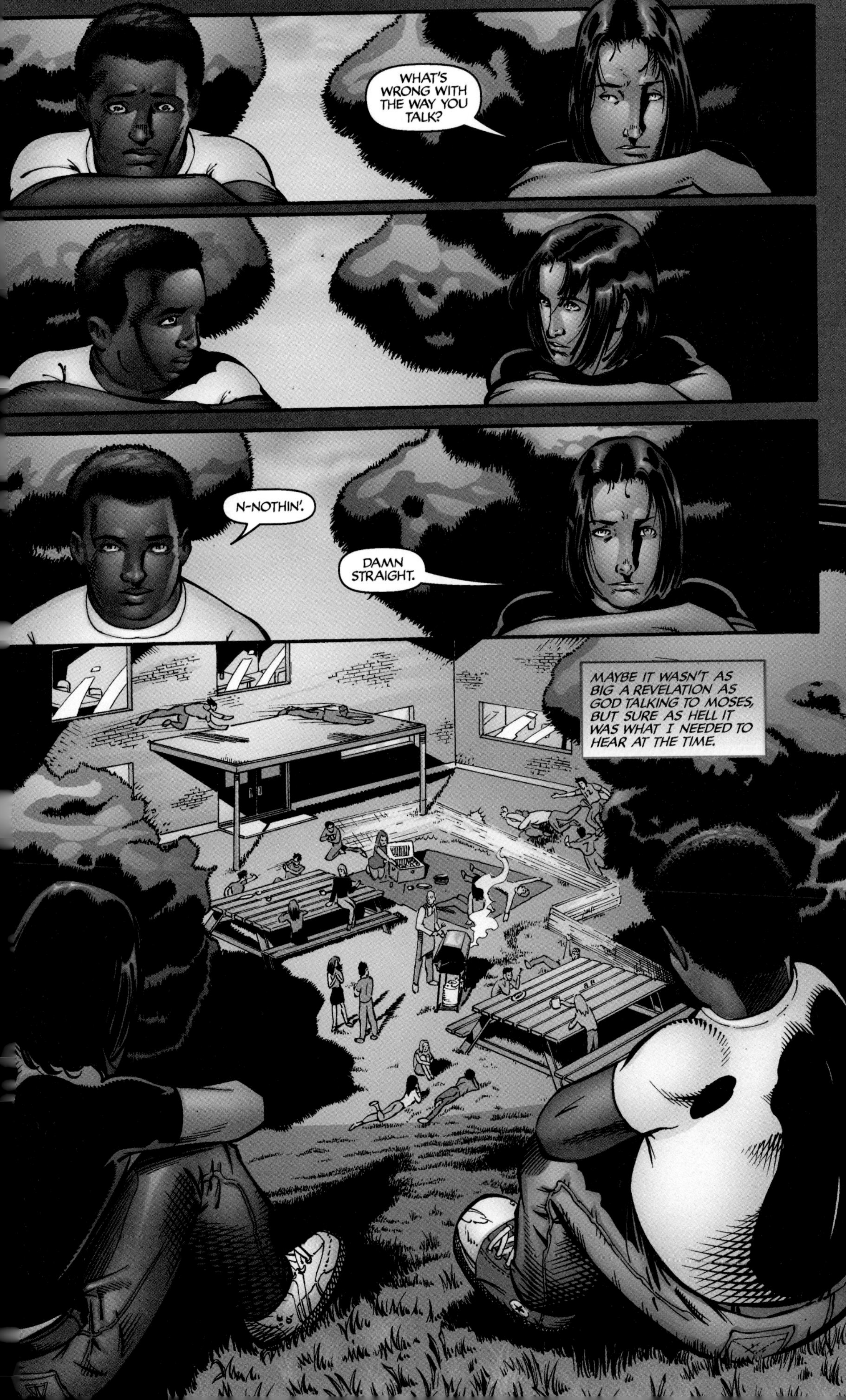
WHAT'S WRONG WITH THE WAY YOU TALK?
N-NOTHIN'.
DAMN STRAIGHT.
MAYBE IT WASN'T AS BIG A REVELATION AS GOD TALKING TO MOSES, BUT SURE AS HELL IT WAS WHAT I NEEDED TO HEAR AT THE TIME.

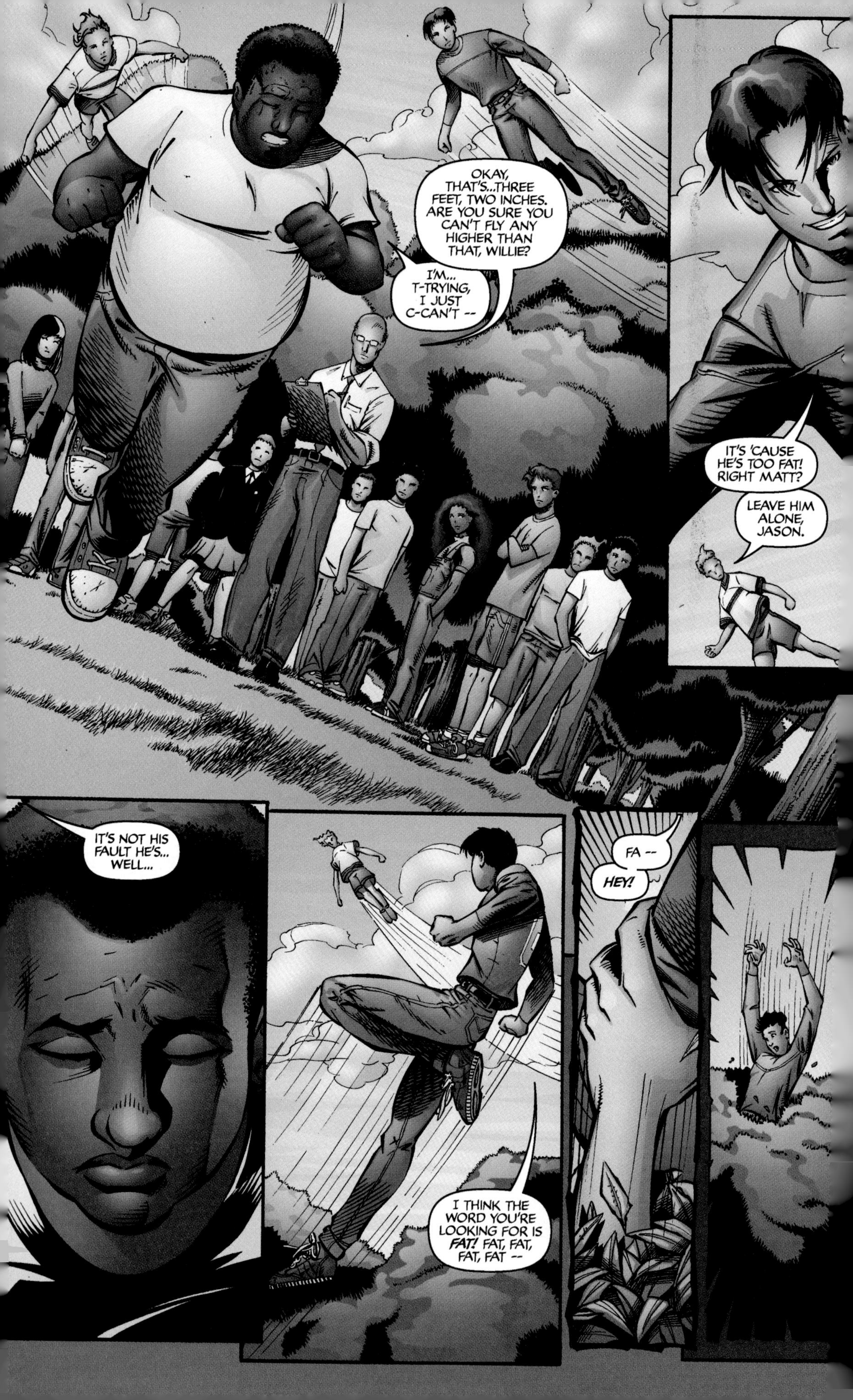
OKAY, THAT'S...THREE FEET, TWO INCHES. ARE YOU SURE YOU CAN'T FLY ANY HIGHER THAN THAT, WILLIE?
I'M... T-TRYING, I JUST C-CAN'T --
IT'S 'CAUSE HE'S TOO FAT! RIGHT MATT?
LEAVE HIM ALONE, JASON.
IT'S NOT HIS FAULT HE'S... WELL...
I THINK THE WORD YOU'RE LOOKING FOR IS FAT! FAT, FAT, FAT, FAT --
FA --
HEY!

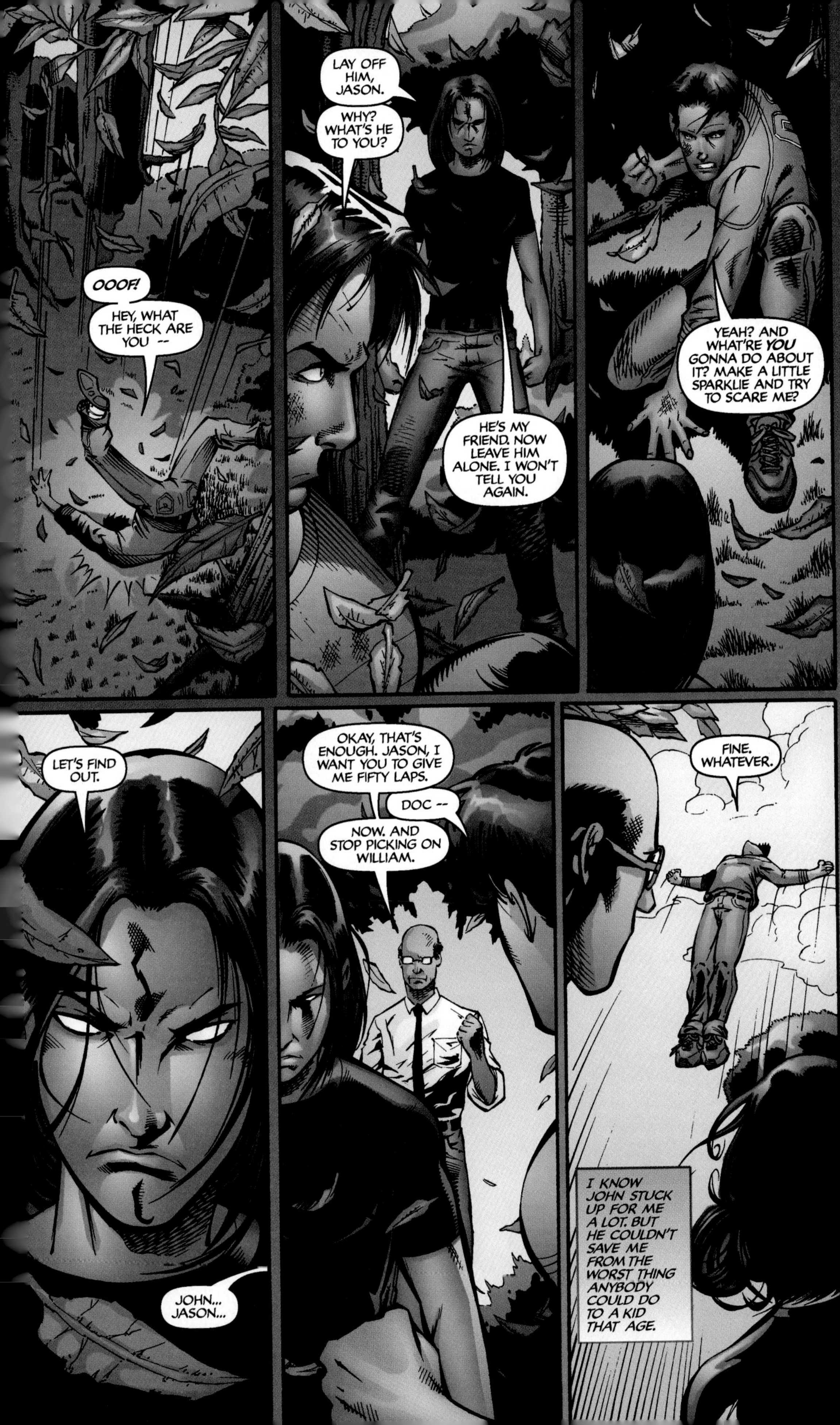
OOOF!
HEY, WHAT THE HECK ARE YOU --
LAY OFF HIM, JASON.
WHY? WHAT'S HE TO YOU?
HE'S MY FRIEND. NOW LEAVE HIM ALONE. I WON'T TELL YOU AGAIN.
YEAH? AND WHAT'RE YOU GONNA DO ABOUT IT? MAKE A LITTLE SPARKLIE AND TRY TO SCARE ME?
LET'S FIND OUT.
JOHN... JASON...
OKAY, THAT'S ENOUGH. JASON, I WANT YOU TO GIVE ME FIFTY LAPS.
DOC --
NOW. AND STOP PICKING ON WILLIAM.
FINE. WHATEVER.
I KNOW JOHN STUCK UP FOR ME A LOT. BUT HE COULDN'T SAVE ME FROM THE WORST THING ANYBODY COULD DO TO A KID THAT AGE.

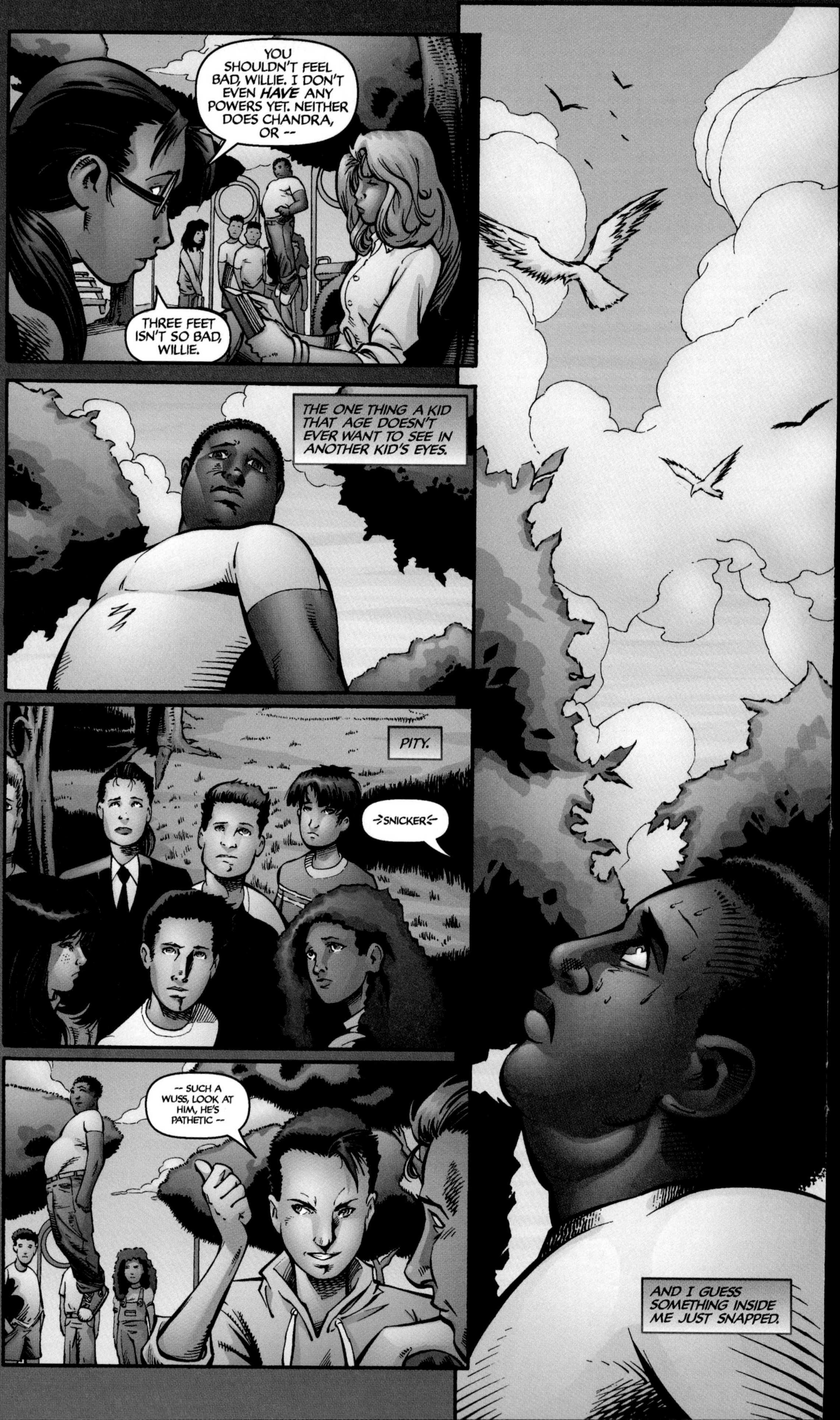
YOU SHOULDN'T FEEL BAD, WILLIE. I DON'T EVEN HAVE ANY POWERS YET. NEITHER DOES CHANDRA, OR --
THREE FEET ISN'T SO BAD, WILLIE.
THE ONE THING A KID THAT AGE DOESN'T EVER WANT TO SEE IN ANOTHER KID'S EYES.
PITY.
SNICKER
-- SUCH A WUSS, LOOK AT HIM, HE'S PATHETIC --
AND I GUESS SOMETHING INSIDE ME JUST SNAPPED.

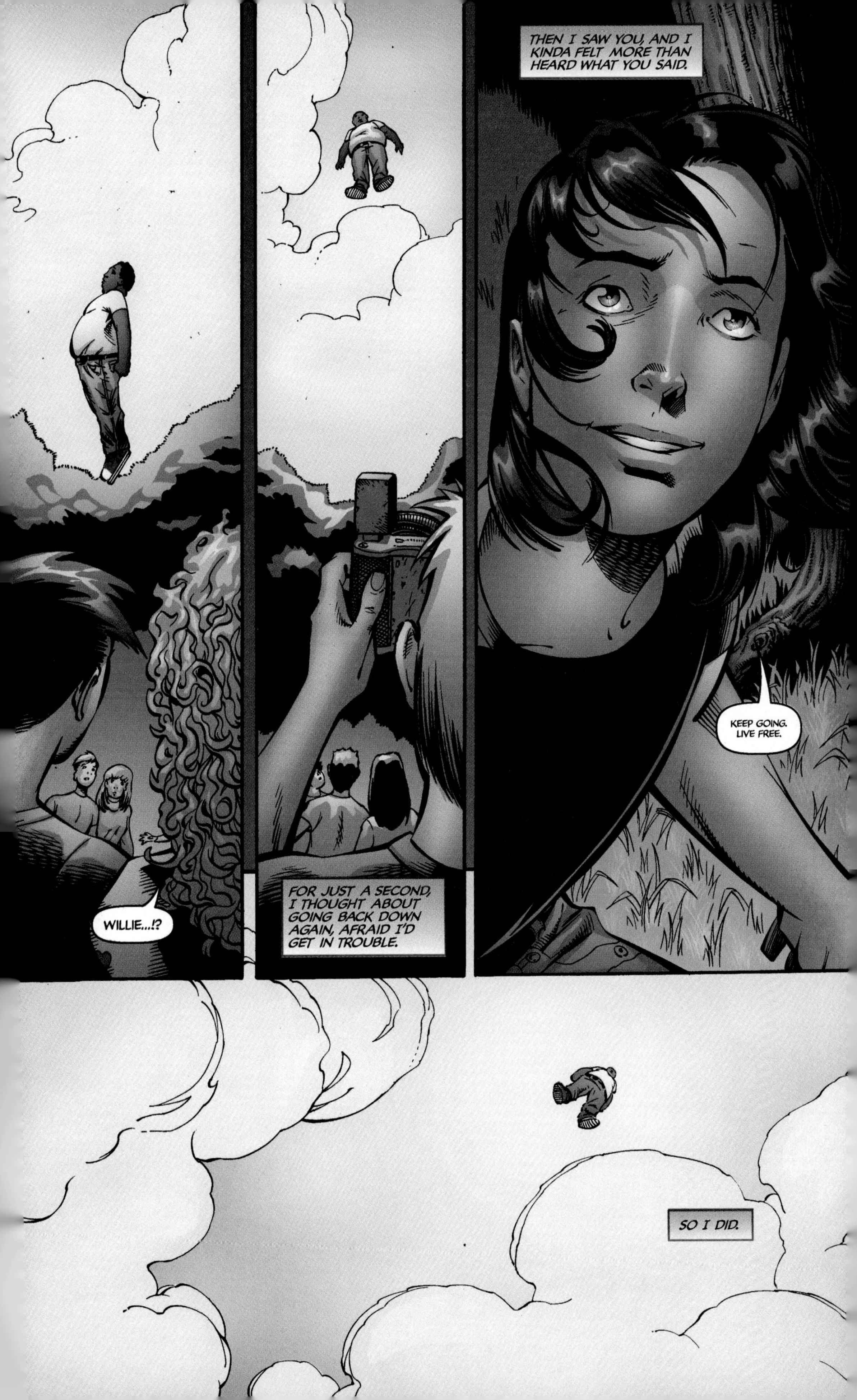

WILLIE...!?
FOR JUST A SECOND, I THOUGHT ABOUT GOING BACK DOWN AGAIN, AFRAID I'D GET IN TROUBLE.
THEN I SAW YOU, AND I KINDA FELT MORE THAN HEARD WHAT YOU SAID.
KEEP GOING. LIVE FREE.
SO I DID.

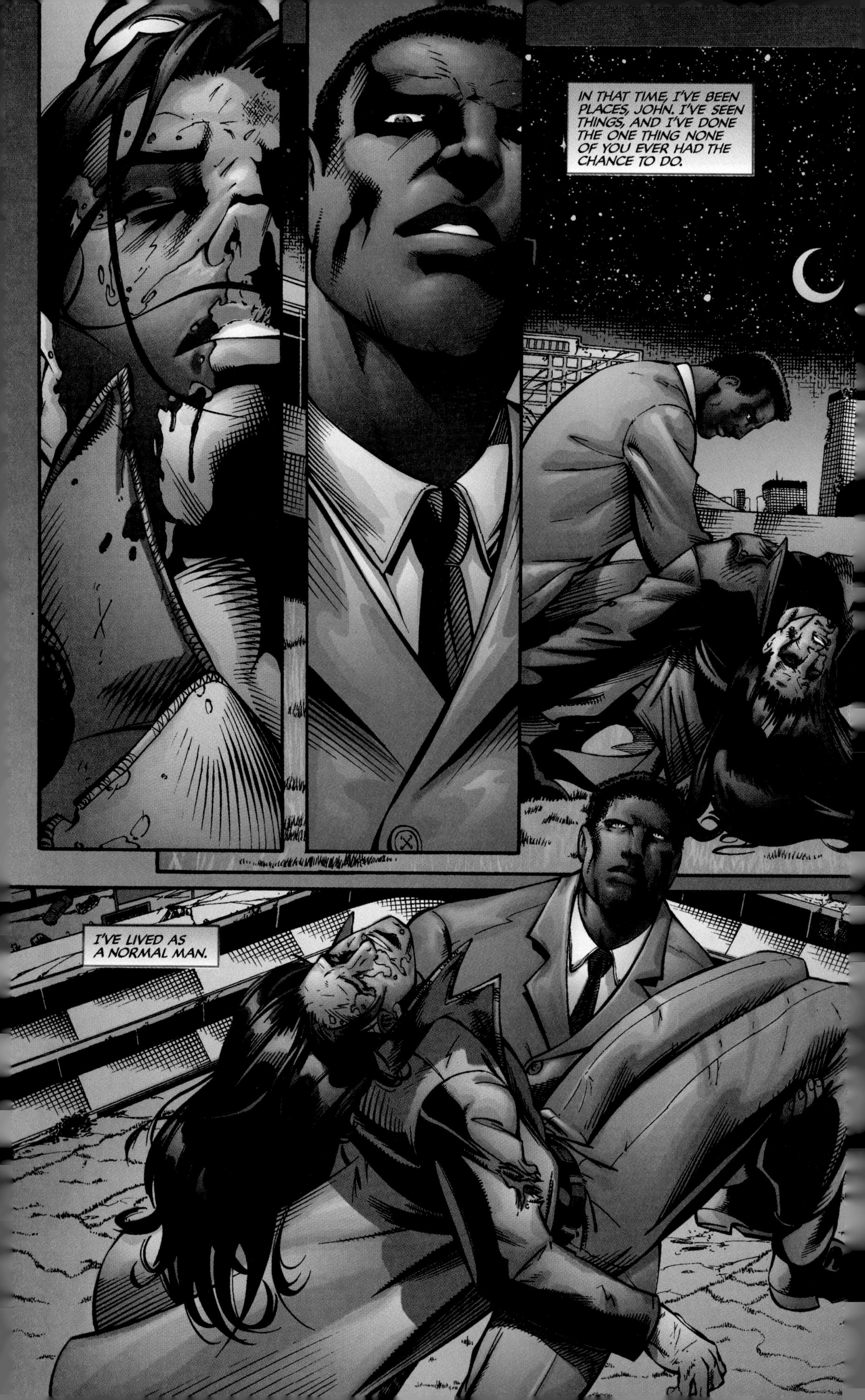
IN THAT TIME, I'VE BEEN PLACES, JOHN. I'VE SEEN THINGS, AND I'VE DONE THE ONE THING NONE OF YOU EVER HAD THE CHANCE TO DO.
I'VE LIVED AS A NORMAL MAN.

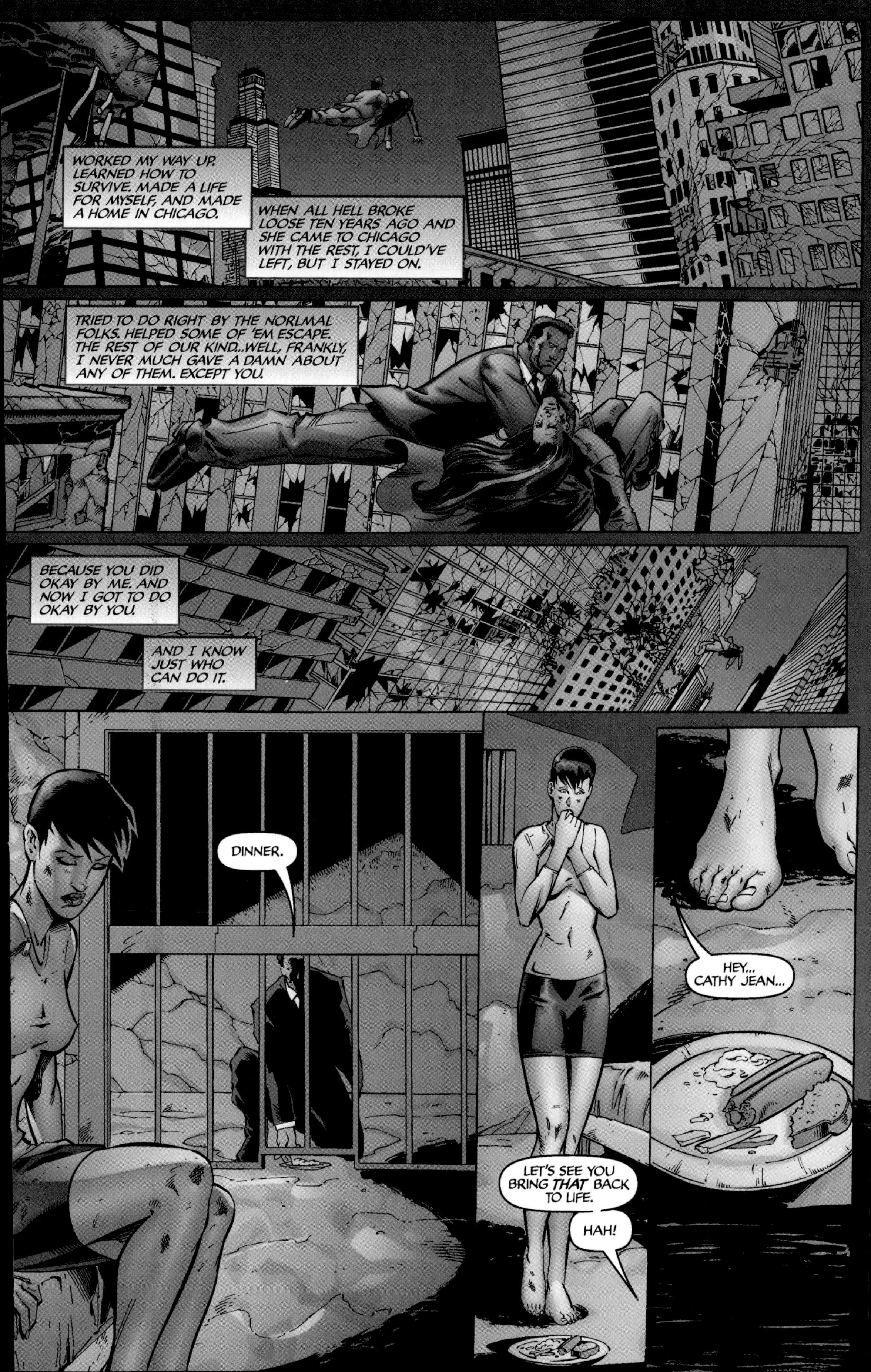
WORKED MY WAY UP. LEARNED HOW TO SURVIVE. MADE A LIFE FOR MYSELF, AND MADE A HOME IN CHICAGO.
WHEN ALL HELL BROKE LOOSE TEN YEARS AGO AND SHE CAME TO CHICAGO WITH THE REST, I COULD'VE LEFT, BUT I STAYED ON.
TRIED TO DO RIGHT BY THE NORLMAL FOLKS. HELPED SOME OF 'EM ESCAPE. THE REST OF OUR KIND...WELL, FRANKLY, I NEVER MUCH GAVE A DAMN ABOUT ANY OF THEM. EXCEPT YOU.
BECAUSE YOU DID OKAY BY ME. AND NOW I GOT TO DO OKAY BY YOU.
AND I KNOW JUST WHO CAN DO IT.
DINNER.
HEY... CATHY JEAN...
LET'S SEE YOU BRING *THAT* BACK TO LIFE.
HAH!

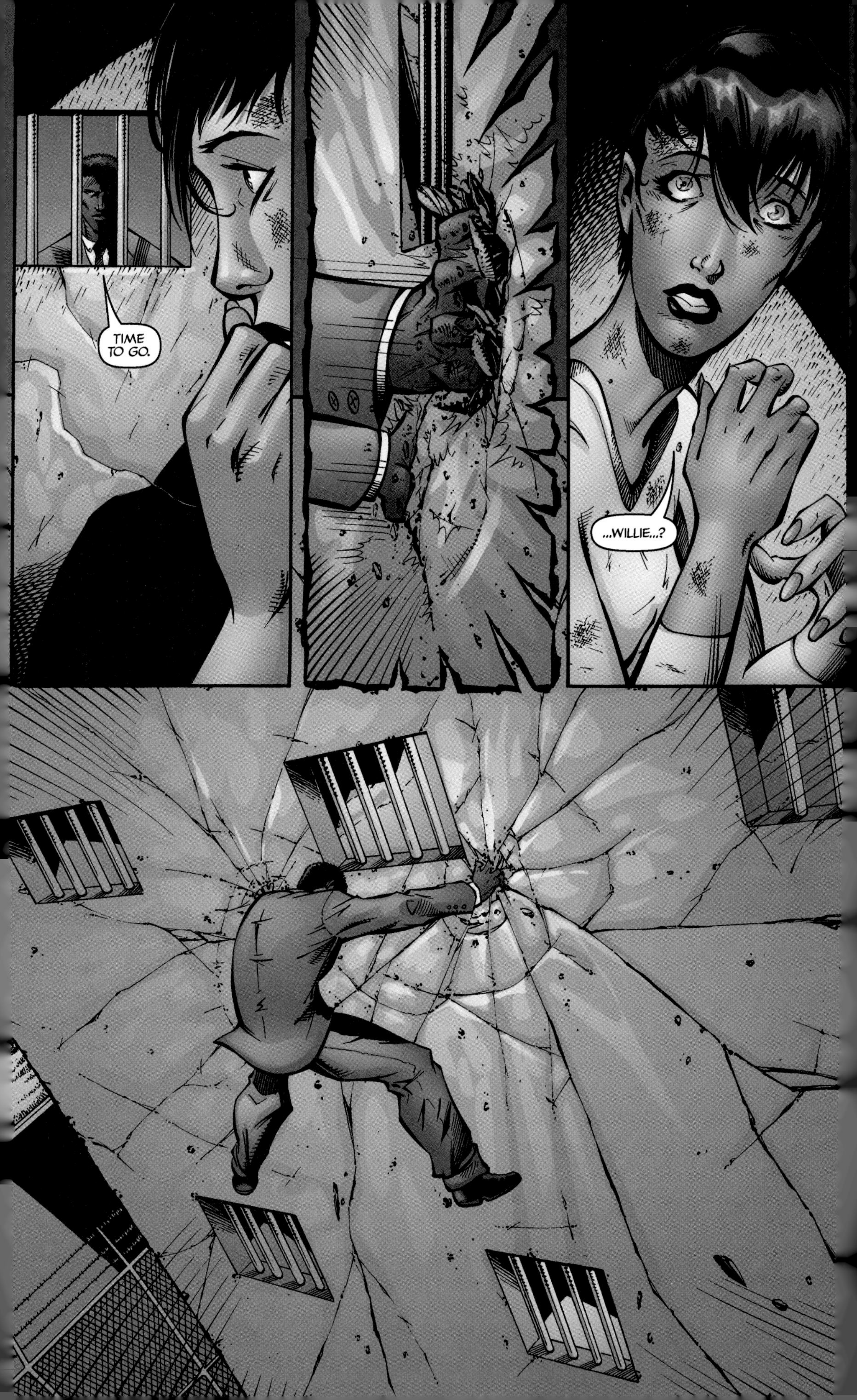
TIME TO GO.
...WILLIE...?

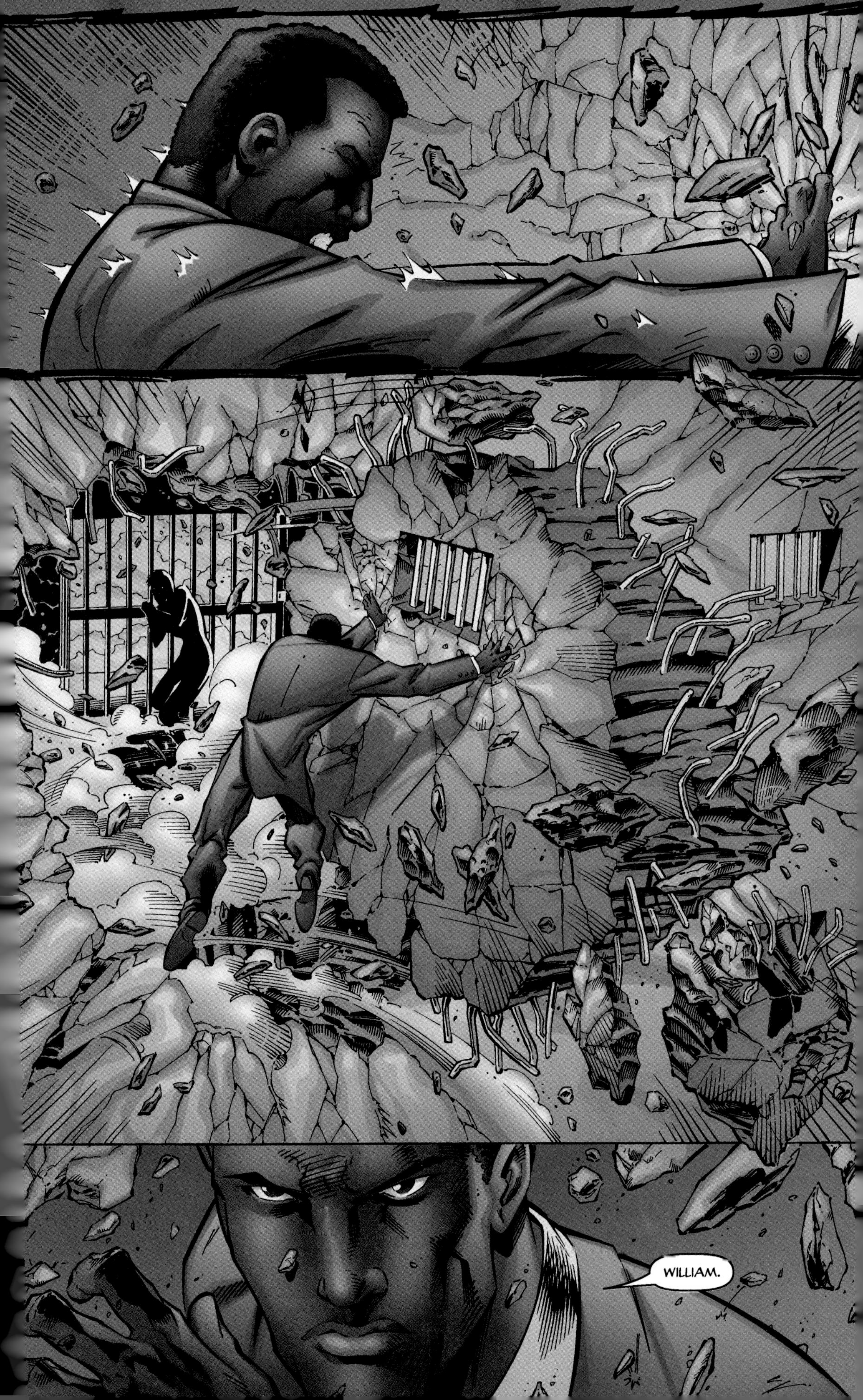
WILLIAM.

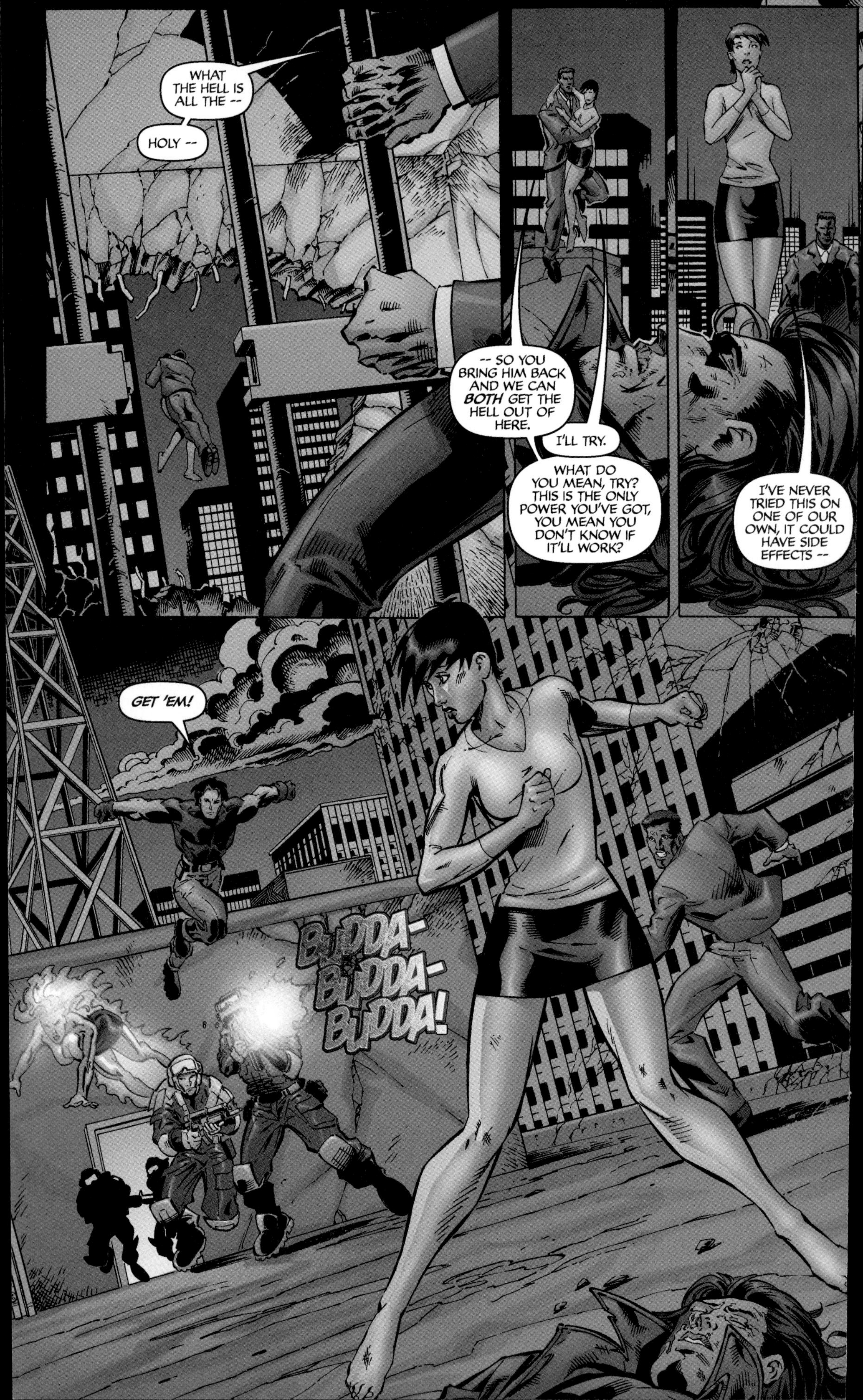
WHAT THE HELL IS ALL THE --
HOLY --
-- SO YOU BRING HIM BACK AND WE CAN *BOTH* GET THE HELL OUT OF HERE.
I'LL TRY.
WHAT DO YOU MEAN, TRY? THIS IS THE ONLY POWER YOU'VE GOT, YOU MEAN YOU DON'T KNOW IF IT'LL WORK?
I'VE NEVER TRIED THIS ON ONE OF OUR OWN, IT COULD HAVE SIDE EFFECTS --
GET 'EM!
BUDDA- BUDDA- BUDDA!

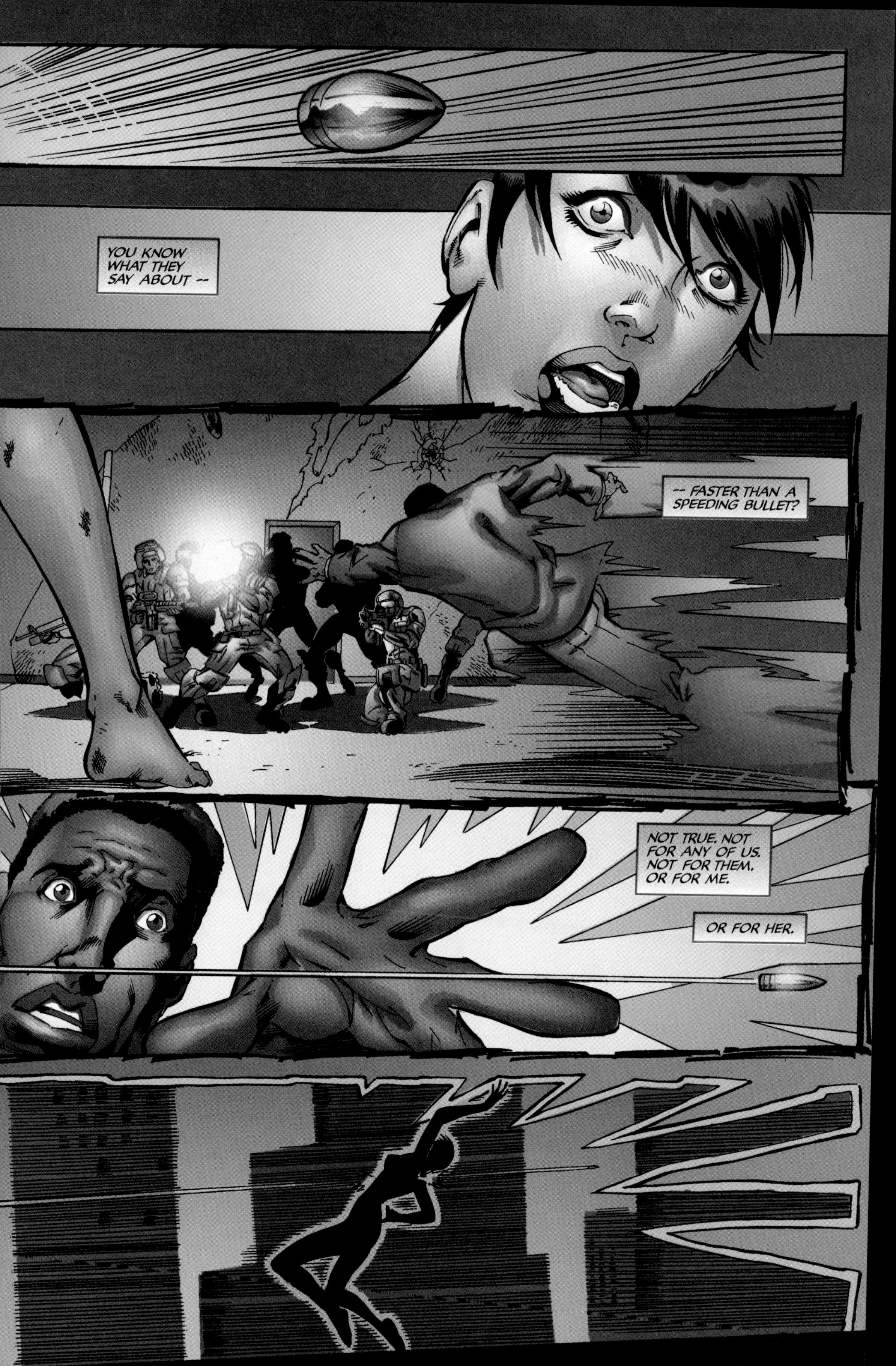
YOU KNOW WHAT THEY SAY ABOUT --
-- FASTER THAN A SPEEDING BULLET?
NOT TRUE. NOT FOR ANY OF US. NOT FOR THEM. OR FOR ME.
OR FOR HER.

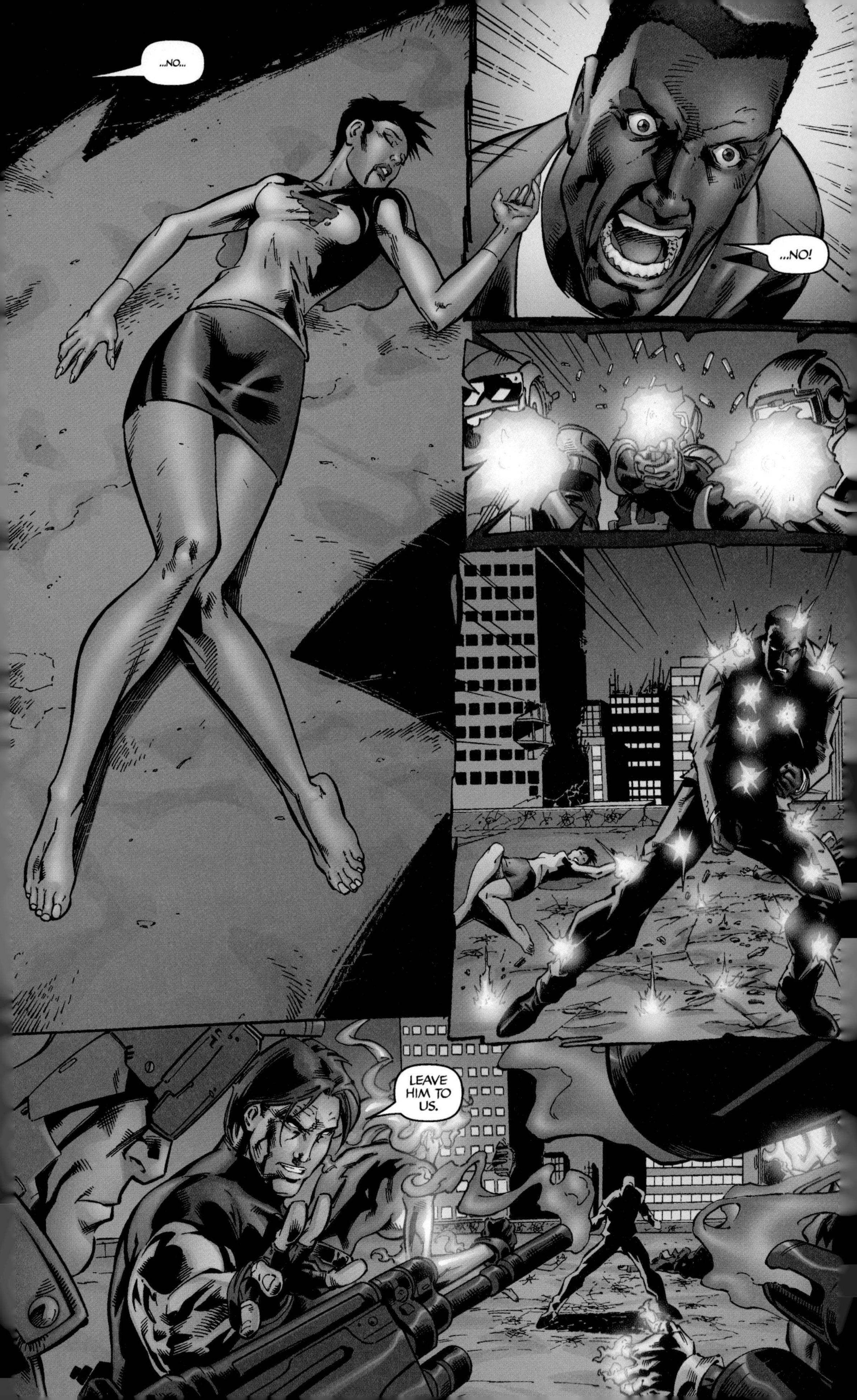
...NO...
...NO!
LEAVE HIM TO US.

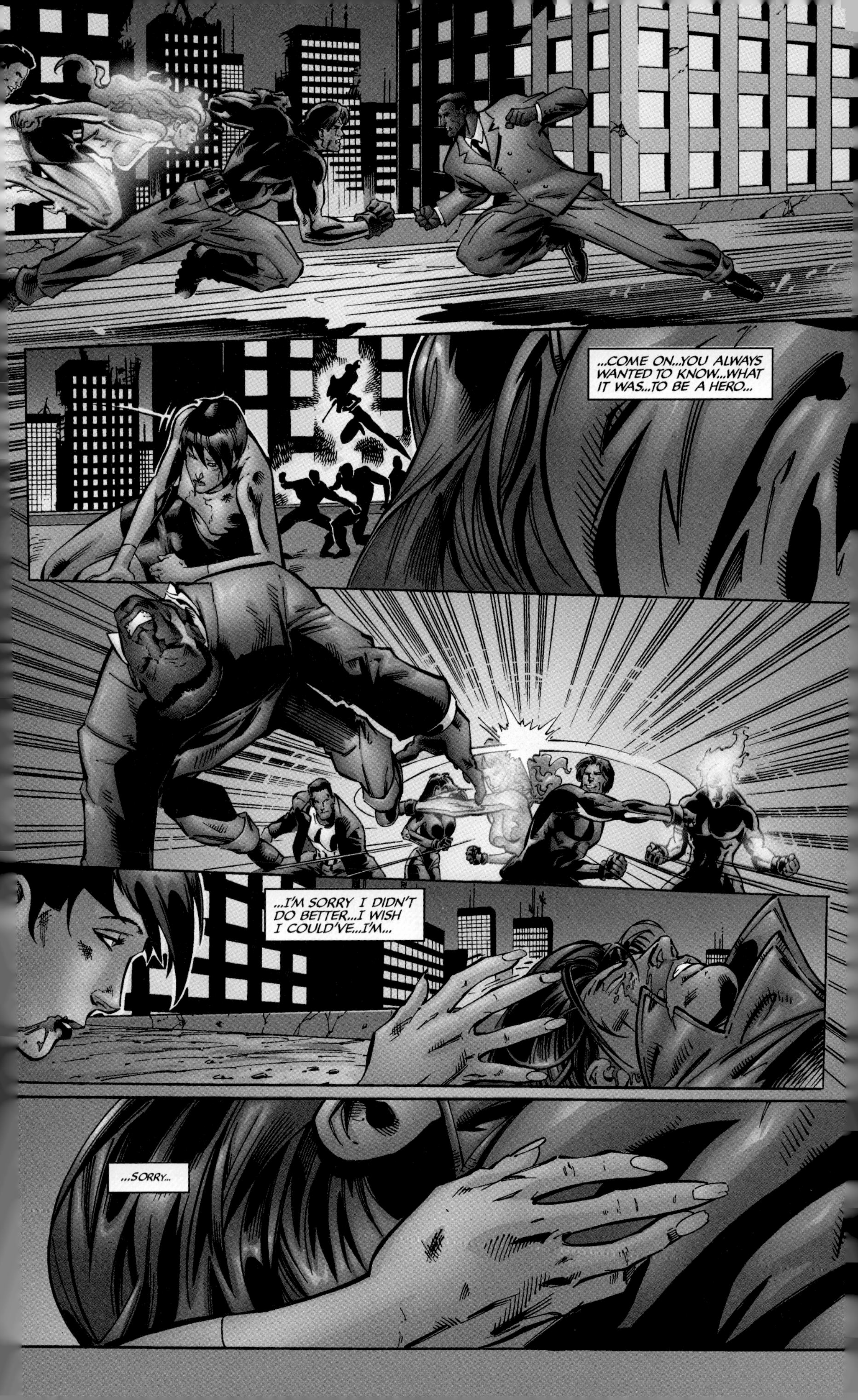
...COME ON...YOU ALWAYS WANTED TO KNOW...WHAT IT WAS...TO BE A HERO...
...I'M SORRY I DIDN'T DO BETTER...I WISH I COULD'VE...I'M...
...SORRY...

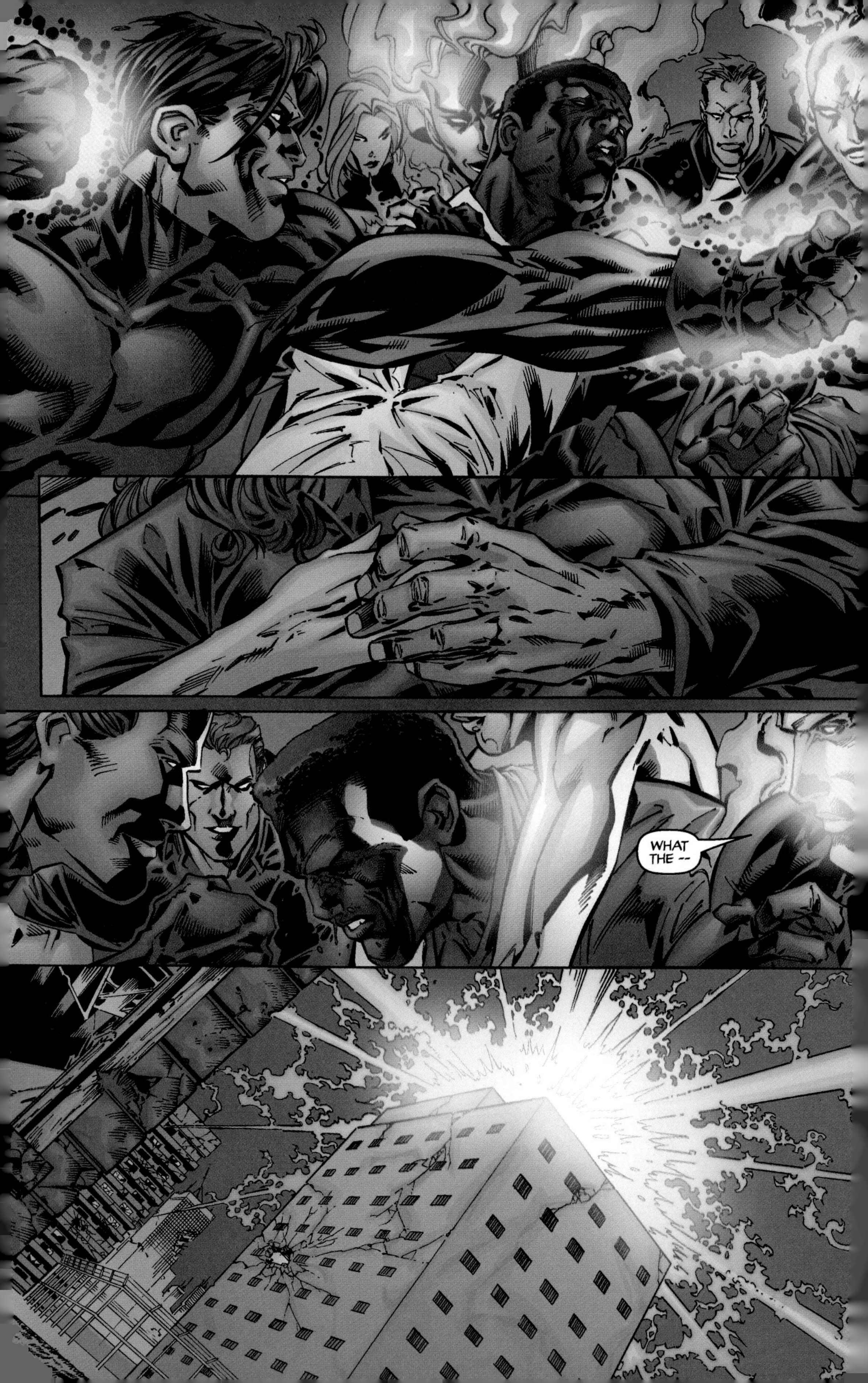
WHAT THE --

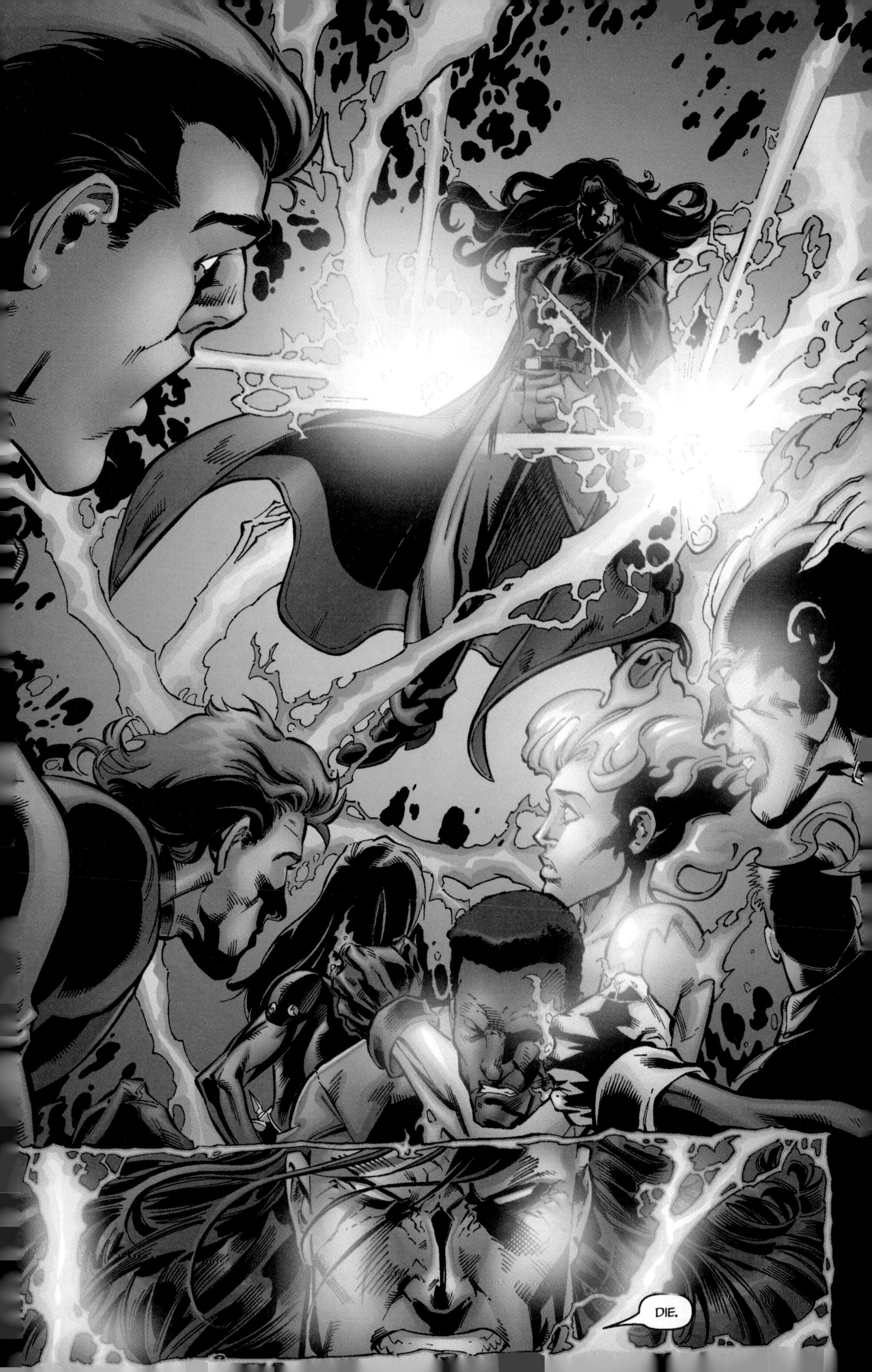
DIE.

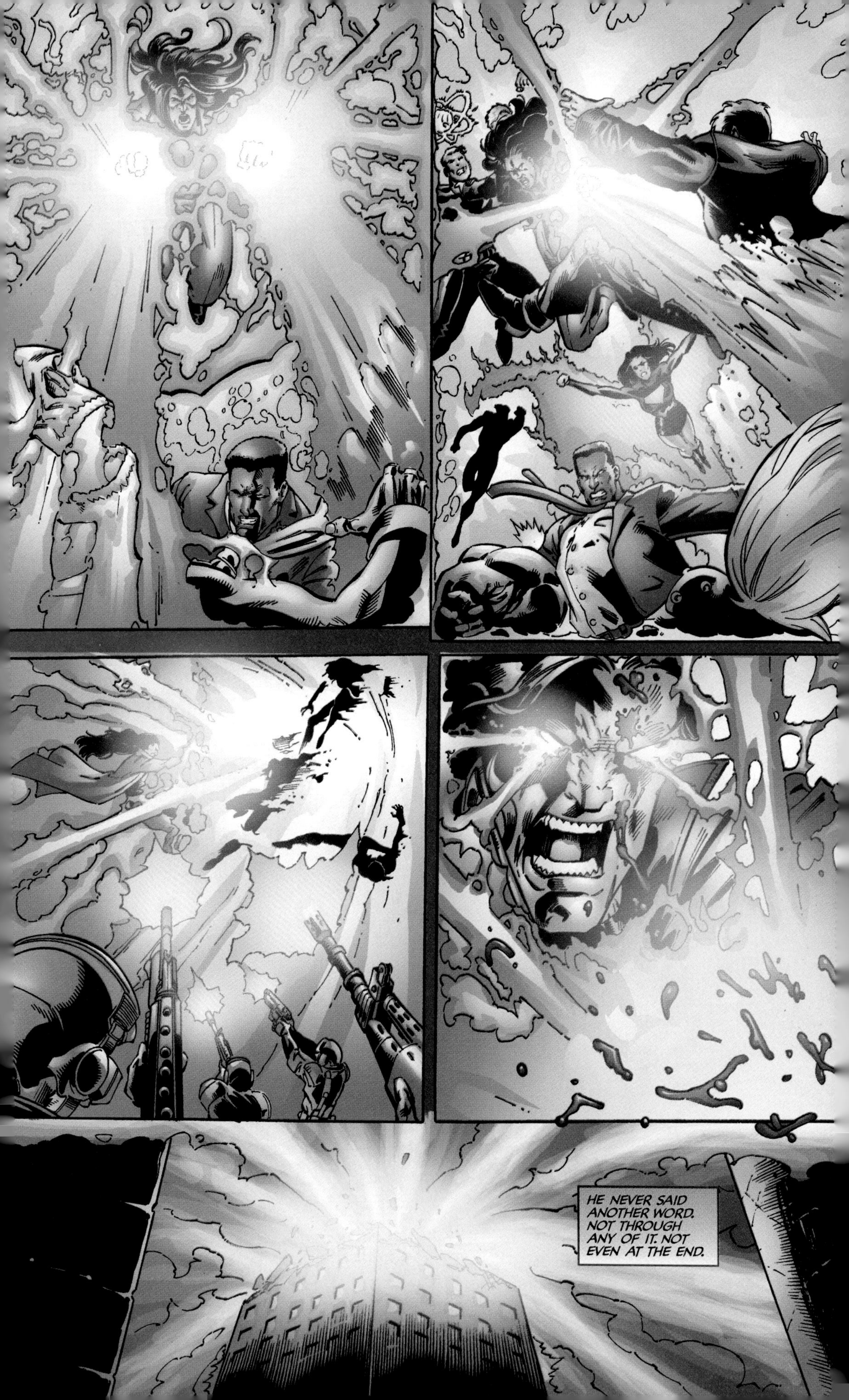
HE NEVER SAID ANOTHER WORD. NOT THROUGH ANY OF IT. NOT EVEN AT THE END.

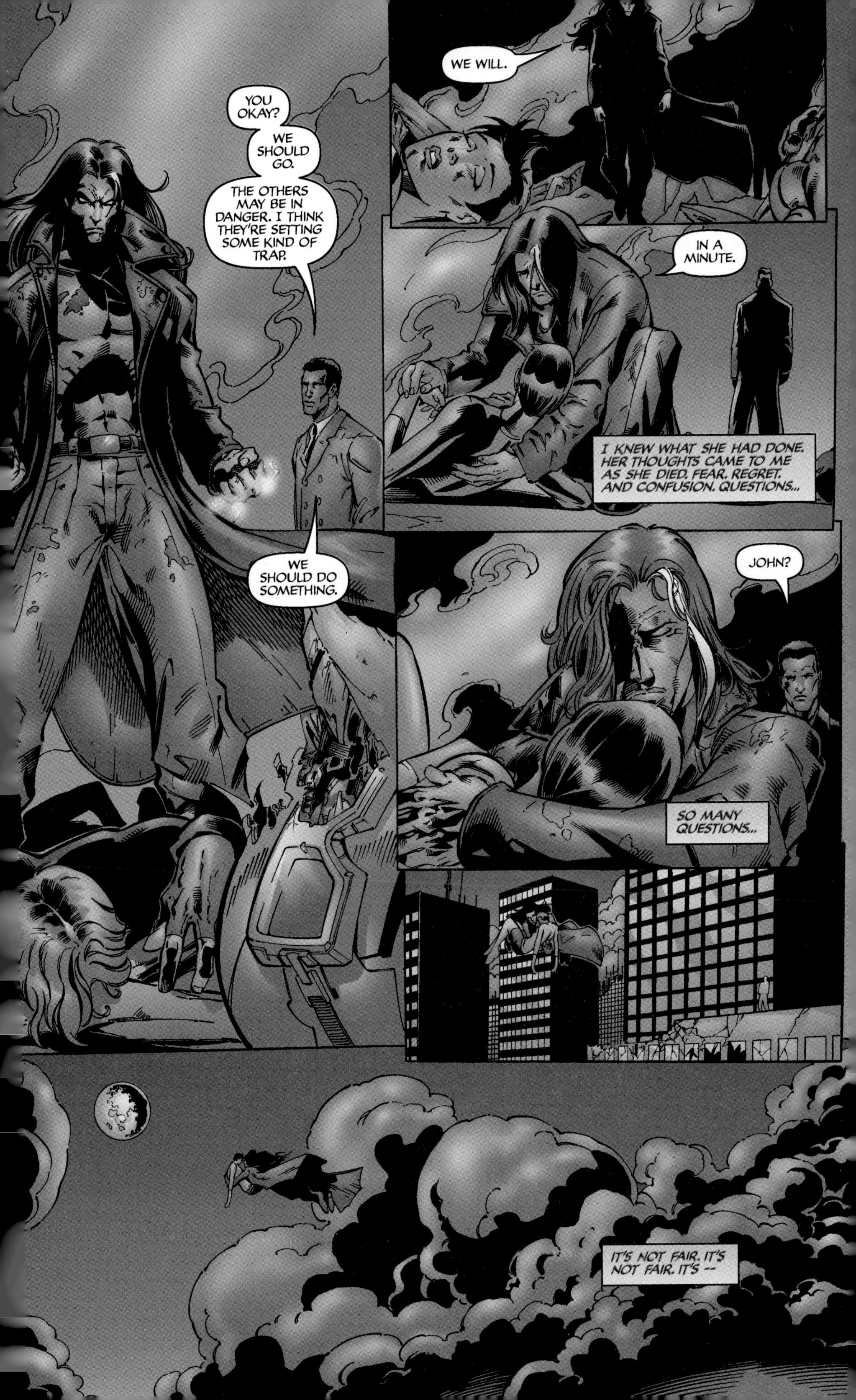

YOU OKAY?
WE SHOULD GO.
THE OTHERS MAY BE IN DANGER. I THINK THEY'RE SETTING SOME KIND OF TRAP.
WE SHOULD DO SOMETHING.
WE WILL.
IN A MINUTE.
I KNEW WHAT SHE HAD DONE. HER THOUGHTS CAME TO ME AS SHE DIED. FEAR. REGRET. AND CONFUSION. QUESTIONS...
JOHN?
SO MANY QUESTIONS...
IT'S NOT FAIR. IT'S NOT FAIR. IT'S --

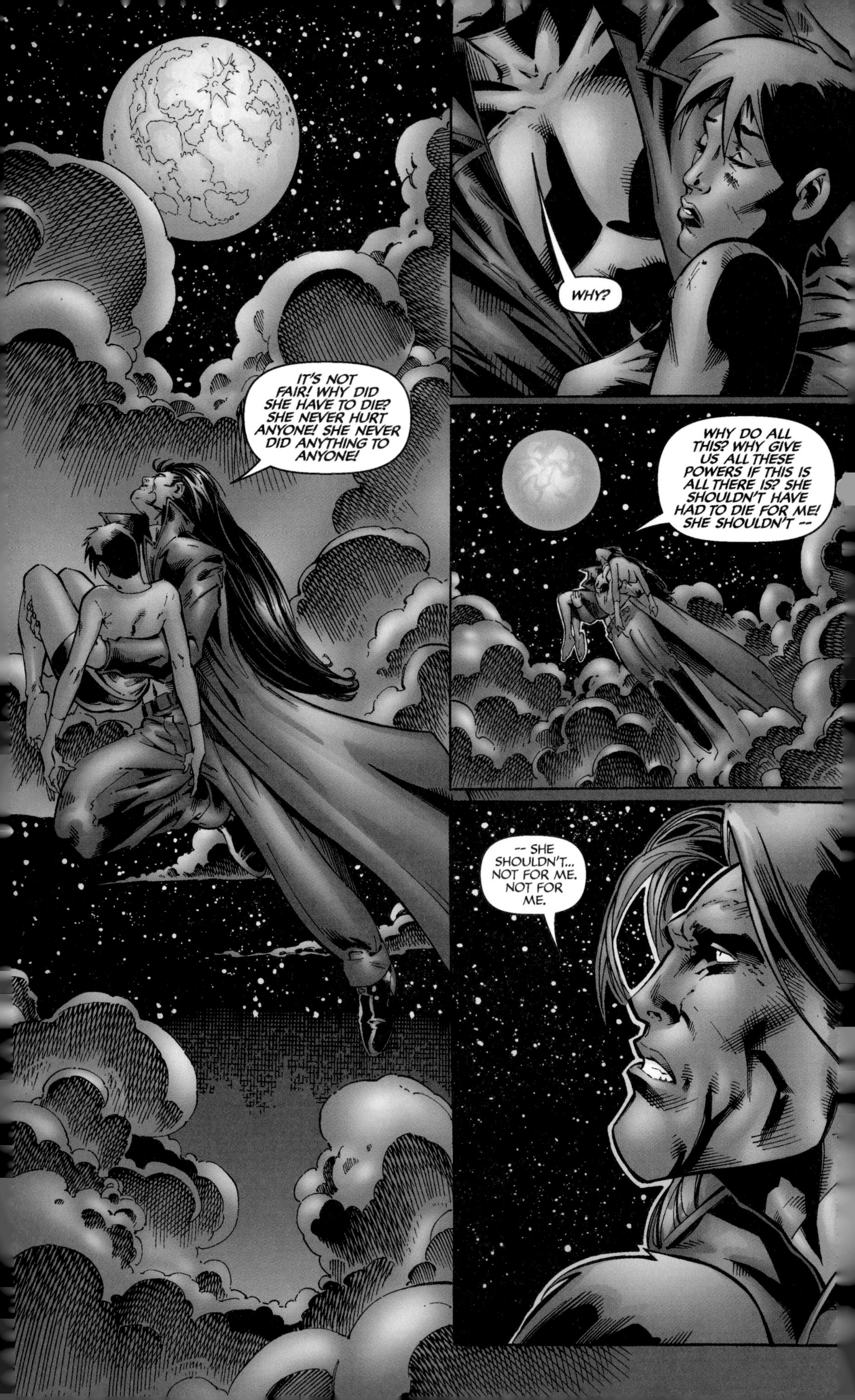
IT'S NOT FAIR! WHY DID SHE HAVE TO DIE? SHE NEVER HURT ANYONE! SHE NEVER DID ANYTHING TO ANYONE!
WHY?
WHY DO ALL THIS? WHY GIVE US ALL THESE POWERS IF THIS IS ALL THERE IS? SHE SHOULDN'T HAVE HAD TO DIE FOR ME! SHE SHOULDN'T --
-- SHE SHOULDN'T... NOT FOR ME. NOT FOR ME.

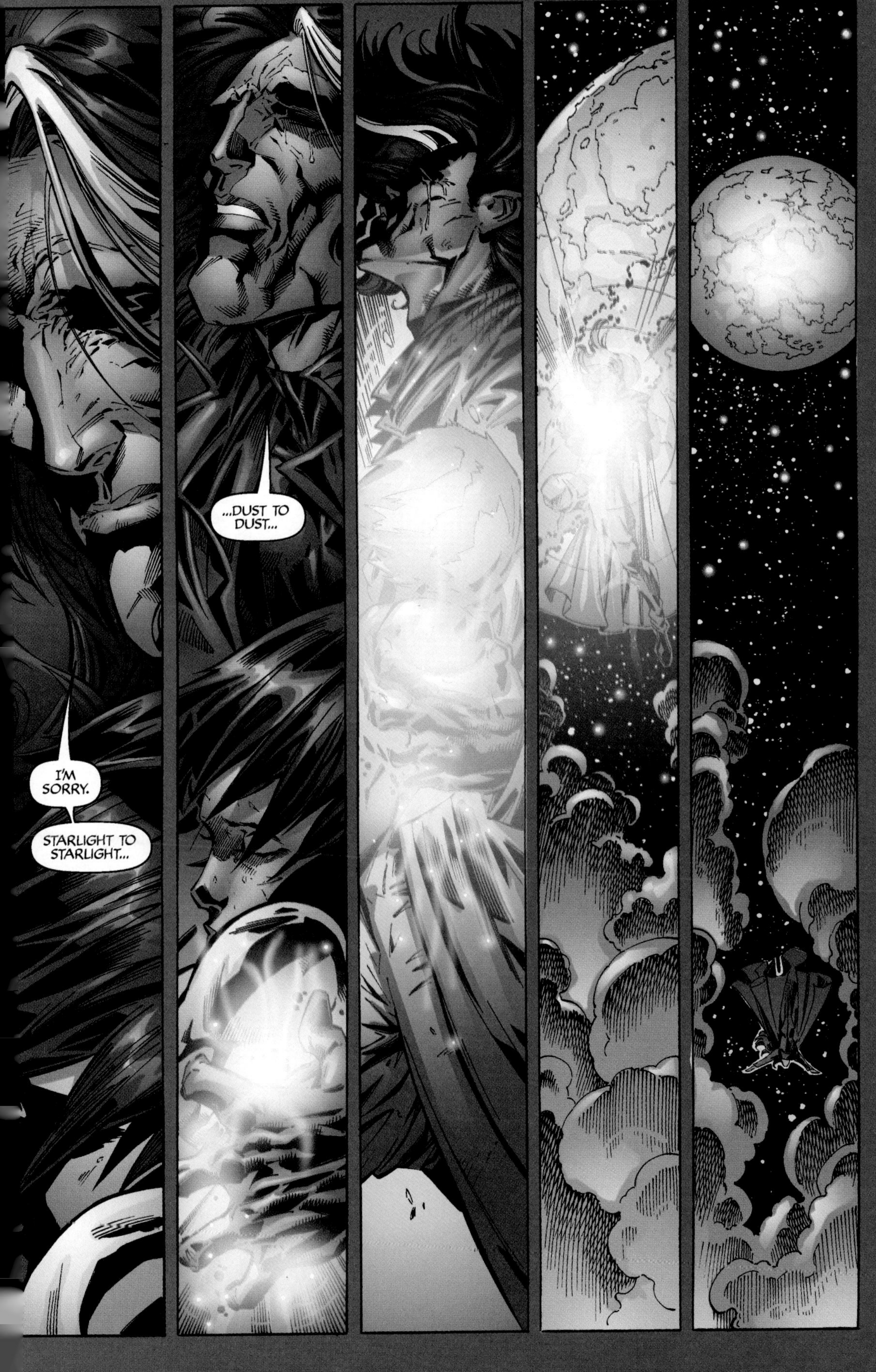
I'M SORRY.
STARLIGHT TO STARLIGHT...
...DUST TO DUST...

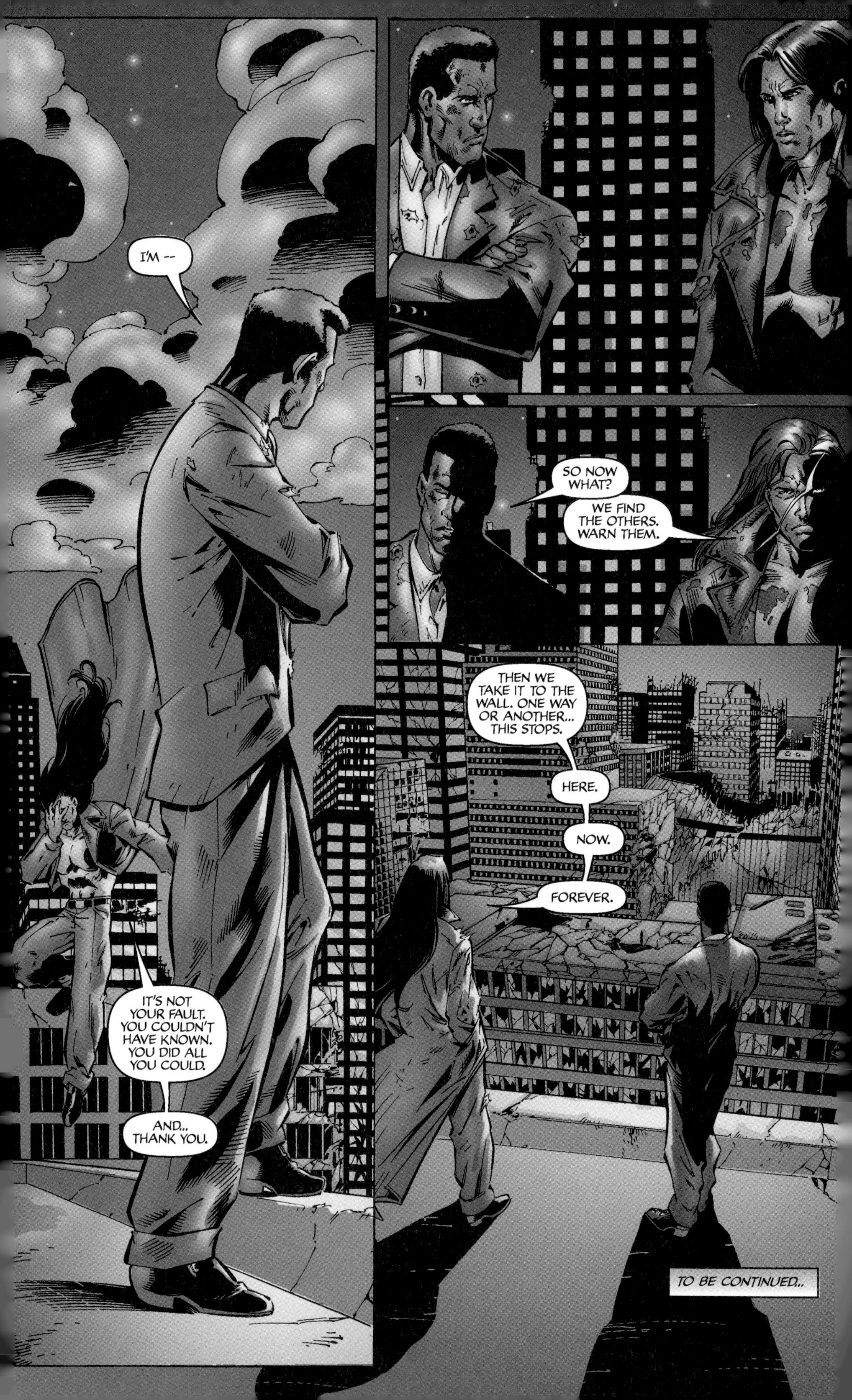
I'M --
IT'S NOT YOUR FAULT. YOU COULDN'T HAVE KNOWN. YOU DID ALL YOU COULD.
AND... THANK YOU.
SO NOW WHAT?
WE FIND THE OTHERS. WARN THEM.
THEN WE TAKE IT TO THE WALL. ONE WAY OR ANOTHER... THIS STOPS.
HERE.
NOW.
FOREVER.
TO BE CONTINUED...

"A, B, C and D"

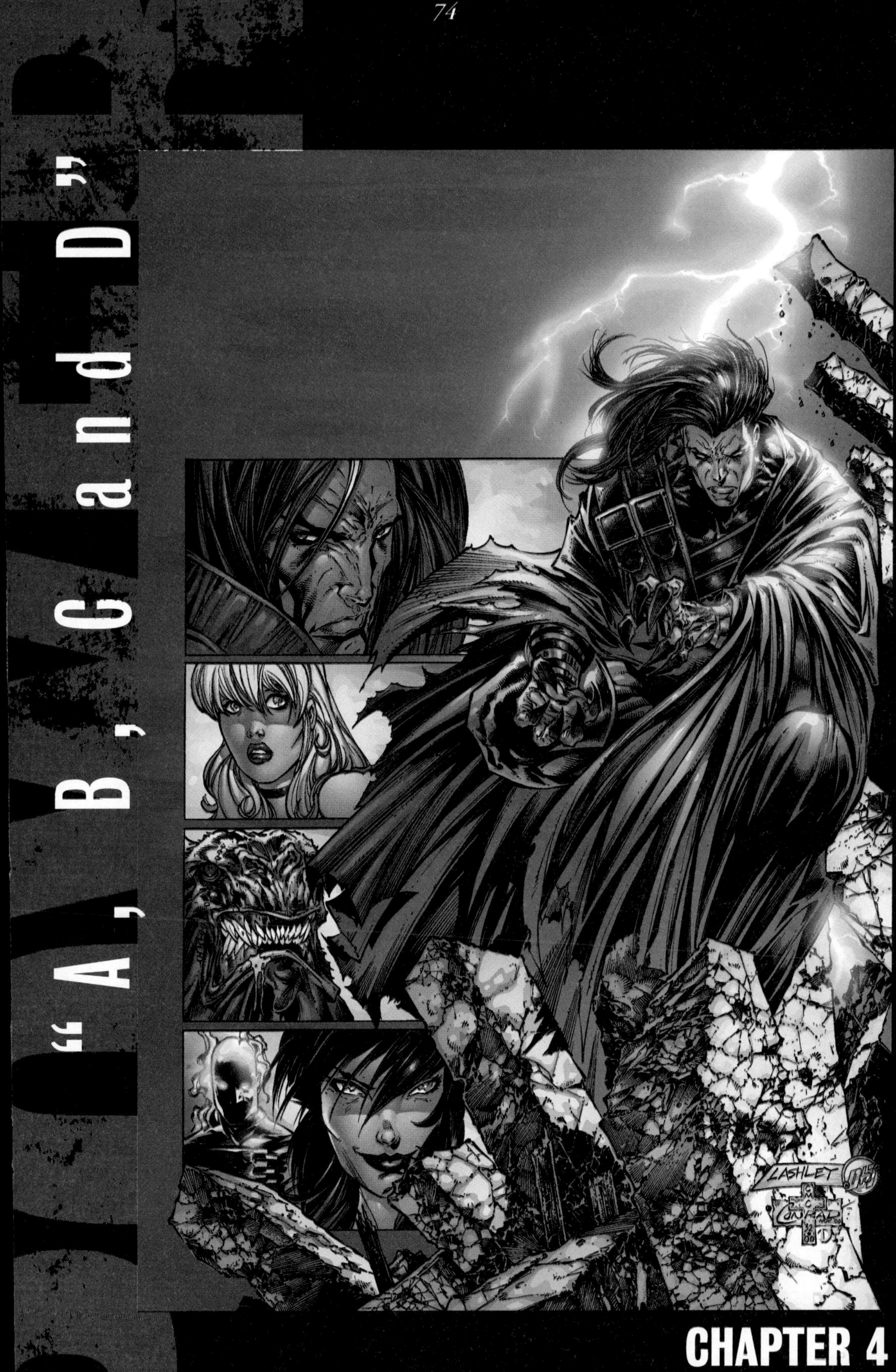

CHAPTER 4

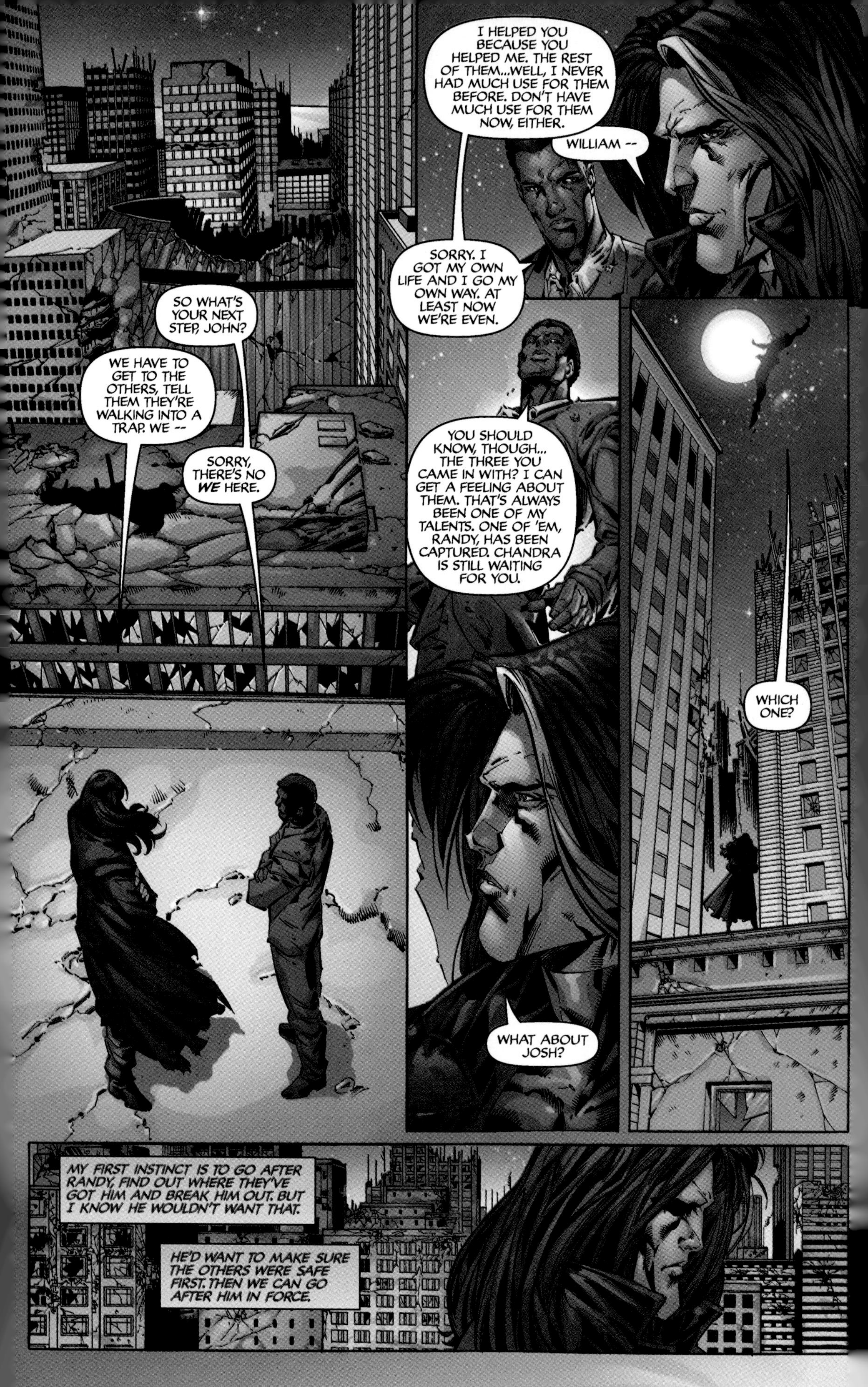
SO WHAT'S YOUR NEXT STEP, JOHN?
WE HAVE TO GET TO THE OTHERS, TELL THEM THEY'RE WALKING INTO A TRAP. WE --
SORRY, THERE'S NO *WE* HERE.
I HELPED YOU BECAUSE YOU HELPED ME. THE REST OF THEM...WELL, I NEVER HAD MUCH USE FOR THEM BEFORE. DON'T HAVE MUCH USE FOR THEM NOW, EITHER.
WILLIAM --
SORRY. I GOT MY OWN LIFE AND I GO MY OWN WAY. AT LEAST NOW WE'RE EVEN.
YOU SHOULD KNOW, THOUGH... THE THREE YOU CAME IN WITH? I CAN GET A FEELING ABOUT THEM. THAT'S ALWAYS BEEN ONE OF MY TALENTS. ONE OF 'EM, RANDY, HAS BEEN CAPTURED. CHANDRA IS STILL WAITING FOR YOU.
WHAT ABOUT JOSH?
WHICH ONE?
MY FIRST INSTINCT IS TO GO AFTER RANDY, FIND OUT WHERE THEY'VE GOT HIM AND BREAK HIM OUT. BUT I KNOW HE WOULDN'T WANT THAT.
HE'D WANT TO MAKE SURE THE OTHERS WERE SAFE FIRST. THEN WE CAN GO AFTER HIM IN FORCE.

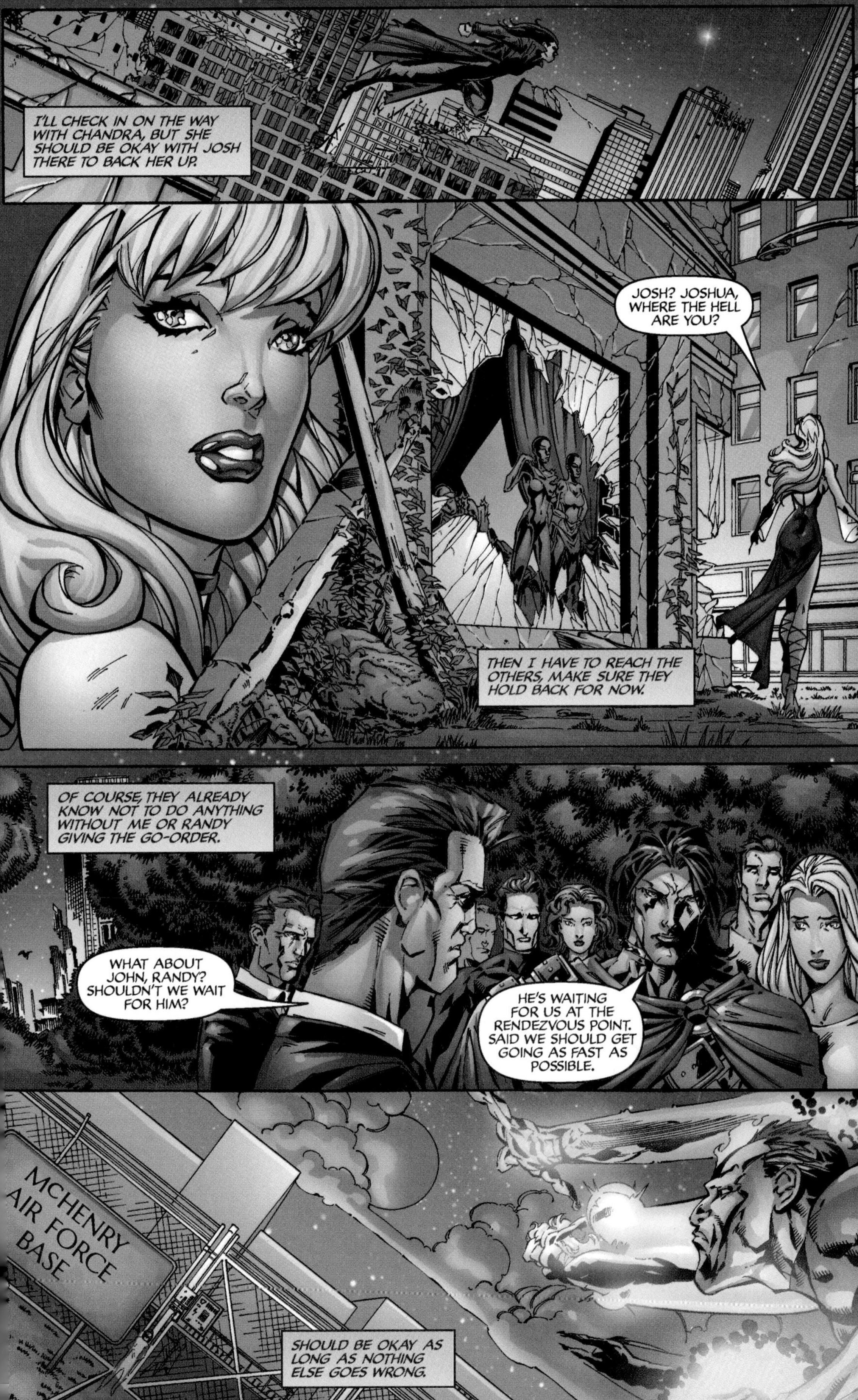
I'LL CHECK IN ON THE WAY WITH CHANDRA, BUT SHE SHOULD BE OKAY WITH JOSH THERE TO BACK HER UP.
JOSH? JOSHUA, WHERE THE HELL ARE YOU?
THEN I HAVE TO REACH THE OTHERS, MAKE SURE THEY HOLD BACK FOR NOW.
OF COURSE, THEY ALREADY KNOW NOT TO DO ANYTHING WITHOUT ME OR RANDY GIVING THE GO-ORDER.
WHAT ABOUT JOHN, RANDY? SHOULDN'T WE WAIT FOR HIM?
HE'S WAITING FOR US AT THE RENDEZVOUS POINT. SAID WE SHOULD GET GOING AS FAST AS POSSIBLE.
MCHENRY AIR FORCE BASE
SHOULD BE OKAY AS LONG AS NOTHING ELSE GOES WRONG.

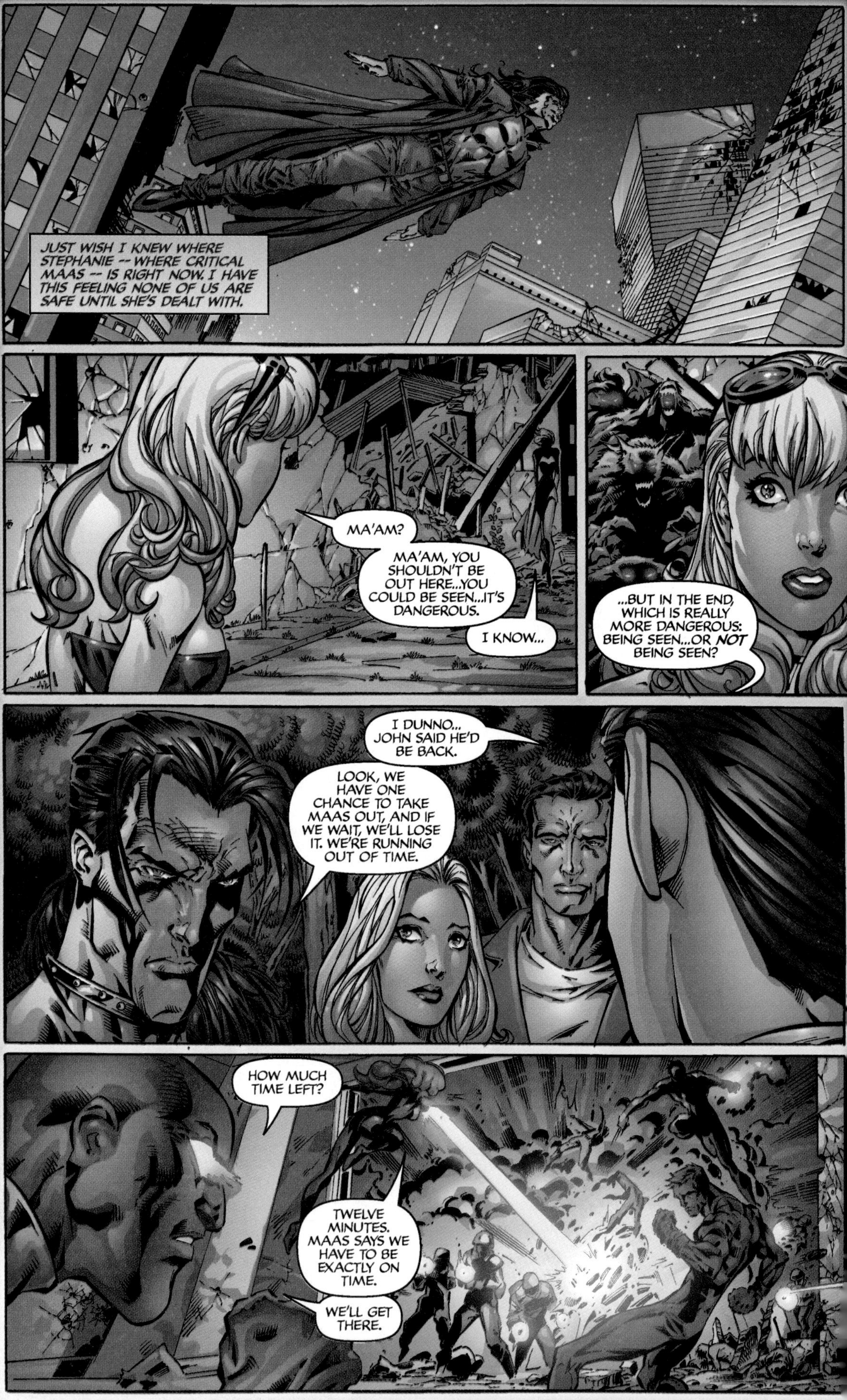
JUST WISH I KNEW WHERE STEPHANIE -- WHERE CRITICAL MAAS -- IS RIGHT NOW. I HAVE THIS FEELING NONE OF US ARE SAFE UNTIL SHE'S DEALT WITH.
MA'AM?
MA'AM, YOU SHOULDN'T BE OUT HERE...YOU COULD BE SEEN...IT'S DANGEROUS.
I KNOW...
...BUT IN THE END, WHICH IS REALLY MORE DANGEROUS: BEING SEEN...OR *NOT* BEING SEEN?
I DUNNO... JOHN SAID HE'D BE BACK.
LOOK, WE HAVE ONE CHANCE TO TAKE MAAS OUT, AND IF WE WAIT, WE'LL LOSE IT. WE'RE RUNNING OUT OF TIME.
HOW MUCH TIME LEFT?
TWELVE MINUTES. MAAS SAYS WE HAVE TO BE EXACTLY ON TIME.
WE'LL GET THERE.

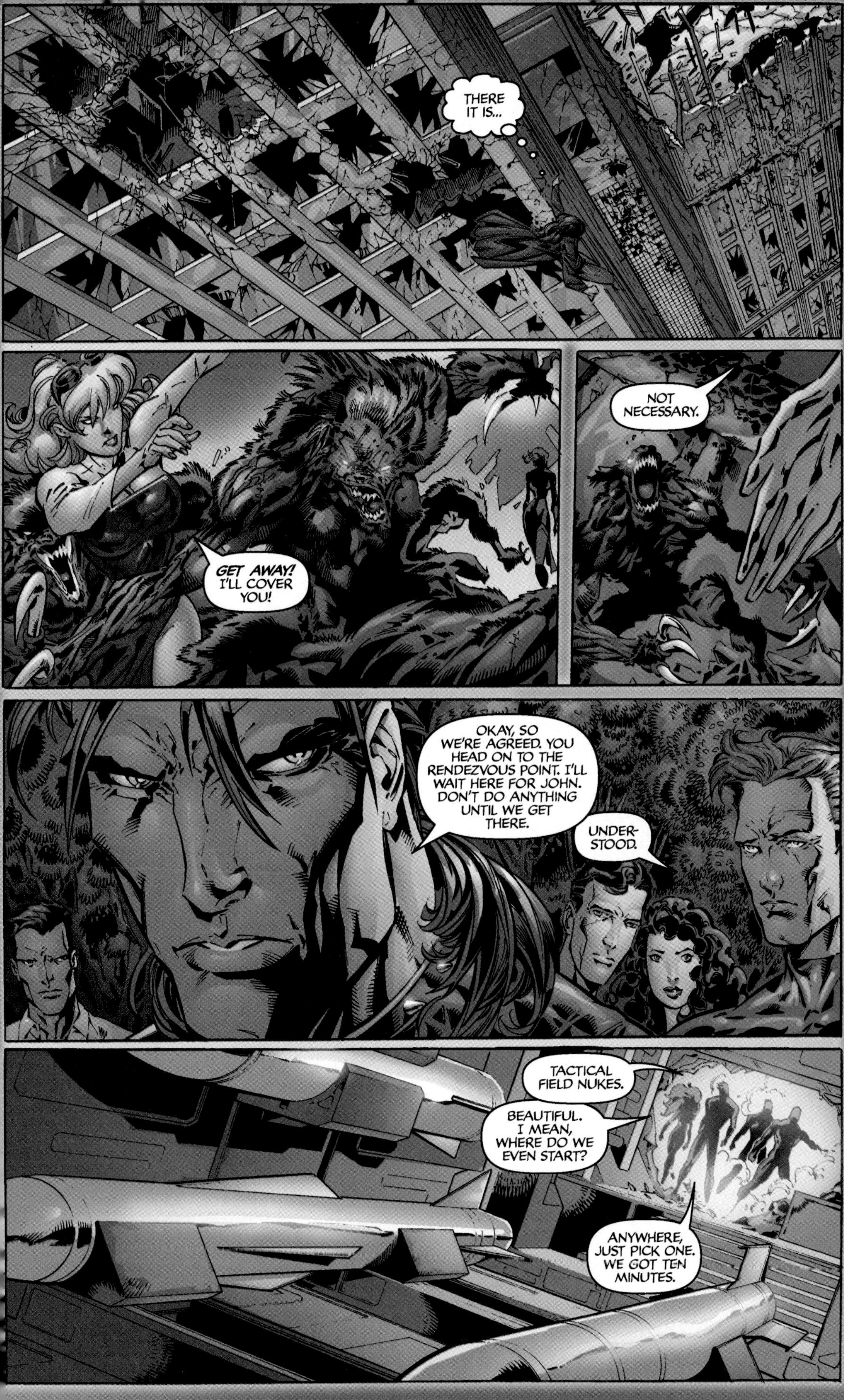
THERE IT IS...
GET AWAY! I'LL COVER YOU!
NOT NECESSARY.
OKAY, SO WE'RE AGREED. YOU HEAD ON TO THE RENDEZVOUS POINT. I'LL WAIT HERE FOR JOHN. DON'T DO ANYTHING UNTIL WE GET THERE.
UNDER-STOOD.
TACTICAL FIELD NUKES.
BEAUTIFUL. I MEAN, WHERE DO WE EVEN START?
ANYWHERE, JUST PICK ONE. WE GOT TEN MINUTES.

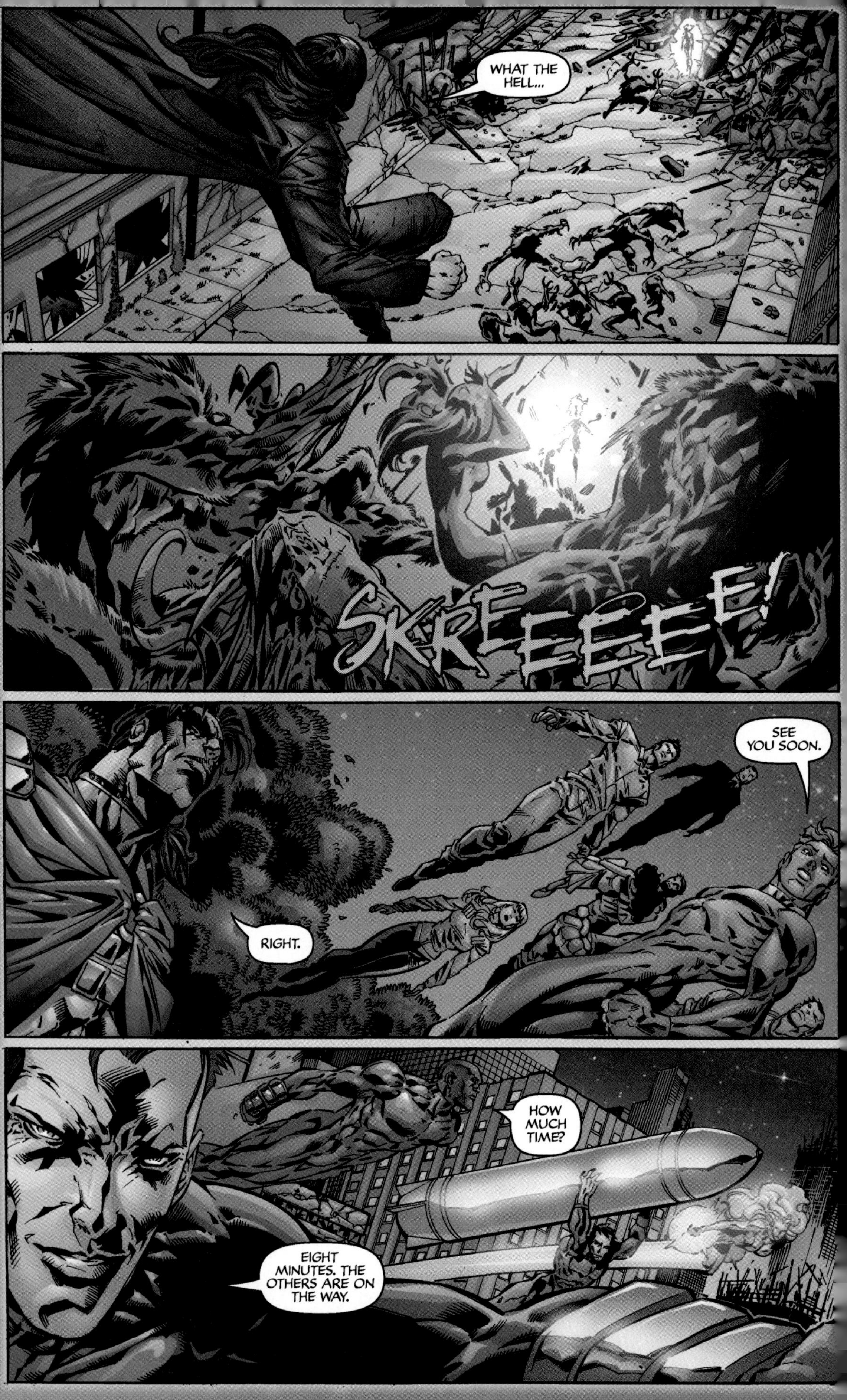
WHAT THE HELL...
SKREEEEEE!
SEE YOU SOON.
RIGHT.
HOW MUCH TIME?
EIGHT MINUTES. THE OTHERS ARE ON THE WAY.

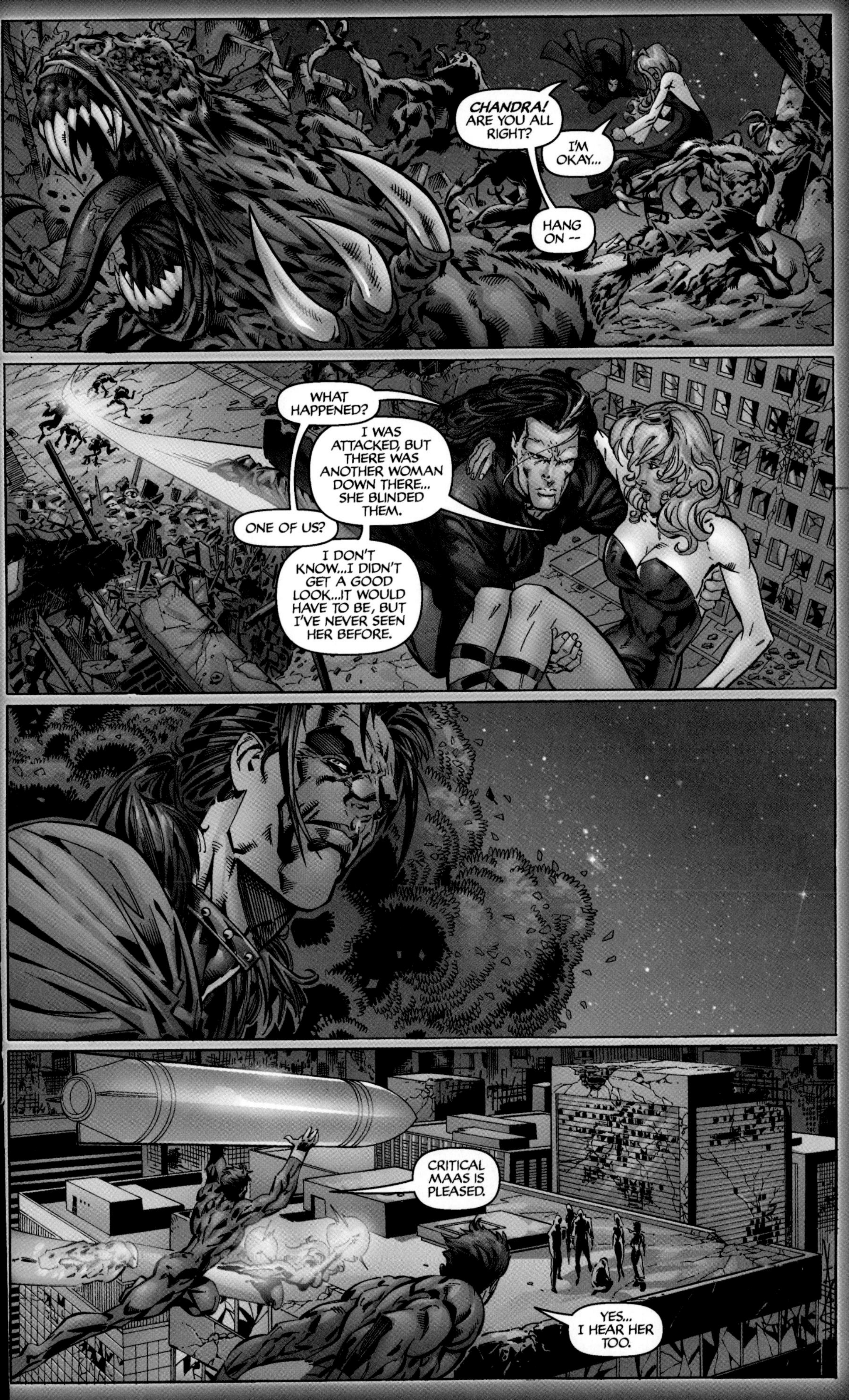
CHANDRA! ARE YOU ALL RIGHT?
I'M OKAY...
HANG ON --
WHAT HAPPENED?
I WAS ATTACKED, BUT THERE WAS ANOTHER WOMAN DOWN THERE... SHE BLINDED THEM.
ONE OF US?
I DON'T KNOW...I DIDN'T GET A GOOD LOOK...IT WOULD HAVE TO BE, BUT I'VE NEVER SEEN HER BEFORE.
CRITICAL MAAS IS PLEASED.
YES... I HEAR HER TOO.

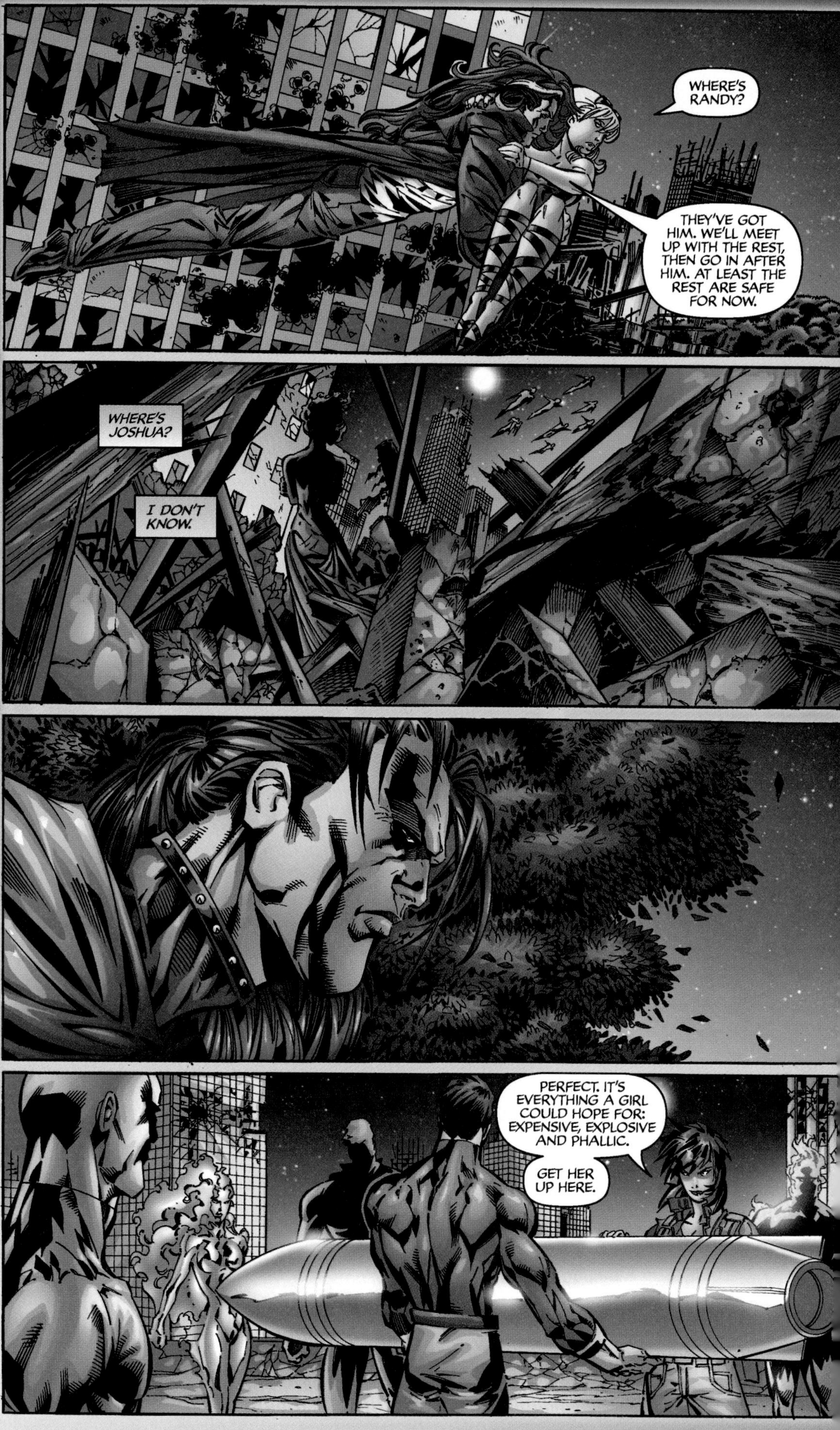
WHERE'S RANDY?
THEY'VE GOT HIM. WE'LL MEET UP WITH THE REST, THEN GO IN AFTER HIM. AT LEAST THE REST ARE SAFE FOR NOW.
WHERE'S JOSHUA?
I DON'T KNOW.
PERFECT. IT'S EVERYTHING A GIRL COULD HOPE FOR: EXPENSIVE, EXPLOSIVE AND PHALLIC.
GET HER UP HERE.

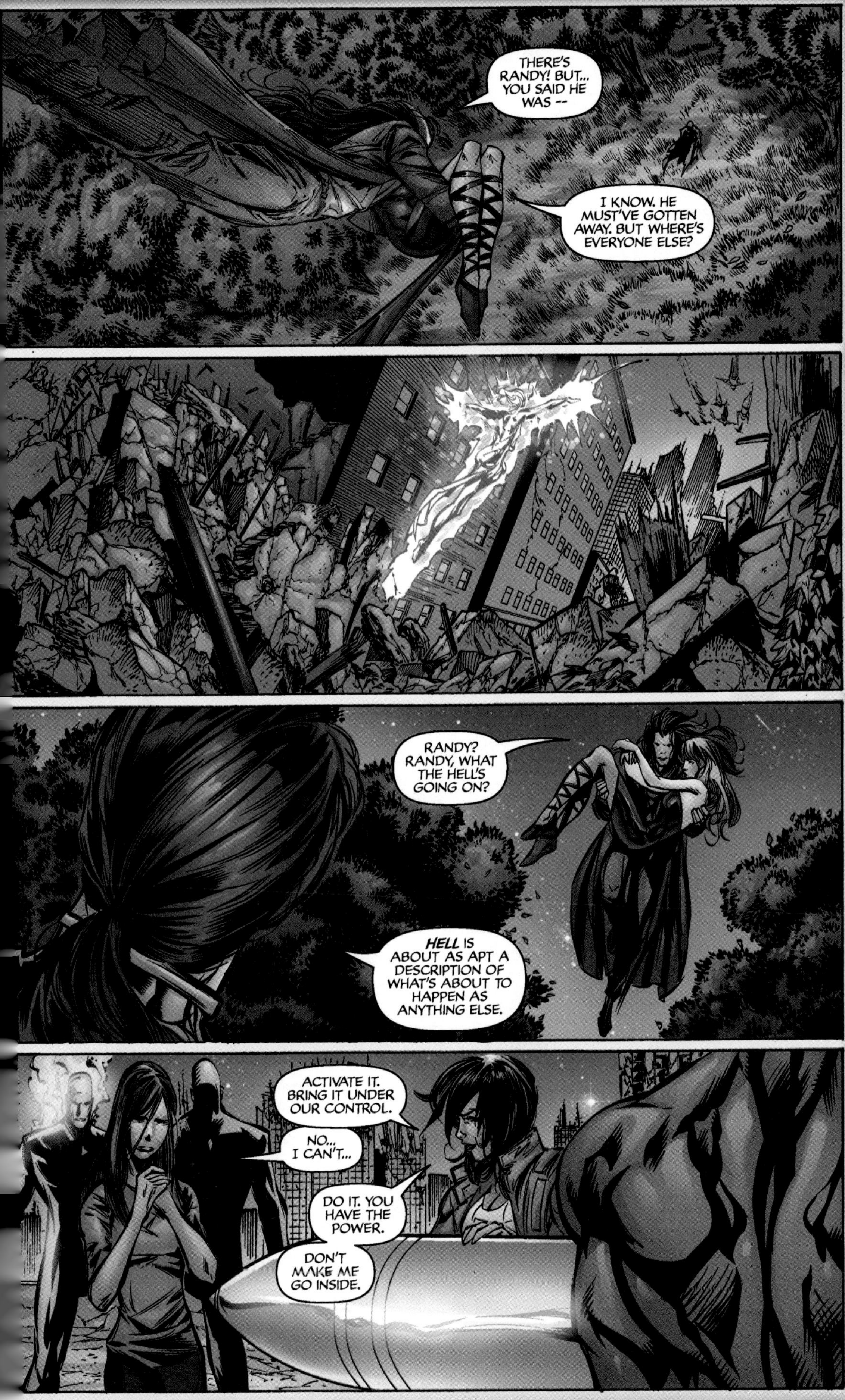
THERE'S RANDY! BUT... YOU SAID HE WAS --
I KNOW. HE MUST'VE GOTTEN AWAY. BUT WHERE'S EVERYONE ELSE?
RANDY? RANDY, WHAT THE HELL'S GOING ON?
HELL IS ABOUT AS APT A DESCRIPTION OF WHAT'S ABOUT TO HAPPEN AS ANYTHING ELSE.
ACTIVATE IT. BRING IT UNDER OUR CONTROL.
NO... I CAN'T...
DO IT. YOU HAVE THE POWER.
DON'T MAKE ME GO INSIDE.

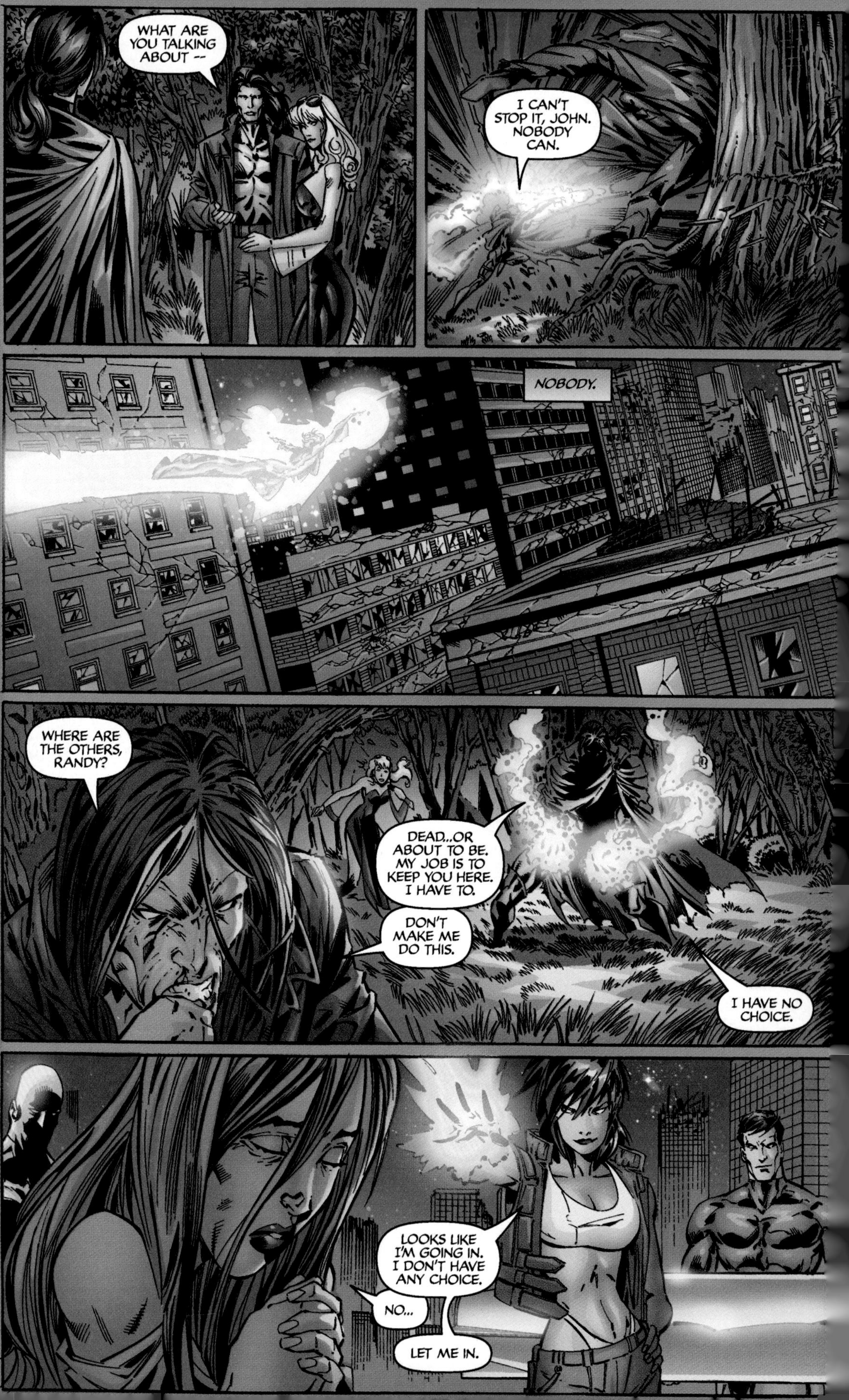
WHAT ARE YOU TALKING ABOUT --
I CAN'T STOP IT, JOHN. NOBODY CAN.
NOBODY.
WHERE ARE THE OTHERS, RANDY?
DEAD...OR ABOUT TO BE. MY JOB IS TO KEEP YOU HERE. I HAVE TO.
DON'T MAKE ME DO THIS.
I HAVE NO CHOICE.
LOOKS LIKE I'M GOING IN. I DON'T HAVE ANY CHOICE.
NO...
LET ME IN.

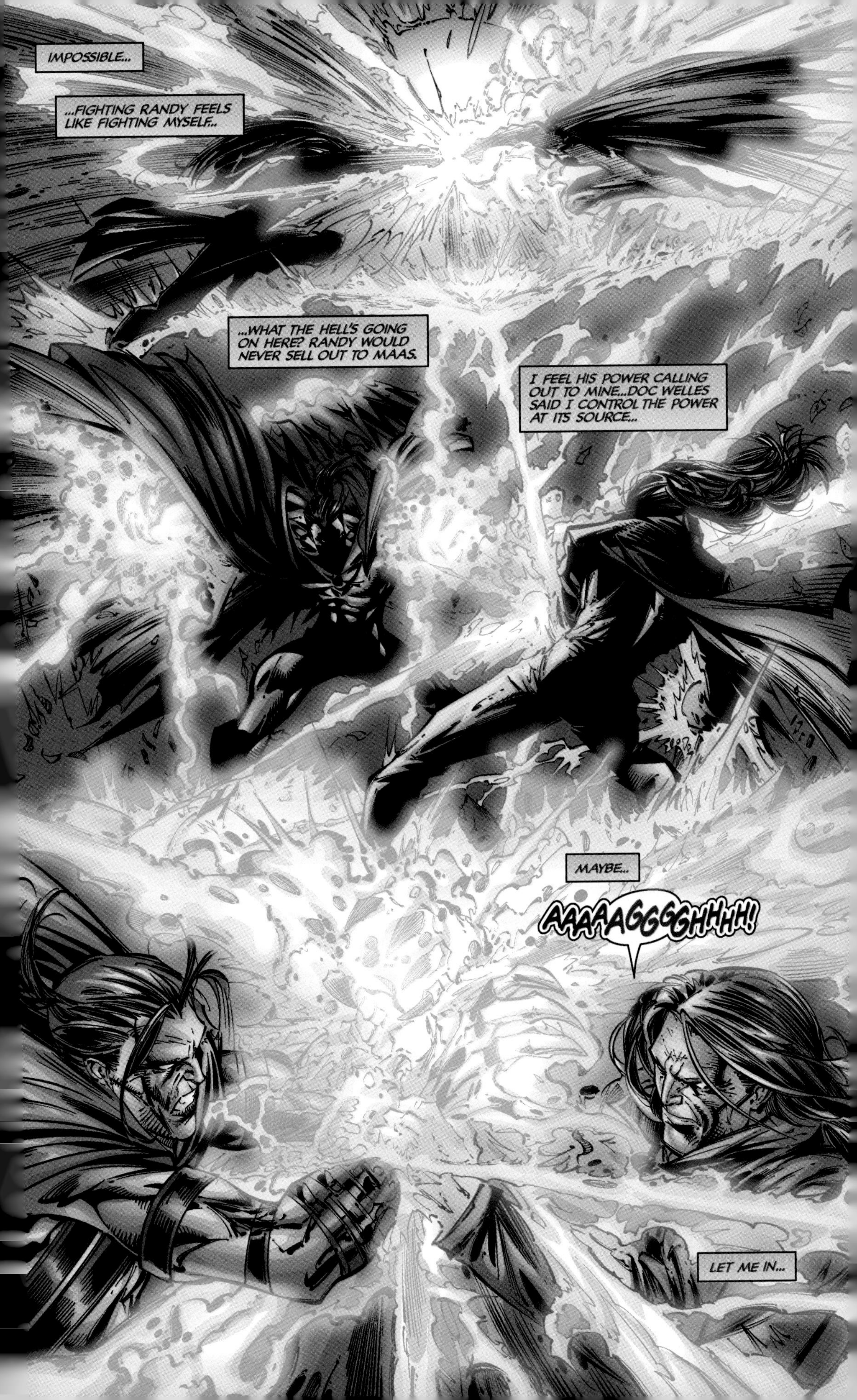
IMPOSSIBLE...
...FIGHTING RANDY FEELS LIKE FIGHTING MYSELF...
...WHAT THE HELL'S GOING ON HERE? RANDY WOULD NEVER SELL OUT TO MAAS.
I FEEL HIS POWER CALLING OUT TO MINE...DOC WELLES SAID I CONTROL THE POWER AT ITS SOURCE...
MAYBE...
AAAAAGGGGHHHH!
LET ME IN...

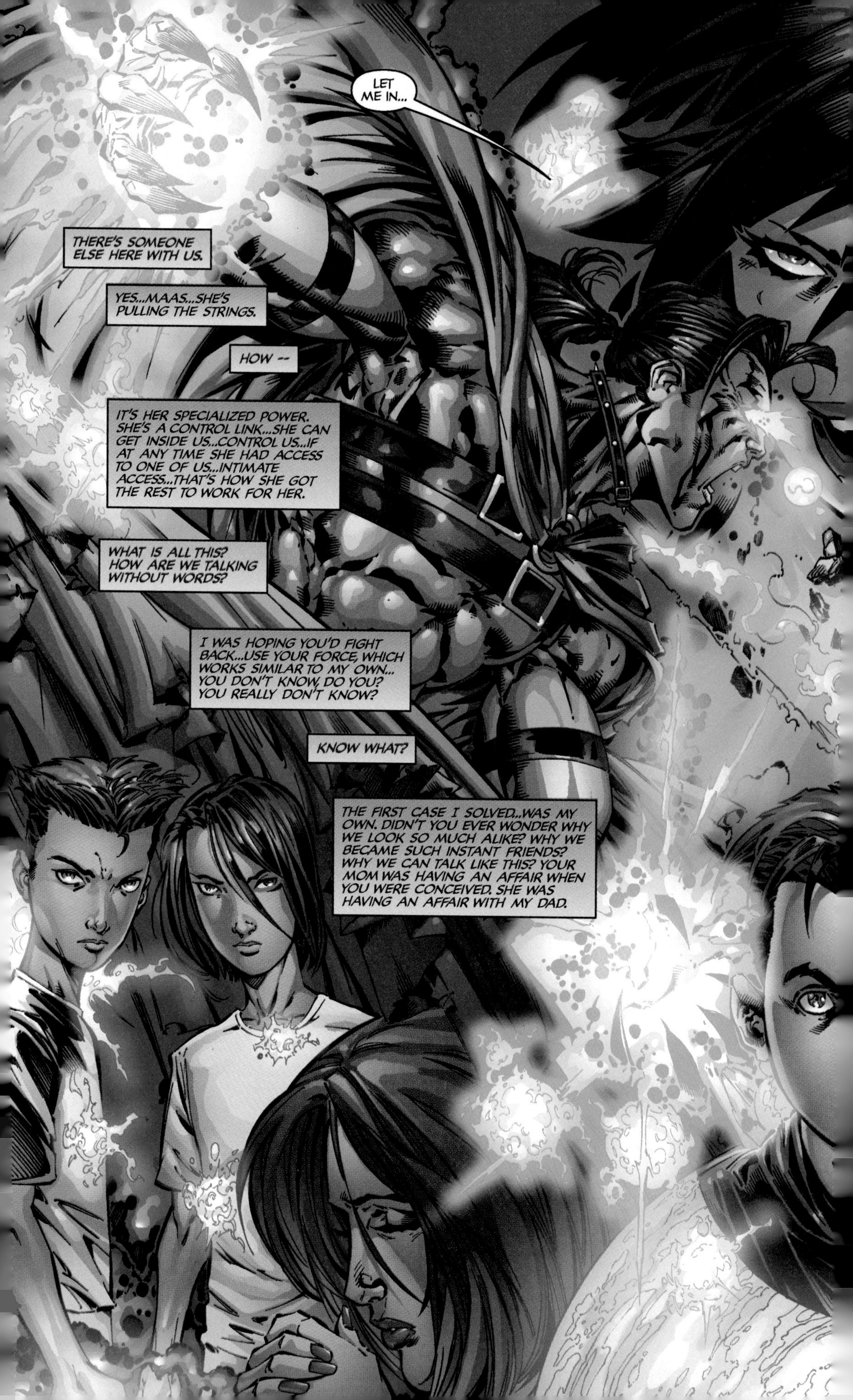
LET ME IN...
THERE'S SOMEONE ELSE HERE WITH US.
YES...MAAS...SHE'S PULLING THE STRINGS.
HOW --
IT'S HER SPECIALIZED POWER. SHE'S A CONTROL LINK...SHE CAN GET INSIDE US...CONTROL US...IF AT ANY TIME SHE HAD ACCESS TO ONE OF US...INTIMATE ACCESS...THAT'S HOW SHE GOT THE REST TO WORK FOR HER.
WHAT IS ALL THIS? HOW ARE WE TALKING WITHOUT WORDS?
I WAS HOPING YOU'D FIGHT BACK...USE YOUR FORCE, WHICH WORKS SIMILAR TO MY OWN... YOU DON'T KNOW, DO YOU? YOU REALLY DON'T KNOW?
KNOW WHAT?
THE FIRST CASE I SOLVED...WAS MY OWN. DIDN'T YOU EVER WONDER WHY WE LOOK SO MUCH ALIKE? WHY WE BECAME SUCH INSTANT FRIENDS? WHY WE CAN TALK LIKE THIS? YOUR MOM WAS HAVING AN AFFAIR WHEN YOU WERE CONCEIVED. SHE WAS HAVING AN AFFAIR WITH MY DAD.

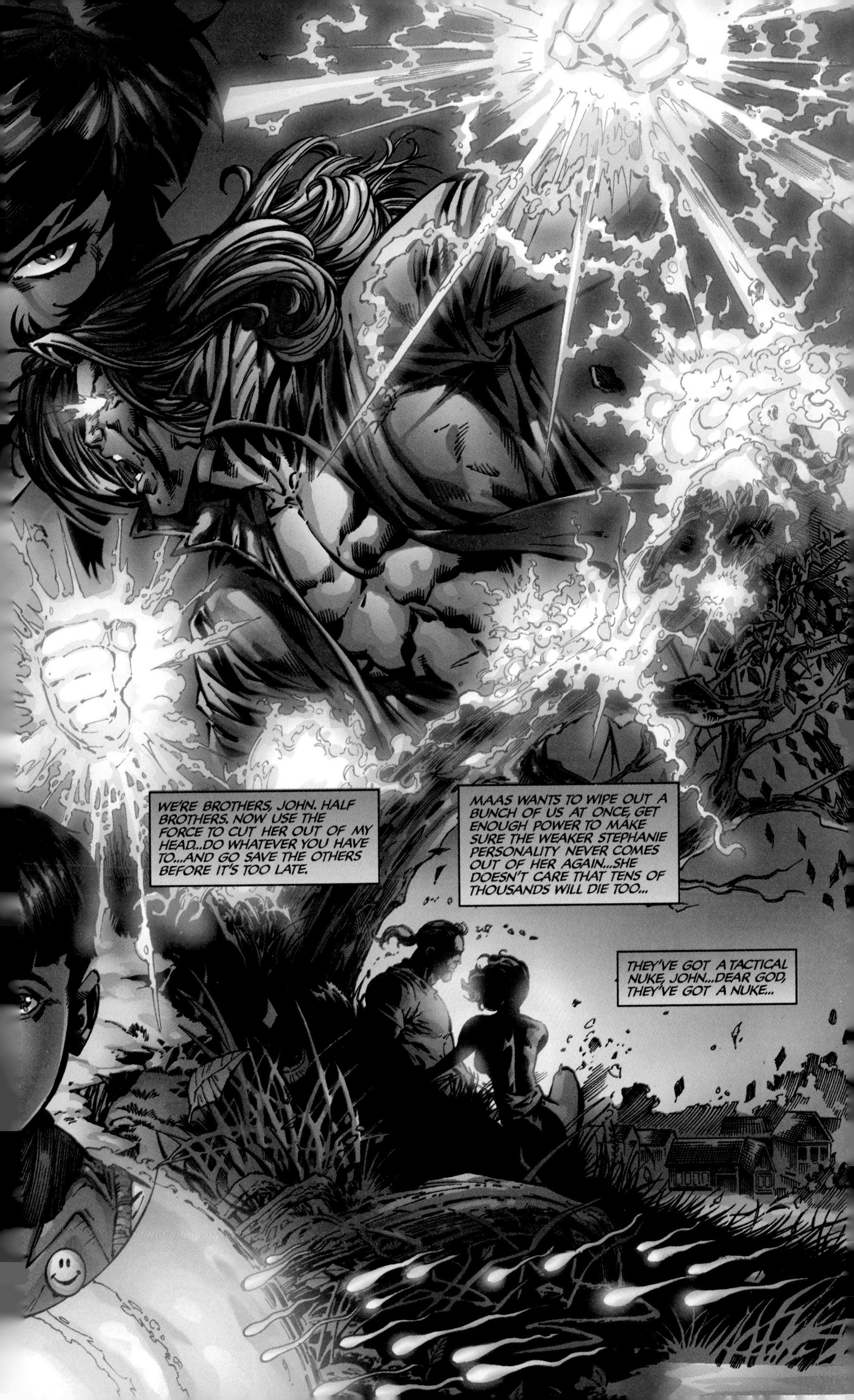
WE'RE BROTHERS, JOHN. HALF BROTHERS. NOW USE THE FORCE TO CUT HER OUT OF MY HEAD...DO WHATEVER YOU HAVE TO...AND GO SAVE THE OTHERS BEFORE IT'S TOO LATE.
MAAS WANTS TO WIPE OUT A BUNCH OF US AT ONCE, GET ENOUGH POWER TO MAKE SURE THE WEAKER STEPHANIE PERSONALITY NEVER COMES OUT OF HER AGAIN...SHE DOESN'T CARE THAT TENS OF THOUSANDS WILL DIE TOO...
THEY'VE GOT A TACTICAL NUKE, JOHN...DEAR GOD, THEY'VE GOT A NUKE...

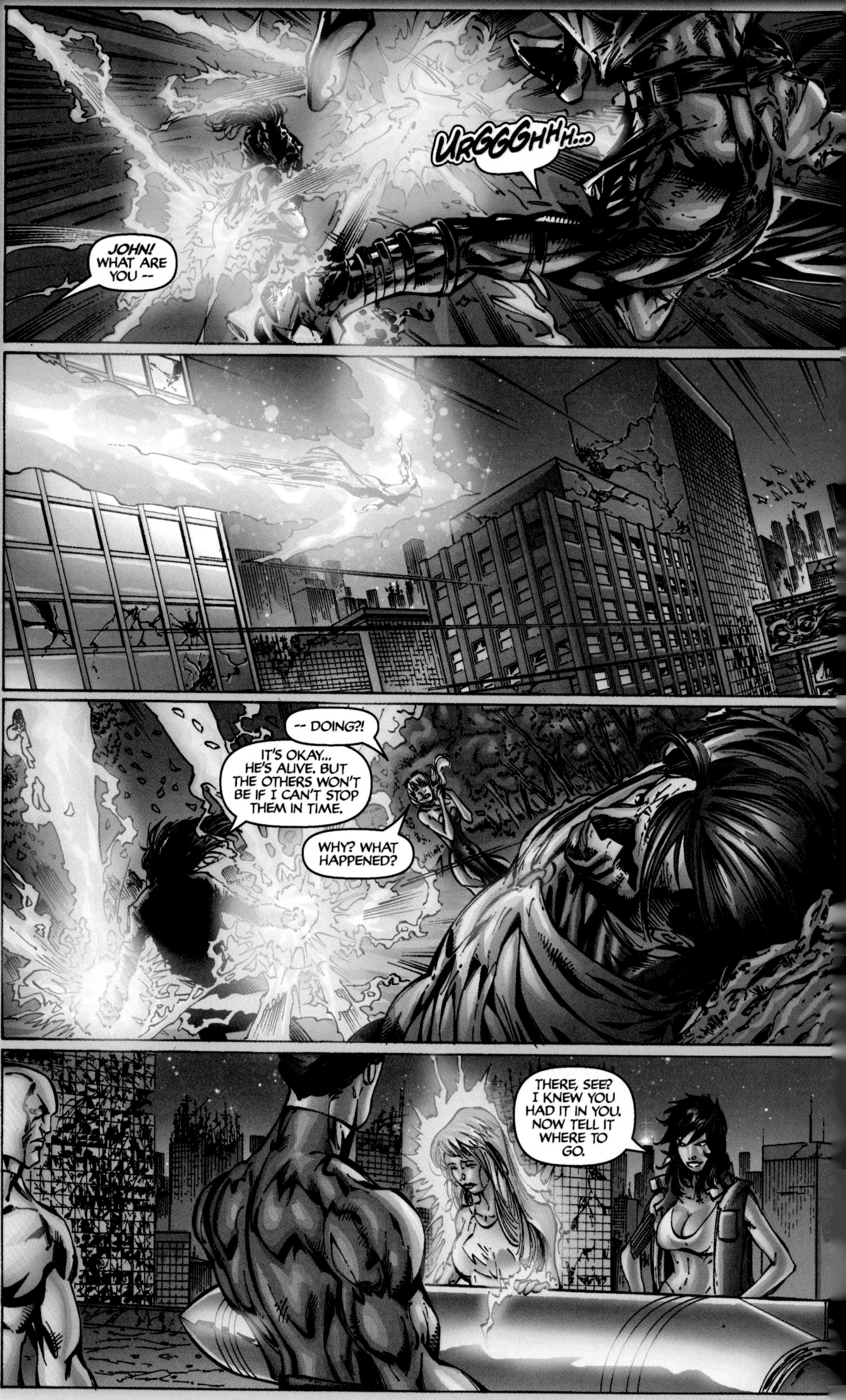
URGGGHHH...
JOHN! WHAT ARE YOU --
-- DOING?!
IT'S OKAY... HE'S ALIVE. BUT THE OTHERS WON'T BE IF I CAN'T STOP THEM IN TIME.
WHY? WHAT HAPPENED?
THERE, SEE? I KNEW YOU HAD IT IN YOU. NOW TELL IT WHERE TO GO.

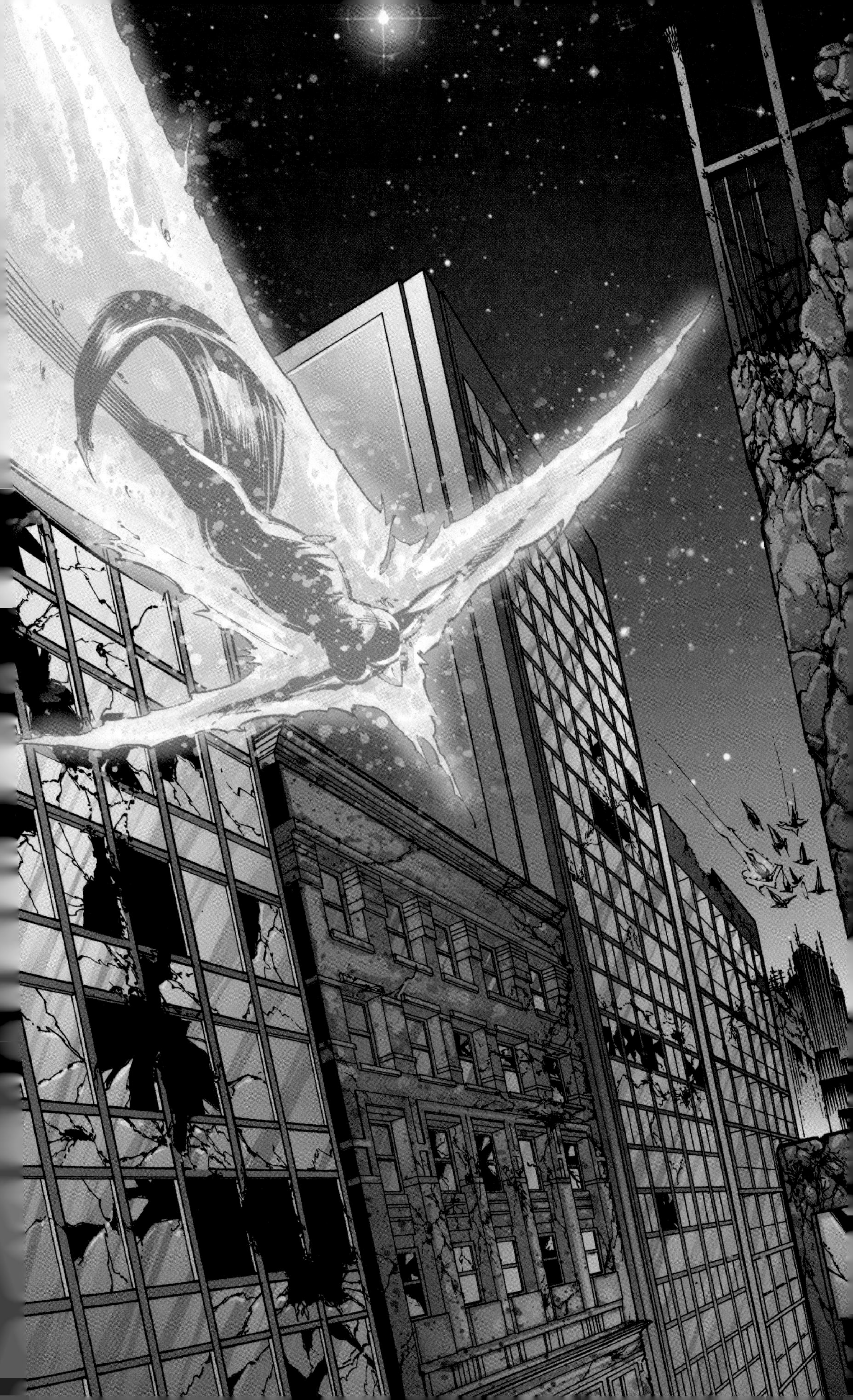

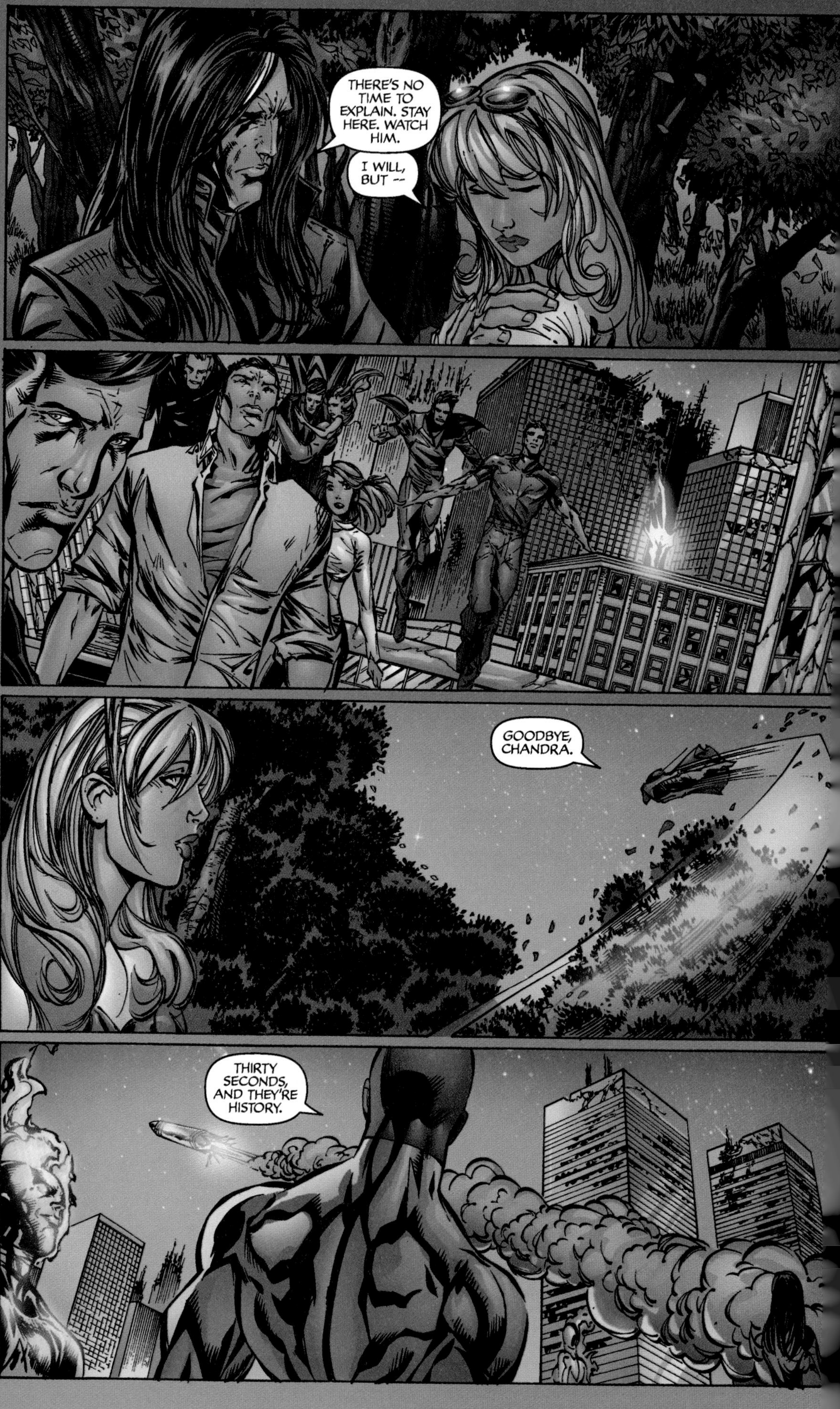
THERE'S NO TIME TO EXPLAIN. STAY HERE. WATCH HIM.
I WILL, BUT --
GOODBYE, CHANDRA.
THIRTY SECONDS, AND THEY'RE HISTORY.

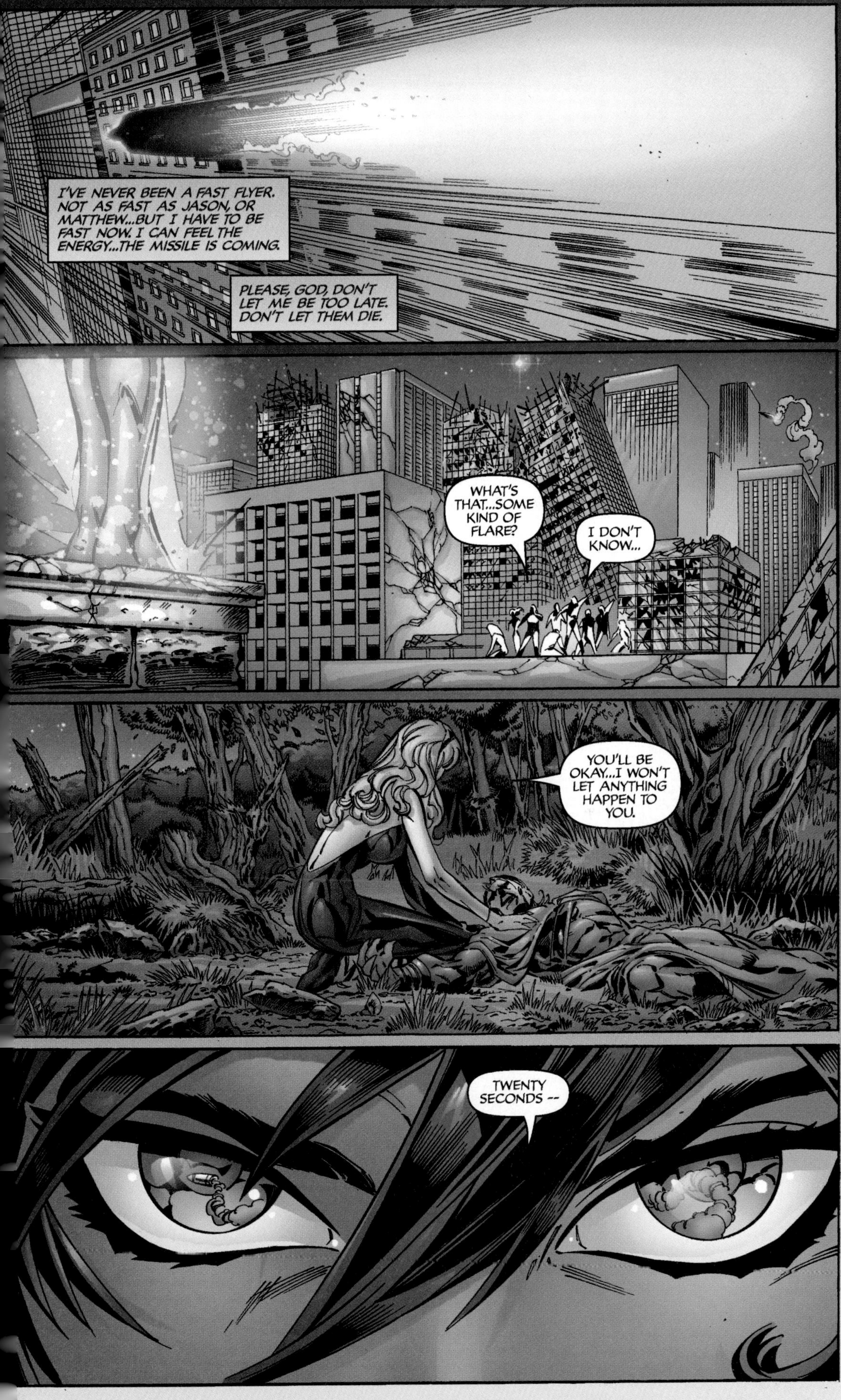
I'VE NEVER BEEN A FAST FLYER. NOT AS FAST AS JASON, OR MATTHEW...BUT I HAVE TO BE FAST NOW. I CAN FEEL THE ENERGY...THE MISSILE IS COMING.
PLEASE, GOD, DON'T LET ME BE TOO LATE. DON'T LET THEM DIE.
WHAT'S THAT...SOME KIND OF FLARE?
I DON'T KNOW...
YOU'LL BE OKAY...I WON'T LET ANYTHING HAPPEN TO YOU.
TWENTY SECONDS --

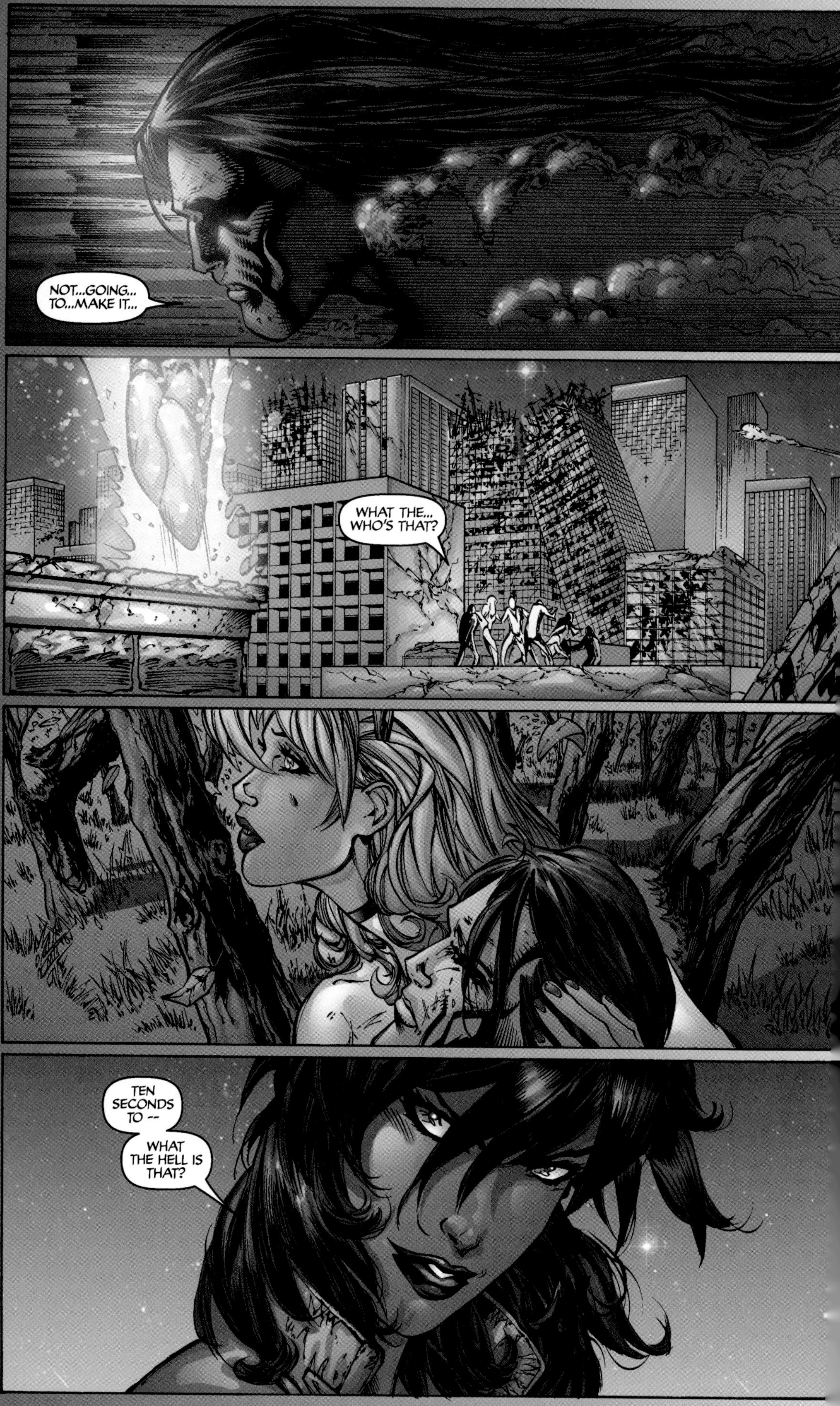

NOT...GOING... TO...MAKE IT...
WHAT THE... WHO'S THAT?
TEN SECONDS TO --
WHAT THE HELL IS THAT?

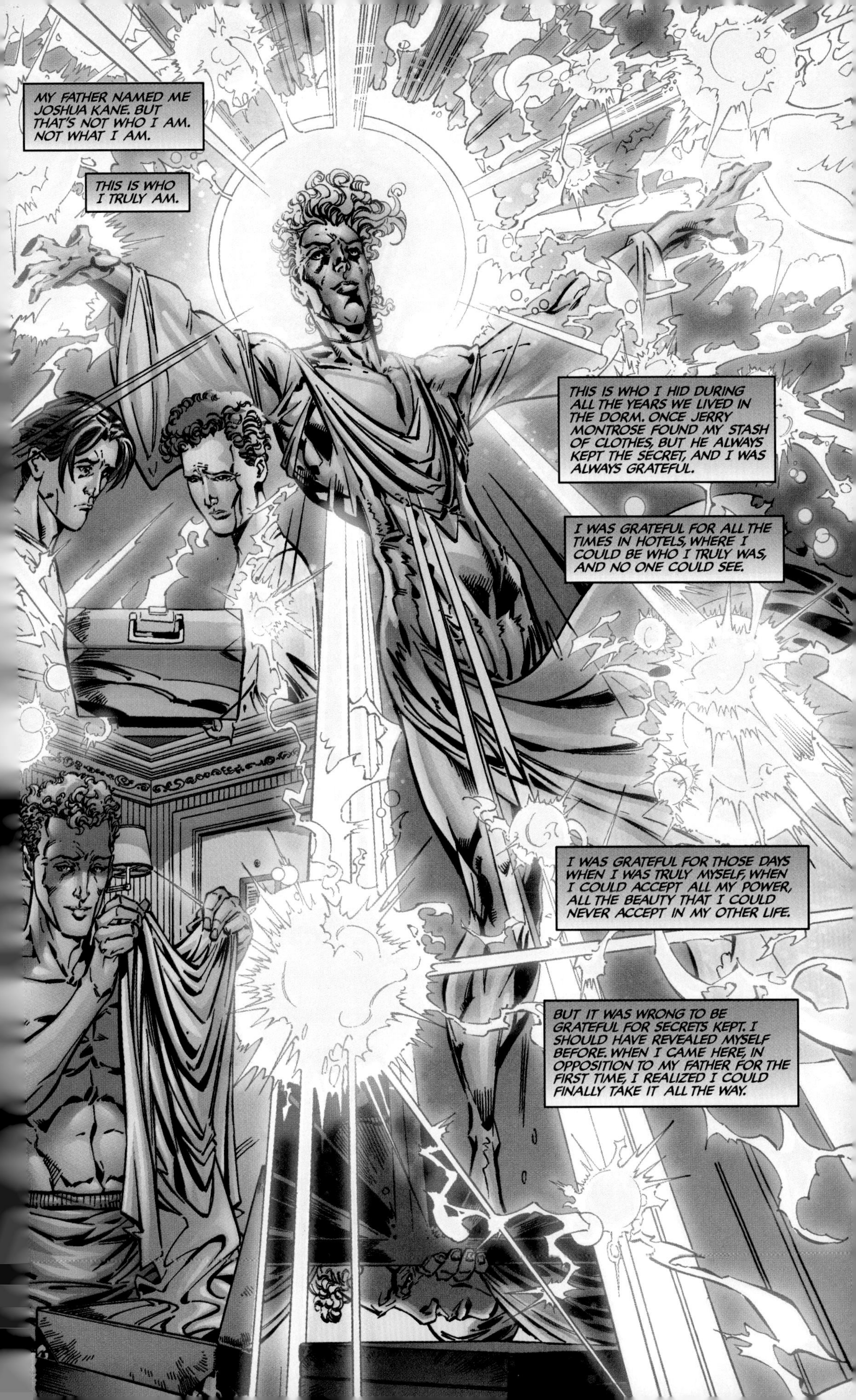
MY FATHER NAMED ME JOSHUA KANE. BUT THAT'S NOT WHO I AM. NOT WHAT I AM.
THIS IS WHO I TRULY AM.
THIS IS WHO I HID DURING ALL THE YEARS WE LIVED IN THE DORM. ONCE JERRY MONTROSE FOUND MY STASH OF CLOTHES, BUT HE ALWAYS KEPT THE SECRET, AND I WAS ALWAYS GRATEFUL.
I WAS GRATEFUL FOR ALL THE TIMES IN HOTELS, WHERE I COULD BE WHO I TRULY WAS, AND NO ONE COULD SEE.
I WAS GRATEFUL FOR THOSE DAYS WHEN I WAS TRULY MYSELF, WHEN I COULD ACCEPT ALL MY POWER, ALL THE BEAUTY THAT I COULD NEVER ACCEPT IN MY OTHER LIFE.
BUT IT WAS WRONG TO BE GRATEFUL FOR SECRETS KEPT. I SHOULD HAVE REVEALED MYSELF BEFORE. WHEN I CAME HERE, IN OPPOSITION TO MY FATHER FOR THE FIRST TIME, I REALIZED I COULD FINALLY TAKE IT ALL THE WAY.

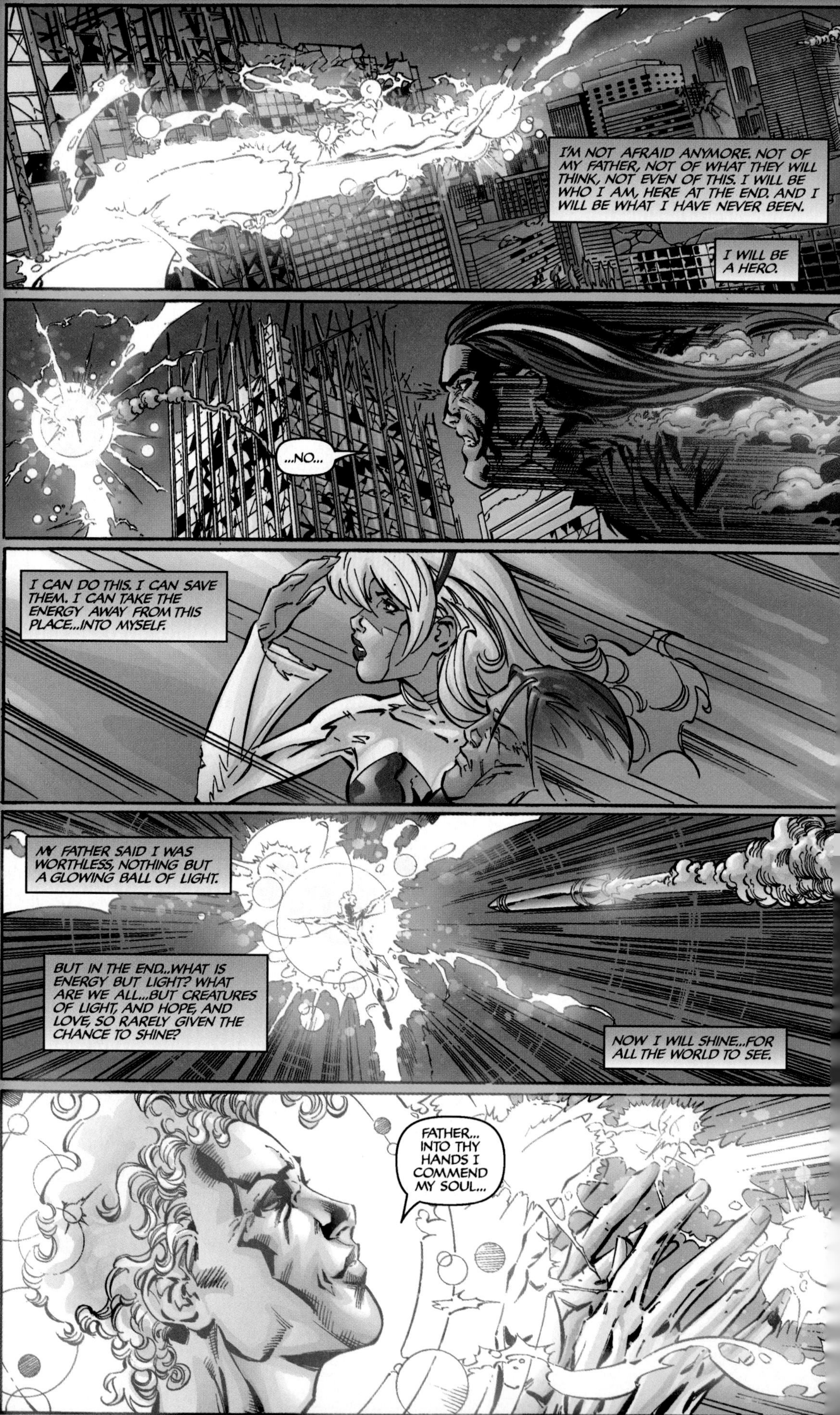
I'M NOT AFRAID ANYMORE. NOT OF MY FATHER, NOT OF WHAT THEY WILL THINK, NOT EVEN OF THIS. I WILL BE WHO I AM, HERE AT THE END. AND I WILL BE WHAT I HAVE NEVER BEEN.
I WILL BE A HERO.
...NO...
I CAN DO THIS. I CAN SAVE THEM. I CAN TAKE THE ENERGY AWAY FROM THIS PLACE...INTO MYSELF.
MY FATHER SAID I WAS WORTHLESS, NOTHING BUT A GLOWING BALL OF LIGHT.
BUT IN THE END...WHAT IS ENERGY BUT LIGHT? WHAT ARE WE ALL...BUT CREATURES OF LIGHT, AND HOPE, AND LOVE, SO RARELY GIVEN THE CHANCE TO SHINE?
NOW I WILL SHINE...FOR ALL THE WORLD TO SEE.
FATHER... INTO THY HANDS I COMMEND MY SOUL...

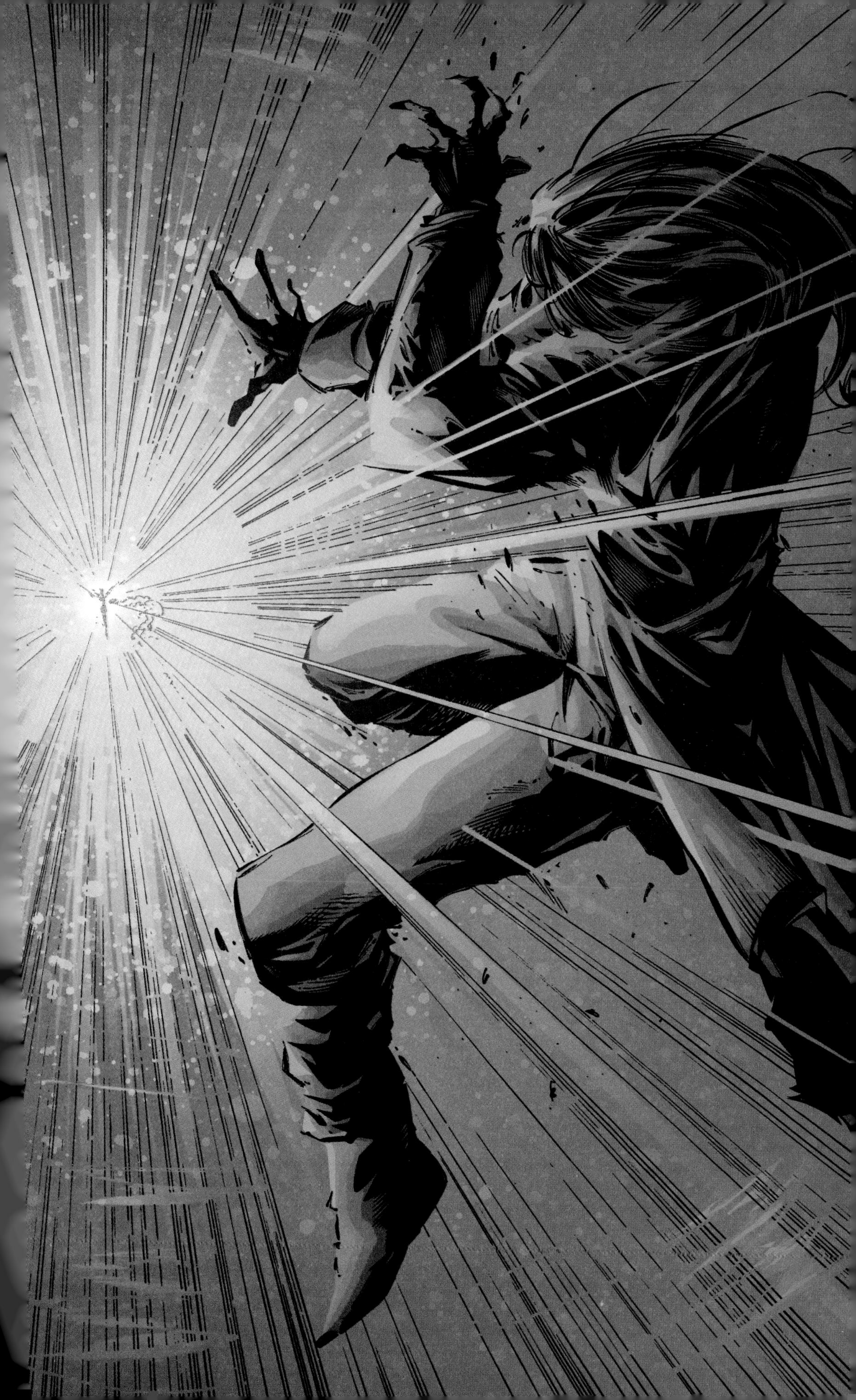

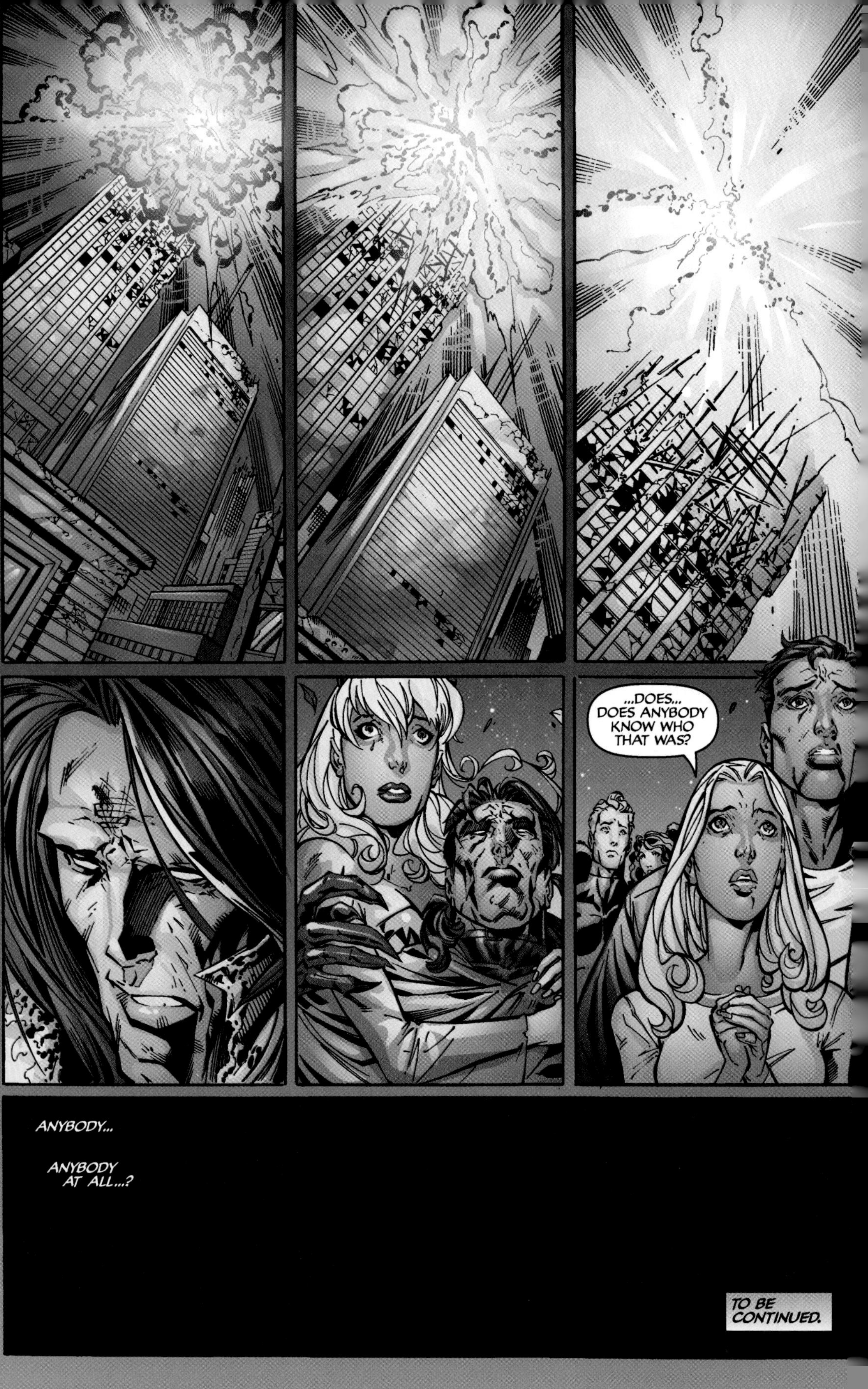
...DOES... DOES ANYBODY KNOW WHO THAT WAS?
ANYBODY...
ANYBODY AT ALL...?
TO BE CONTINUED.

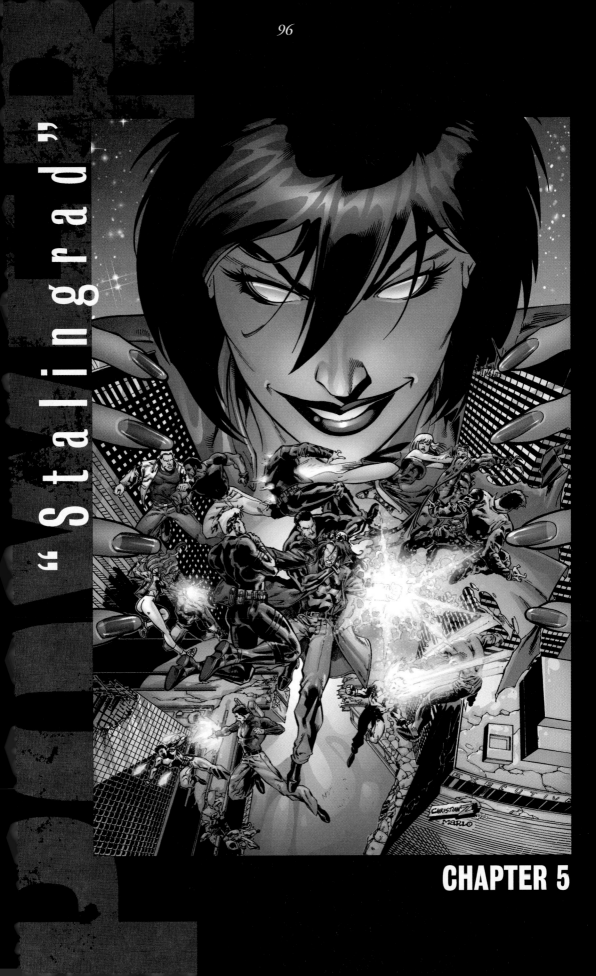

"Stalingrad"

CHAPTER 5

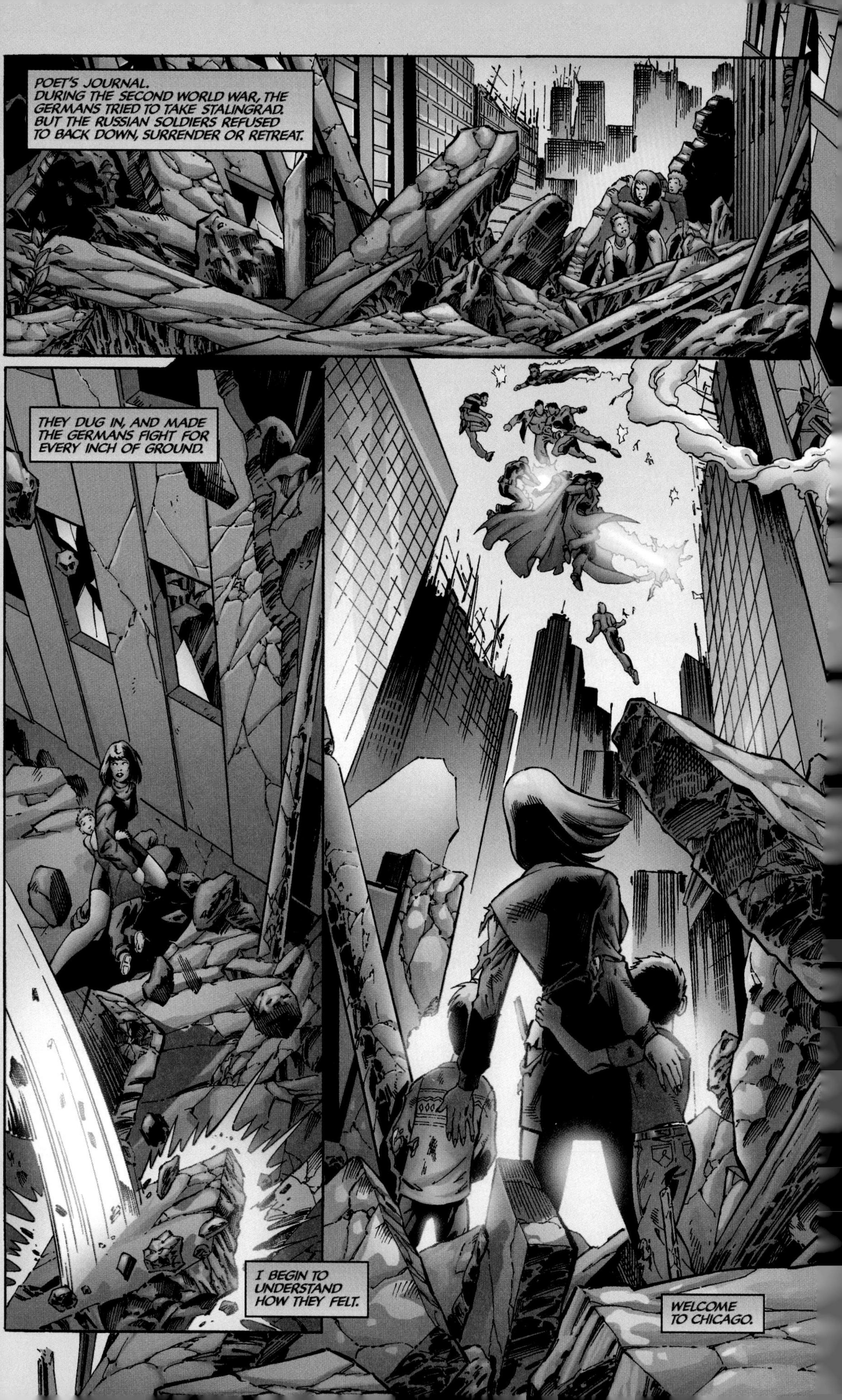
POET'S JOURNAL.
DURING THE SECOND WORLD WAR, THE GERMANS TRIED TO TAKE STALINGRAD. BUT THE RUSSIAN SOLDIERS REFUSED TO BACK DOWN, SURRENDER OR RETREAT.
THEY DUG IN, AND MADE THE GERMANS FIGHT FOR EVERY INCH OF GROUND.
I BEGIN TO UNDERSTAND HOW THEY FELT.
WELCOME TO CHICAGO.

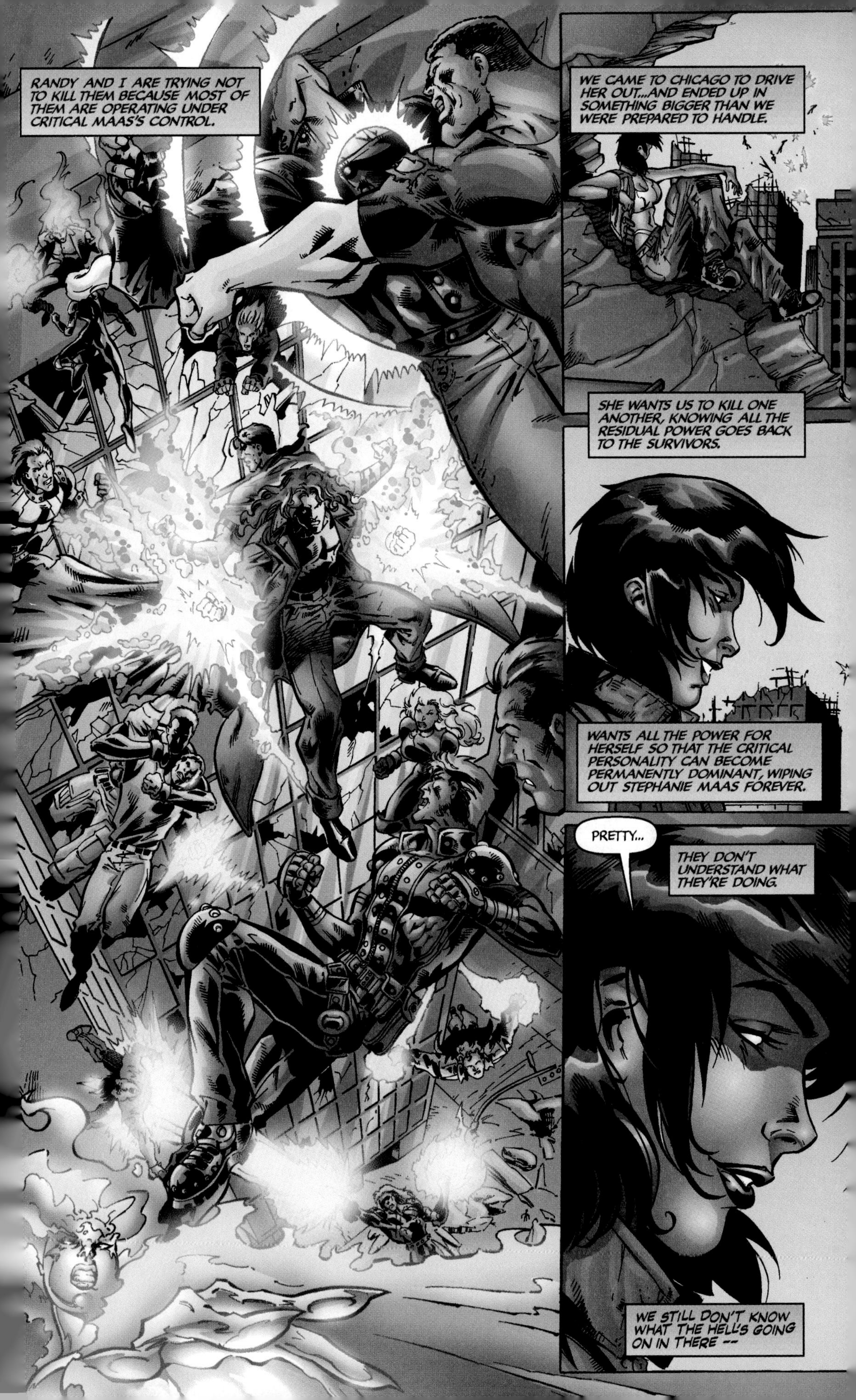
RANDY AND I ARE TRYING NOT TO KILL THEM BECAUSE MOST OF THEM ARE OPERATING UNDER CRITICAL MAAS'S CONTROL.
WE CAME TO CHICAGO TO DRIVE HER OUT...AND ENDED UP IN SOMETHING BIGGER THAN WE WERE PREPARED TO HANDLE.
SHE WANTS US TO KILL ONE ANOTHER, KNOWING ALL THE RESIDUAL POWER GOES BACK TO THE SURVIVORS.
WANTS ALL THE POWER FOR HERSELF SO THAT THE CRITICAL PERSONALITY CAN BECOME PERMANENTLY DOMINANT, WIPING OUT STEPHANIE MAAS FOREVER.
PRETTY...
THEY DON'T UNDERSTAND WHAT THEY'RE DOING.
WE STILL DON'T KNOW WHAT THE HELL'S GOING ON IN THERE --

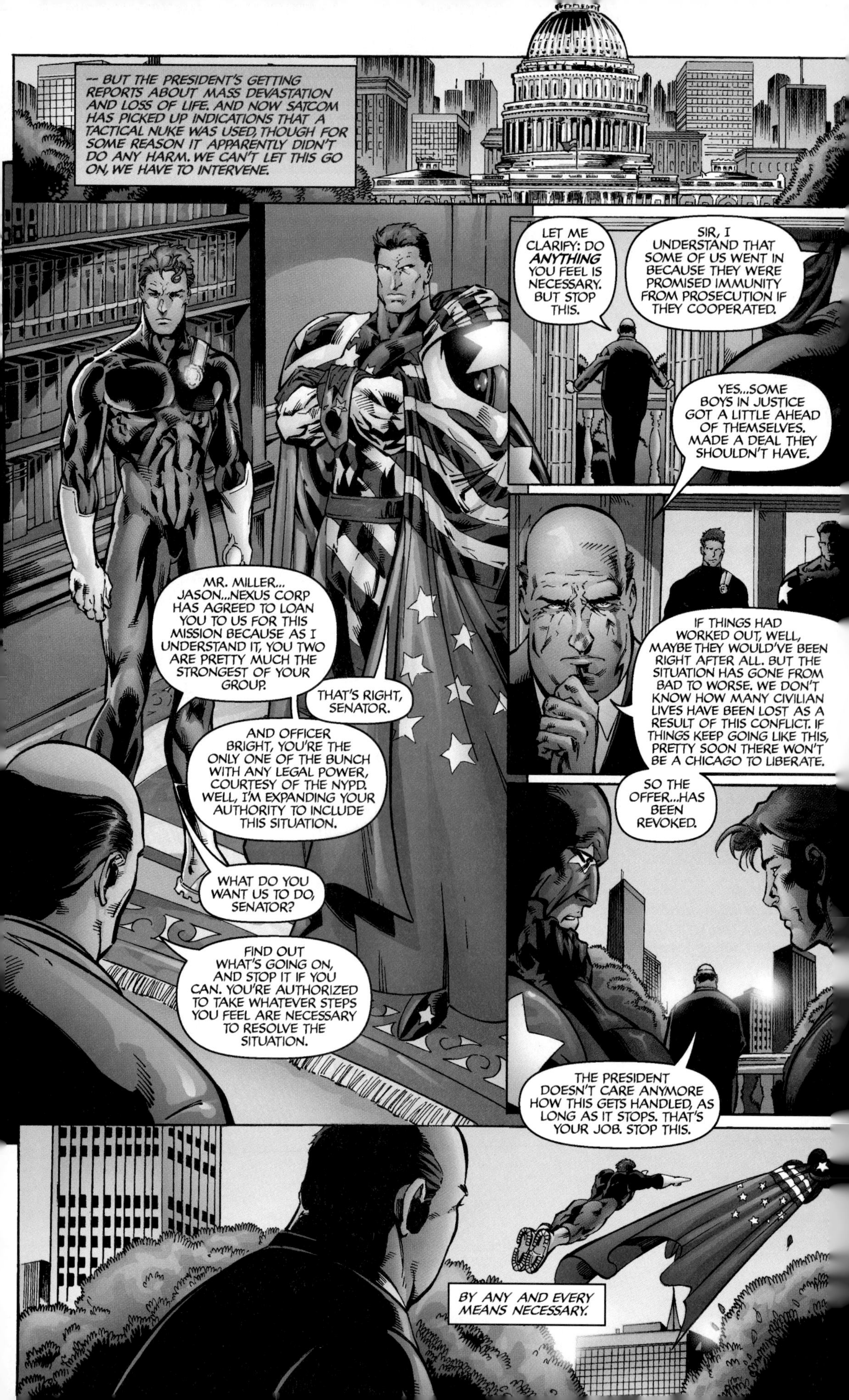
-- BUT THE PRESIDENT'S GETTING REPORTS ABOUT MASS DEVASTATION AND LOSS OF LIFE. AND NOW SATCOM HAS PICKED UP INDICATIONS THAT A TACTICAL NUKE WAS USED, THOUGH FOR SOME REASON IT APPARENTLY DIDN'T DO ANY HARM. WE CAN'T LET THIS GO ON, WE HAVE TO INTERVENE.
MR. MILLER... JASON...NEXUS CORP HAS AGREED TO LOAN YOU TO US FOR THIS MISSION BECAUSE AS I UNDERSTAND IT, YOU TWO ARE PRETTY MUCH THE STRONGEST OF YOUR GROUP.
THAT'S RIGHT, SENATOR.
AND OFFICER BRIGHT, YOU'RE THE ONLY ONE OF THE BUNCH WITH ANY LEGAL POWER, COURTESY OF THE NYPD. WELL, I'M EXPANDING YOUR AUTHORITY TO INCLUDE THIS SITUATION.
WHAT DO YOU WANT US TO DO, SENATOR?
FIND OUT WHAT'S GOING ON, AND STOP IT IF YOU CAN. YOU'RE AUTHORIZED TO TAKE WHATEVER STEPS YOU FEEL ARE NECESSARY TO RESOLVE THE SITUATION.
SIR, I UNDERSTAND THAT SOME OF US WENT IN BECAUSE THEY WERE PROMISED IMMUNITY FROM PROSECUTION IF THEY COOPERATED.
LET ME CLARIFY: DO ANYTHING YOU FEEL IS NECESSARY. BUT STOP THIS.
YES...SOME BOYS IN JUSTICE GOT A LITTLE AHEAD OF THEMSELVES. MADE A DEAL THEY SHOULDN'T HAVE.
IF THINGS HAD WORKED OUT, WELL, MAYBE THEY WOULD'VE BEEN RIGHT AFTER ALL. BUT THE SITUATION HAS GONE FROM BAD TO WORSE. WE DON'T KNOW HOW MANY CIVILIAN LIVES HAVE BEEN LOST AS A RESULT OF THIS CONFLICT. IF THINGS KEEP GOING LIKE THIS, PRETTY SOON THERE WON'T BE A CHICAGO TO LIBERATE.
SO THE OFFER...HAS BEEN REVOKED.
THE PRESIDENT DOESN'T CARE ANYMORE HOW THIS GETS HANDLED, AS LONG AS IT STOPS. THAT'S YOUR JOB. STOP THIS.
BY ANY AND EVERY MEANS NECESSARY.

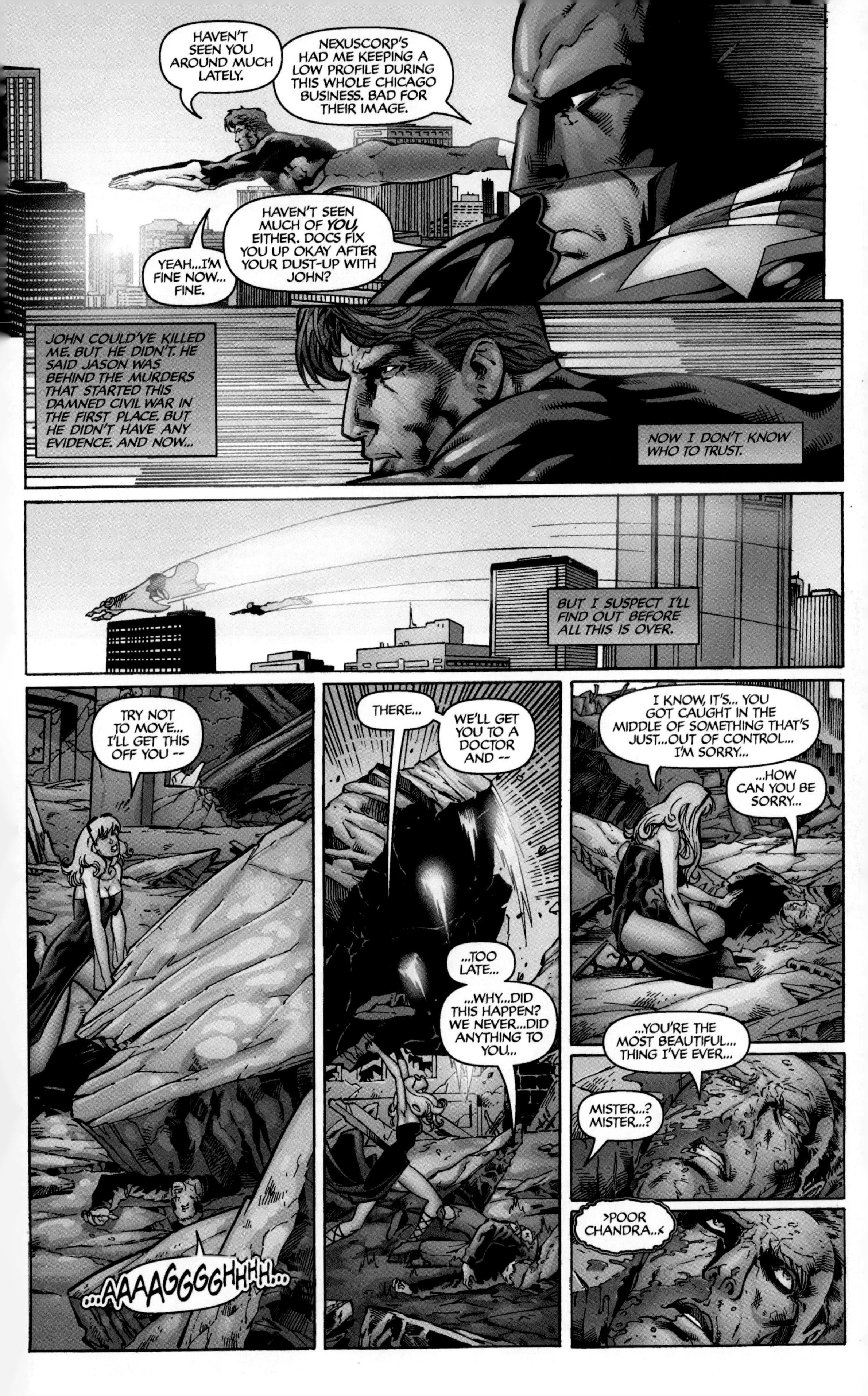

HAVEN'T SEEN YOU AROUND MUCH LATELY.
NEXUSCORP'S HAD ME KEEPING A LOW PROFILE DURING THIS WHOLE CHICAGO BUSINESS. BAD FOR THEIR IMAGE.
HAVEN'T SEEN MUCH OF YOU, EITHER. DOCS FIX YOU UP OKAY AFTER YOUR DUST-UP WITH JOHN?
YEAH...I'M FINE NOW... FINE.
JOHN COULD'VE KILLED ME. BUT HE DIDN'T. HE SAID JASON WAS BEHIND THE MURDERS THAT STARTED THIS DAMNED CIVIL WAR IN THE FIRST PLACE. BUT HE DIDN'T HAVE ANY EVIDENCE. AND NOW...
NOW I DON'T KNOW WHO TO TRUST.
BUT I SUSPECT I'LL FIND OUT BEFORE ALL THIS IS OVER.
TRY NOT TO MOVE... I'LL GET THIS OFF YOU --
...AAAAGGGGHHHH...
THERE...
WE'LL GET YOU TO A DOCTOR AND --
...TOO LATE...
...WHY...DID THIS HAPPEN? WE NEVER...DID ANYTHING TO YOU...
I KNOW, IT'S... YOU GOT CAUGHT IN THE MIDDLE OF SOMETHING THAT'S JUST...OUT OF CONTROL... I'M SORRY...
...HOW CAN YOU BE SORRY...
...YOU'RE THE MOST BEAUTIFUL... THING I'VE EVER...
MISTER...? MISTER...?
>POOR CHANDRA...<

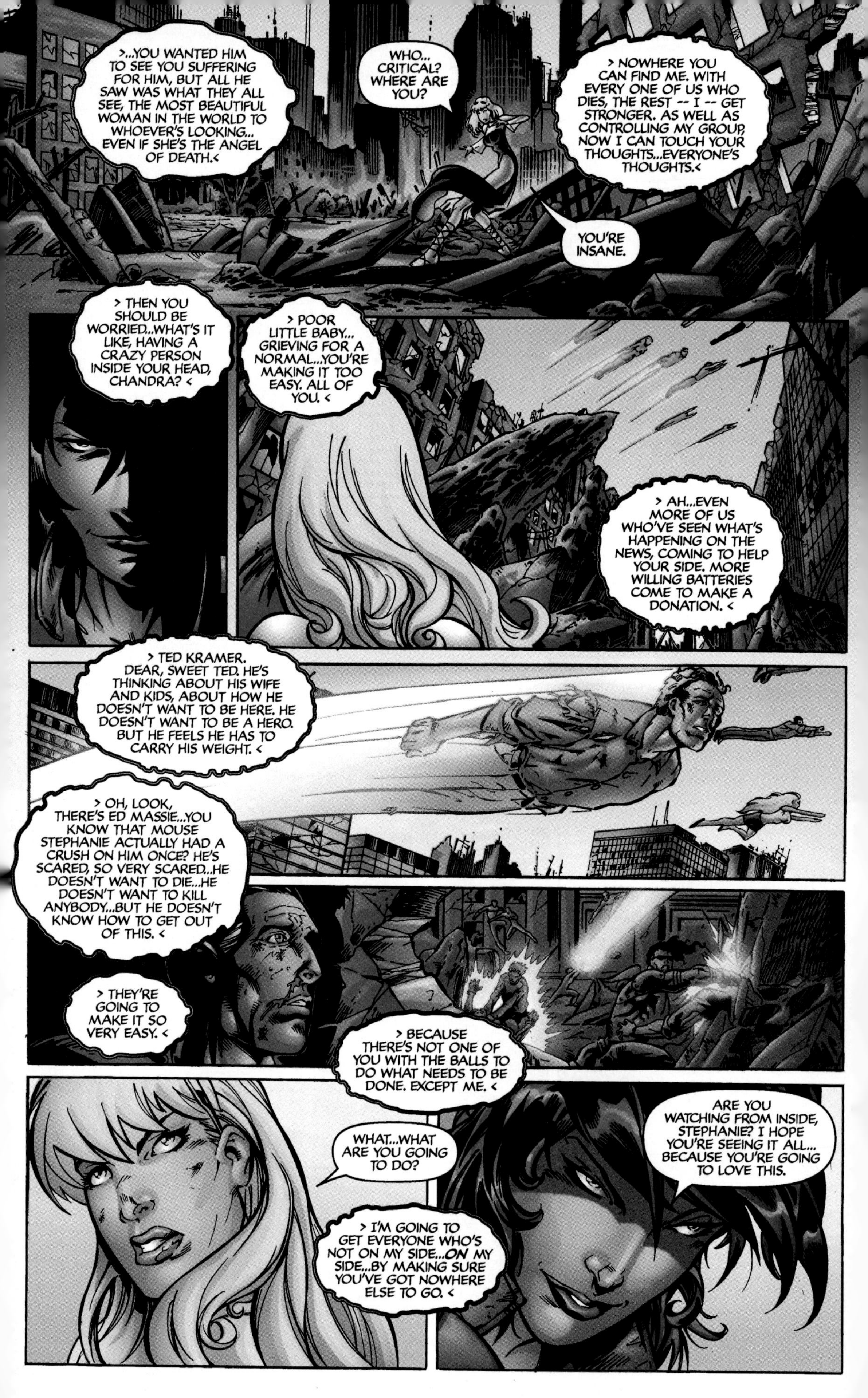
>...YOU WANTED HIM TO SEE YOU SUFFERING FOR HIM, BUT ALL HE SAW WAS WHAT THEY ALL SEE, THE MOST BEAUTIFUL WOMAN IN THE WORLD TO WHOEVER'S LOOKING... EVEN IF SHE'S THE ANGEL OF DEATH.<
WHO... CRITICAL? WHERE ARE YOU?
> NOWHERE YOU CAN FIND ME. WITH EVERY ONE OF US WHO DIES, THE REST -- I -- GET STRONGER. AS WELL AS CONTROLLING MY GROUP, NOW I CAN TOUCH YOUR THOUGHTS...EVERYONE'S THOUGHTS.<
YOU'RE INSANE.
> THEN YOU SHOULD BE WORRIED...WHAT'S IT LIKE, HAVING A CRAZY PERSON INSIDE YOUR HEAD, CHANDRA? <
> POOR LITTLE BABY... GRIEVING FOR A NORMAL...YOU'RE MAKING IT TOO EASY. ALL OF YOU. <
> AH...EVEN MORE OF US WHO'VE SEEN WHAT'S HAPPENING ON THE NEWS, COMING TO HELP YOUR SIDE. MORE WILLING BATTERIES COME TO MAKE A DONATION. <
> TED KRAMER. DEAR, SWEET TED. HE'S THINKING ABOUT HIS WIFE AND KIDS, ABOUT HOW HE DOESN'T WANT TO BE HERE. HE DOESN'T WANT TO BE A HERO. BUT HE FEELS HE HAS TO CARRY HIS WEIGHT. <
> OH, LOOK, THERE'S ED MASSIE...YOU KNOW THAT MOUSE STEPHANIE ACTUALLY HAD A CRUSH ON HIM ONCE? HE'S SCARED, SO VERY SCARED...HE DOESN'T WANT TO DIE...HE DOESN'T WANT TO KILL ANYBODY...BUT HE DOESN'T KNOW HOW TO GET OUT OF THIS. <
> THEY'RE GOING TO MAKE IT SO VERY EASY. <
> BECAUSE THERE'S NOT ONE OF YOU WITH THE BALLS TO DO WHAT NEEDS TO BE DONE. EXCEPT ME. <
WHAT...WHAT ARE YOU GOING TO DO?
ARE YOU WATCHING FROM INSIDE, STEPHANIE? I HOPE YOU'RE SEEING IT ALL... BECAUSE YOU'RE GOING TO LOVE THIS.
> I'M GOING TO GET EVERYONE WHO'S NOT ON MY SIDE...ON MY SIDE...BY MAKING SURE YOU'VE GOT NOWHERE ELSE TO GO. <

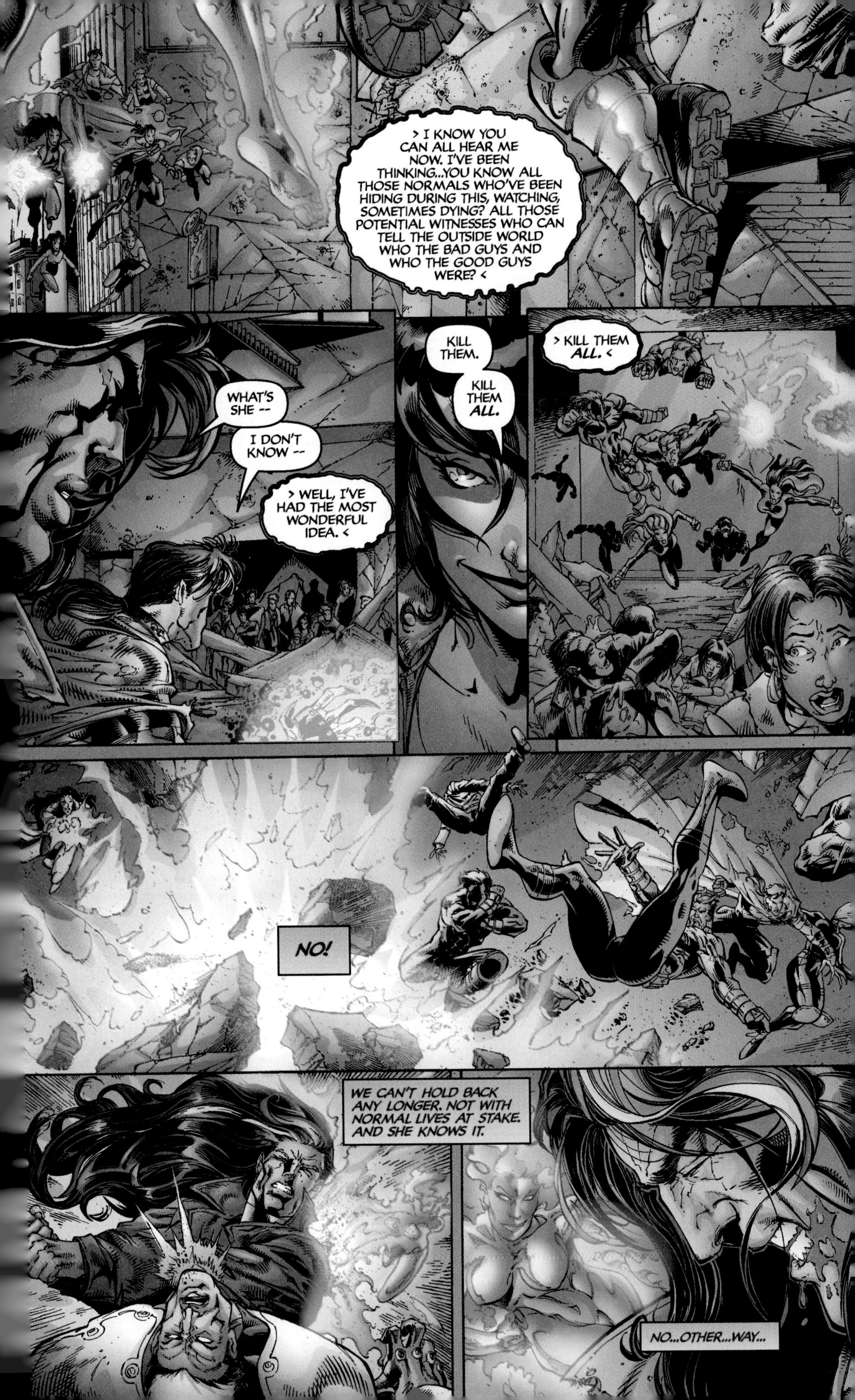
> I KNOW YOU CAN ALL HEAR ME NOW. I'VE BEEN THINKING...YOU KNOW ALL THOSE NORMALS WHO'VE BEEN HIDING DURING THIS, WATCHING, SOMETIMES DYING? ALL THOSE POTENTIAL WITNESSES WHO CAN TELL THE OUTSIDE WORLD WHO THE BAD GUYS AND WHO THE GOOD GUYS WERE? <
WHAT'S SHE --
I DON'T KNOW --
> WELL, I'VE HAD THE MOST WONDERFUL IDEA. <
KILL THEM.
KILL THEM ALL.
> KILL THEM ALL. <
NO!
WE CAN'T HOLD BACK ANY LONGER. NOT WITH NORMAL LIVES AT STAKE. AND SHE KNOWS IT.
NO...OTHER...WAY...

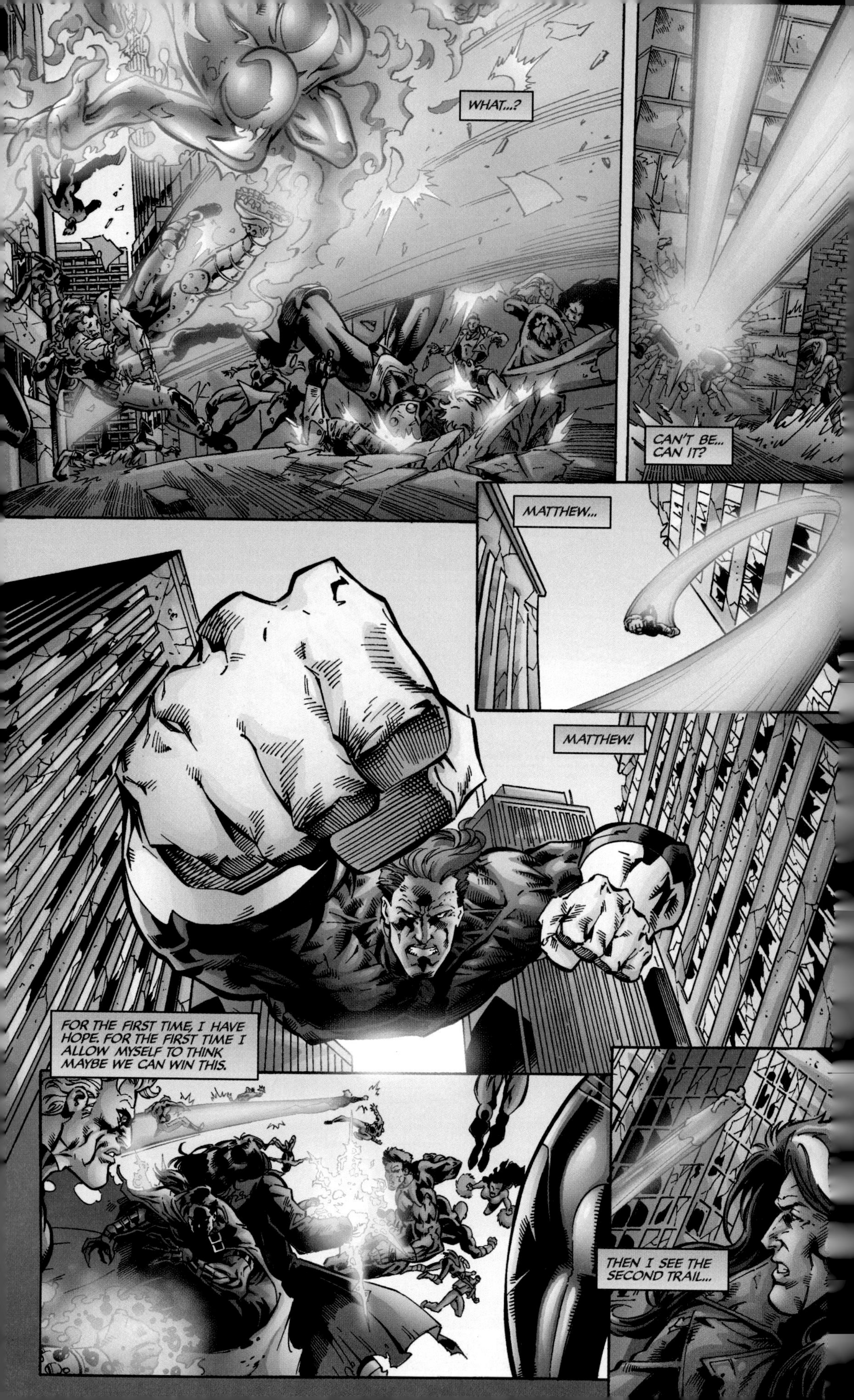
WHAT...?
CAN'T BE...
CAN IT?
MATTHEW...
MATTHEW!
FOR THE FIRST TIME, I HAVE HOPE. FOR THE FIRST TIME I ALLOW MYSELF TO THINK MAYBE WE CAN WIN THIS.
THEN I SEE THE SECOND TRAIL...

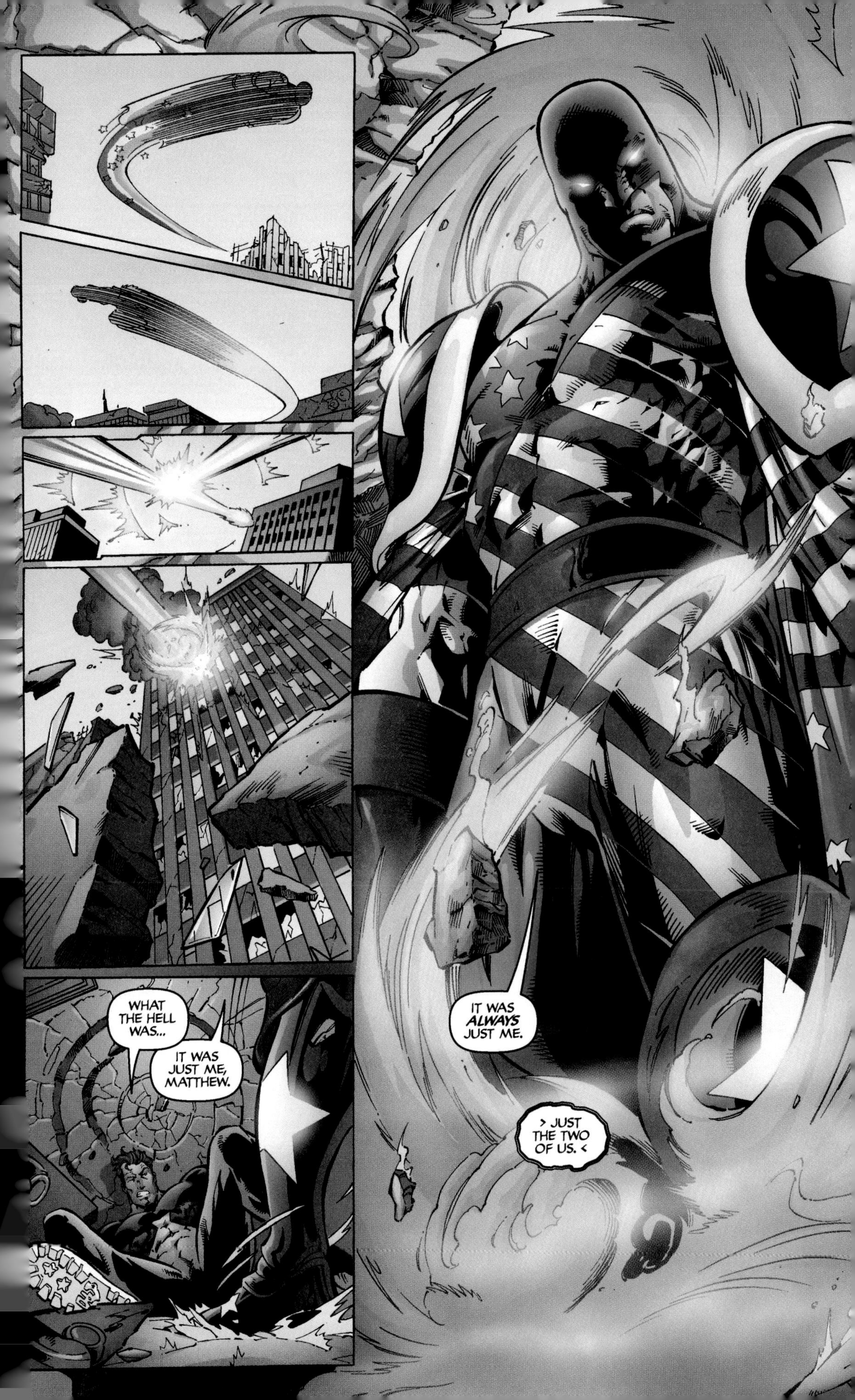
WHAT THE HELL WAS...
IT WAS JUST ME, MATTHEW.
IT WAS *ALWAYS* JUST ME.
> JUST THE TWO OF US. <

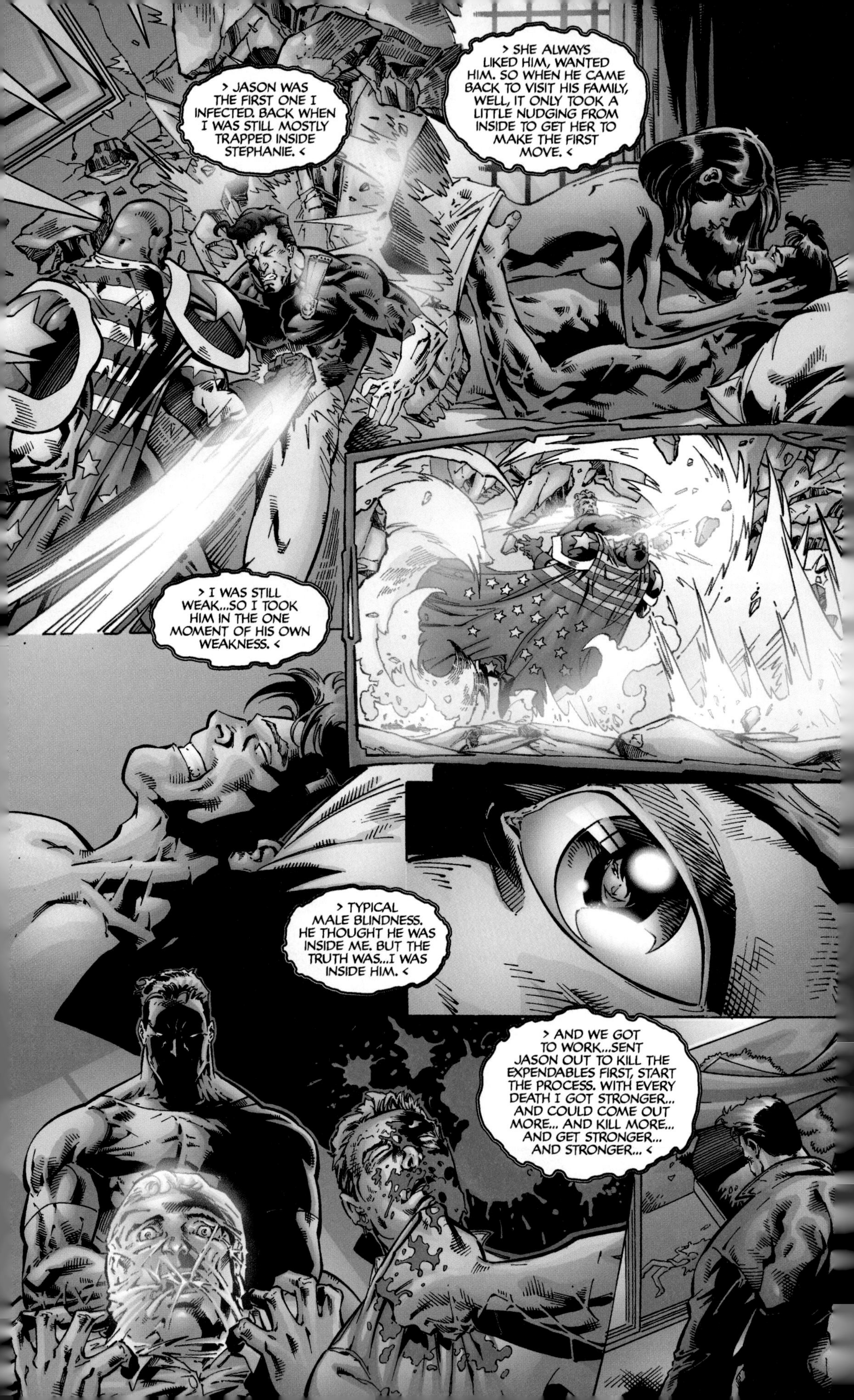
> JASON WAS THE FIRST ONE I INFECTED. BACK WHEN I WAS STILL MOSTLY TRAPPED INSIDE STEPHANIE. <
> SHE ALWAYS LIKED HIM, WANTED HIM. SO WHEN HE CAME BACK TO VISIT HIS FAMILY, WELL, IT ONLY TOOK A LITTLE NUDGING FROM INSIDE TO GET HER TO MAKE THE FIRST MOVE. <
> I WAS STILL WEAK...SO I TOOK HIM IN THE ONE MOMENT OF HIS OWN WEAKNESS. <
> TYPICAL MALE BLINDNESS. HE THOUGHT HE WAS INSIDE ME. BUT THE TRUTH WAS...I WAS INSIDE HIM. <
> AND WE GOT TO WORK...SENT JASON OUT TO KILL THE EXPENDABLES FIRST, START THE PROCESS. WITH EVERY DEATH I GOT STRONGER... AND COULD COME OUT MORE... AND KILL MORE... AND GET STRONGER... AND STRONGER... <

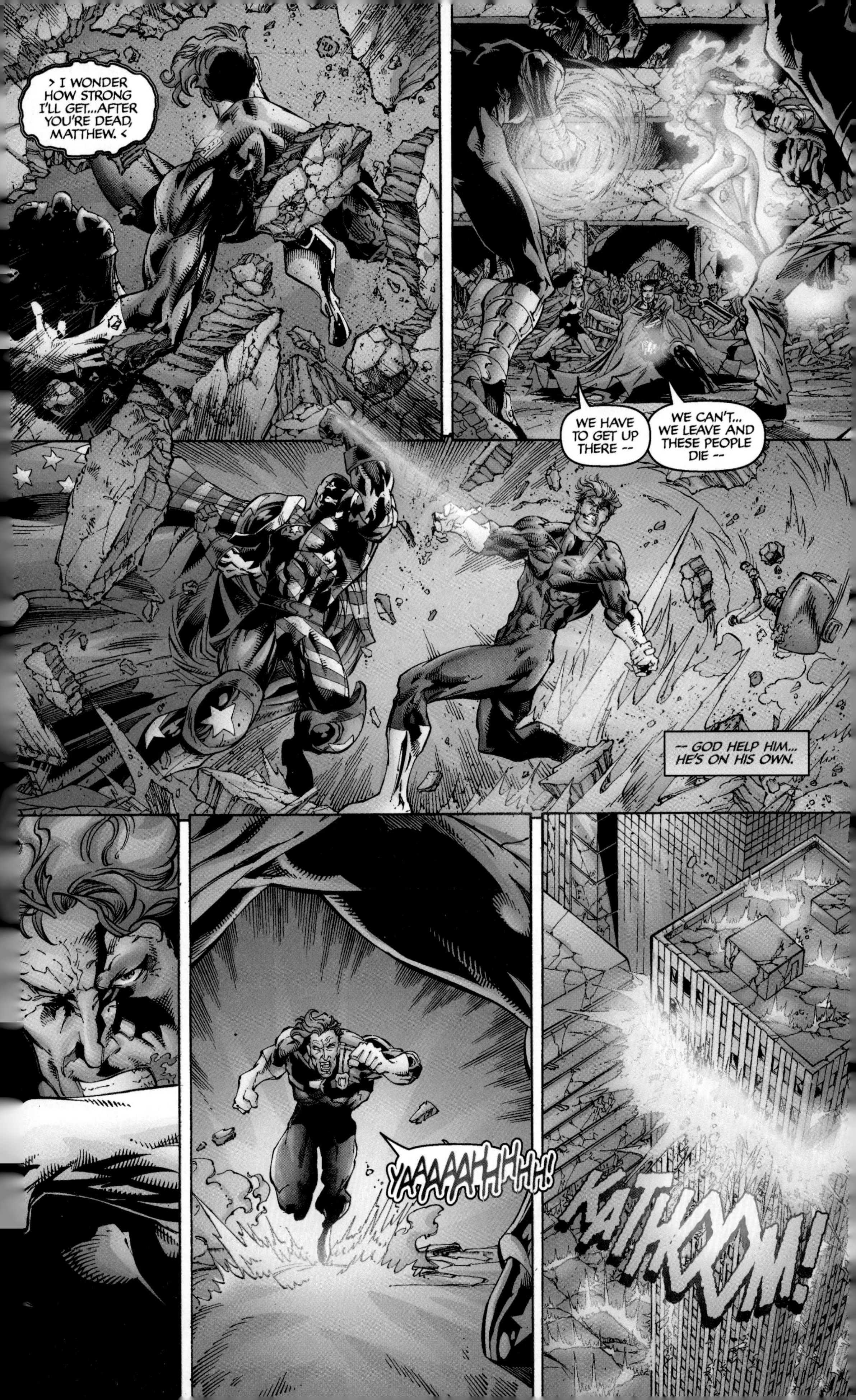
> I WONDER HOW STRONG I'LL GET...AFTER YOU'RE DEAD, MATTHEW. <
WE HAVE TO GET UP THERE --
WE CAN'T... WE LEAVE AND THESE PEOPLE DIE --
-- GOD HELP HIM... HE'S ON HIS OWN.
YAAAAAHHHHH!
KATHOOM!

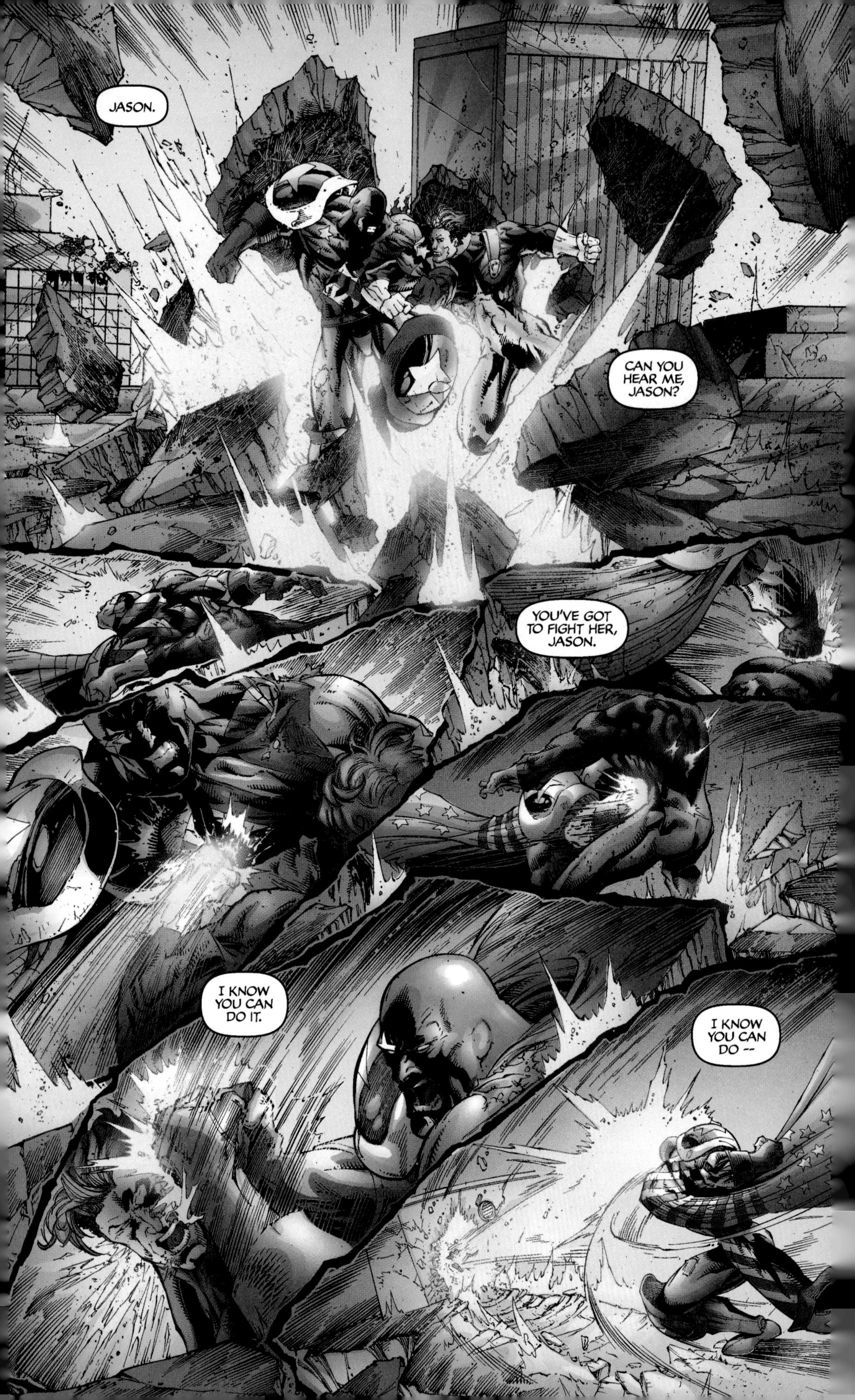
JASON.
CAN YOU HEAR ME, JASON?
YOU'VE GOT TO FIGHT HER, JASON.
I KNOW YOU CAN DO IT.
I KNOW YOU CAN DO --

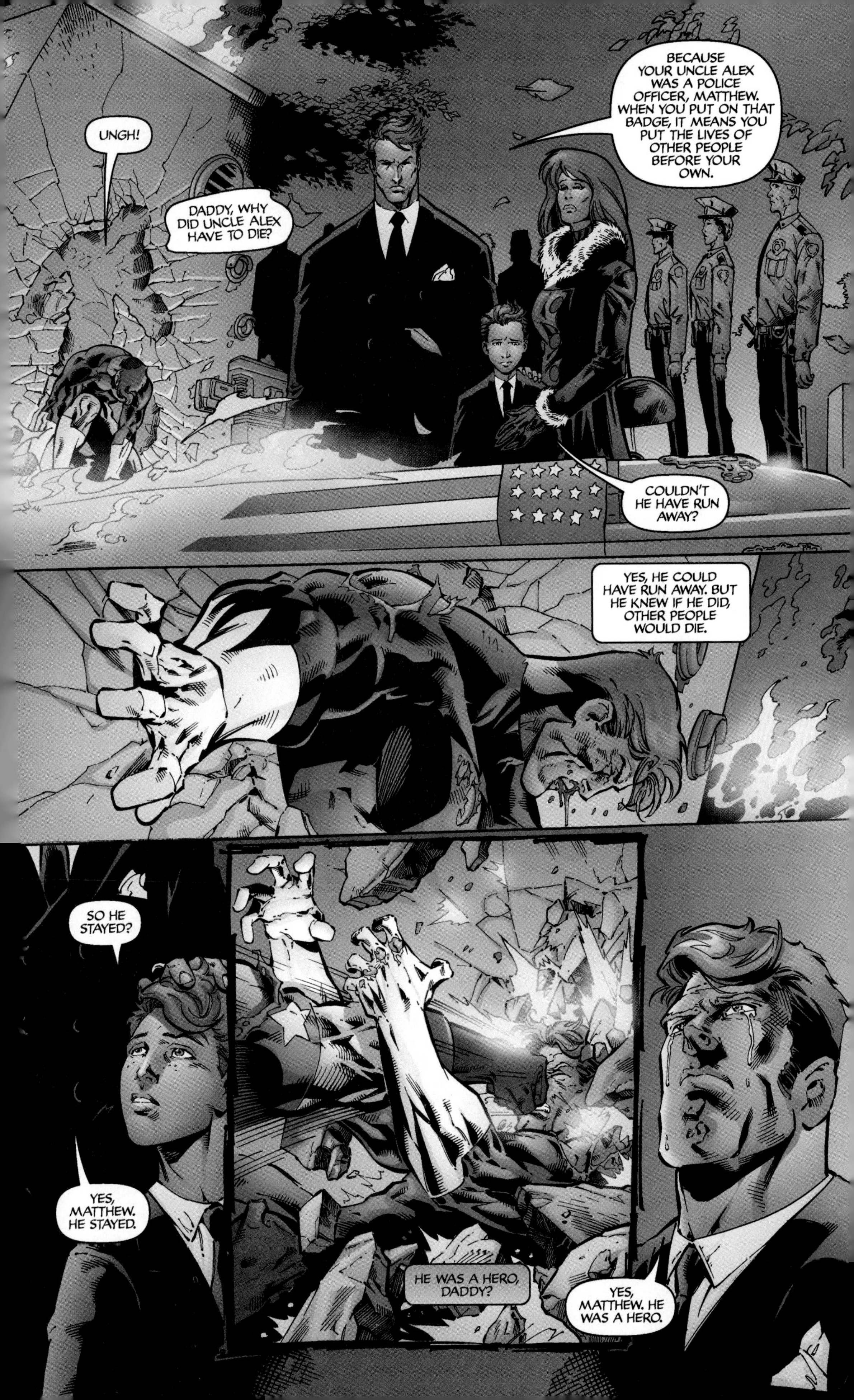
UNGH!
DADDY, WHY DID UNCLE ALEX HAVE TO DIE?
BECAUSE YOUR UNCLE ALEX WAS A POLICE OFFICER, MATTHEW. WHEN YOU PUT ON THAT BADGE, IT MEANS YOU PUT THE LIVES OF OTHER PEOPLE BEFORE YOUR OWN.
COULDN'T HE HAVE RUN AWAY?
YES, HE COULD HAVE RUN AWAY. BUT HE KNEW IF HE DID, OTHER PEOPLE WOULD DIE.
SO HE STAYED?
YES, MATTHEW. HE STAYED.
HE WAS A HERO, DADDY?
YES, MATTHEW. HE WAS A HERO.

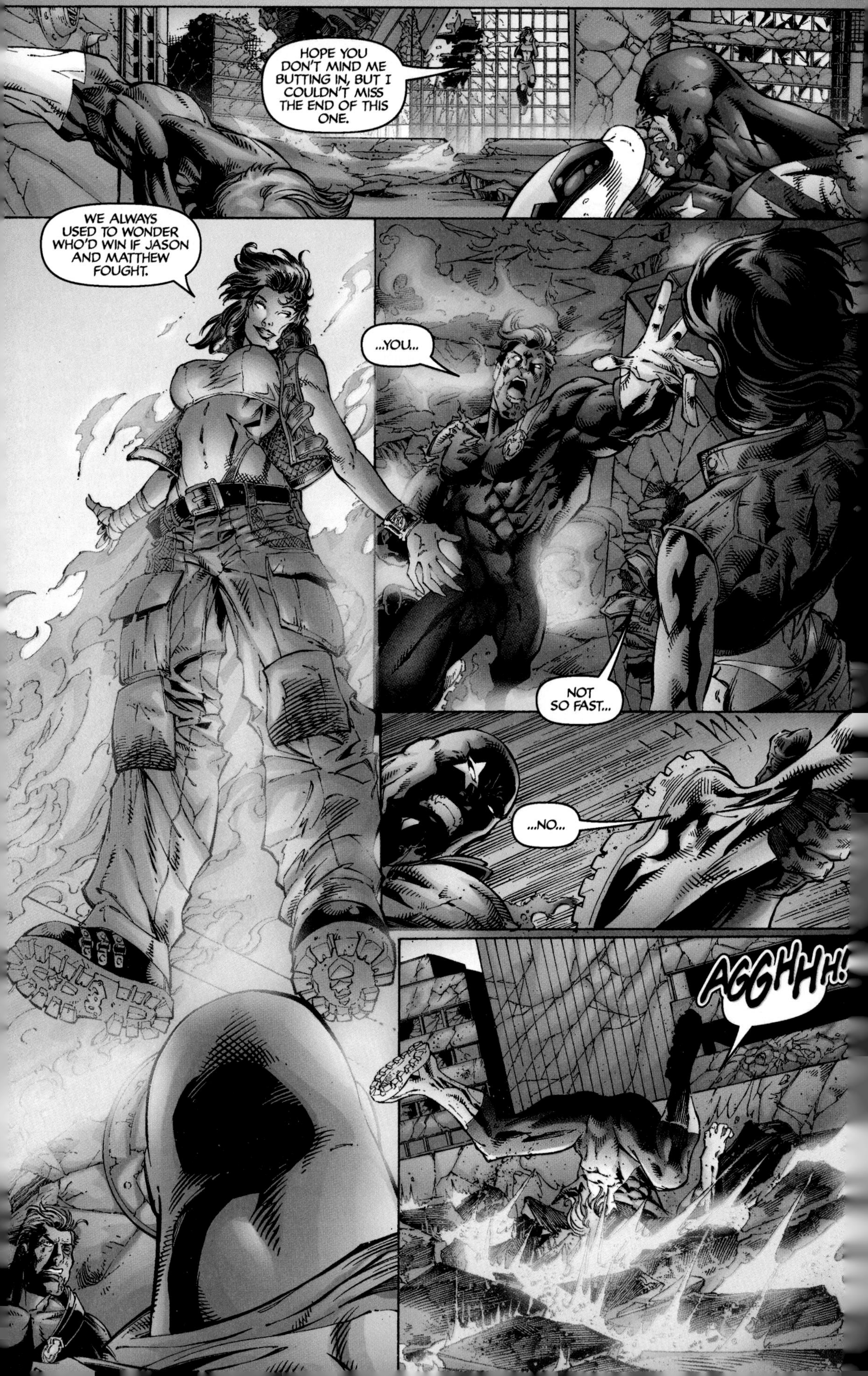
HOPE YOU DON'T MIND ME BUTTING IN, BUT I COULDN'T MISS THE END OF THIS ONE.
WE ALWAYS USED TO WONDER WHO'D WIN IF JASON AND MATTHEW FOUGHT.
...YOU...
NOT SO FAST...
...NO...
AGGHHH!

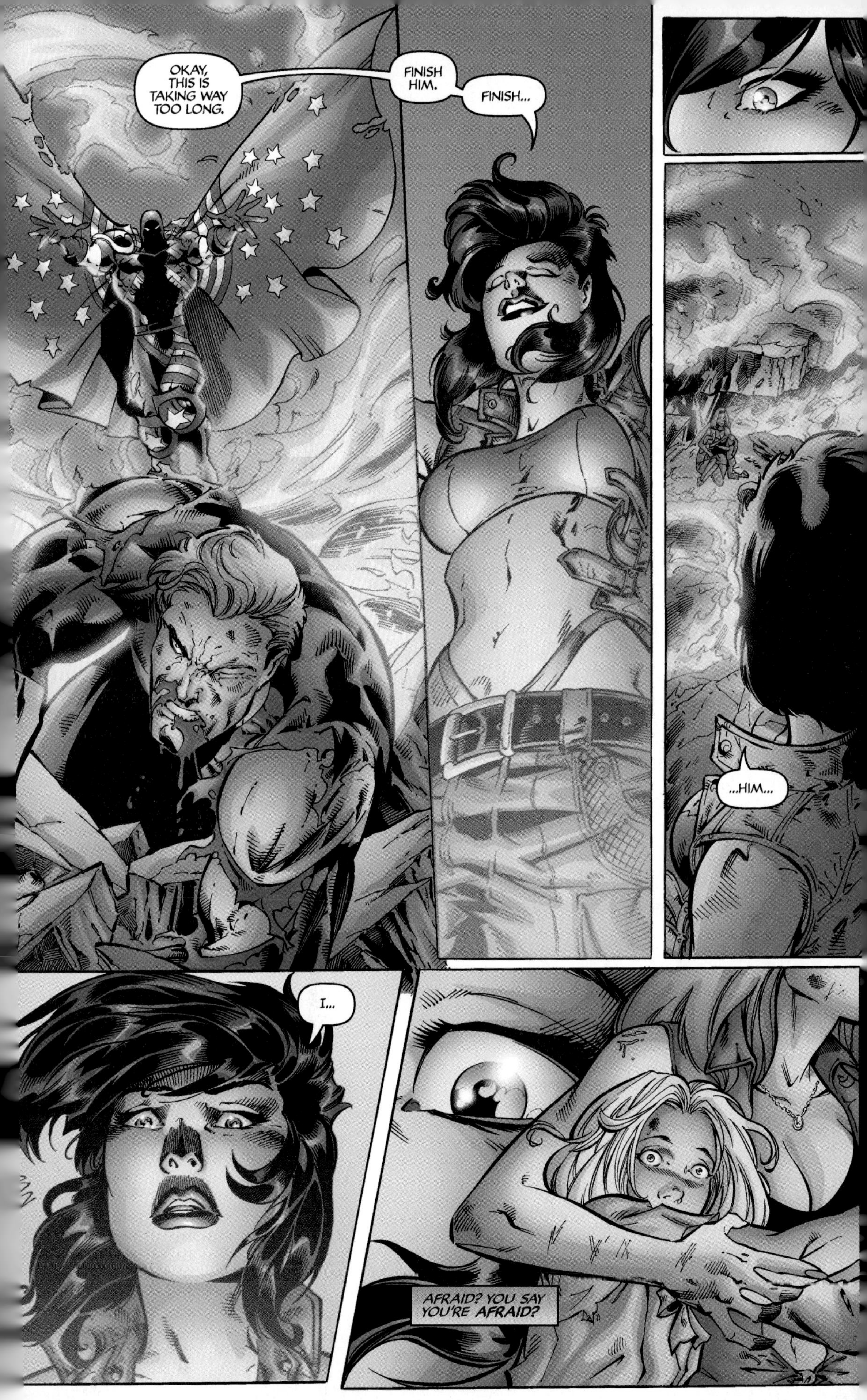
OKAY, THIS IS TAKING WAY TOO LONG.
FINISH HIM.
FINISH...
...HIM...
I...
AFRAID? YOU SAY YOU'RE AFRAID?

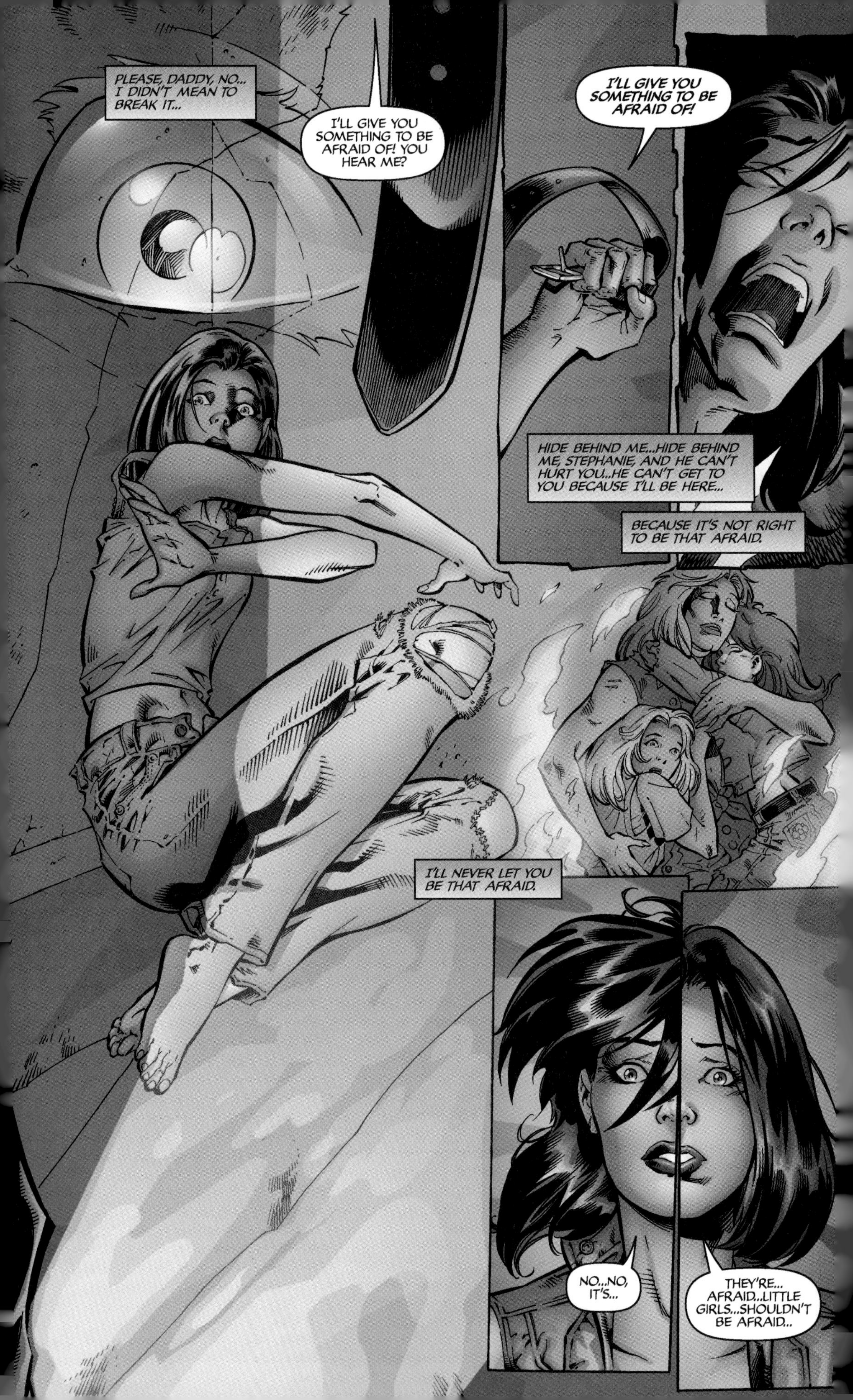
PLEASE, DADDY, NO... I DIDN'T MEAN TO BREAK IT...
I'LL GIVE YOU SOMETHING TO BE AFRAID OF! YOU HEAR ME?
I'LL GIVE YOU SOMETHING TO BE AFRAID OF!
HIDE BEHIND ME...HIDE BEHIND ME, STEPHANIE, AND HE CAN'T HURT YOU...HE CAN'T GET TO YOU BECAUSE I'LL BE HERE...
BECAUSE IT'S NOT RIGHT TO BE THAT AFRAID.
I'LL NEVER LET YOU BE THAT AFRAID.
NO...NO, IT'S...
THEY'RE... AFRAID...LITTLE GIRLS...SHOULDN'T BE AFRAID...

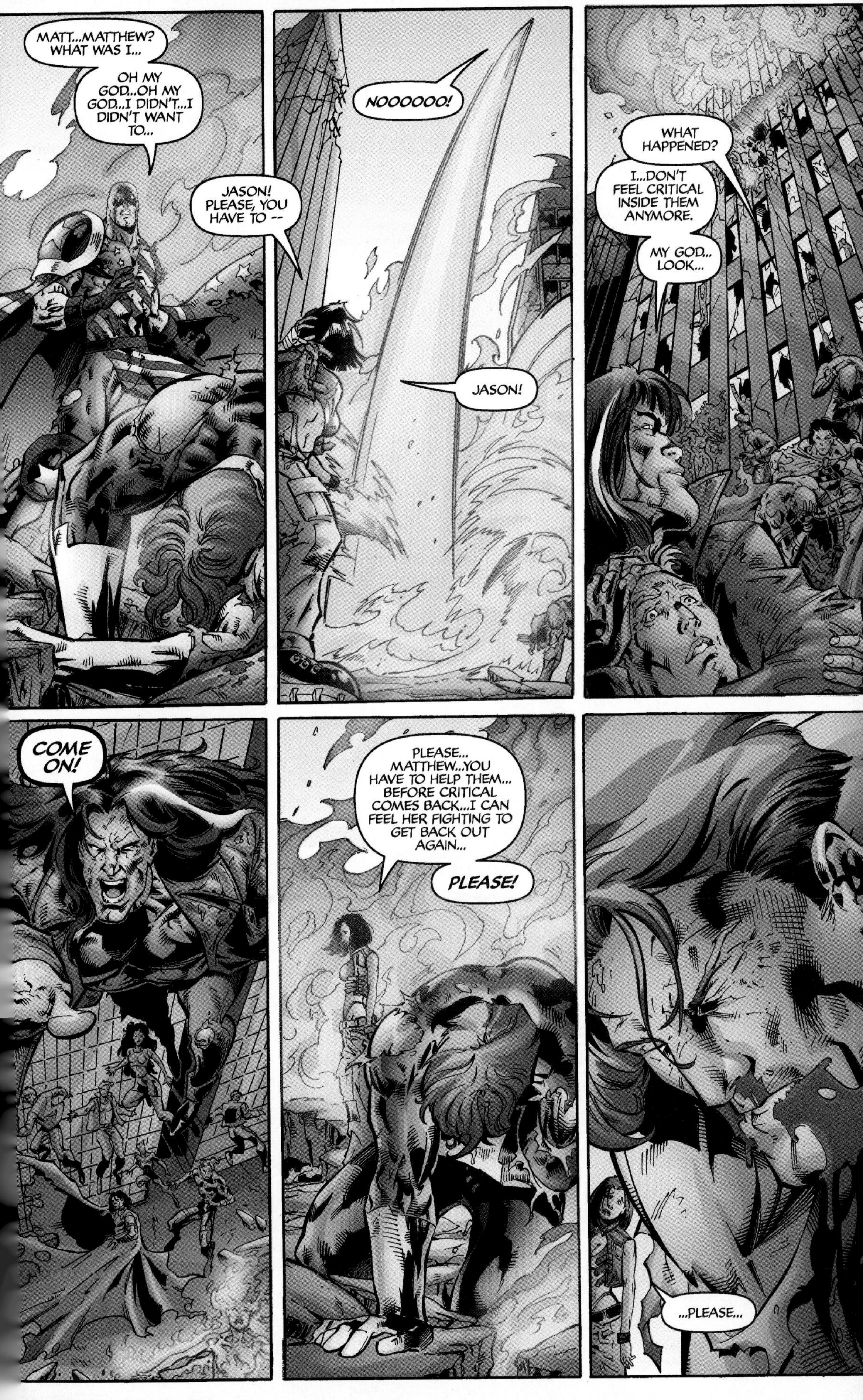
MATT...MATTHEW? WHAT WAS I...
OH MY GOD...OH MY GOD...I DIDN'T...I DIDN'T WANT TO...
JASON! PLEASE, YOU HAVE TO --
NOOOOOO!
JASON!
WHAT HAPPENED?
I...DON'T FEEL CRITICAL INSIDE THEM ANYMORE.
MY GOD... LOOK...
COME ON!
PLEASE... MATTHEW...YOU HAVE TO HELP THEM... BEFORE CRITICAL COMES BACK...I CAN FEEL HER FIGHTING TO GET BACK OUT AGAIN...
PLEASE!
...PLEASE...

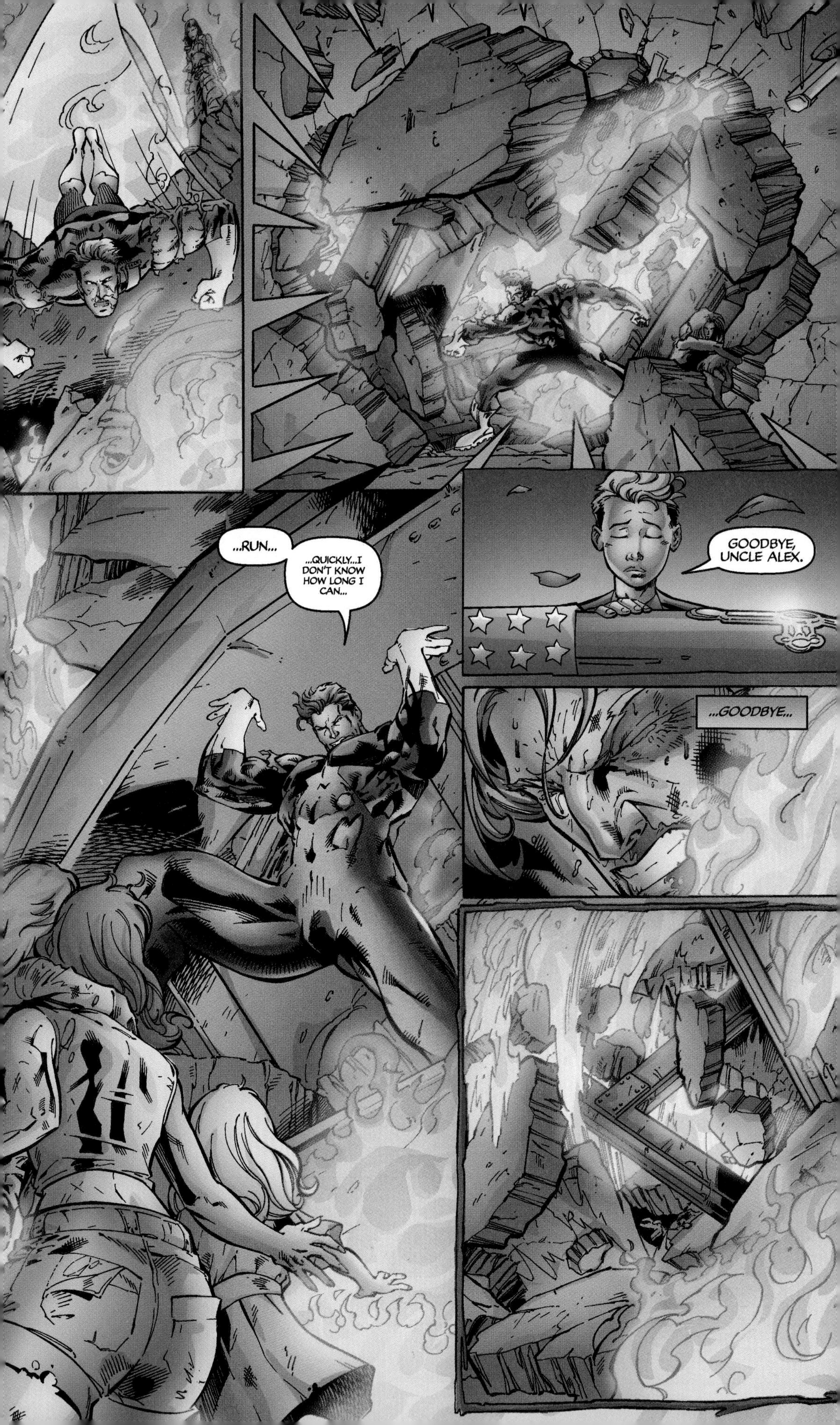
...RUN...
...QUICKLY...I DON'T KNOW HOW LONG I CAN...
GOODBYE, UNCLE ALEX.
...GOODBYE...

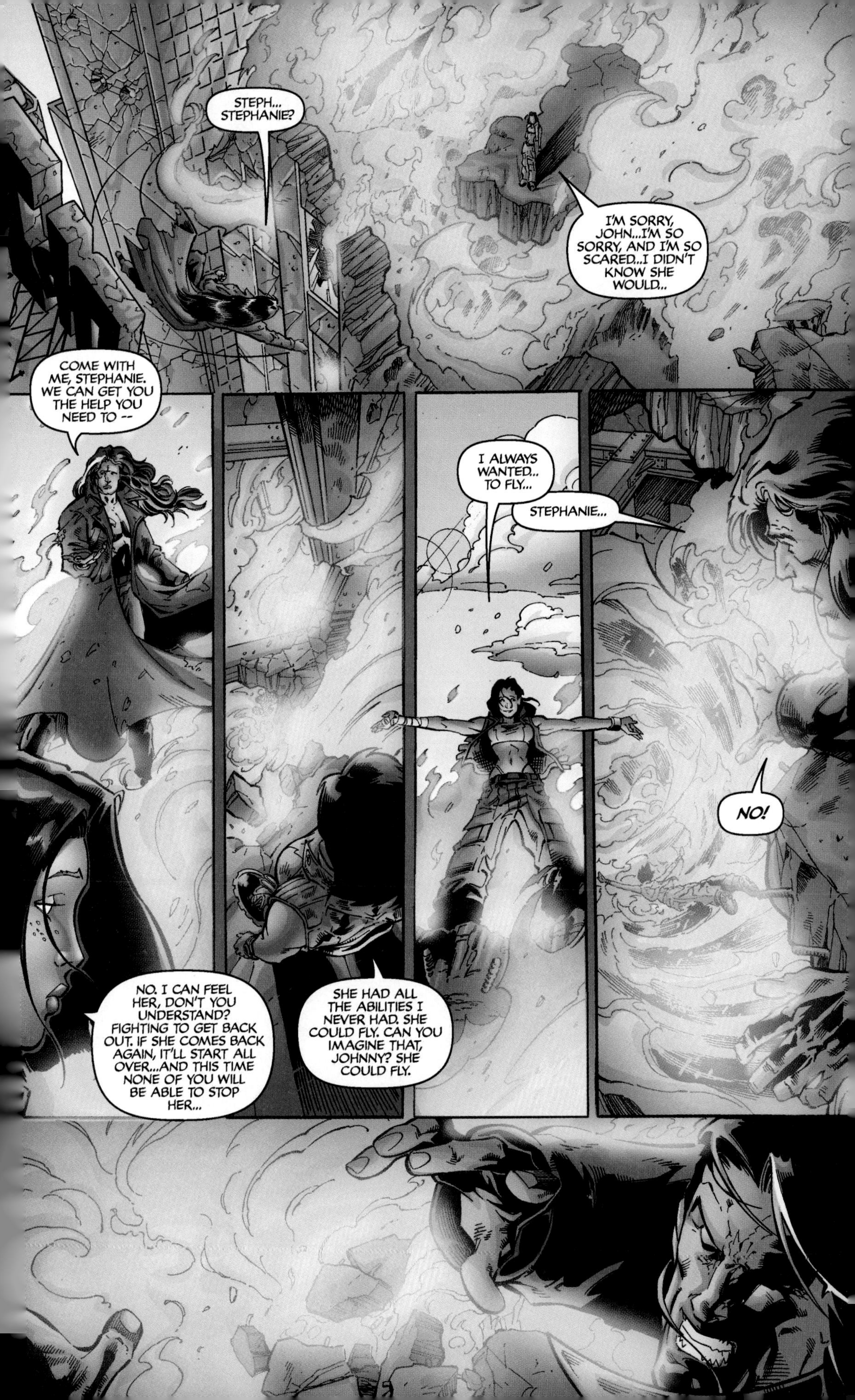
STEPH... STEPHANIE?
I'M SORRY, JOHN...I'M SO SORRY, AND I'M SO SCARED...I DIDN'T KNOW SHE WOULD...
COME WITH ME, STEPHANIE. WE CAN GET YOU THE HELP YOU NEED TO --
NO. I CAN FEEL HER, DON'T YOU UNDERSTAND? FIGHTING TO GET BACK OUT. IF SHE COMES BACK AGAIN, IT'LL START ALL OVER...AND THIS TIME NONE OF YOU WILL BE ABLE TO STOP HER...
SHE HAD ALL THE ABILITIES I NEVER HAD. SHE COULD FLY. CAN YOU IMAGINE THAT, JOHNNY? SHE COULD FLY.
I ALWAYS WANTED... TO FLY...
STEPHANIE...
NO!

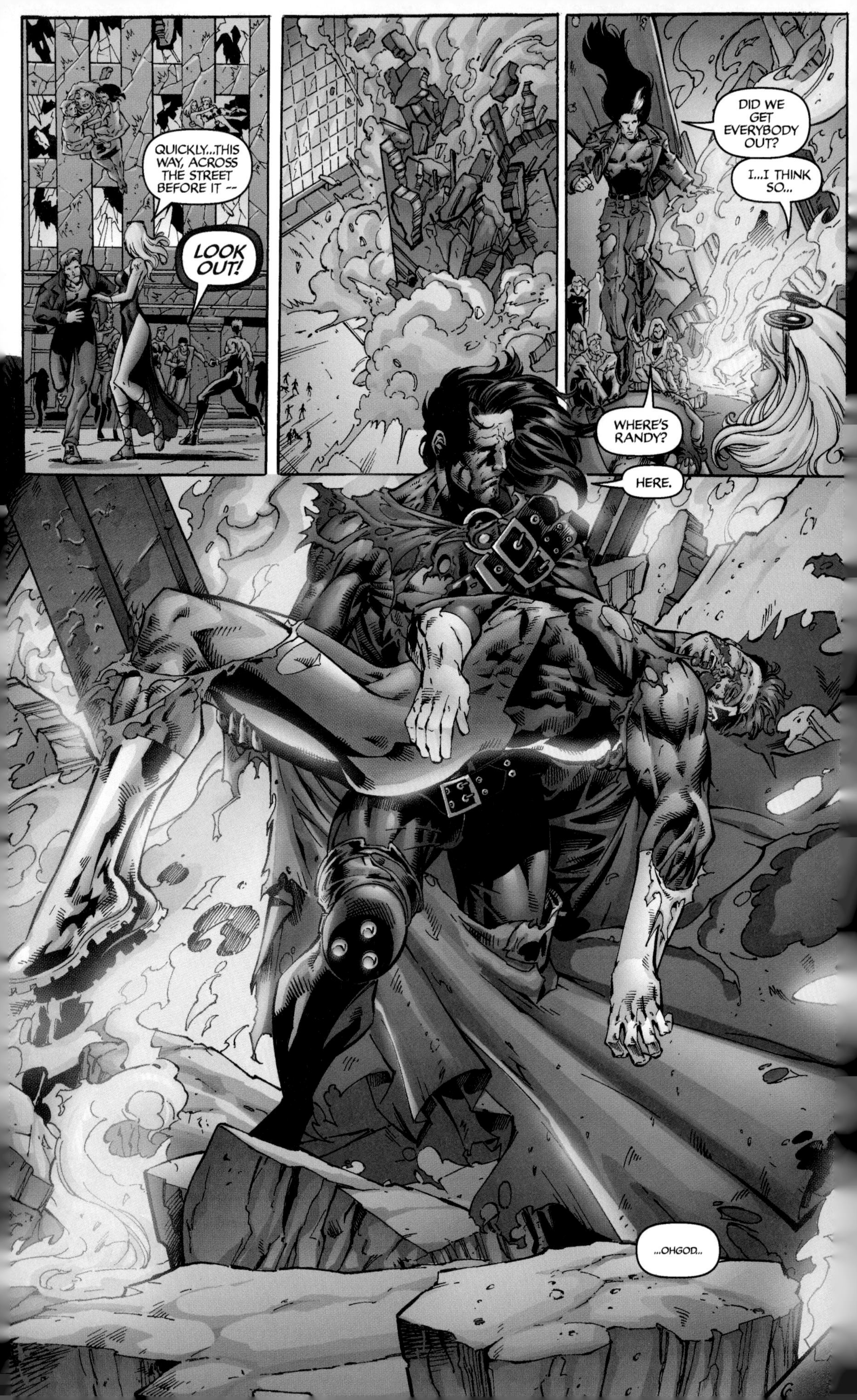
QUICKLY...THIS WAY, ACROSS THE STREET BEFORE IT --
LOOK OUT!
DID WE GET EVERYBODY OUT?
I...I THINK SO...
WHERE'S RANDY?
HERE.
...OHGOD...

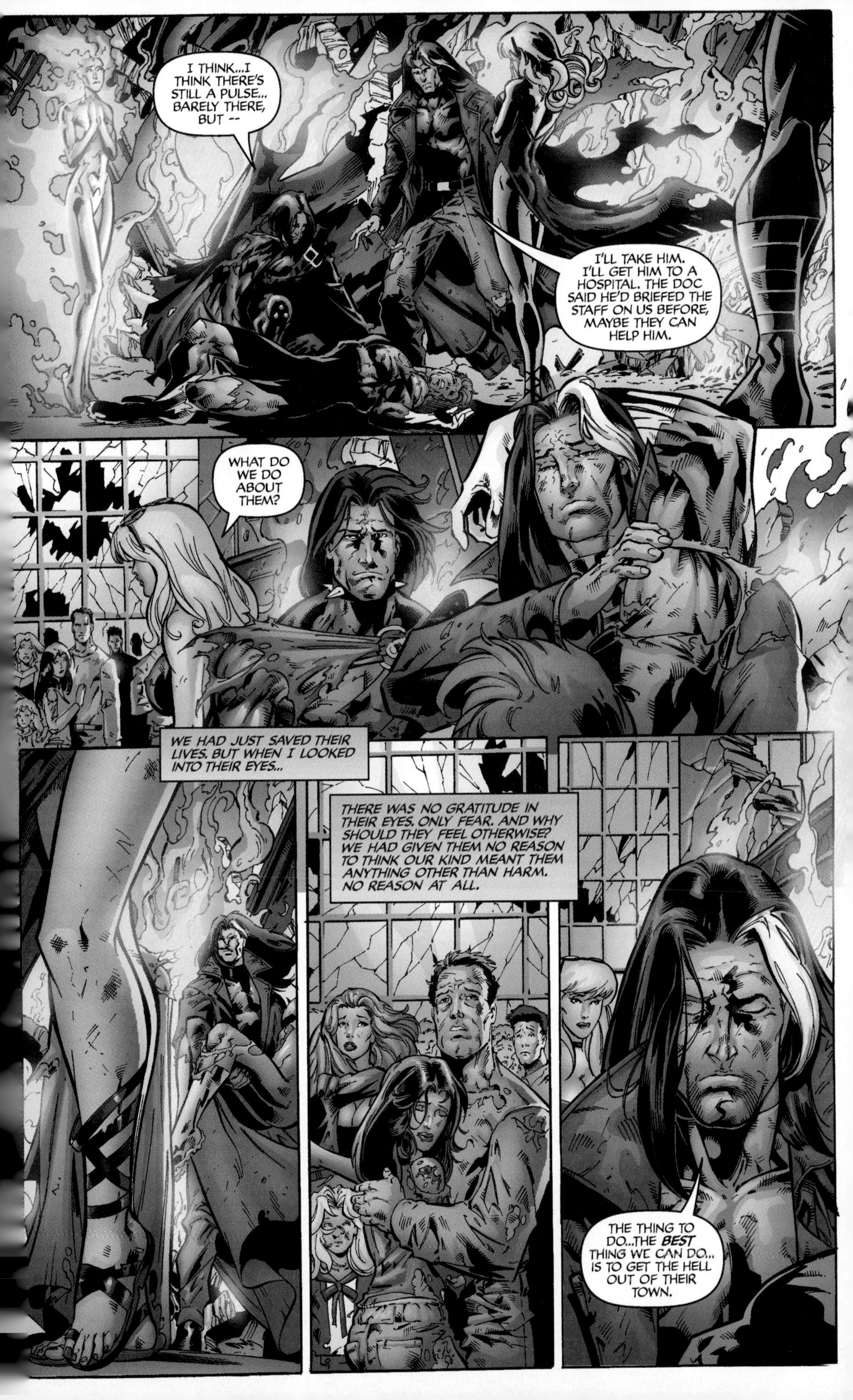
I THINK...I THINK THERE'S STILL A PULSE... BARELY THERE, BUT --
I'LL TAKE HIM. I'LL GET HIM TO A HOSPITAL. THE DOC SAID HE'D BRIEFED THE STAFF ON US BEFORE, MAYBE THEY CAN HELP HIM.
WHAT DO WE DO ABOUT THEM?
WE HAD JUST SAVED THEIR LIVES. BUT WHEN I LOOKED INTO THEIR EYES...
THERE WAS NO GRATITUDE IN THEIR EYES. ONLY FEAR. AND WHY SHOULD THEY FEEL OTHERWISE? WE HAD GIVEN THEM NO REASON TO THINK OUR KIND MEANT THEM ANYTHING OTHER THAN HARM. NO REASON AT ALL.
THE THING TO DO...THE BEST THING WE CAN DO... IS TO GET THE HELL OUT OF THEIR TOWN.

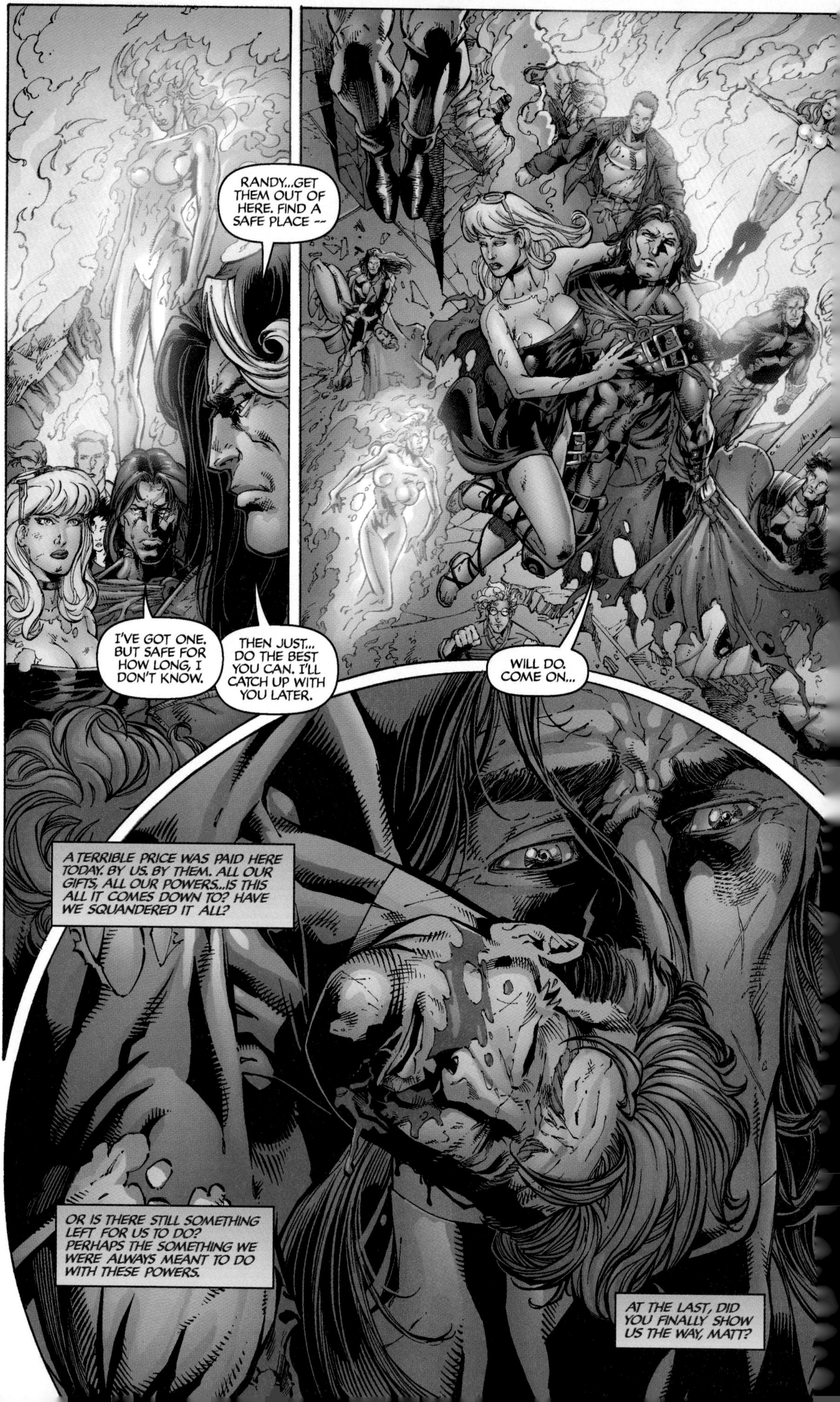
RANDY...GET THEM OUT OF HERE. FIND A SAFE PLACE --
I'VE GOT ONE. BUT SAFE FOR HOW LONG, I DON'T KNOW.
THEN JUST... DO THE BEST YOU CAN. I'LL CATCH UP WITH YOU LATER.
WILL DO. COME ON...
A TERRIBLE PRICE WAS PAID HERE TODAY. BY US. BY THEM. ALL OUR GIFTS, ALL OUR POWERS...IS THIS ALL IT COMES DOWN TO? HAVE WE SQUANDERED IT ALL?
OR IS THERE STILL SOMETHING LEFT FOR US TO DO? PERHAPS THE SOMETHING WE WERE ALWAYS MEANT TO DO WITH THESE POWERS.
AT THE LAST, DID YOU FINALLY SHOW US THE WAY, MATT?

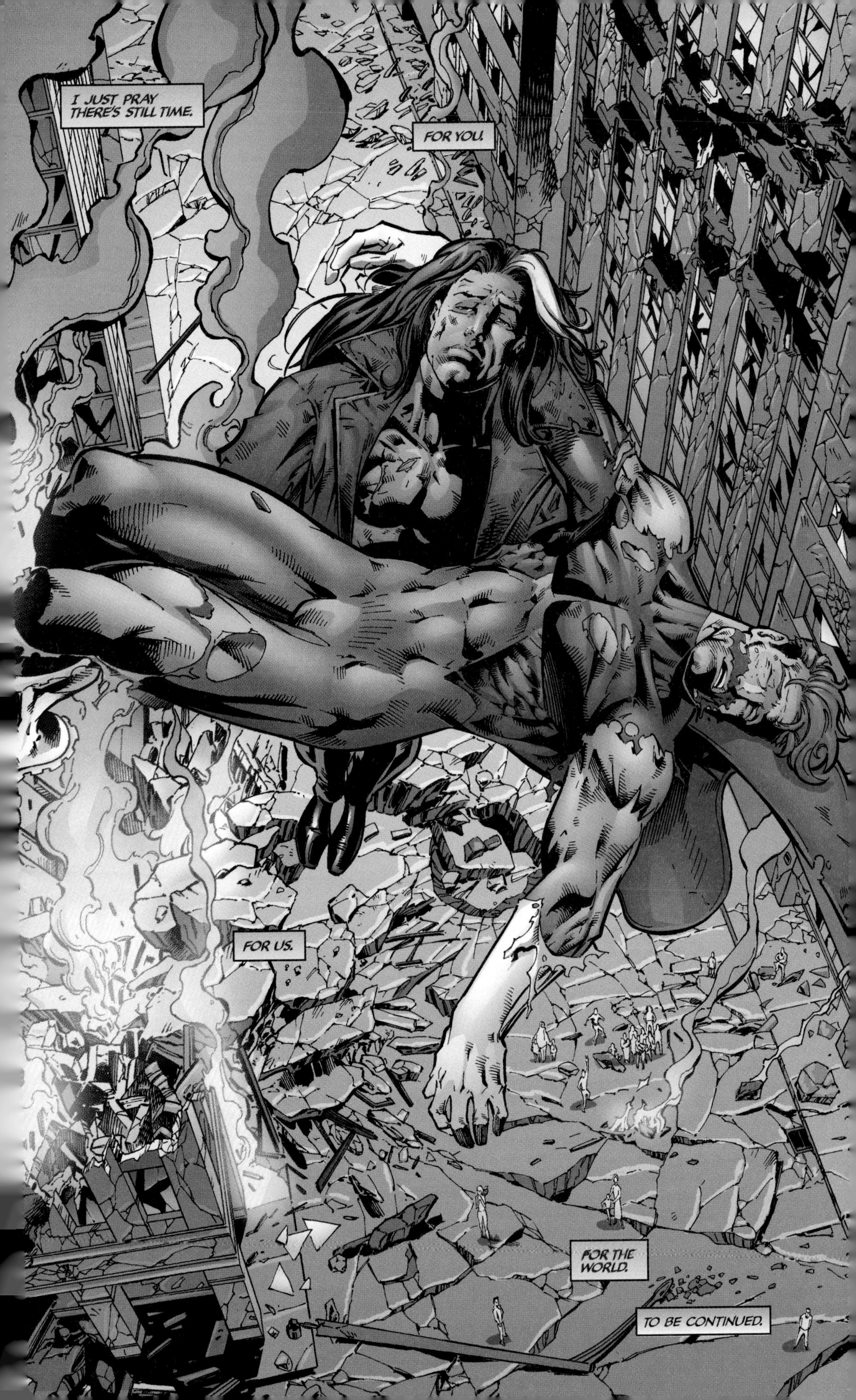
I JUST PRAY THERE'S STILL TIME.
FOR YOU.
FOR US.
FOR THE WORLD.
TO BE CONTINUED.

“Things Change”

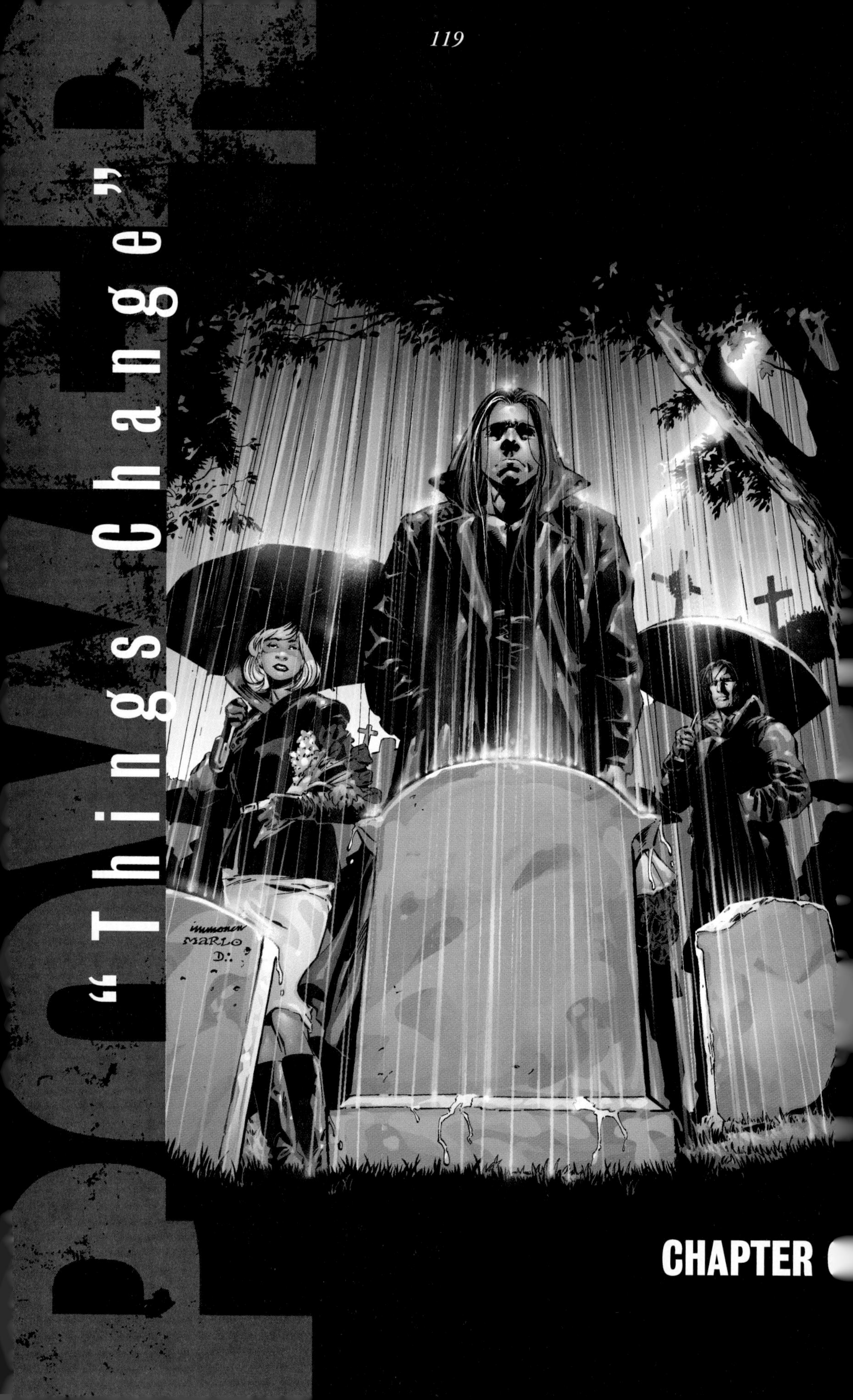

CHAPTER

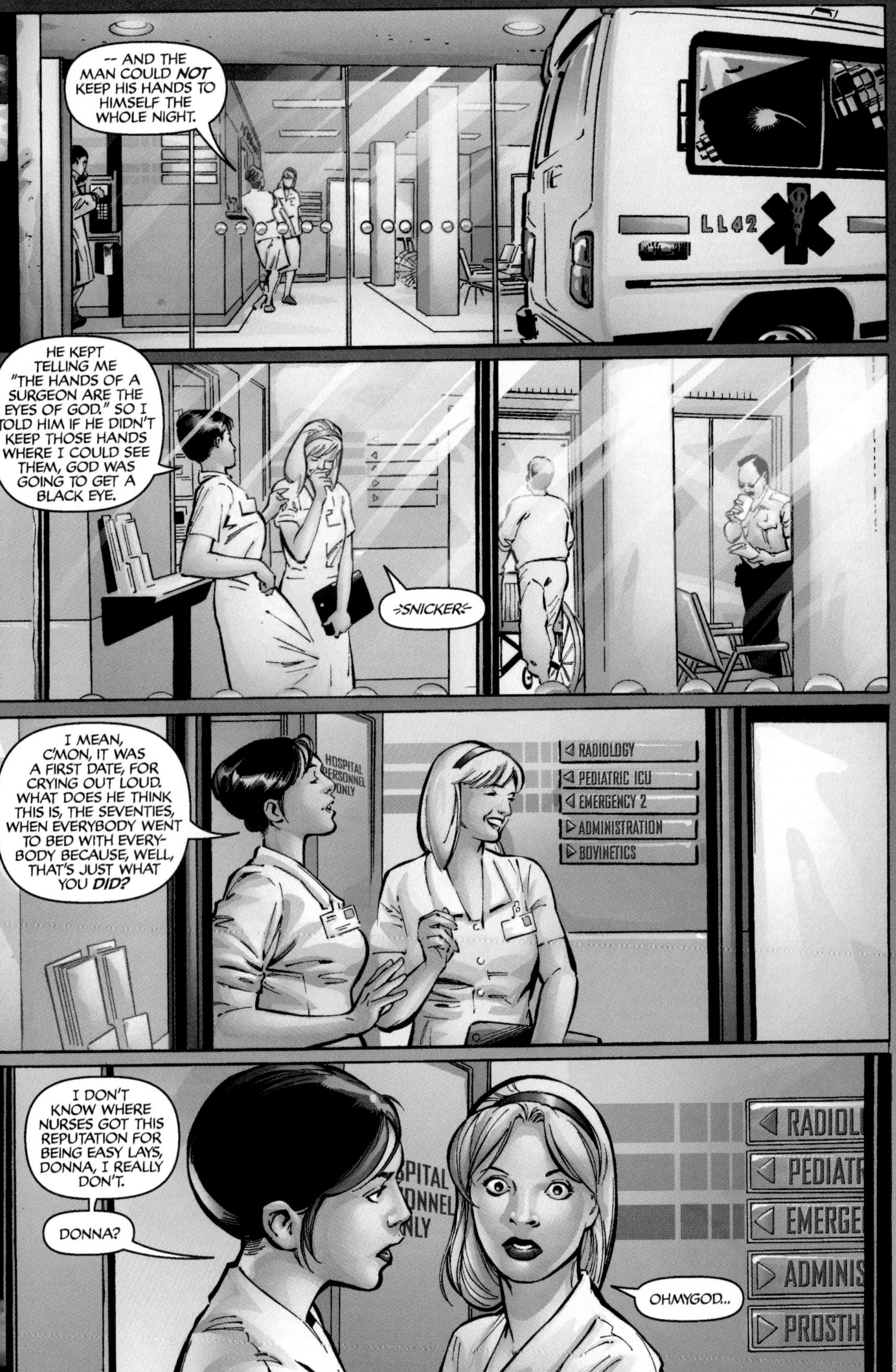

-- AND THE MAN COULD NOT KEEP HIS HANDS TO HIMSELF THE WHOLE NIGHT.
LL42
HE KEPT TELLING ME "THE HANDS OF A SURGEON ARE THE EYES OF GOD." SO I TOLD HIM IF HE DIDN'T KEEP THOSE HANDS WHERE I COULD SEE THEM, GOD WAS GOING TO GET A BLACK EYE.
-SNICKER-
I MEAN, C'MON, IT WAS A FIRST DATE, FOR CRYING OUT LOUD. WHAT DOES HE THINK THIS IS, THE SEVENTIES, WHEN EVERYBODY WENT TO BED WITH EVERYBODY BECAUSE, WELL, THAT'S JUST WHAT YOU DID?
HOSPITAL PERSONNEL ONLY
RADIOLOGY
PEDIATRIC ICU
EMERGENCY 2
ADMINISTRATION
BOVINETICS
I DON'T KNOW WHERE NURSES GOT THIS REPUTATION FOR BEING EASY LAYS, DONNA, I REALLY DON'T.
DONNA?
OHMYGOD...

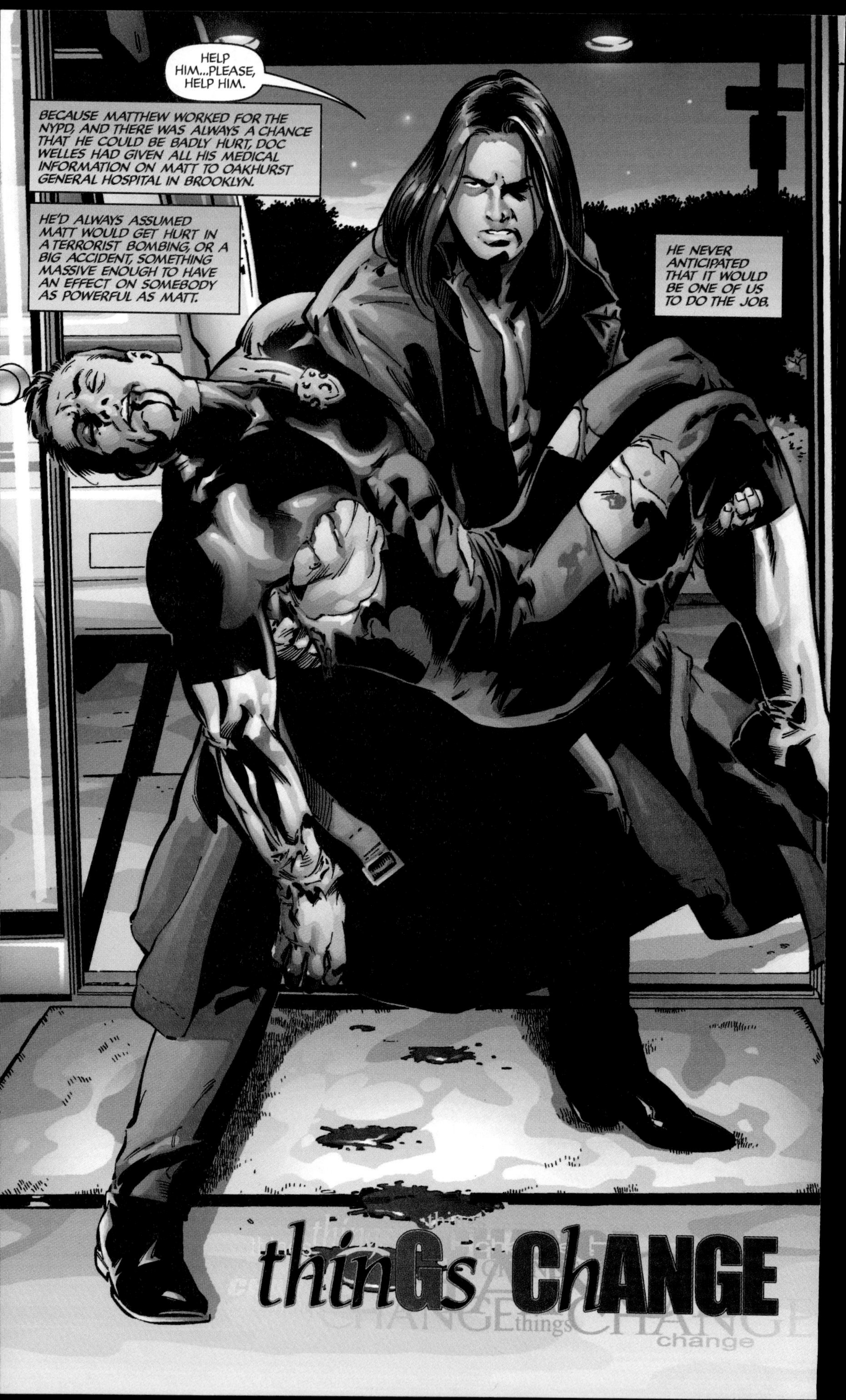
HELP HIM...PLEASE, HELP HIM.
BECAUSE MATTHEW WORKED FOR THE NYPD, AND THERE WAS ALWAYS A CHANCE THAT HE COULD BE BADLY HURT, DOC WELLES HAD GIVEN ALL HIS MEDICAL INFORMATION ON MATT TO OAKHURST GENERAL HOSPITAL IN BROOKLYN.
HE'D ALWAYS ASSUMED MATT WOULD GET HURT IN A TERRORIST BOMBING, OR A BIG ACCIDENT, SOMETHING MASSIVE ENOUGH TO HAVE AN EFFECT ON SOMEBODY AS POWERFUL AS MATT.
HE NEVER ANTICIPATED THAT IT WOULD BE ONE OF US TO DO THE JOB.
thinGs ChANGE
CHANGEthingsCHANGE
change

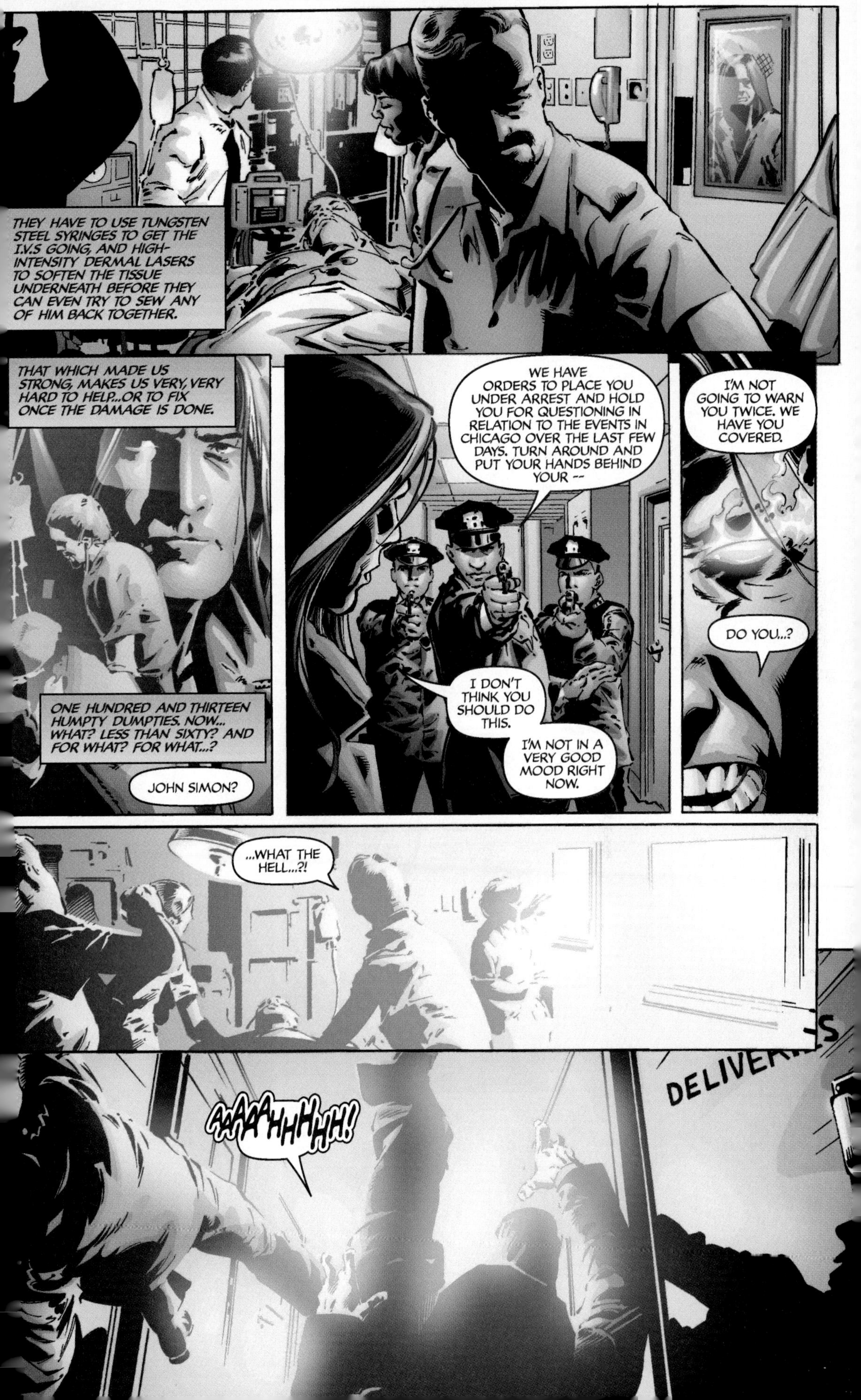
THEY HAVE TO USE TUNGSTEN STEEL SYRINGES TO GET THE I.V.S GOING, AND HIGH-INTENSITY DERMAL LASERS TO SOFTEN THE TISSUE UNDERNEATH BEFORE THEY CAN EVEN TRY TO SEW ANY OF HIM BACK TOGETHER.
THAT WHICH MADE US STRONG, MAKES US VERY, VERY HARD TO HELP...OR TO FIX ONCE THE DAMAGE IS DONE.
ONE HUNDRED AND THIRTEEN HUMPTY DUMPTIES. NOW... WHAT? LESS THAN SIXTY? AND FOR WHAT? FOR WHAT...?
JOHN SIMON?
WE HAVE ORDERS TO PLACE YOU UNDER ARREST AND HOLD YOU FOR QUESTIONING IN RELATION TO THE EVENTS IN CHICAGO OVER THE LAST FEW DAYS. TURN AROUND AND PUT YOUR HANDS BEHIND YOUR --
I DON'T THINK YOU SHOULD DO THIS.
I'M NOT IN A VERY GOOD MOOD RIGHT NOW.
I'M NOT GOING TO WARN YOU TWICE. WE HAVE YOU COVERED.
DO YOU...?
...WHAT THE HELL...?!
AAAAAHHHHHH!
DELIVER
S

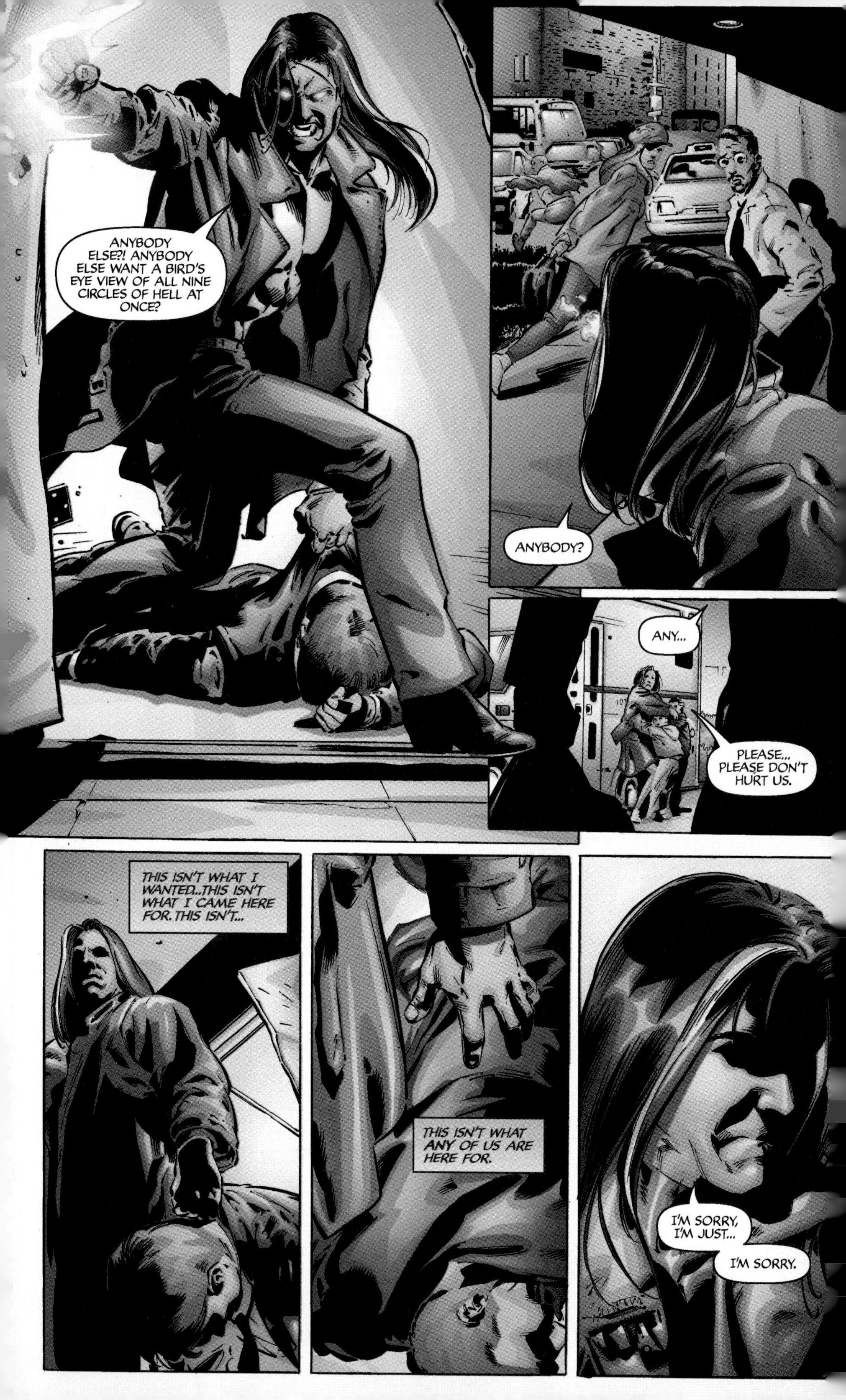
ANYBODY ELSE?! ANYBODY ELSE WANT A BIRD'S EYE VIEW OF ALL NINE CIRCLES OF HELL AT ONCE?
ANYBODY?
ANY...
PLEASE... PLEASE DON'T HURT US.
THIS ISN'T WHAT I WANTED...THIS ISN'T WHAT I CAME HERE FOR. THIS ISN'T...
THIS ISN'T WHAT ANY OF US ARE HERE FOR.
I'M SORRY, I'M JUST...
I'M SORRY.

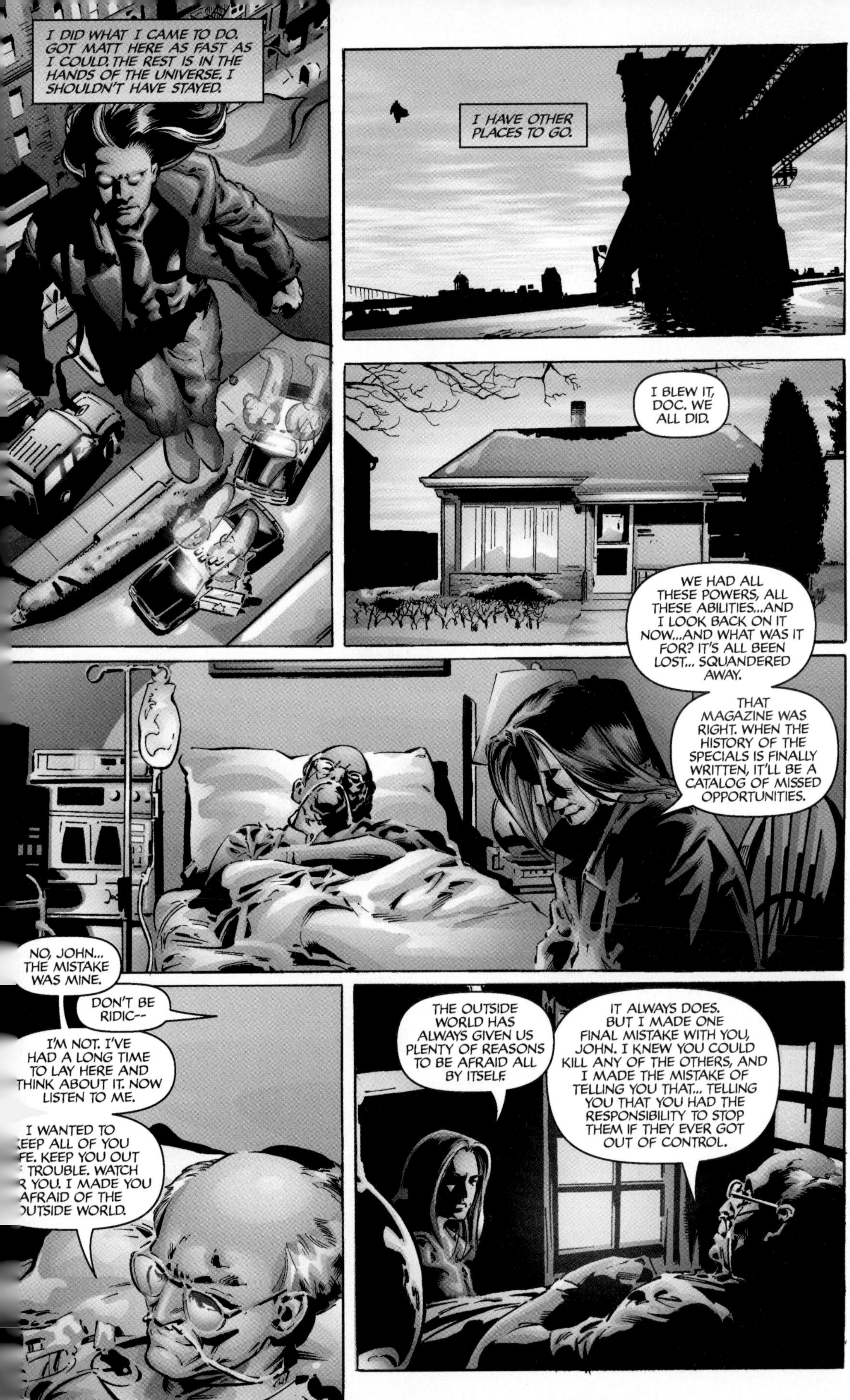

I DID WHAT I CAME TO DO. GOT MATT HERE AS FAST AS I COULD. THE REST IS IN THE HANDS OF THE UNIVERSE. I SHOULDN'T HAVE STAYED.
I HAVE OTHER PLACES TO GO.
I BLEW IT, DOC. WE ALL DID.
WE HAD ALL THESE POWERS, ALL THESE ABILITIES...AND I LOOK BACK ON IT NOW...AND WHAT WAS IT FOR? IT'S ALL BEEN LOST... SQUANDERED AWAY.
THAT MAGAZINE WAS RIGHT. WHEN THE HISTORY OF THE SPECIALS IS FINALLY WRITTEN, IT'LL BE A CATALOG OF MISSED OPPORTUNITIES.
NO, JOHN... THE MISTAKE WAS MINE.
DON'T BE RIDIC--
I'M NOT. I'VE HAD A LONG TIME TO LAY HERE AND THINK ABOUT IT. NOW LISTEN TO ME.
I WANTED TO EEP ALL OF YOU FE. KEEP YOU OUT TROUBLE. WATCH R YOU. I MADE YOU AFRAID OF THE UTSIDE WORLD.
THE OUTSIDE WORLD HAS ALWAYS GIVEN US PLENTY OF REASONS TO BE AFRAID ALL BY ITSELF.
IT ALWAYS DOES. BUT I MADE ONE FINAL MISTAKE WITH YOU, JOHN. I KNEW YOU COULD KILL ANY OF THE OTHERS, AND I MADE THE MISTAKE OF TELLING YOU THAT... TELLING YOU THAT YOU HAD THE RESPONSIBILITY TO STOP THEM IF THEY EVER GOT OUT OF CONTROL.

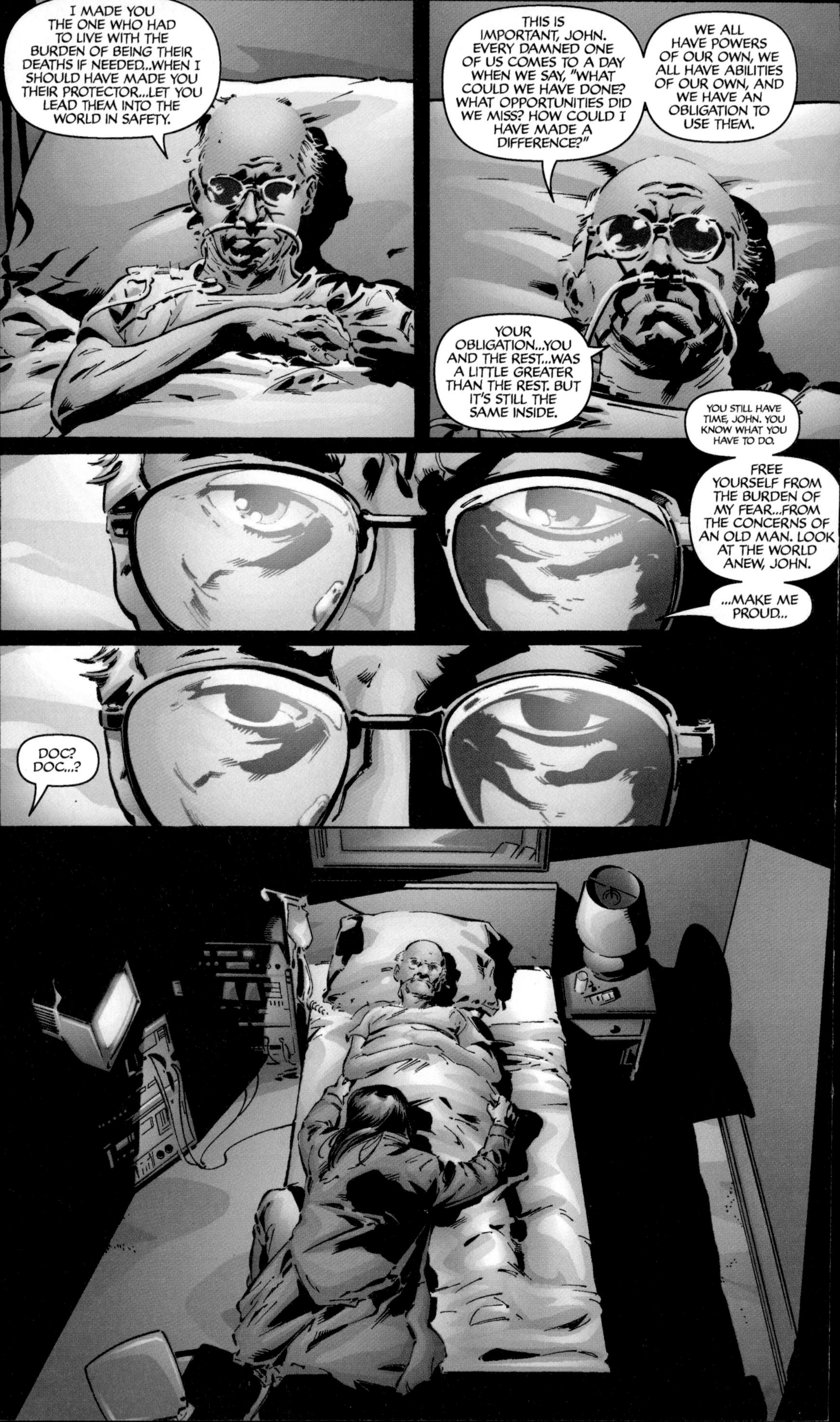
I MADE YOU THE ONE WHO HAD TO LIVE WITH THE BURDEN OF BEING THEIR DEATHS IF NEEDED...WHEN I SHOULD HAVE MADE YOU THEIR PROTECTOR...LET YOU LEAD THEM INTO THE WORLD IN SAFETY.
THIS IS IMPORTANT, JOHN. EVERY DAMNED ONE OF US COMES TO A DAY WHEN WE SAY, "WHAT COULD WE HAVE DONE? WHAT OPPORTUNITIES DID WE MISS? HOW COULD I HAVE MADE A DIFFERENCE?"
WE ALL HAVE POWERS OF OUR OWN, WE ALL HAVE ABILITIES OF OUR OWN, AND WE HAVE AN OBLIGATION TO USE THEM.
YOUR OBLIGATION...YOU AND THE REST...WAS A LITTLE GREATER THAN THE REST. BUT IT'S STILL THE SAME INSIDE.
YOU STILL HAVE TIME, JOHN. YOU KNOW WHAT YOU HAVE TO DO.
FREE YOURSELF FROM THE BURDEN OF MY FEAR...FROM THE CONCERNS OF AN OLD MAN. LOOK AT THE WORLD ANEW, JOHN.
...MAKE ME PROUD...
DOC? DOC...?

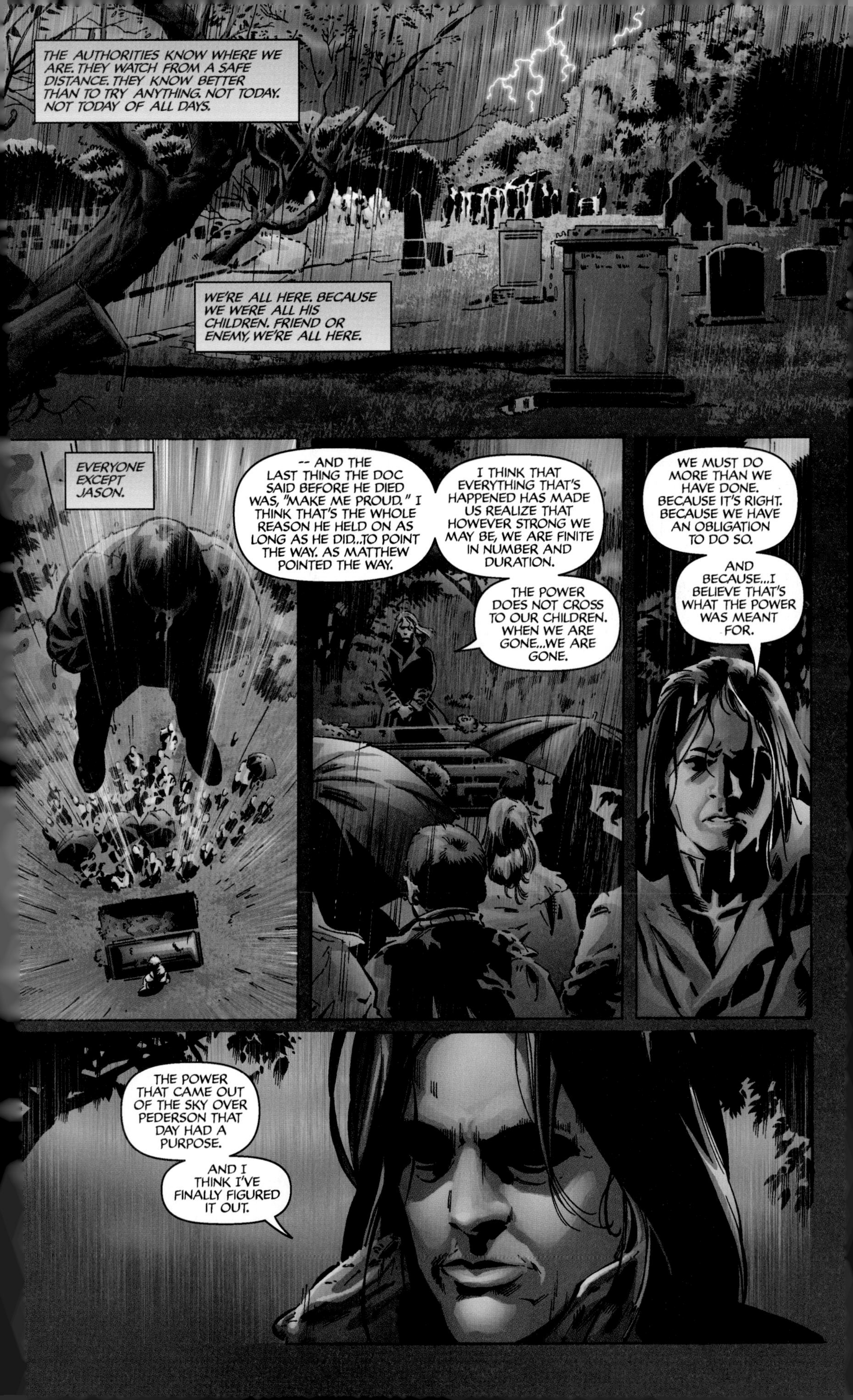
THE AUTHORITIES KNOW WHERE WE ARE. THEY WATCH FROM A SAFE DISTANCE. THEY KNOW BETTER THAN TO TRY ANYTHING. NOT TODAY. NOT TODAY OF ALL DAYS.
WE'RE ALL HERE. BECAUSE WE WERE ALL HIS CHILDREN. FRIEND OR ENEMY, WE'RE ALL HERE.
EVERYONE EXCEPT JASON.
-- AND THE LAST THING THE DOC SAID BEFORE HE DIED WAS, "MAKE ME PROUD." I THINK THAT'S THE WHOLE REASON HE HELD ON AS LONG AS HE DID...TO POINT THE WAY. AS MATTHEW POINTED THE WAY.
I THINK THAT EVERYTHING THAT'S HAPPENED HAS MADE US REALIZE THAT HOWEVER STRONG WE MAY BE, WE ARE FINITE IN NUMBER AND DURATION.
THE POWER DOES NOT CROSS TO OUR CHILDREN. WHEN WE ARE GONE...WE ARE GONE.
WE MUST DO MORE THAN WE HAVE DONE. BECAUSE IT'S RIGHT. BECAUSE WE HAVE AN OBLIGATION TO DO SO.
AND BECAUSE...I BELIEVE THAT'S WHAT THE POWER WAS MEANT FOR.
THE POWER THAT CAME OUT OF THE SKY OVER PEDERSON THAT DAY HAD A PURPOSE.
AND I THINK I'VE FINALLY FIGURED IT OUT.

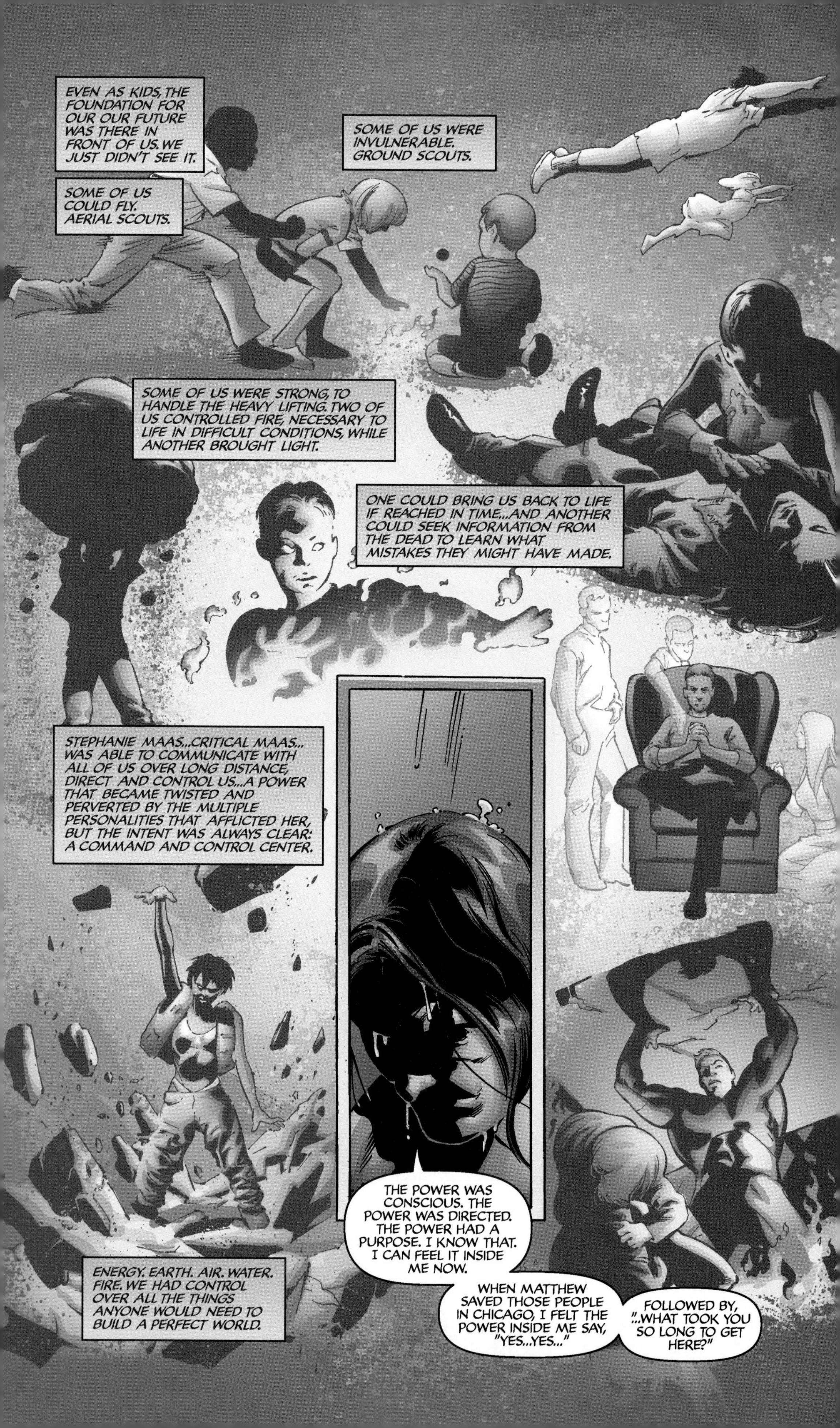
EVEN AS KIDS, THE FOUNDATION FOR OUR OUR FUTURE WAS THERE IN FRONT OF US. WE JUST DIDN'T SEE IT.
SOME OF US COULD FLY. AERIAL SCOUTS.
SOME OF US WERE INVULNERABLE. GROUND SCOUTS.
SOME OF US WERE STRONG, TO HANDLE THE HEAVY LIFTING. TWO OF US CONTROLLED FIRE, NECESSARY TO LIFE IN DIFFICULT CONDITIONS, WHILE ANOTHER BROUGHT LIGHT.
ONE COULD BRING US BACK TO LIFE IF REACHED IN TIME...AND ANOTHER COULD SEEK INFORMATION FROM THE DEAD TO LEARN WHAT MISTAKES THEY MIGHT HAVE MADE.
STEPHANIE MAAS...CRITICAL MAAS... WAS ABLE TO COMMUNICATE WITH ALL OF US OVER LONG DISTANCE, DIRECT AND CONTROL US...A POWER THAT BECAME TWISTED AND PERVERTED BY THE MULTIPLE PERSONALITIES THAT AFFLICTED HER, BUT THE INTENT WAS ALWAYS CLEAR: A COMMAND AND CONTROL CENTER.
ENERGY. EARTH. AIR. WATER. FIRE. WE HAD CONTROL OVER ALL THE THINGS ANYONE WOULD NEED TO BUILD A PERFECT WORLD.
THE POWER WAS CONSCIOUS. THE POWER WAS DIRECTED. THE POWER HAD A PURPOSE. I KNOW THAT. I CAN FEEL IT INSIDE ME NOW.
WHEN MATTHEW SAVED THOSE PEOPLE IN CHICAGO, I FELT THE POWER INSIDE ME SAY, "YES...YES..."
FOLLOWED BY, "...WHAT TOOK YOU SO LONG TO GET HERE?"

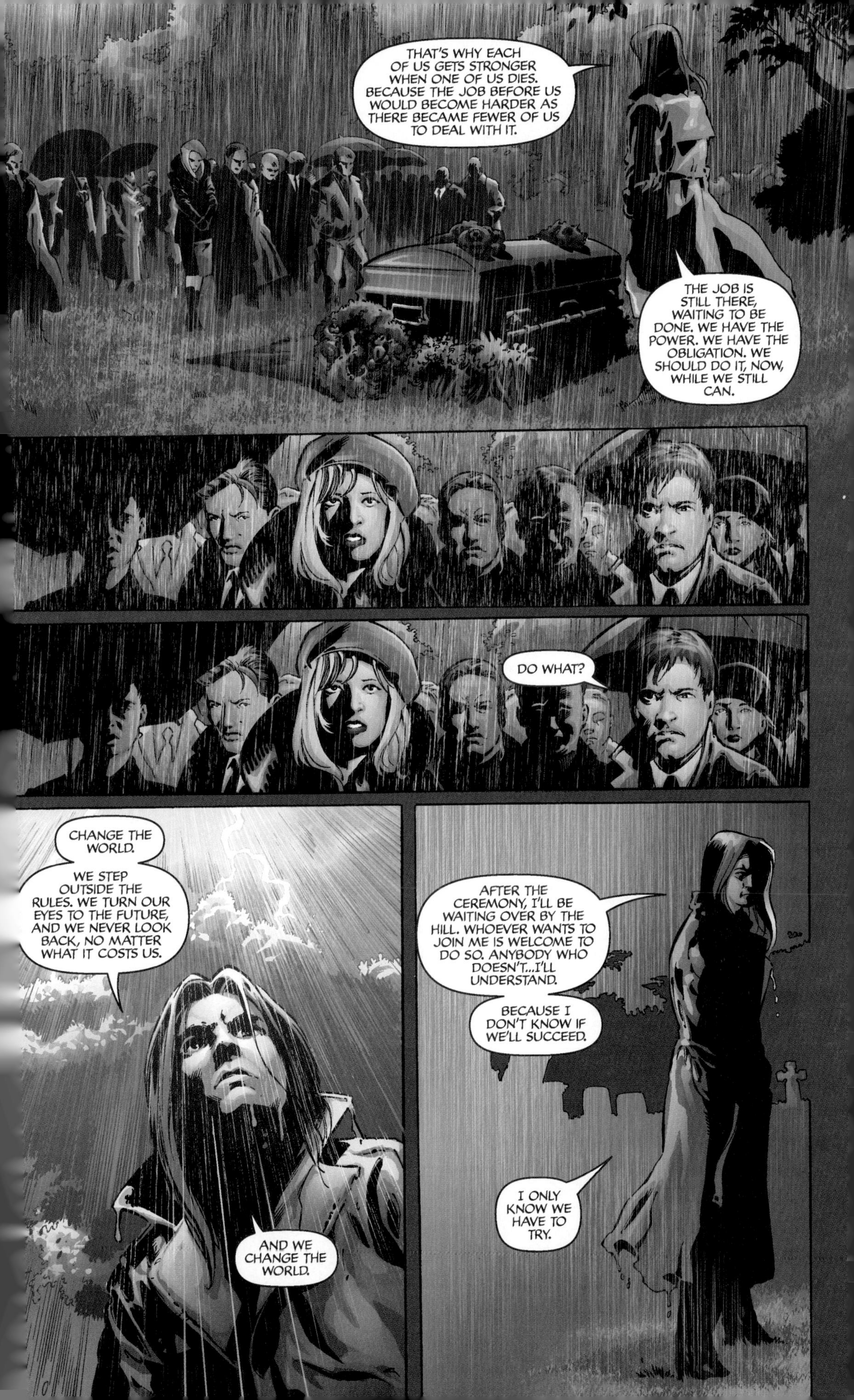
THAT'S WHY EACH OF US GETS STRONGER WHEN ONE OF US DIES. BECAUSE THE JOB BEFORE US WOULD BECOME HARDER AS THERE BECAME FEWER OF US TO DEAL WITH IT.
THE JOB IS STILL THERE, WAITING TO BE DONE. WE HAVE THE POWER. WE HAVE THE OBLIGATION. WE SHOULD DO IT, NOW, WHILE WE STILL CAN.
DO WHAT?
CHANGE THE WORLD.
WE STEP OUTSIDE THE RULES. WE TURN OUR EYES TO THE FUTURE, AND WE NEVER LOOK BACK, NO MATTER WHAT IT COSTS US.
AND WE CHANGE THE WORLD.
AFTER THE CEREMONY, I'LL BE WAITING OVER BY THE HILL. WHOEVER WANTS TO JOIN ME IS WELCOME TO DO SO. ANYBODY WHO DOESN'T...I'LL UNDERSTAND.
BECAUSE I DON'T KNOW IF WE'LL SUCCEED.
I ONLY KNOW WE HAVE TO TRY.

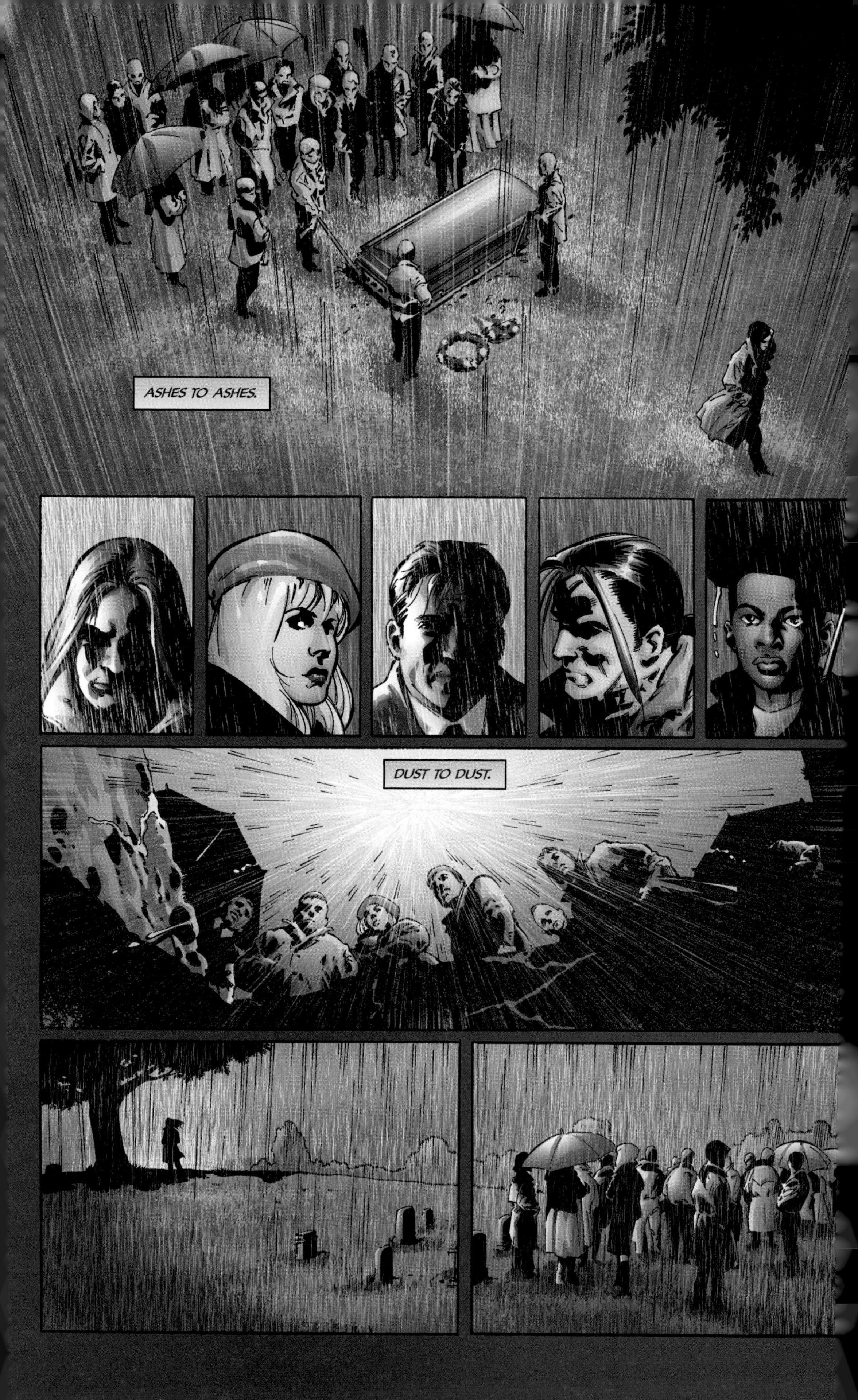
ASHES TO ASHES.
DUST TO DUST.

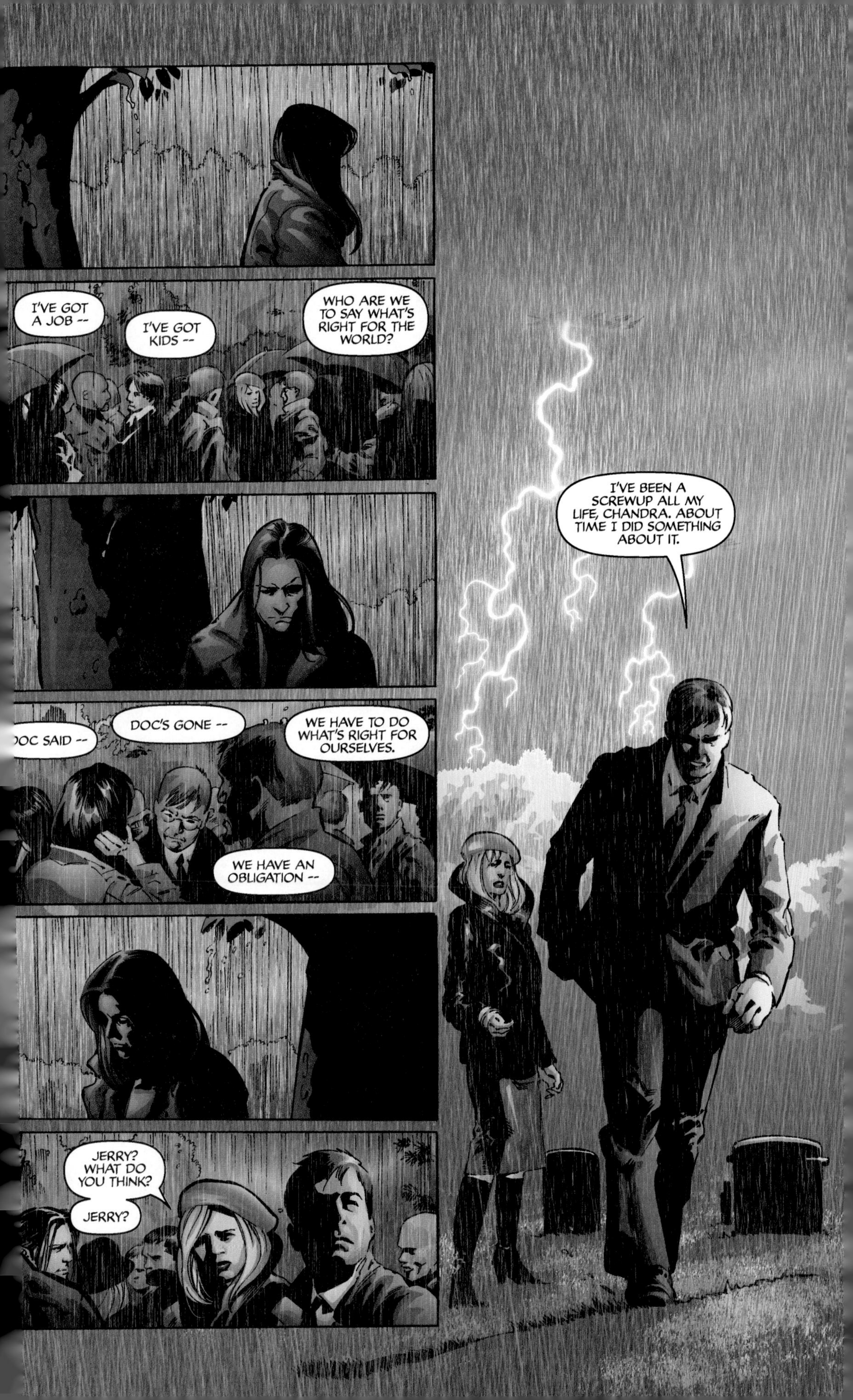
I'VE GOT A JOB --
I'VE GOT KIDS --
WHO ARE WE TO SAY WHAT'S RIGHT FOR THE WORLD?
DOC SAID --
DOC'S GONE --
WE HAVE TO DO WHAT'S RIGHT FOR OURSELVES.
WE HAVE AN OBLIGATION --
JERRY? WHAT DO YOU THINK?
JERRY?
I'VE BEEN A SCREWUP ALL MY LIFE, CHANDRA. ABOUT TIME I DID SOMETHING ABOUT IT.

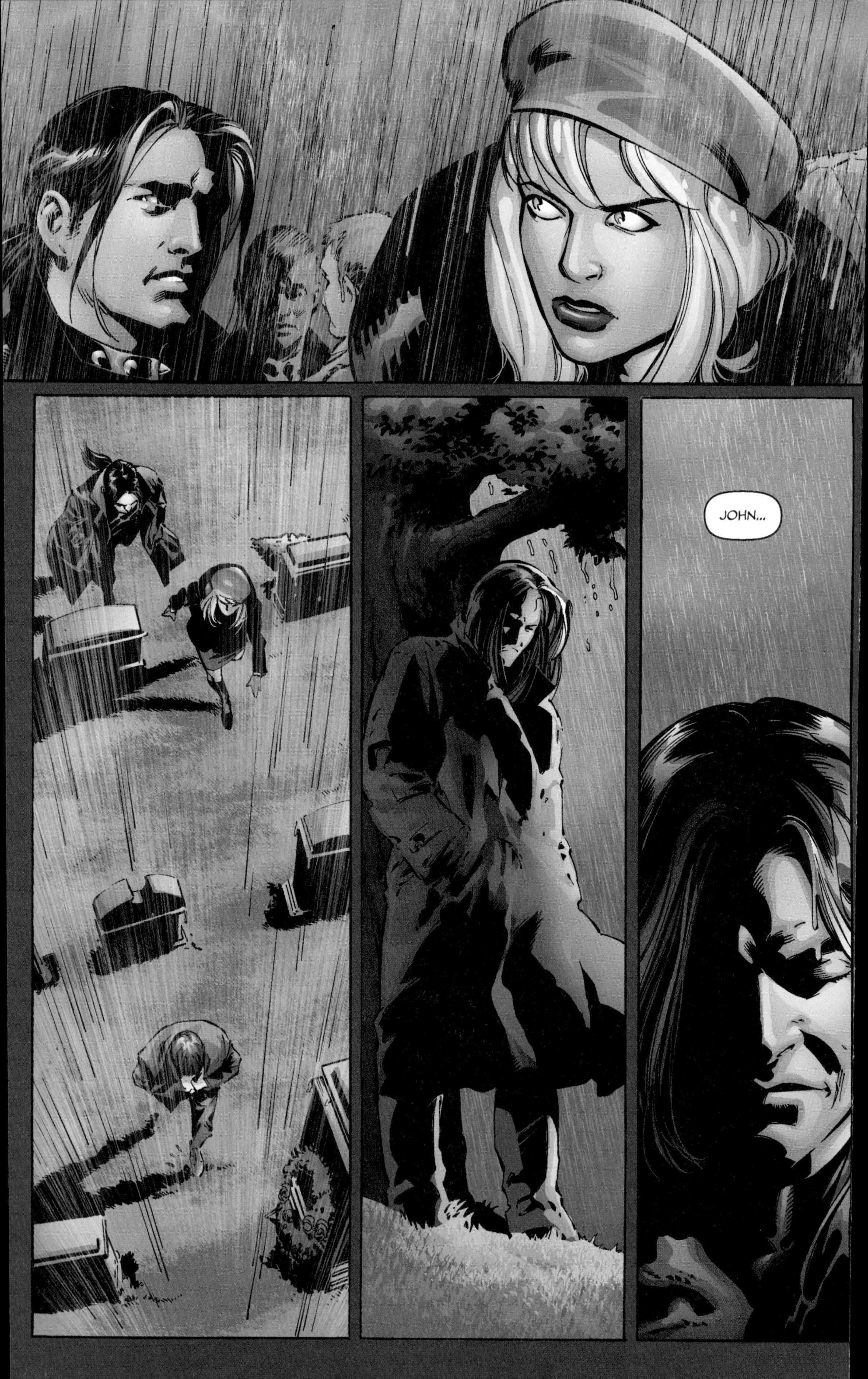
JOHN...

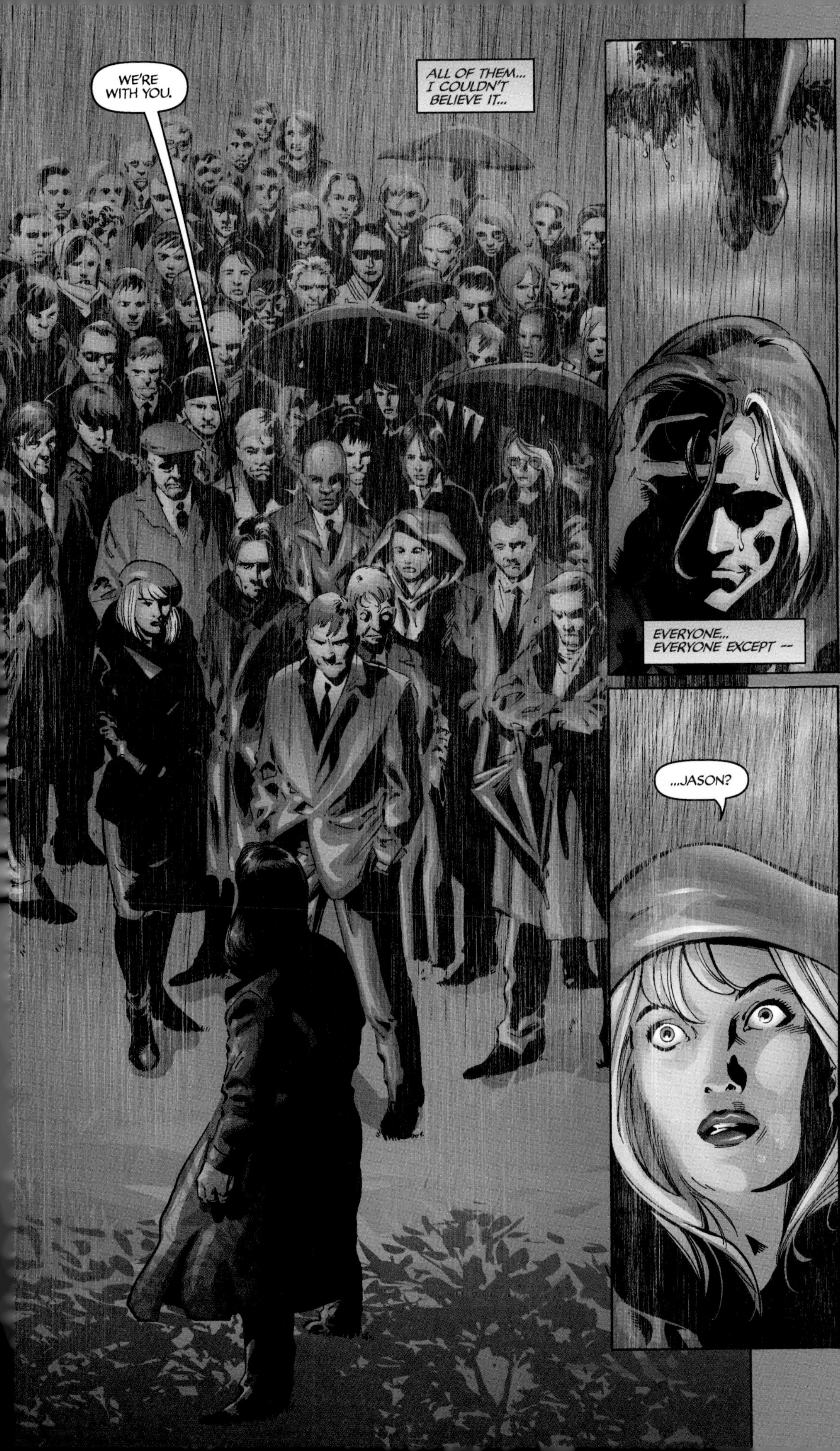
WE'RE WITH YOU.
ALL OF THEM... I COULDN'T BELIEVE IT...
EVERYONE... EVERYONE EXCEPT --
...JASON?

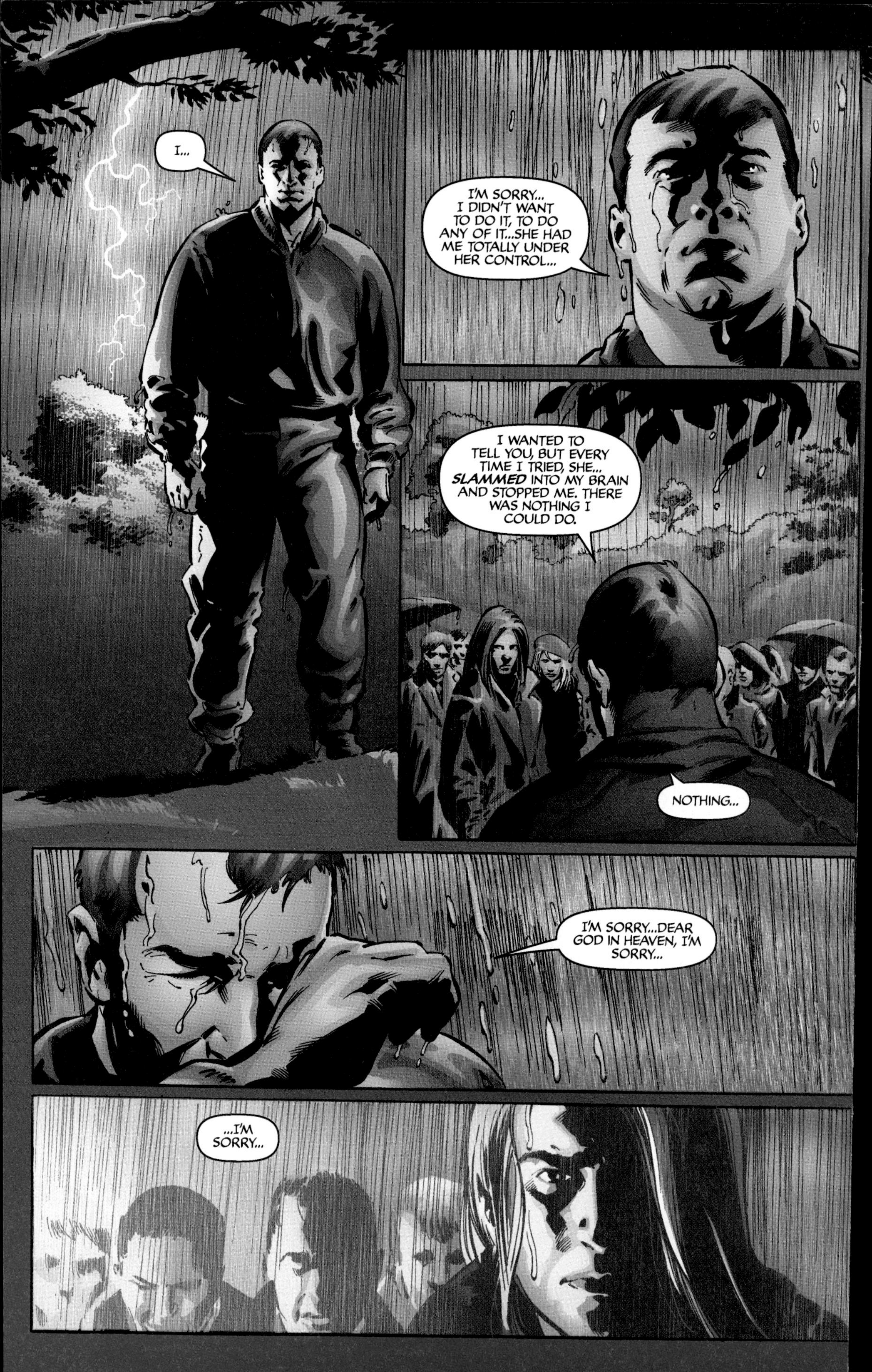
I...
I'M SORRY... I DIDN'T WANT TO DO IT, TO DO ANY OF IT...SHE HAD ME TOTALLY UNDER HER CONTROL...
I WANTED TO TELL YOU, BUT EVERY TIME I TRIED, SHE... SLAMMED INTO MY BRAIN AND STOPPED ME. THERE WAS NOTHING I COULD DO.
NOTHING...
I'M SORRY...DEAR GOD IN HEAVEN, I'M SORRY...
...I'M SORRY...

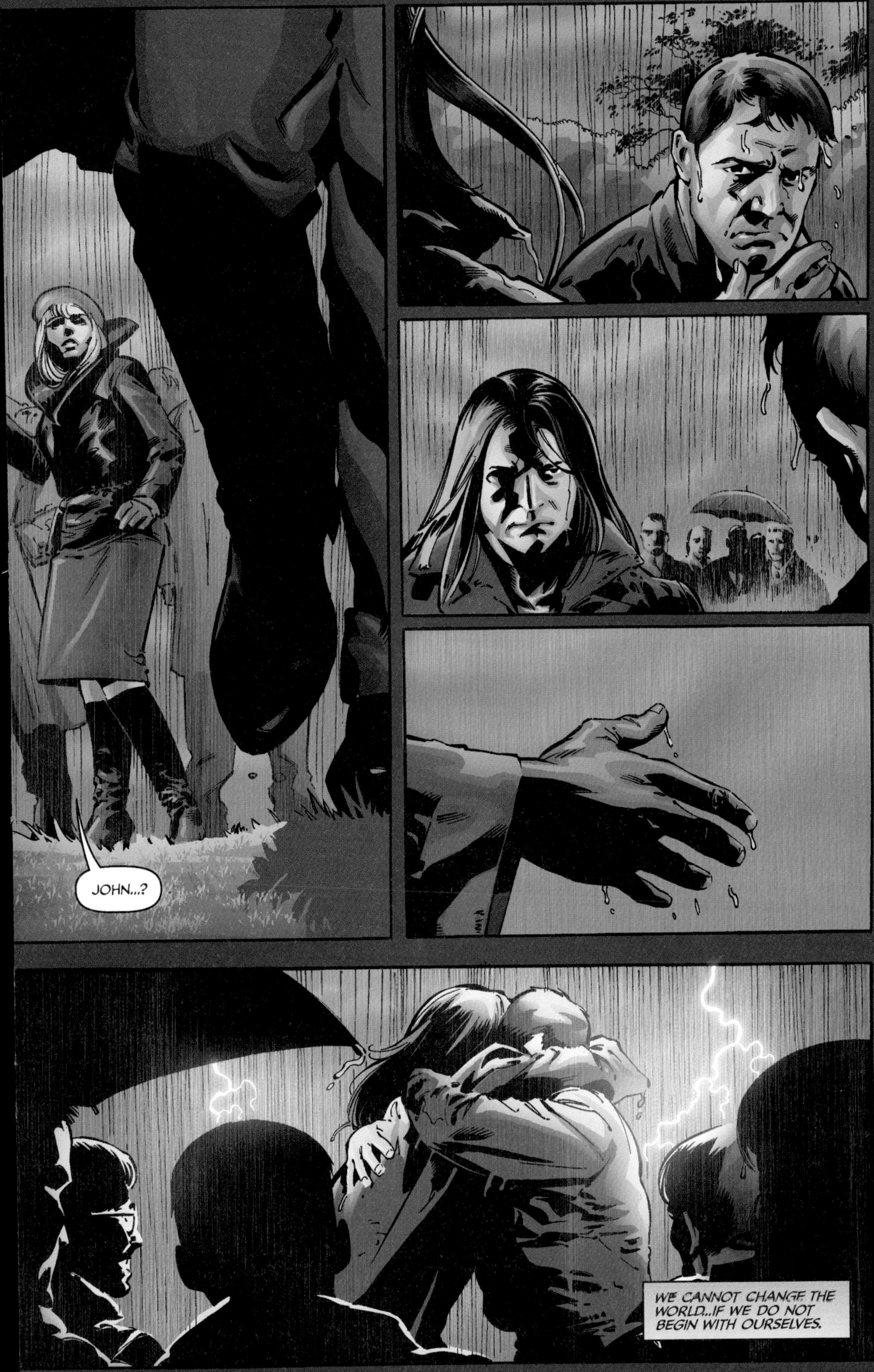
JOHN...?
WE CANNOT CHANGE THE WORLD...IF WE DO NOT BEGIN WITH OURSELVES.

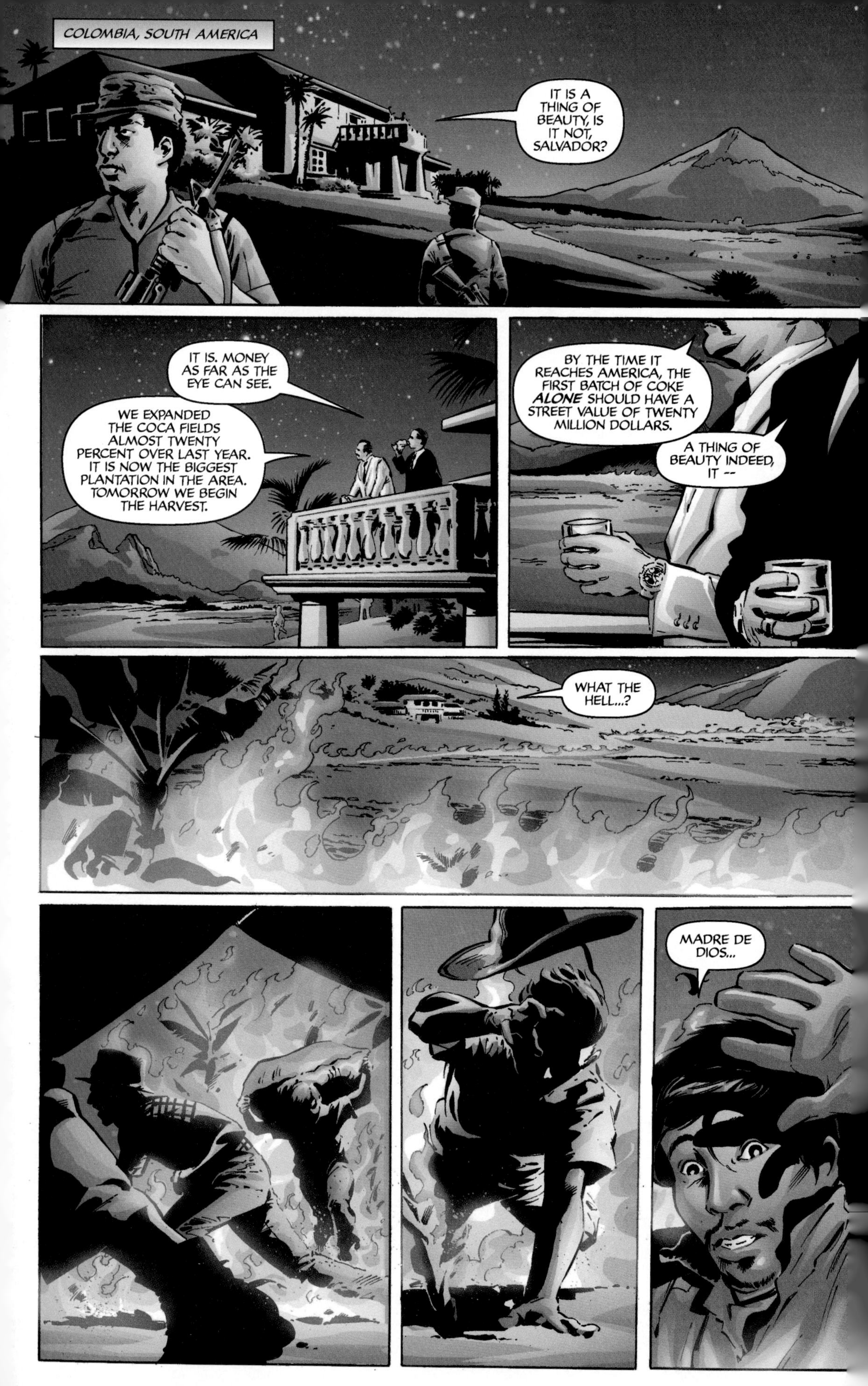
COLOMBIA, SOUTH AMERICA
IT IS A THING OF BEAUTY, IS IT NOT, SALVADOR?
IT IS. MONEY AS FAR AS THE EYE CAN SEE.
WE EXPANDED THE COCA FIELDS ALMOST TWENTY PERCENT OVER LAST YEAR. IT IS NOW THE BIGGEST PLANTATION IN THE AREA. TOMORROW WE BEGIN THE HARVEST.
BY THE TIME IT REACHES AMERICA, THE FIRST BATCH OF COKE ALONE SHOULD HAVE A STREET VALUE OF TWENTY MILLION DOLLARS.
A THING OF BEAUTY INDEED, IT --
WHAT THE HELL...?
MADRE DE DIOS...

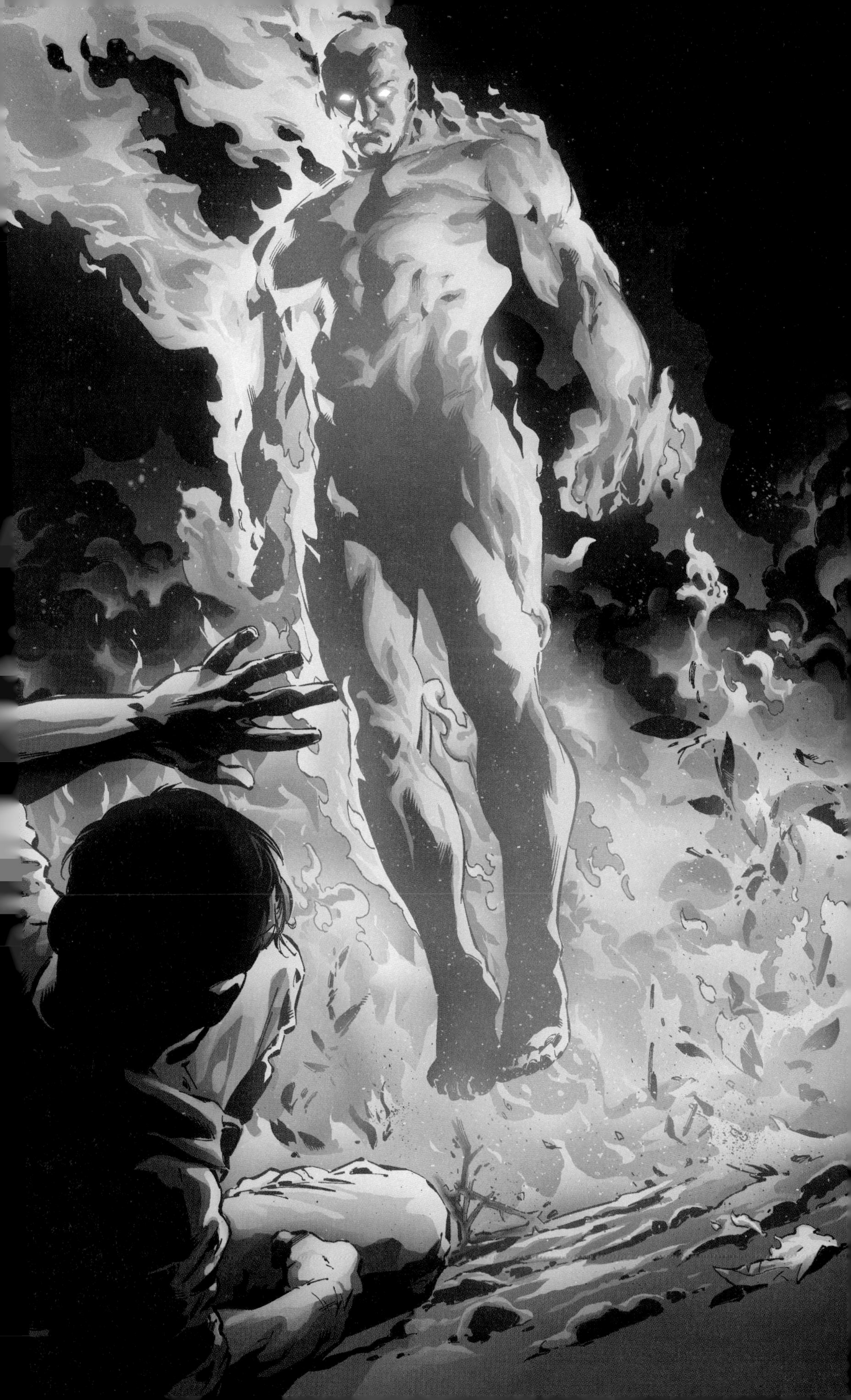

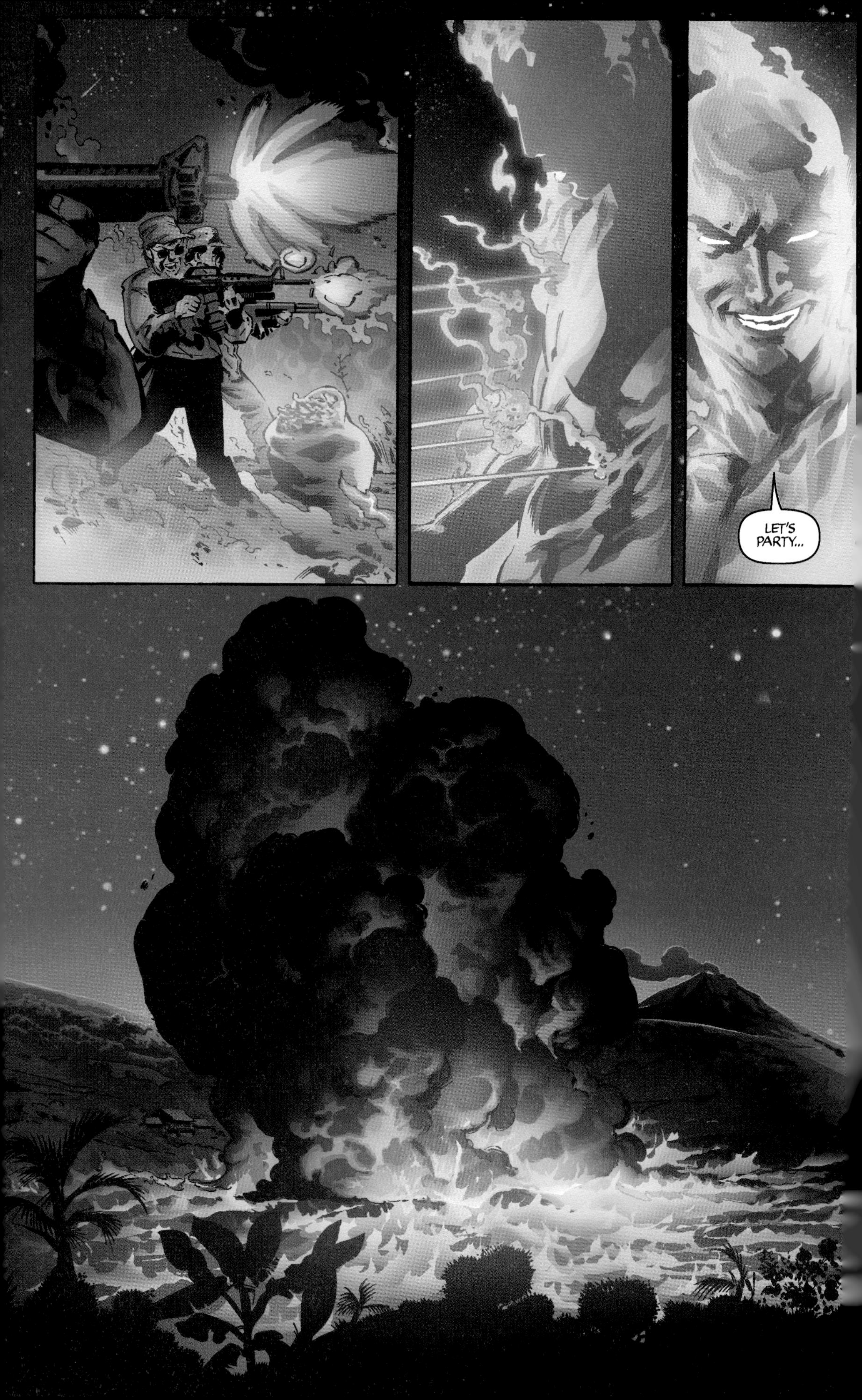
LET'S PARTY...

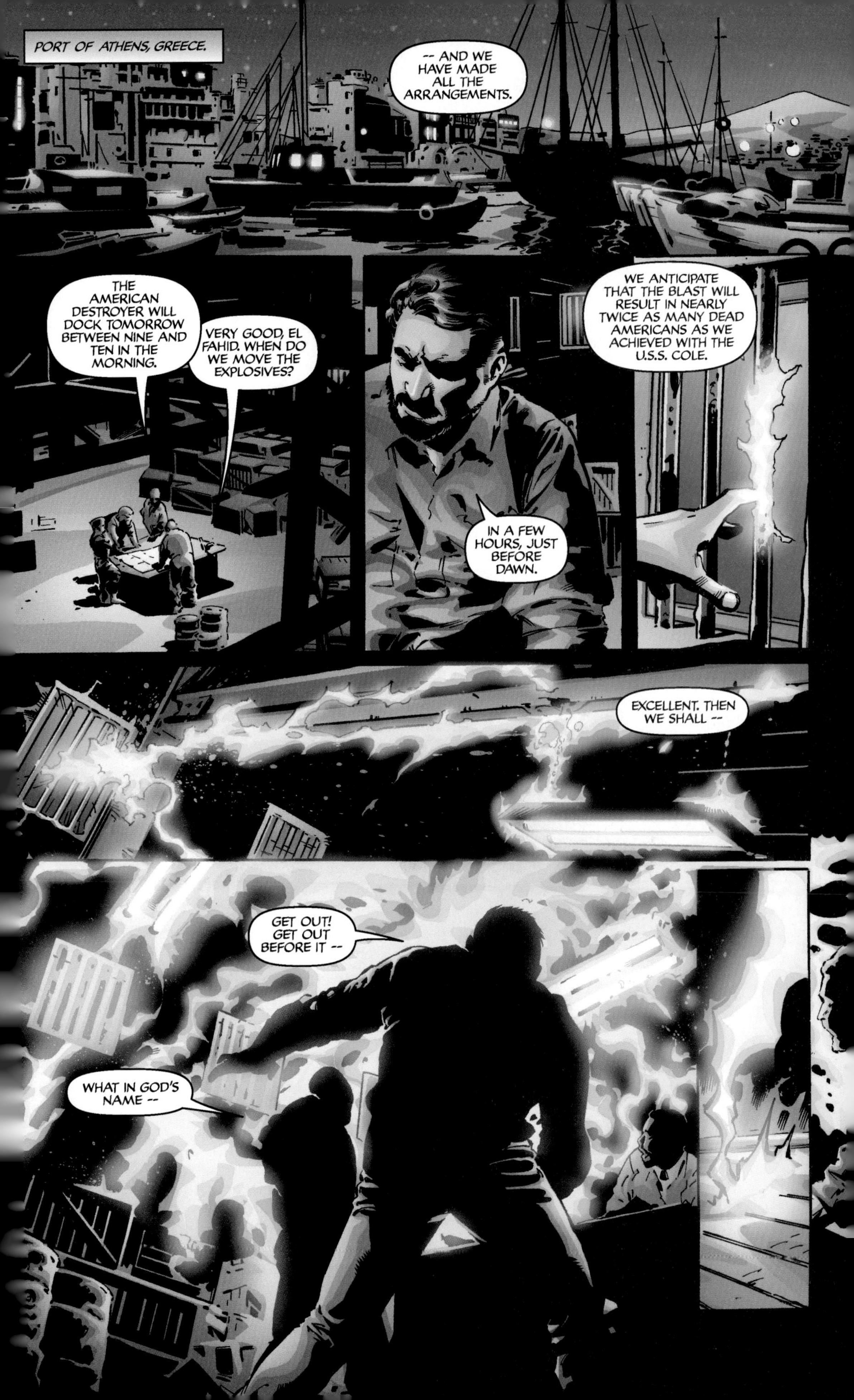
PORT OF ATHENS, GREECE.
-- AND WE HAVE MADE ALL THE ARRANGEMENTS.
THE AMERICAN DESTROYER WILL DOCK TOMORROW BETWEEN NINE AND TEN IN THE MORNING.
VERY GOOD, EL FAHID. WHEN DO WE MOVE THE EXPLOSIVES?
IN A FEW HOURS, JUST BEFORE DAWN.
WE ANTICIPATE THAT THE BLAST WILL RESULT IN NEARLY TWICE AS MANY DEAD AMERICANS AS WE ACHIEVED WITH THE U.S.S. COLE.
EXCELLENT. THEN WE SHALL --
GET OUT! GET OUT BEFORE IT --
WHAT IN GOD'S NAME --

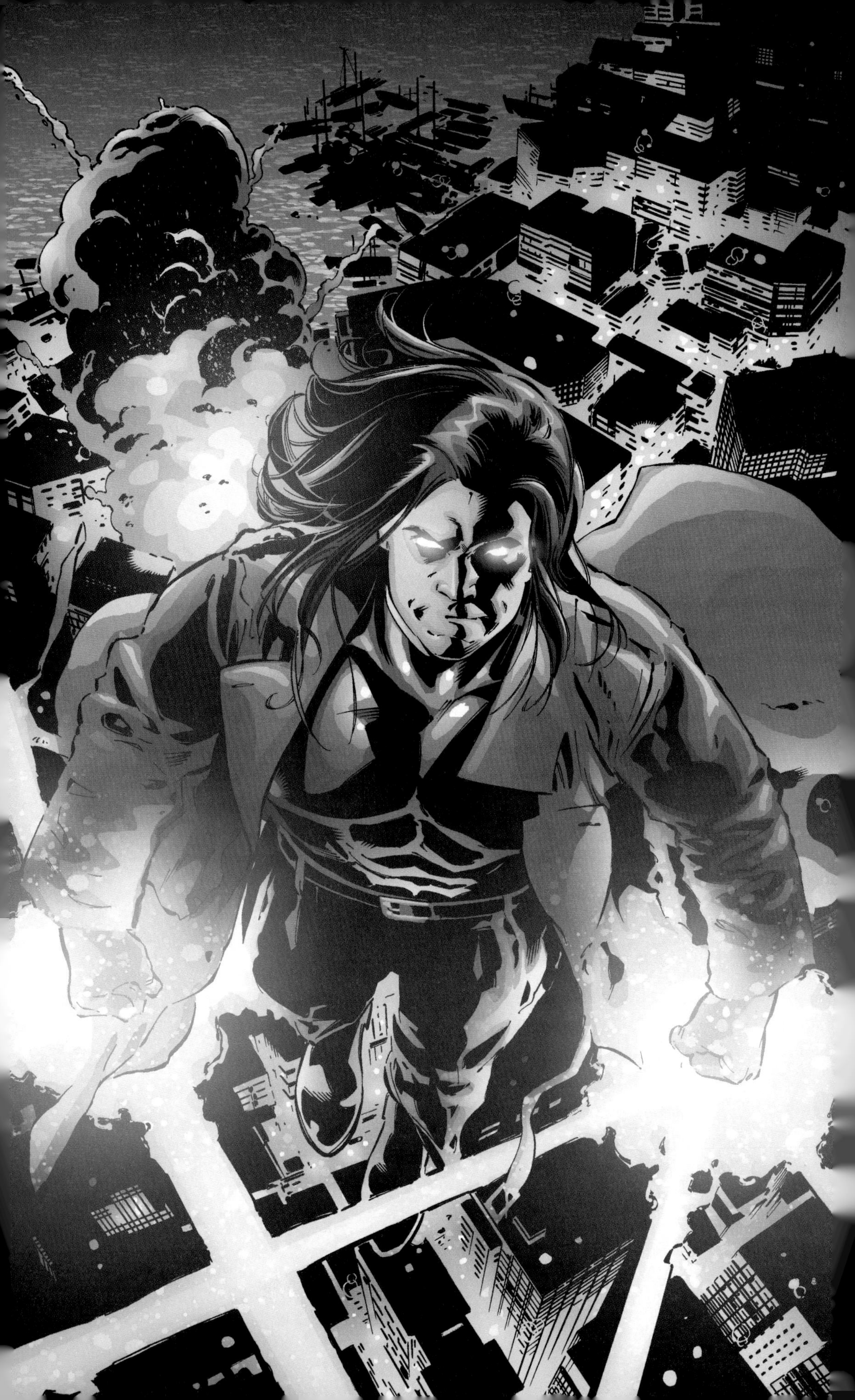

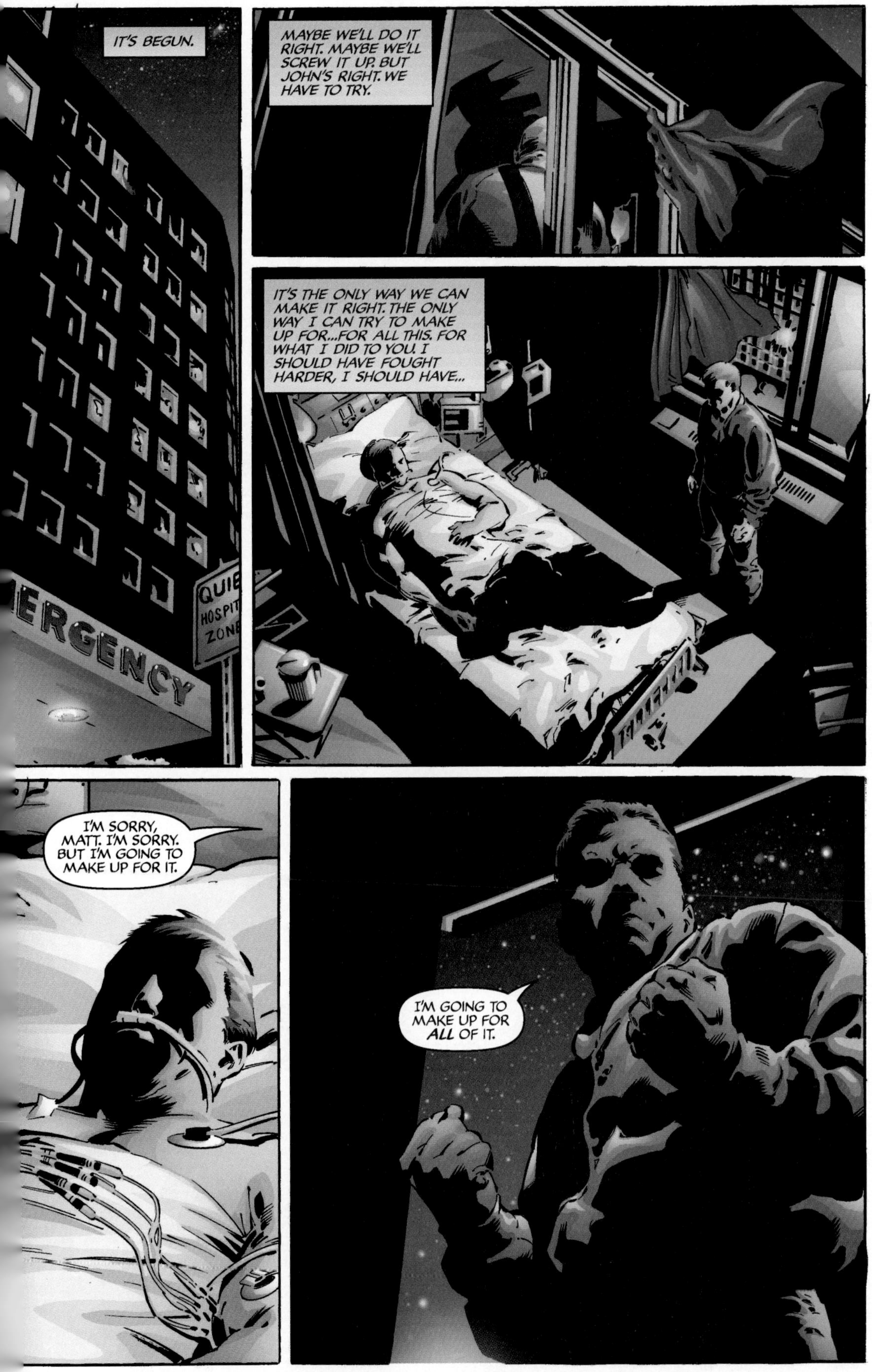
IT'S BEGUN.
MAYBE WE'LL DO IT RIGHT. MAYBE WE'LL SCREW IT UP. BUT JOHN'S RIGHT. WE HAVE TO TRY.
IT'S THE ONLY WAY WE CAN MAKE IT RIGHT. THE ONLY WAY I CAN TRY TO MAKE UP FOR...FOR ALL THIS. FOR WHAT I DID TO YOU. I SHOULD HAVE FOUGHT HARDER, I SHOULD HAVE...
I'M SORRY, MATT. I'M SORRY. BUT I'M GOING TO MAKE UP FOR IT.
I'M GOING TO MAKE UP FOR ALL OF IT.

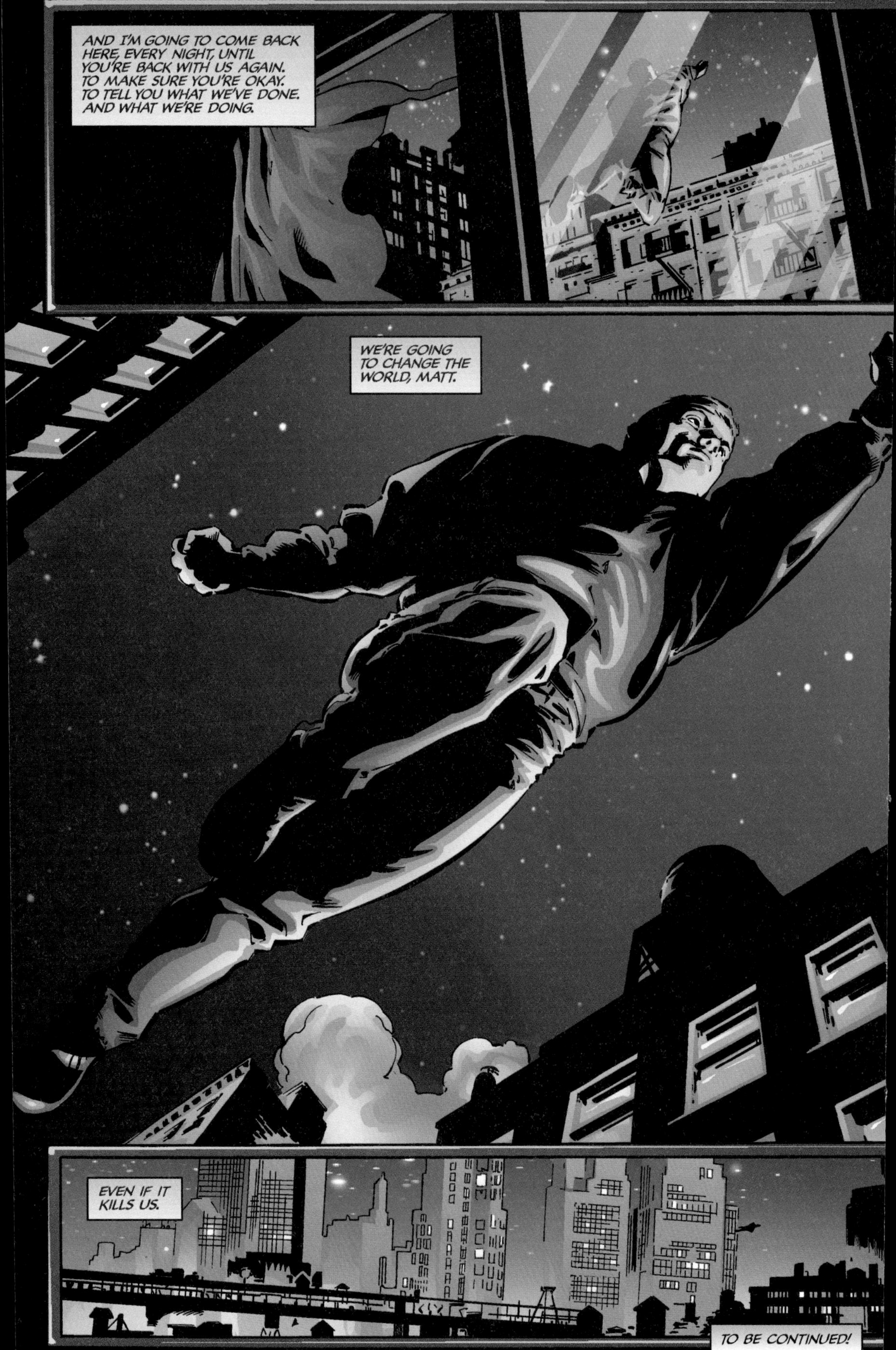
AND I'M GOING TO COME BACK HERE, EVERY NIGHT, UNTIL YOU'RE BACK WITH US AGAIN. TO MAKE SURE YOU'RE OKAY. TO TELL YOU WHAT WE'VE DONE. AND WHAT WE'RE DOING.
WE'RE GOING TO CHANGE THE WORLD, MATT.
EVEN IF IT KILLS US.
TO BE CONTINUED!

“Power”

CHAPTER 7

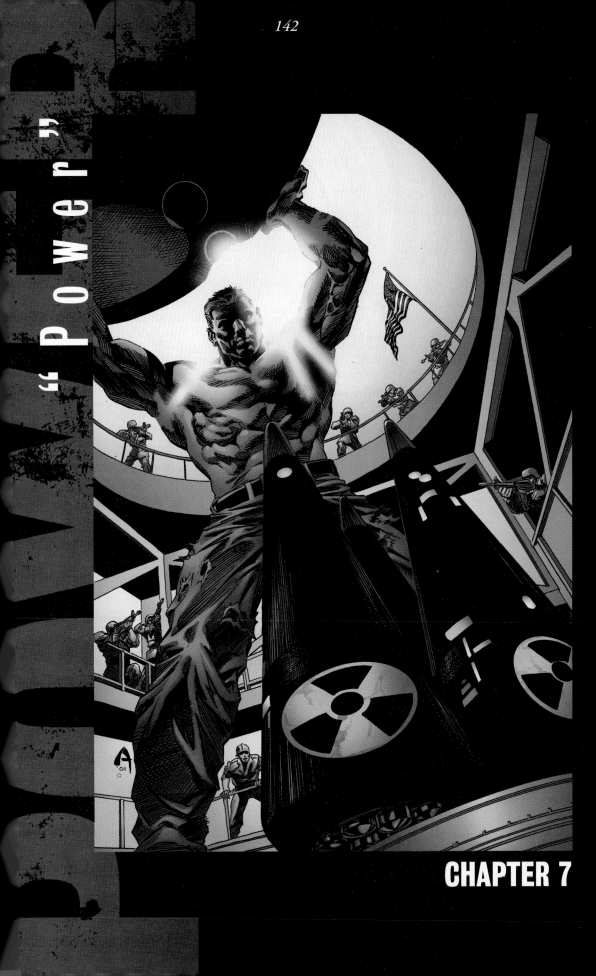

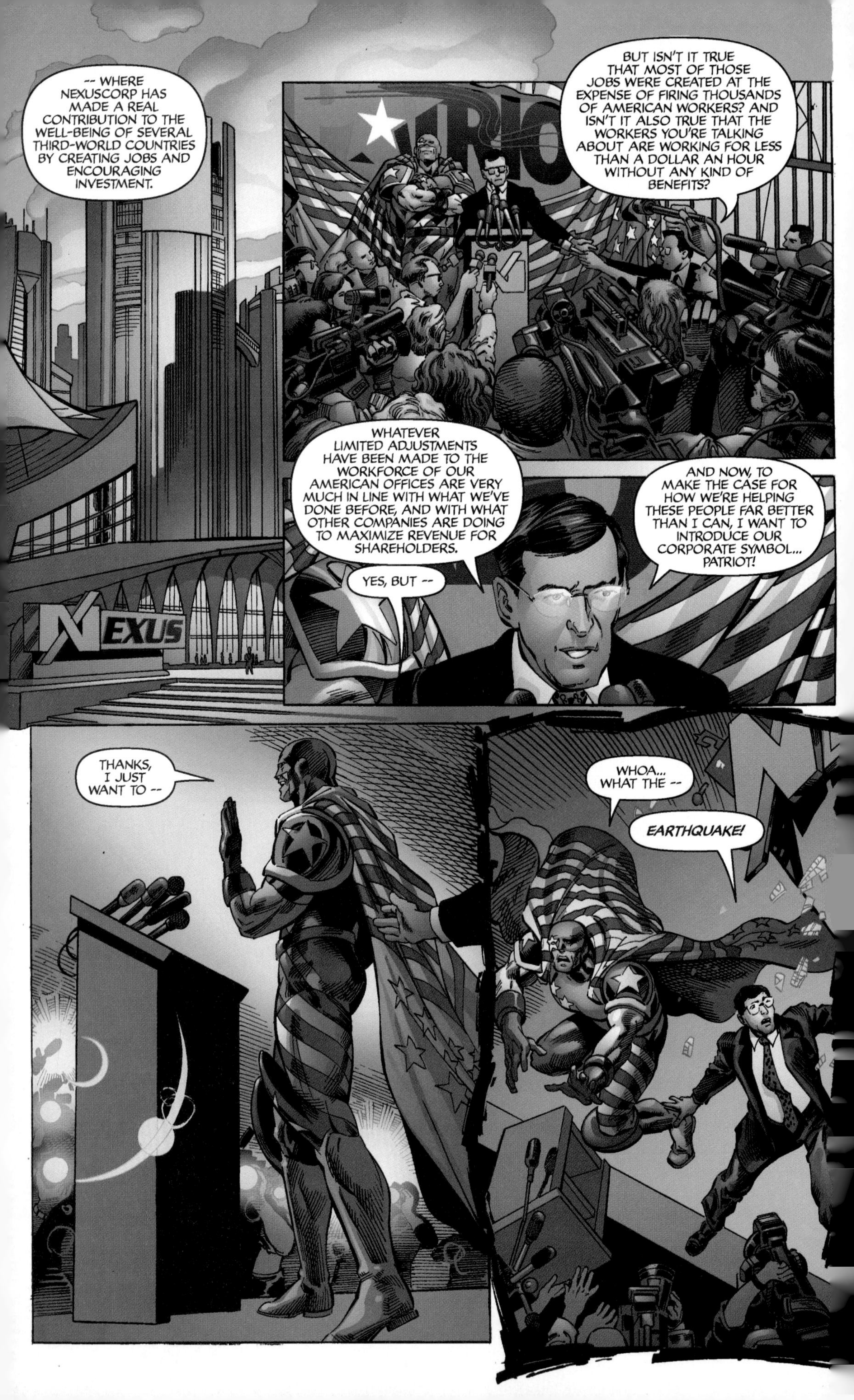
-- WHERE NEXUSCORP HAS MADE A REAL CONTRIBUTION TO THE WELL-BEING OF SEVERAL THIRD-WORLD COUNTRIES BY CREATING JOBS AND ENCOURAGING INVESTMENT.
BUT ISN'T IT TRUE THAT MOST OF THOSE JOBS WERE CREATED AT THE EXPENSE OF FIRING THOUSANDS OF AMERICAN WORKERS? AND ISN'T IT ALSO TRUE THAT THE WORKERS YOU'RE TALKING ABOUT ARE WORKING FOR LESS THAN A DOLLAR AN HOUR WITHOUT ANY KIND OF BENEFITS?
NEXUS
WHATEVER LIMITED ADJUSTMENTS HAVE BEEN MADE TO THE WORKFORCE OF OUR AMERICAN OFFICES ARE VERY MUCH IN LINE WITH WHAT WE'VE DONE BEFORE, AND WITH WHAT OTHER COMPANIES ARE DOING TO MAXIMIZE REVENUE FOR SHAREHOLDERS.
YES, BUT --
AND NOW, TO MAKE THE CASE FOR HOW WE'RE HELPING THESE PEOPLE FAR BETTER THAN I CAN, I WANT TO INTRODUCE OUR CORPORATE SYMBOL... PATRIOT!
THANKS, I JUST WANT TO --
WHOA... WHAT THE --
EARTHQUAKE!

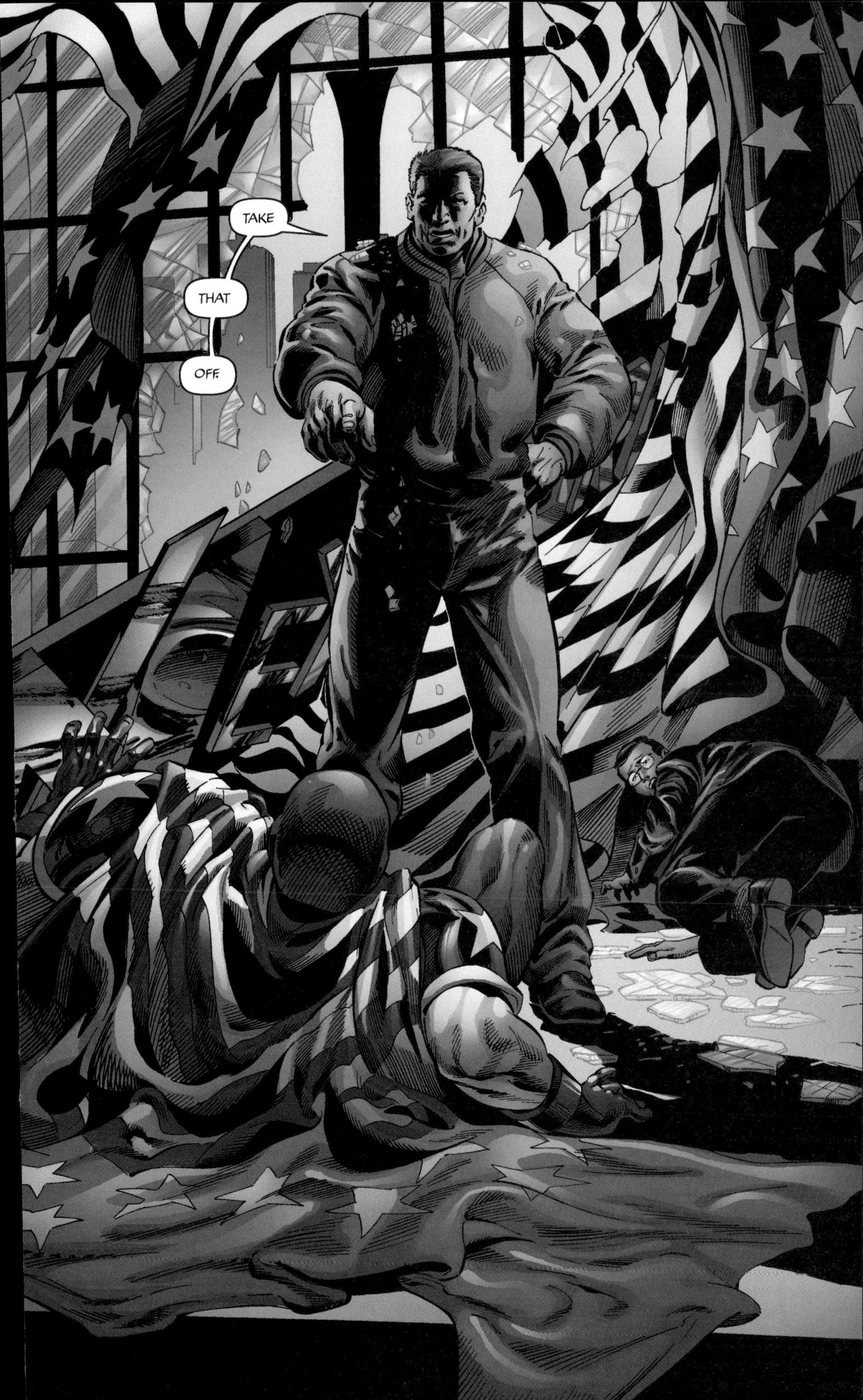
TAKE
THAT
OFF.

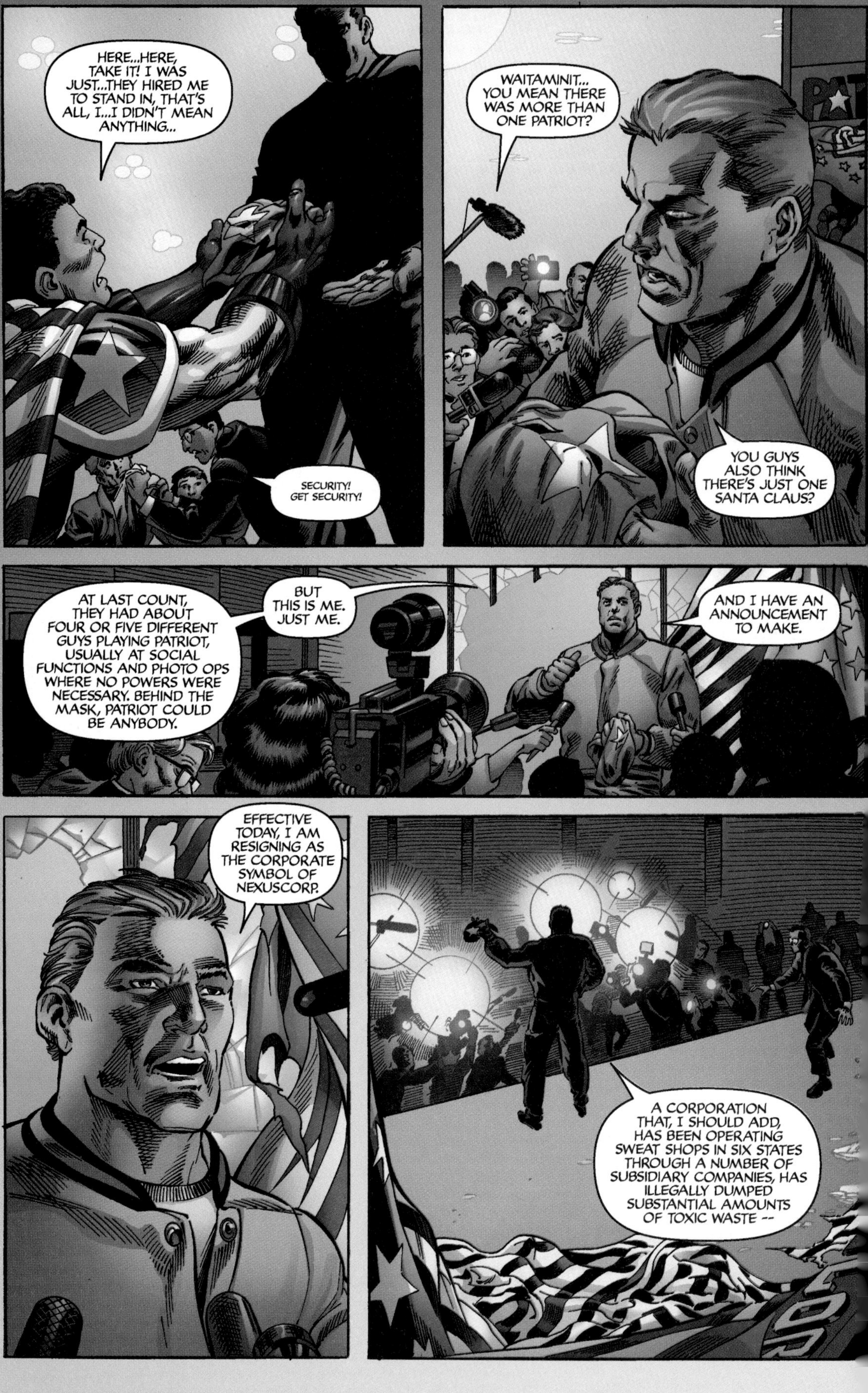
HERE...HERE, TAKE IT! I WAS JUST...THEY HIRED ME TO STAND IN, THAT'S ALL, I...I DIDN'T MEAN ANYTHING...
SECURITY! GET SECURITY!
WAITAMINIT... YOU MEAN THERE WAS MORE THAN ONE PATRIOT?
YOU GUYS ALSO THINK THERE'S JUST ONE SANTA CLAUS?
AT LAST COUNT, THEY HAD ABOUT FOUR OR FIVE DIFFERENT GUYS PLAYING PATRIOT, USUALLY AT SOCIAL FUNCTIONS AND PHOTO OPS WHERE NO POWERS WERE NECESSARY. BEHIND THE MASK, PATRIOT COULD BE ANYBODY.
BUT THIS IS ME. JUST ME.
AND I HAVE AN ANNOUNCEMENT TO MAKE.
EFFECTIVE TODAY, I AM RESIGNING AS THE CORPORATE SYMBOL OF NEXUSCORP.
A CORPORATION THAT, I SHOULD ADD, HAS BEEN OPERATING SWEAT SHOPS IN SIX STATES THROUGH A NUMBER OF SUBSIDIARY COMPANIES, HAS ILLEGALLY DUMPED SUBSTANTIAL AMOUNTS OF TOXIC WASTE --

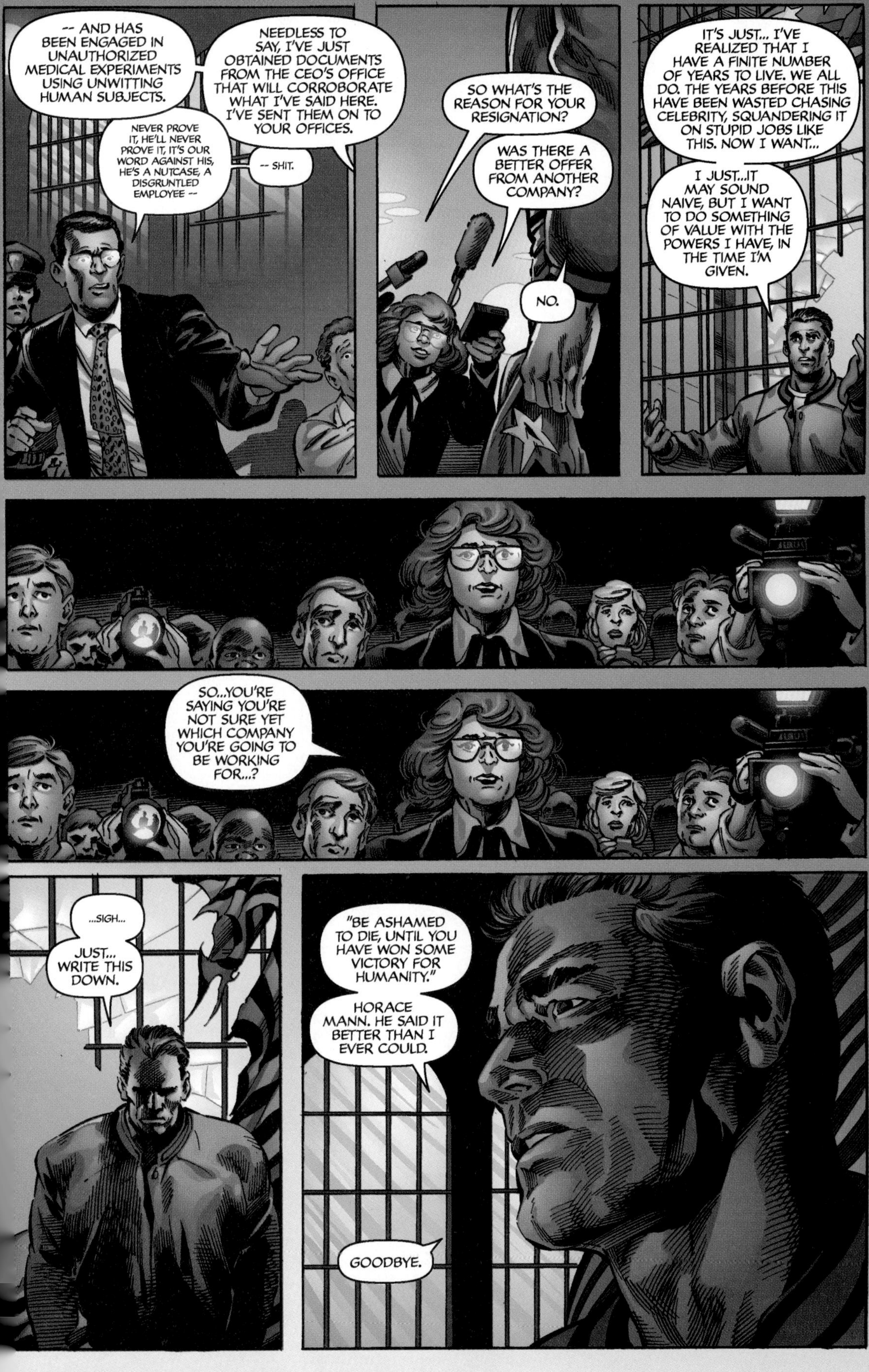
-- AND HAS BEEN ENGAGED IN UNAUTHORIZED MEDICAL EXPERIMENTS USING UNWITTING HUMAN SUBJECTS.
NEEDLESS TO SAY, I'VE JUST OBTAINED DOCUMENTS FROM THE CEO'S OFFICE THAT WILL CORROBORATE WHAT I'VE SAID HERE. I'VE SENT THEM ON TO YOUR OFFICES.
NEVER PROVE IT, HE'LL NEVER PROVE IT, IT'S OUR WORD AGAINST HIS, HE'S A NUTCASE, A DISGRUNTLED EMPLOYEE --
-- SHIT.
SO WHAT'S THE REASON FOR YOUR RESIGNATION?
WAS THERE A BETTER OFFER FROM ANOTHER COMPANY?
NO.
IT'S JUST... I'VE REALIZED THAT I HAVE A FINITE NUMBER OF YEARS TO LIVE. WE ALL DO. THE YEARS BEFORE THIS HAVE BEEN WASTED CHASING CELEBRITY, SQUANDERING IT ON STUPID JOBS LIKE THIS. NOW I WANT...
I JUST...IT MAY SOUND NAIVE, BUT I WANT TO DO SOMETHING OF VALUE WITH THE POWERS I HAVE, IN THE TIME I'M GIVEN.
SO...YOU'RE SAYING YOU'RE NOT SURE YET WHICH COMPANY YOU'RE GOING TO BE WORKING FOR...?
...SIGH...
JUST... WRITE THIS DOWN.
"BE ASHAMED TO DIE, UNTIL YOU HAVE WON SOME VICTORY FOR HUMANITY."
HORACE MANN. HE SAID IT BETTER THAN I EVER COULD.
GOODBYE.

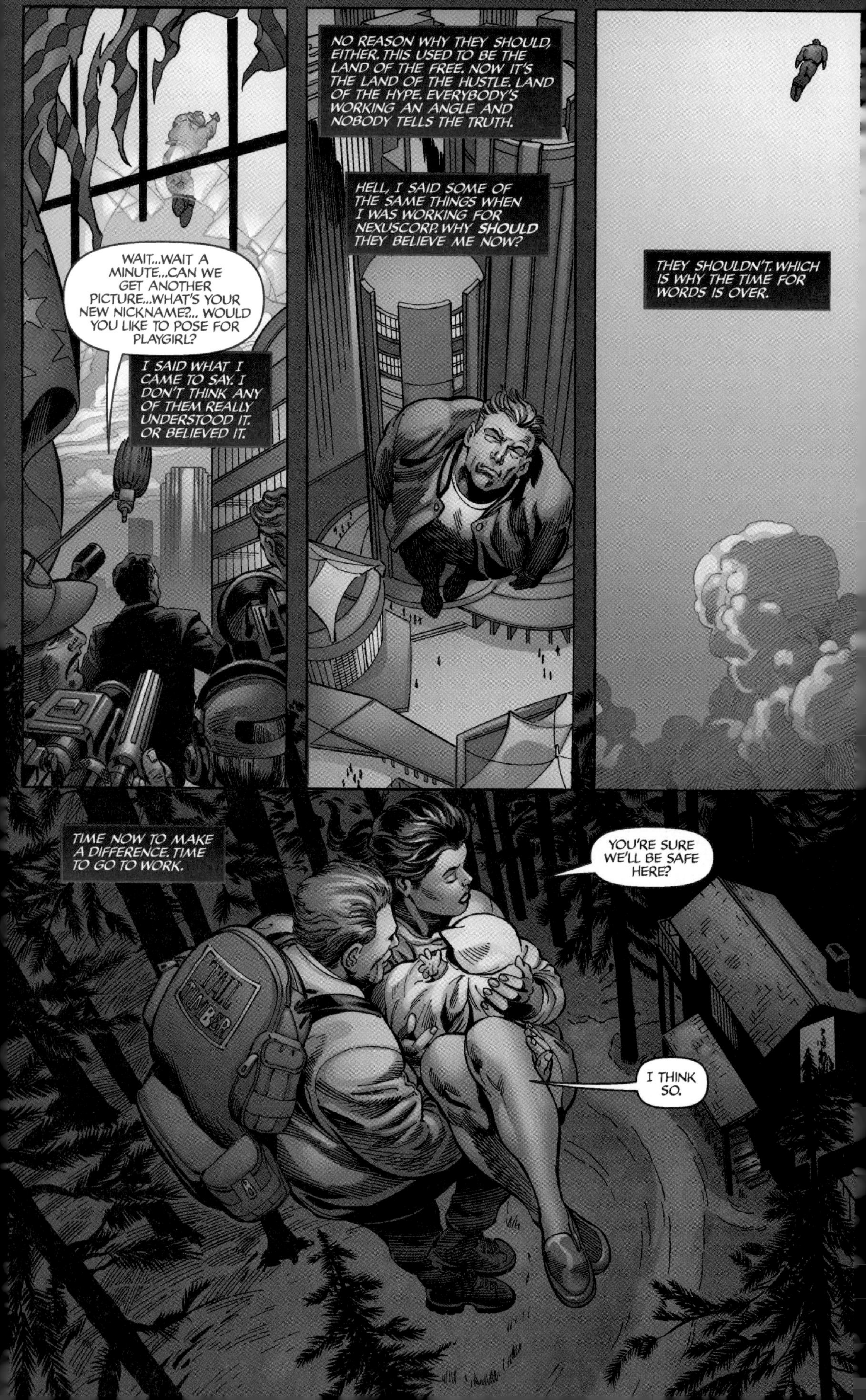
WAIT...WAIT A MINUTE...CAN WE GET ANOTHER PICTURE...WHAT'S YOUR NEW NICKNAME?... WOULD YOU LIKE TO POSE FOR PLAYGIRL?
I SAID WHAT I CAME TO SAY. I DON'T THINK ANY OF THEM REALLY UNDERSTOOD IT. OR BELIEVED IT.
NO REASON WHY THEY SHOULD, EITHER. THIS USED TO BE THE LAND OF THE FREE. NOW IT'S THE LAND OF THE HUSTLE. LAND OF THE HYPE. EVERYBODY'S WORKING AN ANGLE AND NOBODY TELLS THE TRUTH.
HELL, I SAID SOME OF THE SAME THINGS WHEN I WAS WORKING FOR NEXUSCORP. WHY SHOULD THEY BELIEVE ME NOW?
THEY SHOULDN'T. WHICH IS WHY THE TIME FOR WORDS IS OVER.
TIME NOW TO MAKE A DIFFERENCE. TIME TO GO TO WORK.
YOU'RE SURE WE'LL BE SAFE HERE?
I THINK SO.
TALL TIMBER

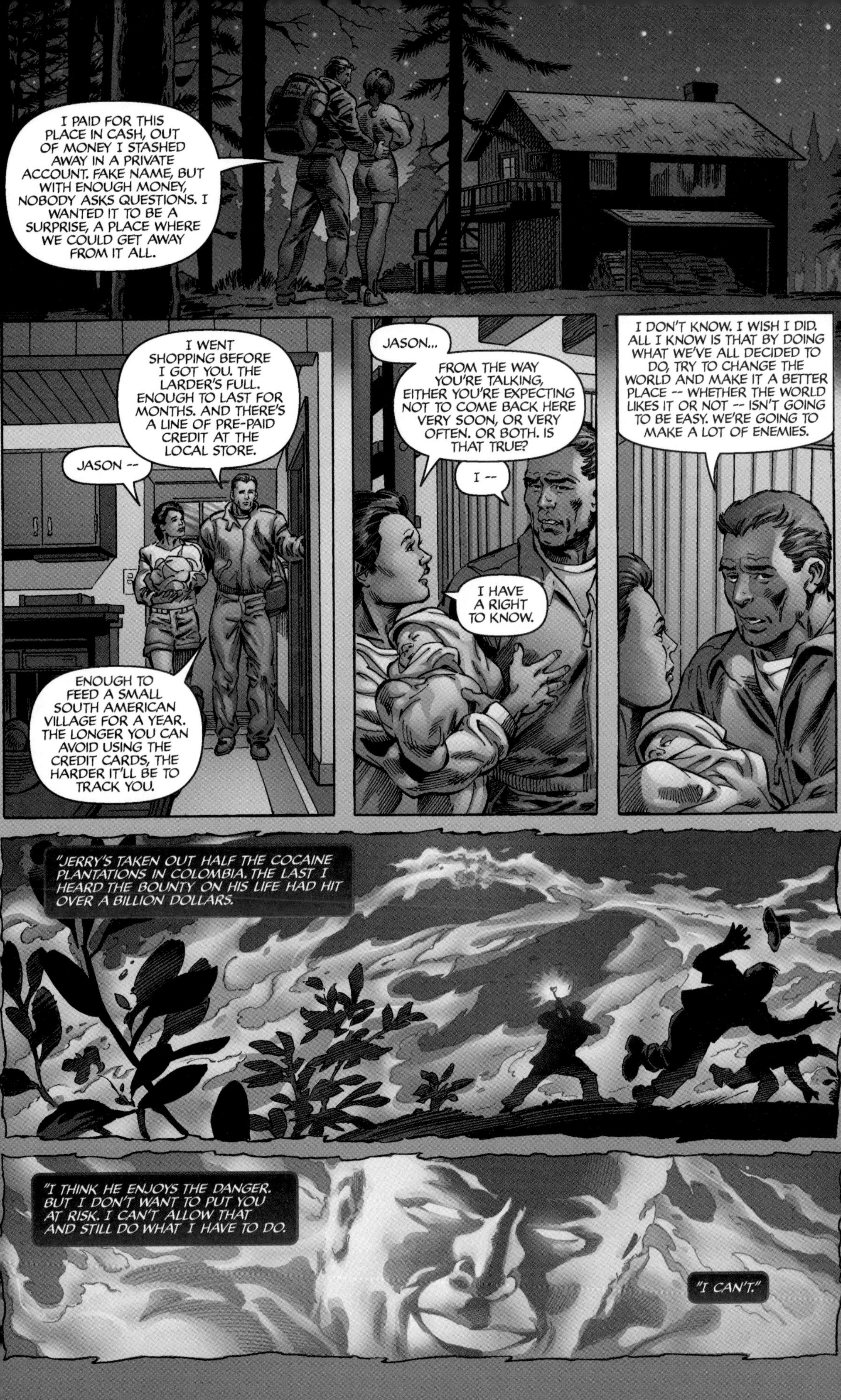
I PAID FOR THIS PLACE IN CASH, OUT OF MONEY I STASHED AWAY IN A PRIVATE ACCOUNT. FAKE NAME, BUT WITH ENOUGH MONEY, NOBODY ASKS QUESTIONS. I WANTED IT TO BE A SURPRISE, A PLACE WHERE WE COULD GET AWAY FROM IT ALL.
I WENT SHOPPING BEFORE I GOT YOU. THE LARDER'S FULL. ENOUGH TO LAST FOR MONTHS. AND THERE'S A LINE OF PRE-PAID CREDIT AT THE LOCAL STORE.
JASON --
ENOUGH TO FEED A SMALL SOUTH AMERICAN VILLAGE FOR A YEAR. THE LONGER YOU CAN AVOID USING THE CREDIT CARDS, THE HARDER IT'LL BE TO TRACK YOU.
JASON...
FROM THE WAY YOU'RE TALKING, EITHER YOU'RE EXPECTING NOT TO COME BACK HERE VERY SOON, OR VERY OFTEN. OR BOTH. IS THAT TRUE?
I --
I HAVE A RIGHT TO KNOW.
I DON'T KNOW. I WISH I DID. ALL I KNOW IS THAT BY DOING WHAT WE'VE ALL DECIDED TO DO, TRY TO CHANGE THE WORLD AND MAKE IT A BETTER PLACE -- WHETHER THE WORLD LIKES IT OR NOT -- ISN'T GOING TO BE EASY. WE'RE GOING TO MAKE A LOT OF ENEMIES.
"JERRY'S TAKEN OUT HALF THE COCAINE PLANTATIONS IN COLOMBIA. THE LAST I HEARD THE BOUNTY ON HIS LIFE HAD HIT OVER A BILLION DOLLARS.
"I THINK HE ENJOYS THE DANGER. BUT I DON'T WANT TO PUT YOU AT RISK. I CAN'T ALLOW THAT AND STILL DO WHAT I HAVE TO DO.
"I CAN'T."

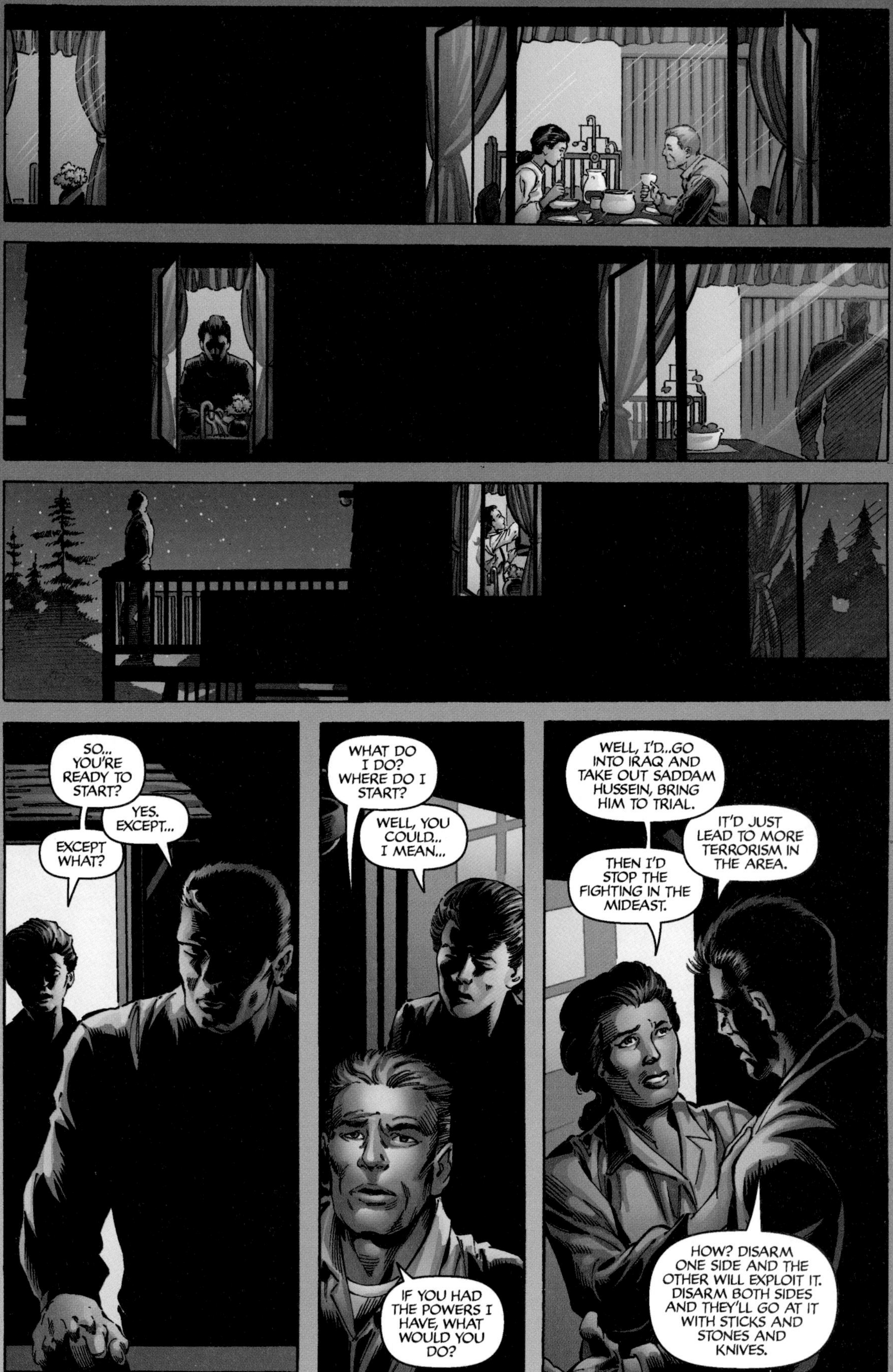
SO... YOU'RE READY TO START?
YES. EXCEPT...
EXCEPT WHAT?
WHAT DO I DO? WHERE DO I START?
WELL, YOU COULD... I MEAN...
IF YOU HAD THE POWERS I HAVE, WHAT WOULD YOU DO?
WELL, I'D...GO INTO IRAQ AND TAKE OUT SADDAM HUSSEIN, BRING HIM TO TRIAL.
IT'D JUST LEAD TO MORE TERRORISM IN THE AREA.
THEN I'D STOP THE FIGHTING IN THE MIDEAST.
HOW? DISARM ONE SIDE AND THE OTHER WILL EXPLOIT IT. DISARM BOTH SIDES AND THEY'LL GO AT IT WITH STICKS AND STONES AND KNIVES.

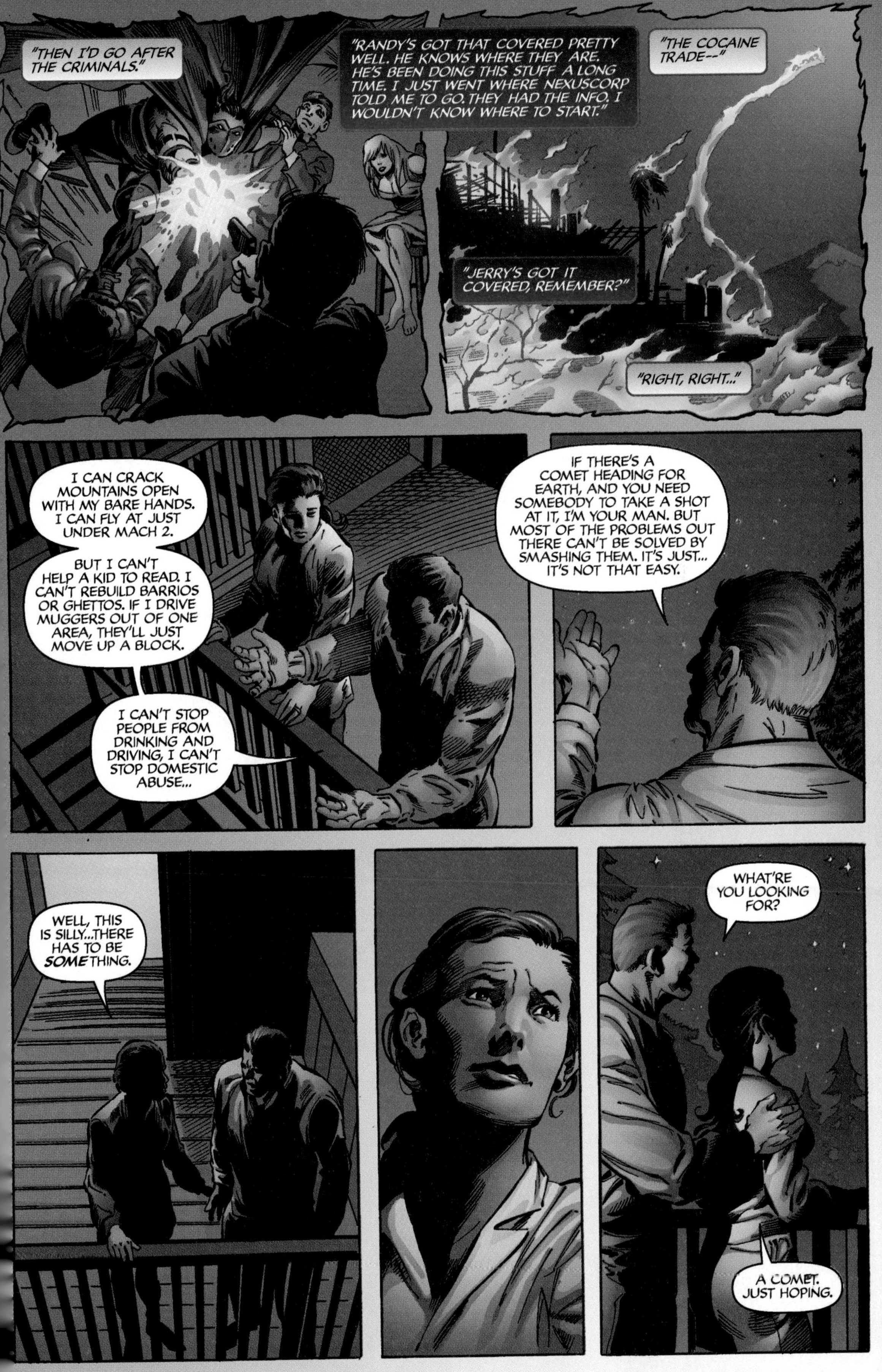
"THEN I'D GO AFTER THE CRIMINALS."
"RANDY'S GOT THAT COVERED PRETTY WELL. HE KNOWS WHERE THEY ARE. HE'S BEEN DOING THIS STUFF A LONG TIME. I JUST WENT WHERE NEXUSCORP TOLD ME TO GO. THEY HAD THE INFO. I WOULDN'T KNOW WHERE TO START."
"THE COCAINE TRADE--"
"JERRY'S GOT IT COVERED, REMEMBER?"
"RIGHT, RIGHT..."
I CAN CRACK MOUNTAINS OPEN WITH MY BARE HANDS. I CAN FLY AT JUST UNDER MACH 2.
BUT I CAN'T HELP A KID TO READ. I CAN'T REBUILD BARRIOS OR GHETTOS. IF I DRIVE MUGGERS OUT OF ONE AREA, THEY'LL JUST MOVE UP A BLOCK.
I CAN'T STOP PEOPLE FROM DRINKING AND DRIVING, I CAN'T STOP DOMESTIC ABUSE...
IF THERE'S A COMET HEADING FOR EARTH, AND YOU NEED SOMEBODY TO TAKE A SHOT AT IT, I'M YOUR MAN. BUT MOST OF THE PROBLEMS OUT THERE CAN'T BE SOLVED BY SMASHING THEM. IT'S JUST... IT'S NOT THAT EASY.
WELL, THIS IS SILLY...THERE HAS TO BE SOMETHING.
WHAT'RE YOU LOOKING FOR?
A COMET. JUST HOPING.

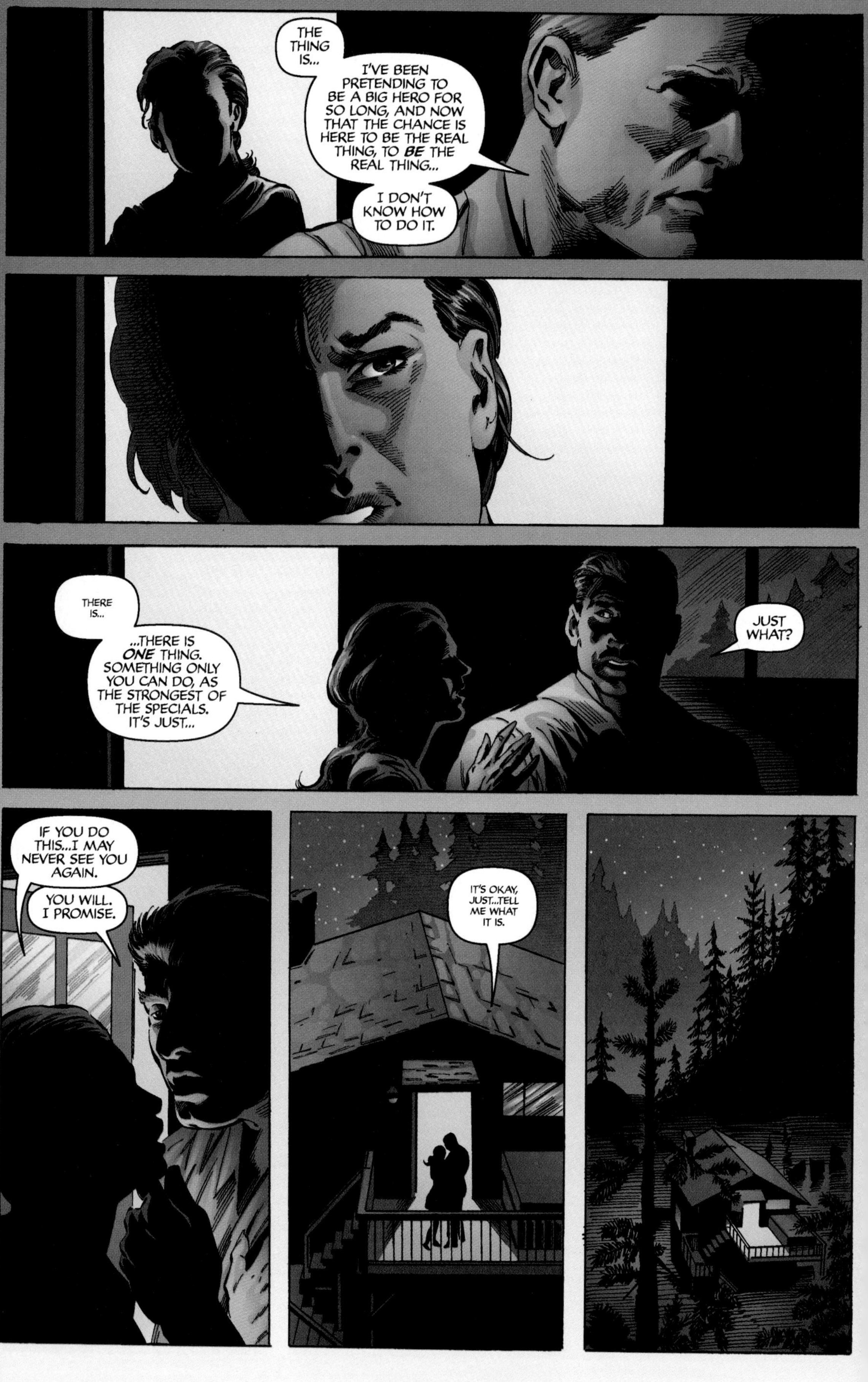
THE THING IS...
I'VE BEEN PRETENDING TO BE A BIG HERO FOR SO LONG, AND NOW THAT THE CHANCE IS HERE TO BE THE REAL THING, TO *BE* THE REAL THING...
I DON'T KNOW HOW TO DO IT.
THERE IS...
...THERE IS *ONE* THING. SOMETHING ONLY YOU CAN DO, AS THE STRONGEST OF THE SPECIALS. IT'S JUST...
JUST WHAT?
IF YOU DO THIS...I MAY NEVER SEE YOU AGAIN.
YOU WILL. I PROMISE.
IT'S OKAY, JUST...TELL ME WHAT IT IS.

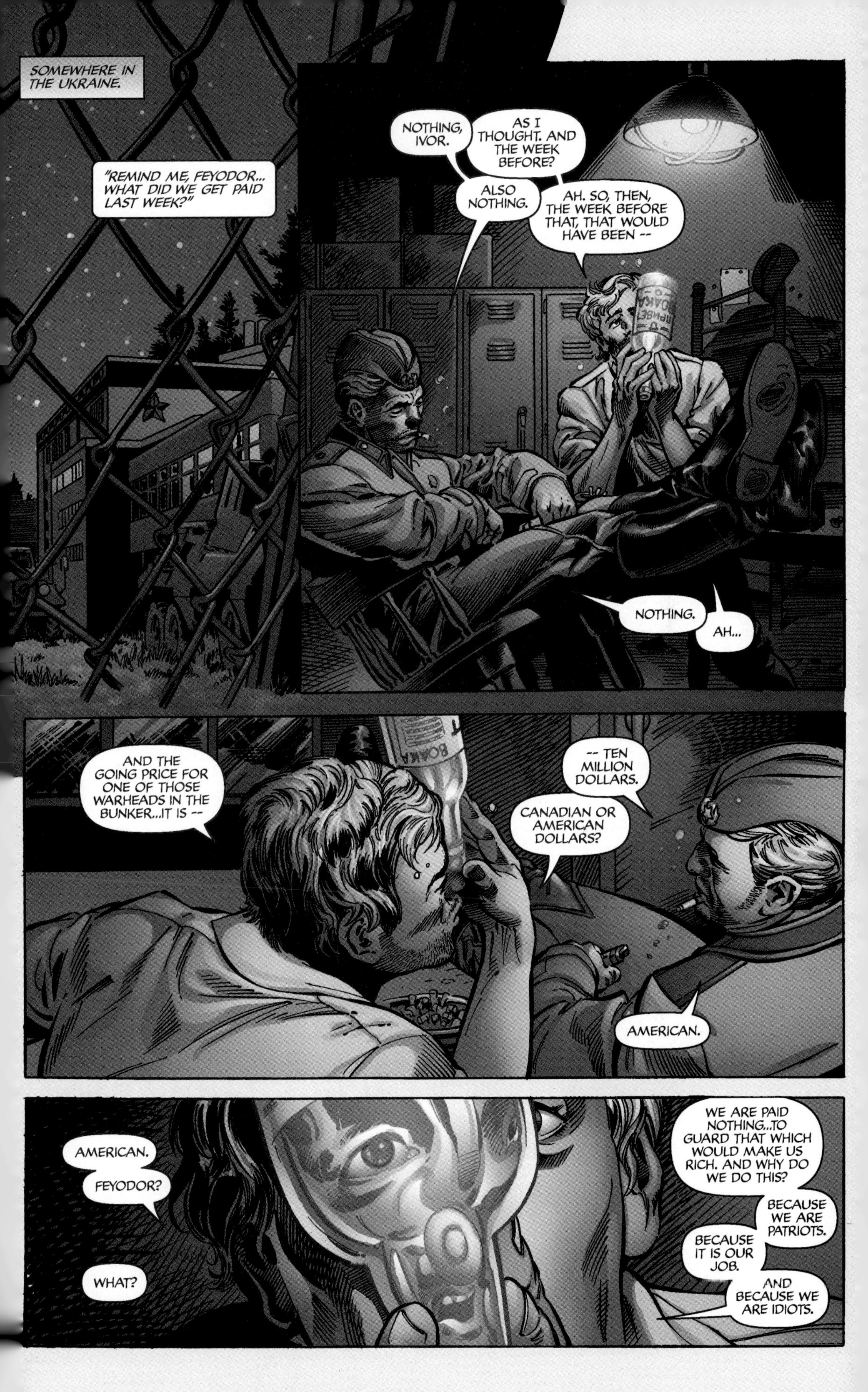
SOMEWHERE IN THE UKRAINE.
"REMIND ME, FEYODOR... WHAT DID WE GET PAID LAST WEEK?"
NOTHING, IVOR.
AS I THOUGHT. AND THE WEEK BEFORE?
ALSO NOTHING.
AH. SO, THEN, THE WEEK BEFORE THAT, THAT WOULD HAVE BEEN --
NOTHING.
AH...
AND THE GOING PRICE FOR ONE OF THOSE WARHEADS IN THE BUNKER...IT IS --
-- TEN MILLION DOLLARS.
CANADIAN OR AMERICAN DOLLARS?
AMERICAN.
AMERICAN.
FEYODOR?
WHAT?
WE ARE PAID NOTHING...TO GUARD THAT WHICH WOULD MAKE US RICH. AND WHY DO WE DO THIS?
BECAUSE WE ARE PATRIOTS.
BECAUSE IT IS OUR JOB.
AND BECAUSE WE ARE IDIOTS.

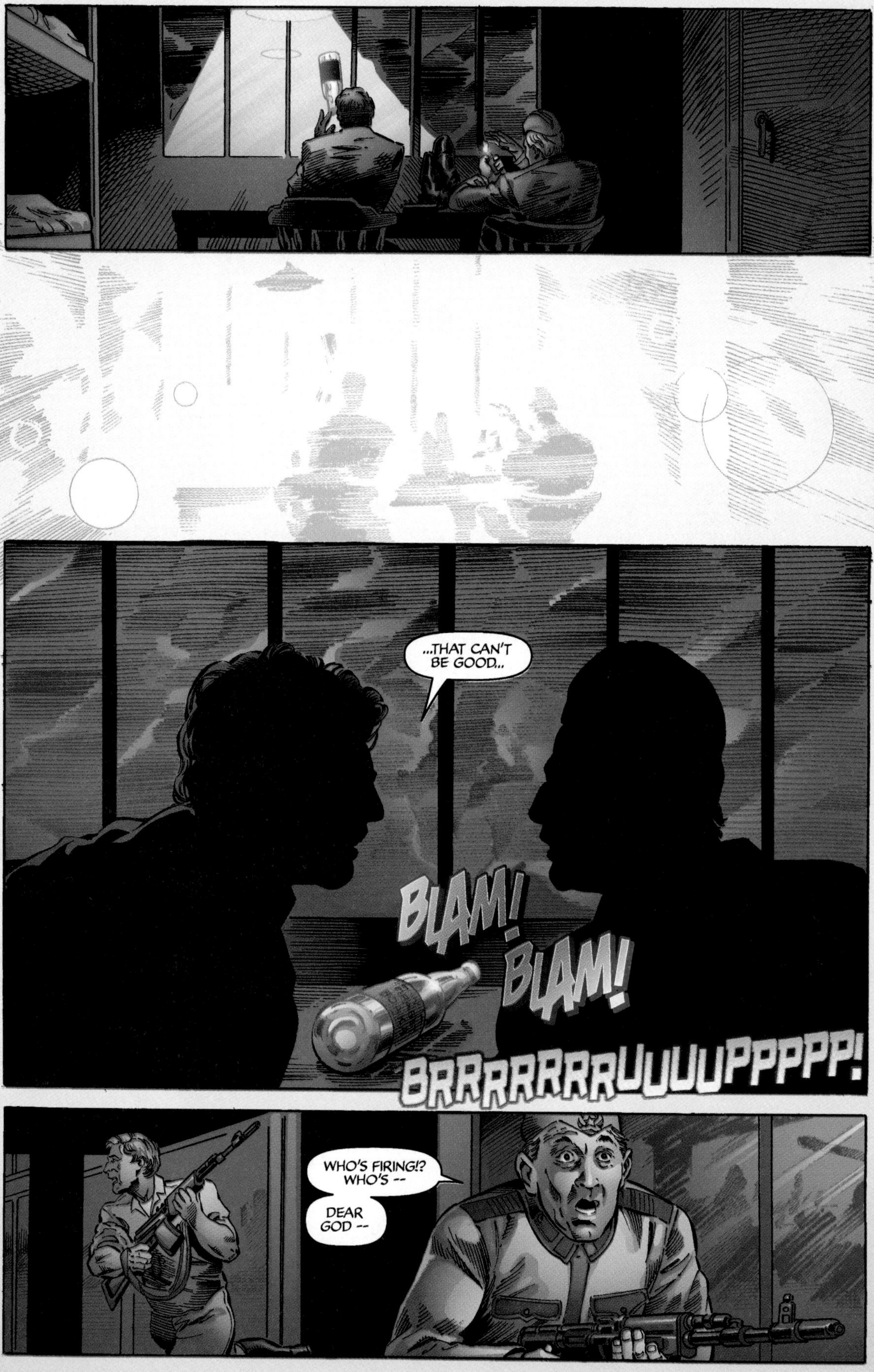
...THAT CAN'T BE GOOD...
BLAM!
BLAM!
BRRRRRRRUUUUPPPPP!
WHO'S FIRING!? WHO'S --
DEAR GOD --

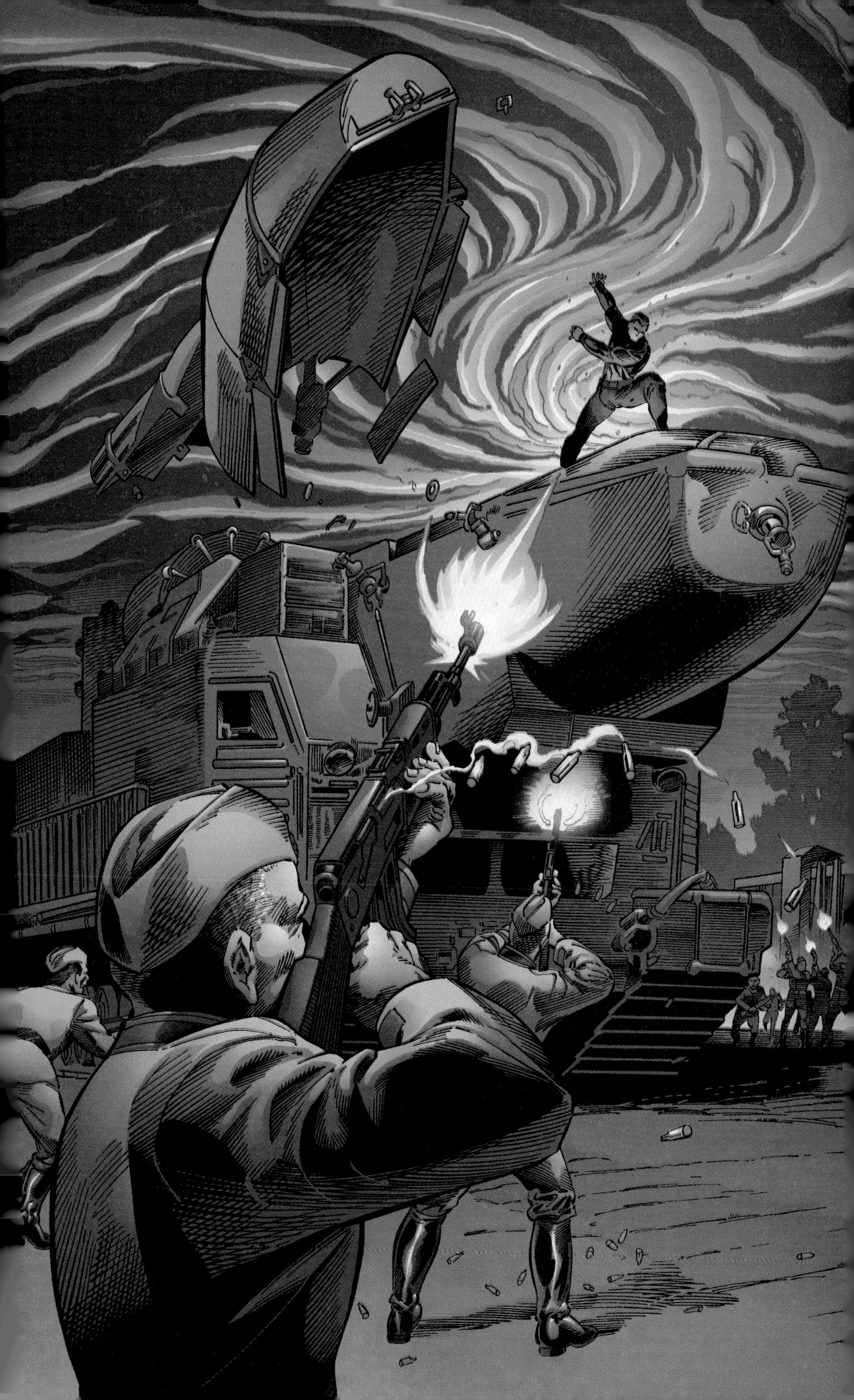

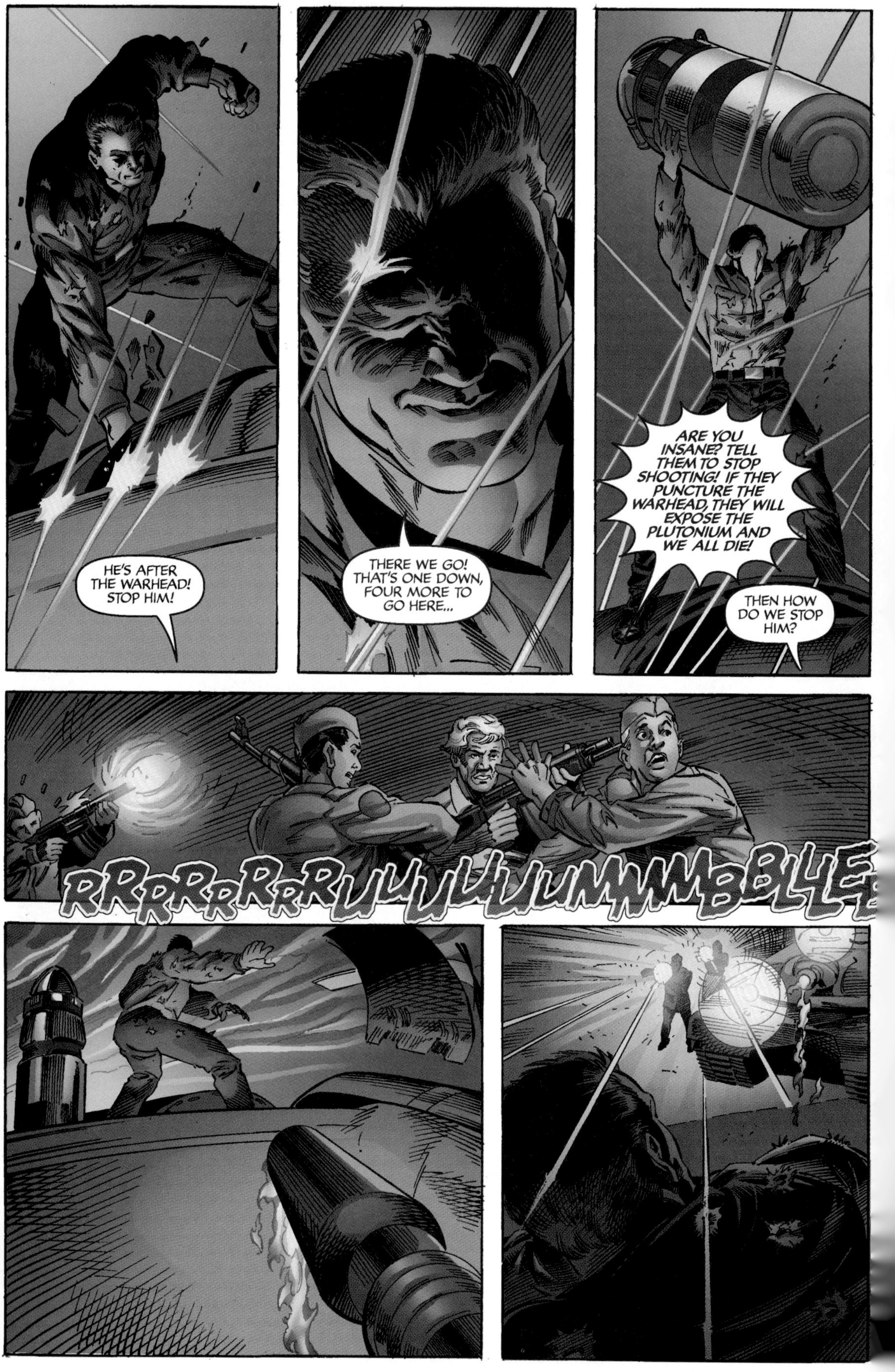
HE'S AFTER THE WARHEAD! STOP HIM!
THERE WE GO! THAT'S ONE DOWN, FOUR MORE TO GO HERE...
ARE YOU INSANE? TELL THEM TO STOP SHOOTING! IF THEY PUNCTURE THE WARHEAD, THEY WILL EXPOSE THE PLUTONIUM AND WE ALL DIE!
THEN HOW DO WE STOP HIM?
RRRRRRRRRUUUUUUUMMMMBBLLE

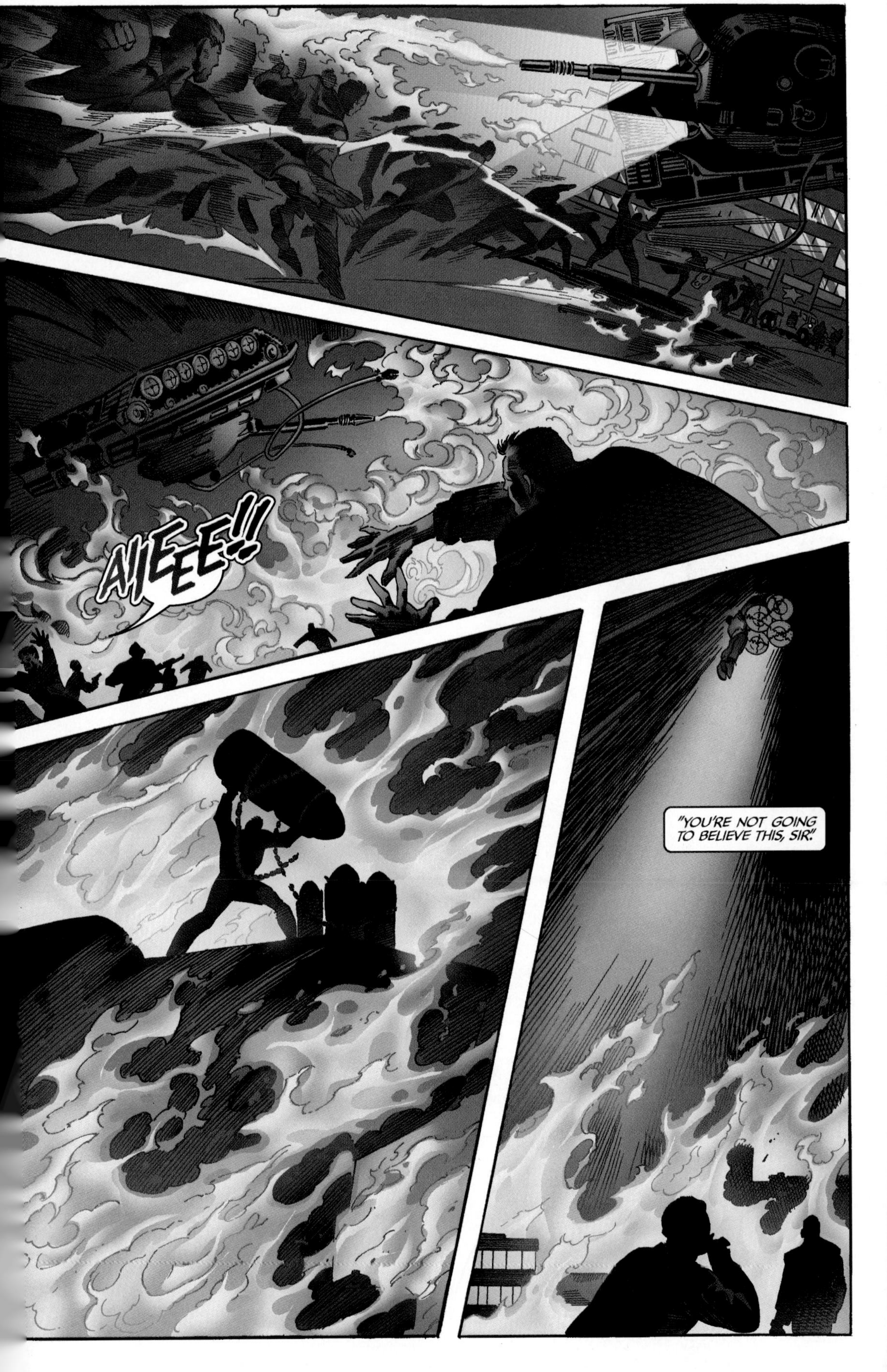
AIIEEE!!
"YOU'RE NOT GOING TO BELIEVE THIS, SIR."

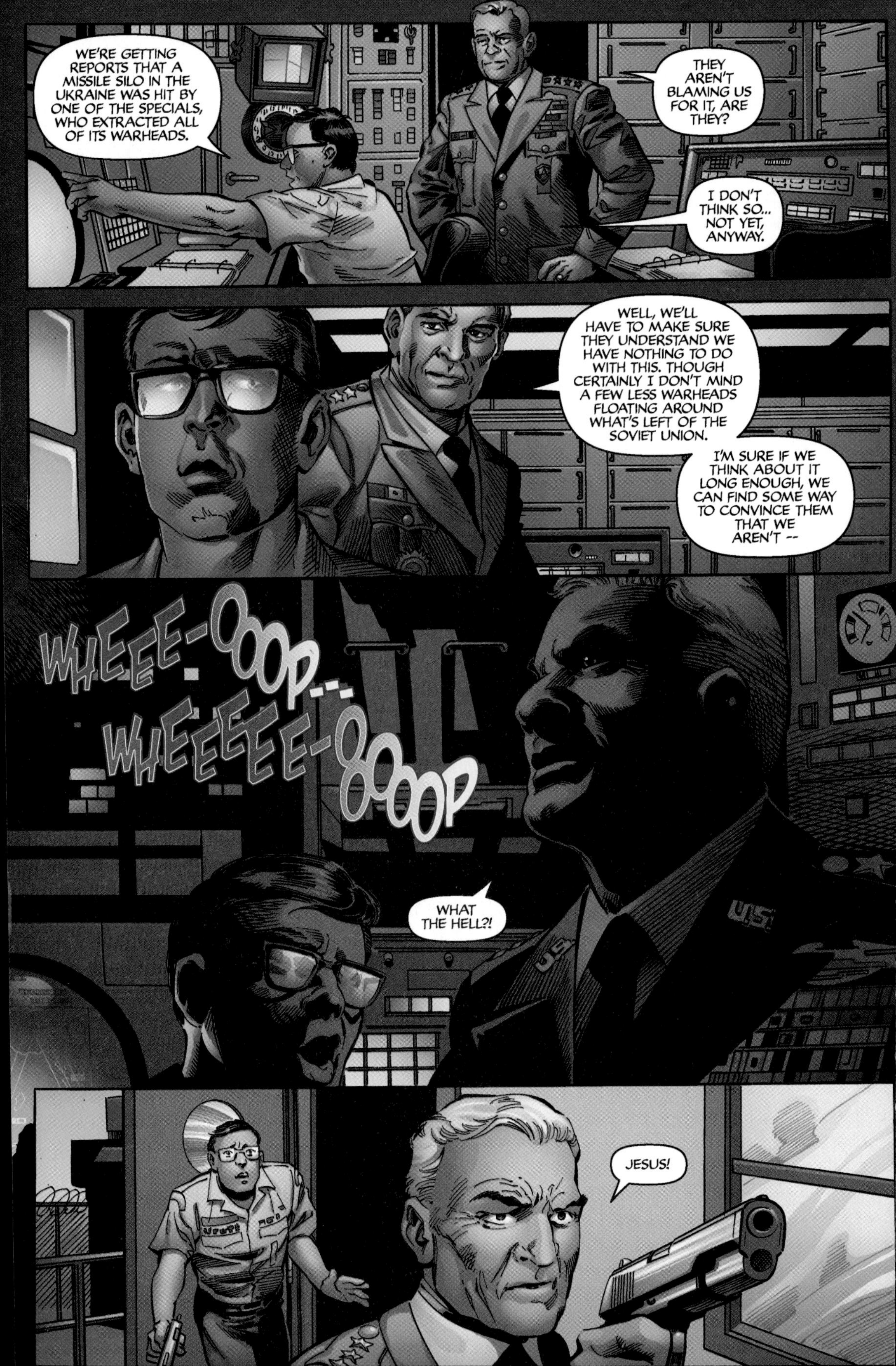
WE'RE GETTING REPORTS THAT A MISSILE SILO IN THE UKRAINE WAS HIT BY ONE OF THE SPECIALS, WHO EXTRACTED ALL OF ITS WARHEADS.
THEY AREN'T BLAMING US FOR IT, ARE THEY?
I DON'T THINK SO... NOT YET, ANYWAY.
WELL, WE'LL HAVE TO MAKE SURE THEY UNDERSTAND WE HAVE NOTHING TO DO WITH THIS. THOUGH CERTAINLY I DON'T MIND A FEW LESS WARHEADS FLOATING AROUND WHAT'S LEFT OF THE SOVIET UNION.
I'M SURE IF WE THINK ABOUT IT LONG ENOUGH, WE CAN FIND SOME WAY TO CONVINCE THEM THAT WE AREN'T --
WHEEE-OOOP... WHEEEEE-OOOOP
WHAT THE HELL?!
JESUS!

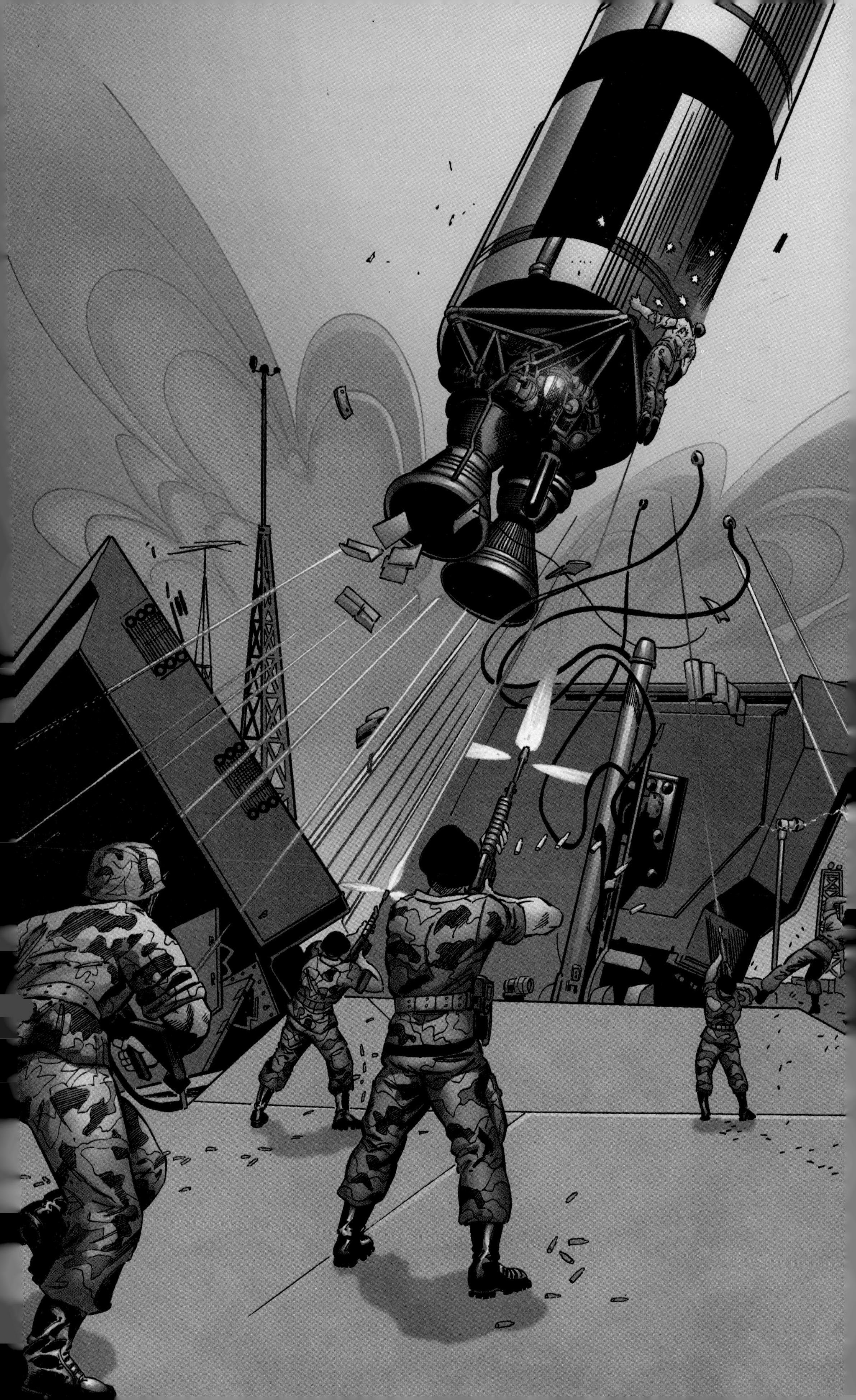

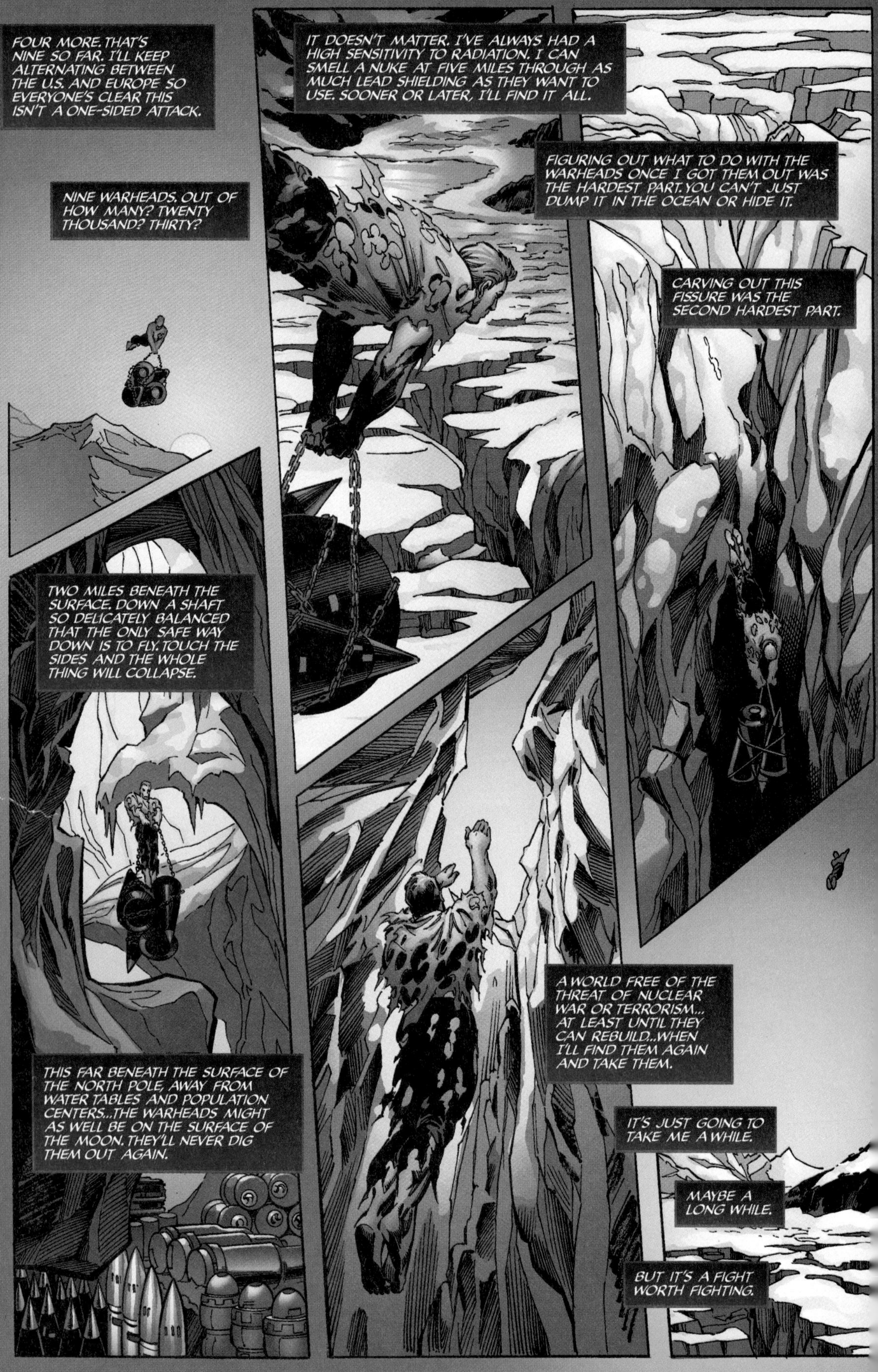
FOUR MORE. THAT'S NINE SO FAR. I'LL KEEP ALTERNATING BETWEEN THE U.S. AND EUROPE SO EVERYONE'S CLEAR THIS ISN'T A ONE-SIDED ATTACK.
NINE WARHEADS. OUT OF HOW MANY? TWENTY THOUSAND? THIRTY?
IT DOESN'T MATTER. I'VE ALWAYS HAD A HIGH SENSITIVITY TO RADIATION. I CAN SMELL A NUKE AT FIVE MILES THROUGH AS MUCH LEAD SHIELDING AS THEY WANT TO USE. SOONER OR LATER, I'LL FIND IT ALL.
FIGURING OUT WHAT TO DO WITH THE WARHEADS ONCE I GOT THEM OUT WAS THE HARDEST PART. YOU CAN'T JUST DUMP IT IN THE OCEAN OR HIDE IT.
CARVING OUT THIS FISSURE WAS THE SECOND HARDEST PART.
TWO MILES BENEATH THE SURFACE. DOWN A SHAFT SO DELICATELY BALANCED THAT THE ONLY SAFE WAY DOWN IS TO FLY. TOUCH THE SIDES AND THE WHOLE THING WILL COLLAPSE.
THIS FAR BENEATH THE SURFACE OF THE NORTH POLE, AWAY FROM WATER TABLES AND POPULATION CENTERS...THE WARHEADS MIGHT AS WELL BE ON THE SURFACE OF THE MOON. THEY'LL NEVER DIG THEM OUT AGAIN.
A WORLD FREE OF THE THREAT OF NUCLEAR WAR OR TERRORISM... AT LEAST UNTIL THEY CAN REBUILD...WHEN I'LL FIND THEM AGAIN AND TAKE THEM.
IT'S JUST GOING TO TAKE ME A WHILE.
MAYBE A LONG WHILE.
BUT IT'S A FIGHT WORTH FIGHTING.

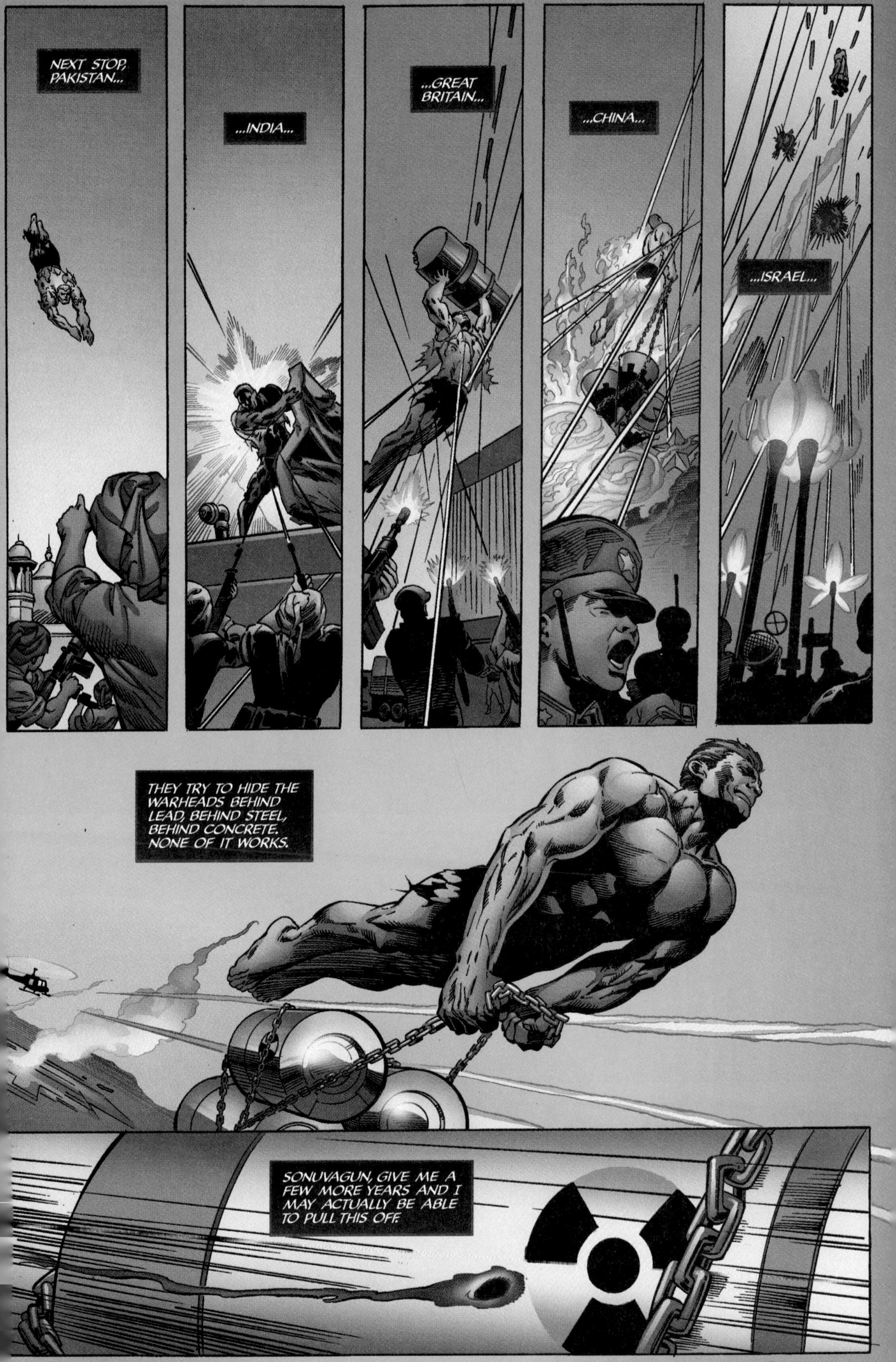
NEXT STOP, PAKISTAN...
...INDIA...
...GREAT BRITAIN...
...CHINA...
...ISRAEL...
THEY TRY TO HIDE THE WARHEADS BEHIND LEAD, BEHIND STEEL, BEHIND CONCRETE. NONE OF IT WORKS.
SONUVAGUN, GIVE ME A FEW MORE YEARS AND I MAY ACTUALLY BE ABLE TO PULL THIS OFF.

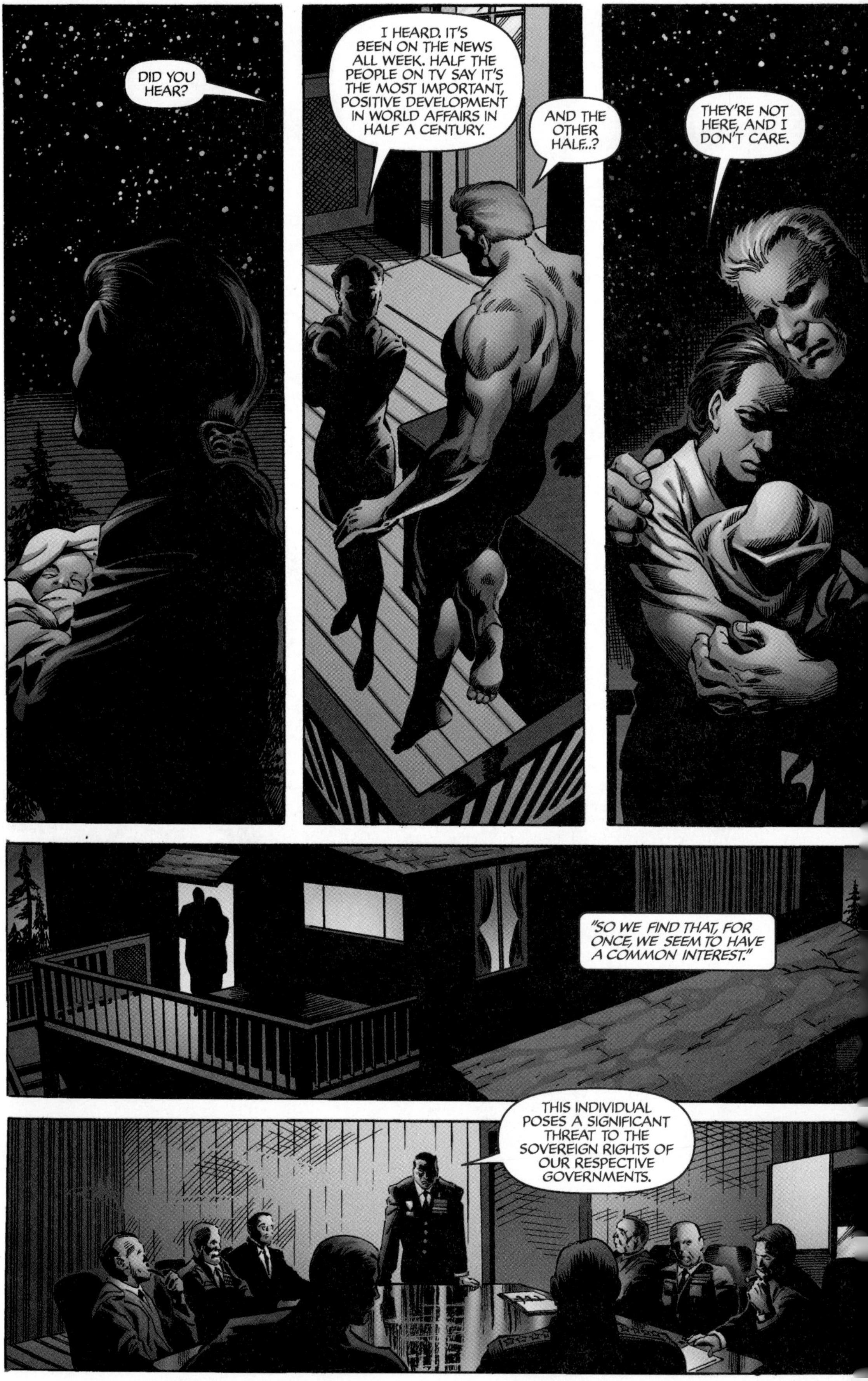
DID YOU HEAR?
I HEARD. IT'S BEEN ON THE NEWS ALL WEEK. HALF THE PEOPLE ON TV SAY IT'S THE MOST IMPORTANT, POSITIVE DEVELOPMENT IN WORLD AFFAIRS IN HALF A CENTURY.
AND THE OTHER HALF..?
THEY'RE NOT HERE, AND I DON'T CARE.
"SO WE FIND THAT, FOR ONCE, WE SEEM TO HAVE A COMMON INTEREST."
THIS INDIVIDUAL POSES A SIGNIFICANT THREAT TO THE SOVEREIGN RIGHTS OF OUR RESPECTIVE GOVERNMENTS.

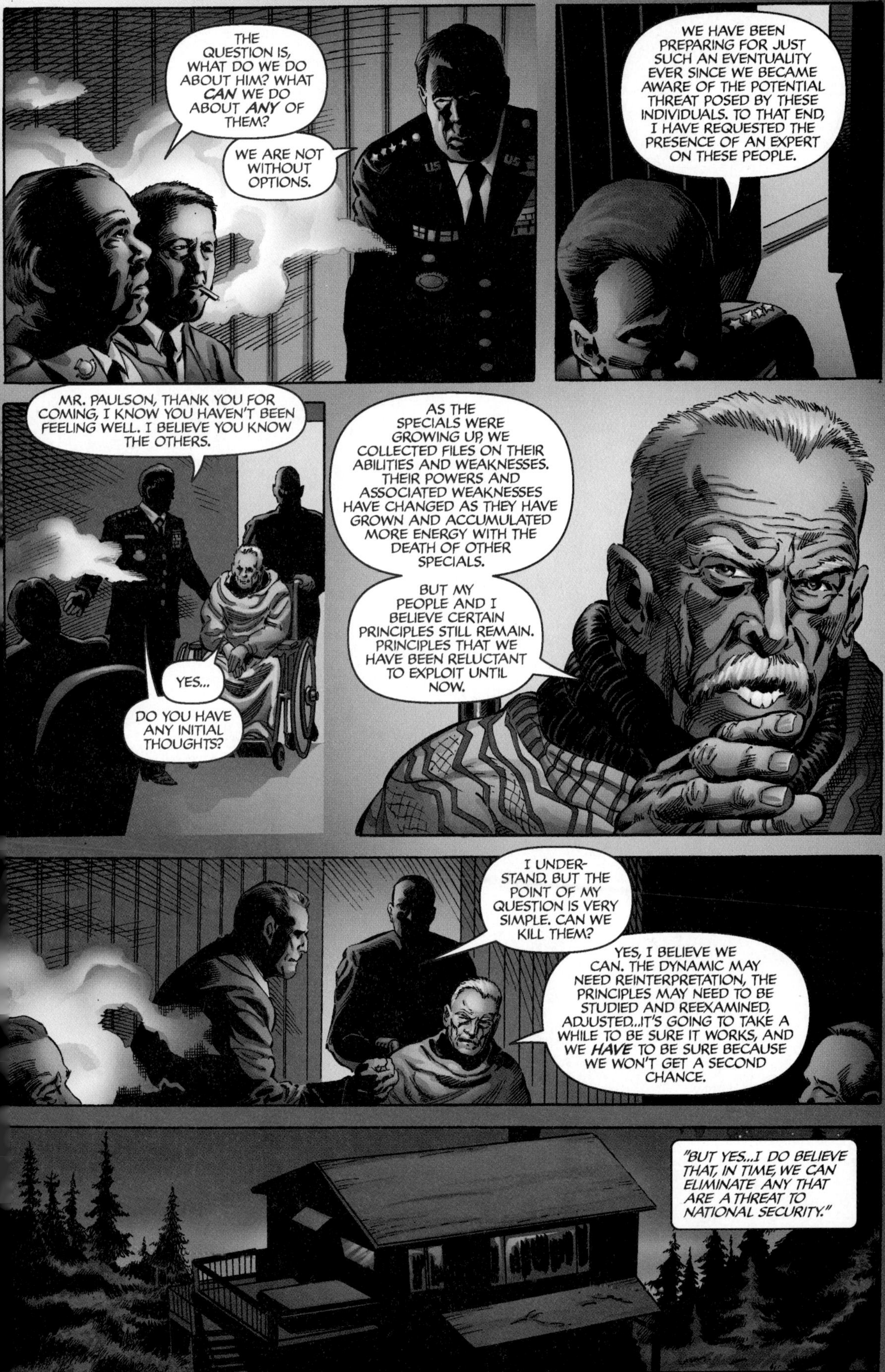

THE QUESTION IS, WHAT DO WE DO ABOUT HIM? WHAT *CAN* WE DO ABOUT *ANY* OF THEM?
WE ARE NOT WITHOUT OPTIONS.
WE HAVE BEEN PREPARING FOR JUST SUCH AN EVENTUALITY EVER SINCE WE BECAME AWARE OF THE POTENTIAL THREAT POSED BY THESE INDIVIDUALS. TO THAT END, I HAVE REQUESTED THE PRESENCE OF AN EXPERT ON THESE PEOPLE.
MR. PAULSON, THANK YOU FOR COMING, I KNOW YOU HAVEN'T BEEN FEELING WELL. I BELIEVE YOU KNOW THE OTHERS.
YES...
DO YOU HAVE ANY INITIAL THOUGHTS?
AS THE SPECIALS WERE GROWING UP, WE COLLECTED FILES ON THEIR ABILITIES AND WEAKNESSES. THEIR POWERS AND ASSOCIATED WEAKNESSES HAVE CHANGED AS THEY HAVE GROWN AND ACCUMULATED MORE ENERGY WITH THE DEATH OF OTHER SPECIALS.
BUT MY PEOPLE AND I BELIEVE CERTAIN PRINCIPLES STILL REMAIN. PRINCIPLES THAT WE HAVE BEEN RELUCTANT TO EXPLOIT UNTIL NOW.
I UNDER-STAND. BUT THE POINT OF MY QUESTION IS VERY SIMPLE. CAN WE KILL THEM?
YES, I BELIEVE WE CAN. THE DYNAMIC MAY NEED REINTERPRETATION, THE PRINCIPLES MAY NEED TO BE STUDIED AND REEXAMINED, ADJUSTED...IT'S GOING TO TAKE A WHILE TO BE SURE IT WORKS, AND WE *HAVE* TO BE SURE BECAUSE WE WON'T GET A SECOND CHANCE.
"BUT YES...I DO BELIEVE THAT, IN TIME, WE CAN ELIMINATE ANY THAT ARE A THREAT TO NATIONAL SECURITY."

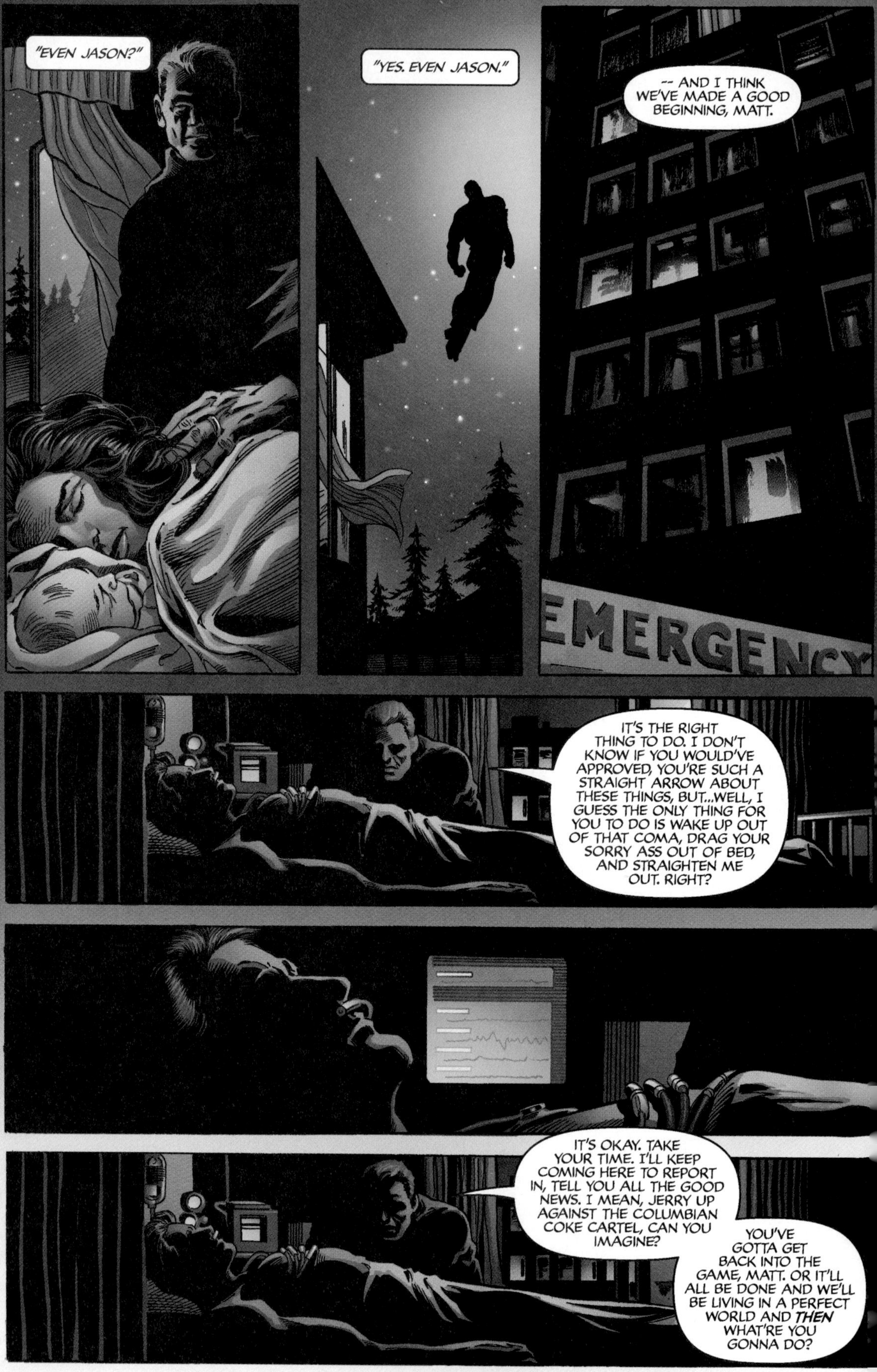
"EVEN JASON?"
"YES. EVEN JASON."
-- AND I THINK WE'VE MADE A GOOD BEGINNING, MATT.
EMERGENCY
IT'S THE RIGHT THING TO DO. I DON'T KNOW IF YOU WOULD'VE APPROVED, YOU'RE SUCH A STRAIGHT ARROW ABOUT THESE THINGS, BUT...WELL, I GUESS THE ONLY THING FOR YOU TO DO IS WAKE UP OUT OF THAT COMA, DRAG YOUR SORRY ASS OUT OF BED, AND STRAIGHTEN ME OUT. RIGHT?
IT'S OKAY. TAKE YOUR TIME. I'LL KEEP COMING HERE TO REPORT IN, TELL YOU ALL THE GOOD NEWS. I MEAN, JERRY UP AGAINST THE COLUMBIAN COKE CARTEL, CAN YOU IMAGINE?
YOU'VE GOTTA GET BACK INTO THE GAME, MATT. OR IT'LL ALL BE DONE AND WE'LL BE LIVING IN A PERFECT WORLD AND *THEN* WHAT'RE YOU GONNA DO?

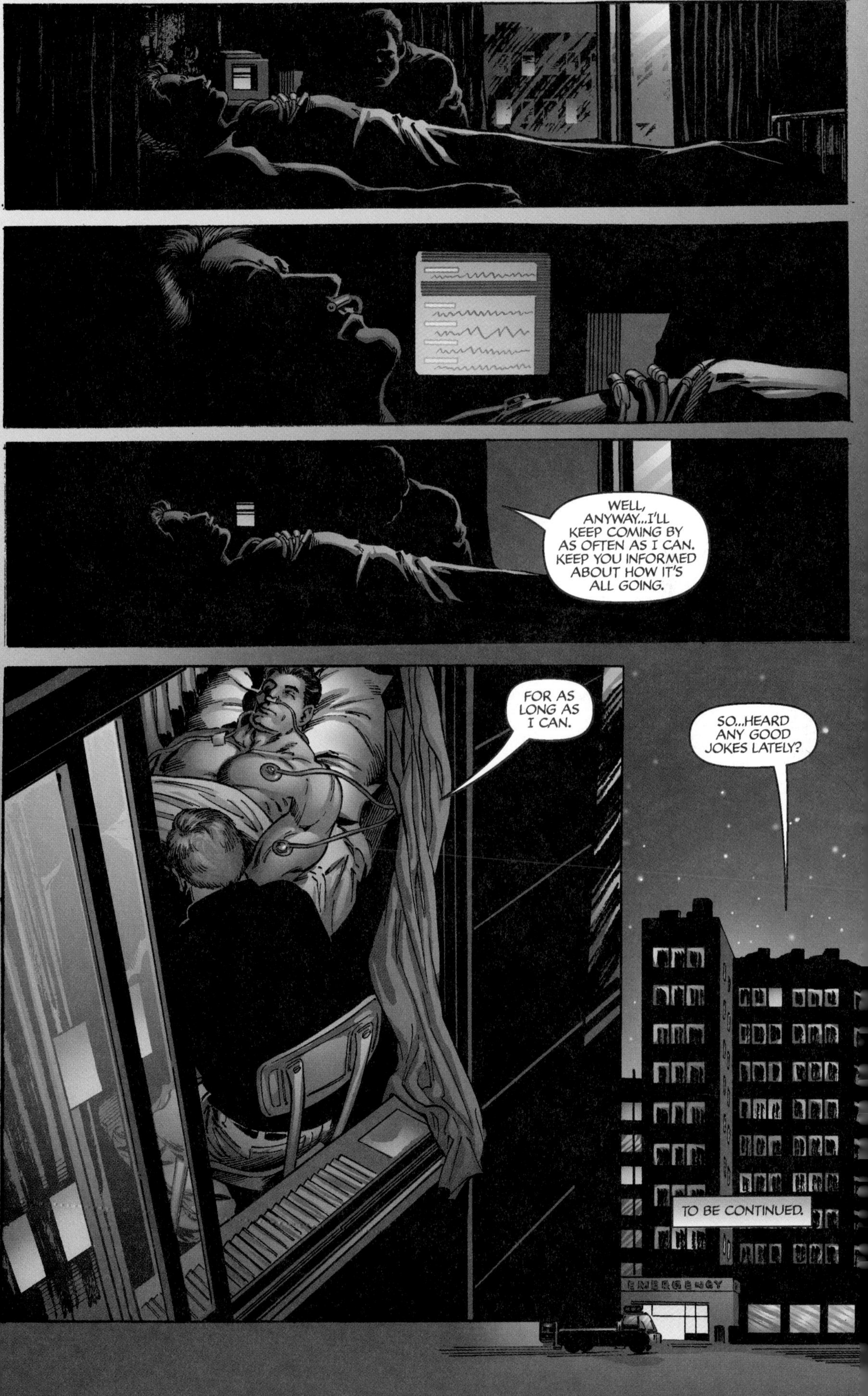
WELL, ANYWAY...I'LL KEEP COMING BY AS OFTEN AS I CAN. KEEP YOU INFORMED ABOUT HOW IT'S ALL GOING.
FOR AS LONG AS I CAN.
SO...HEARD ANY GOOD JOKES LATELY?
EMERGENCY
TO BE CONTINUED.

“Selah”

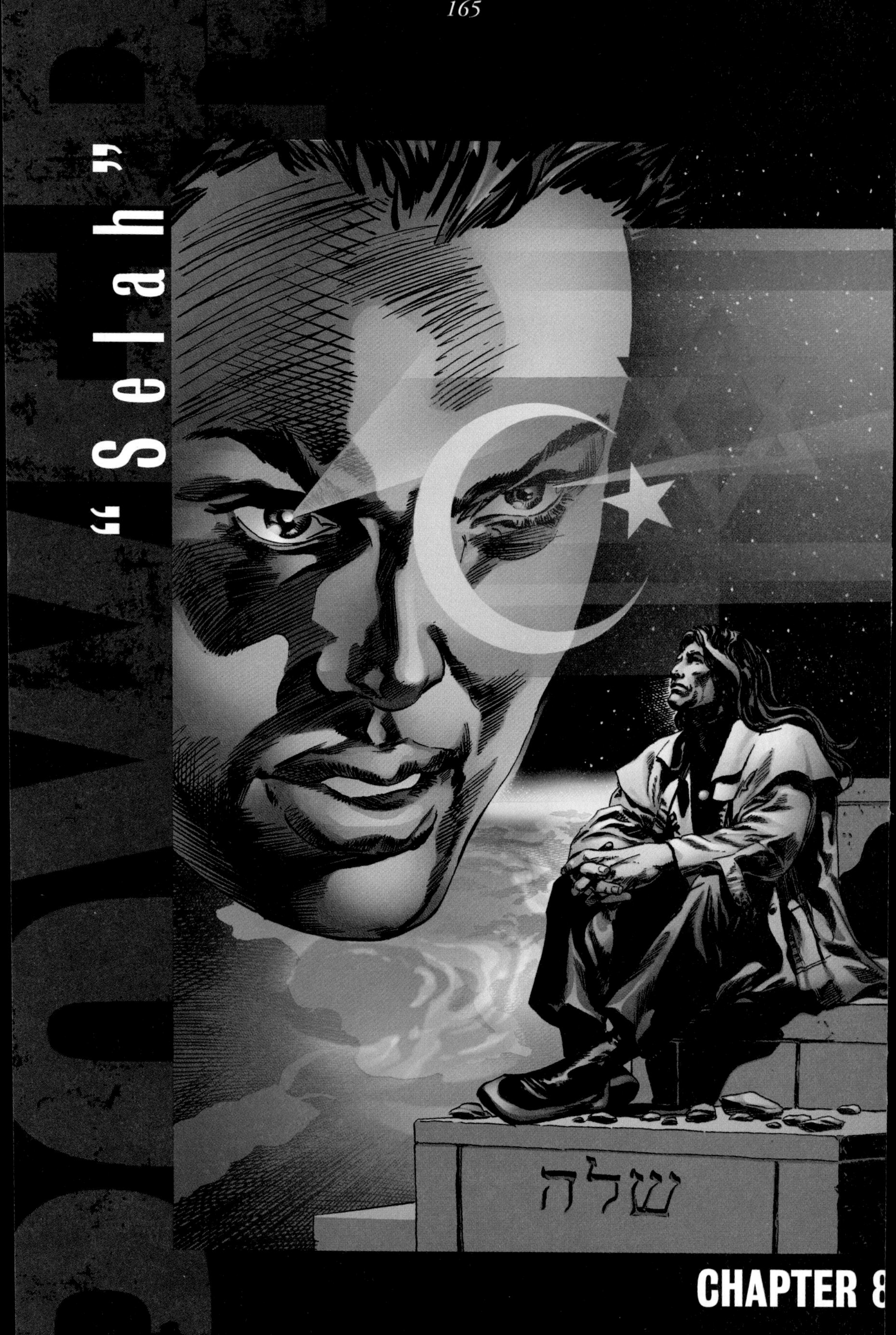
שלה

CHAPTER 8

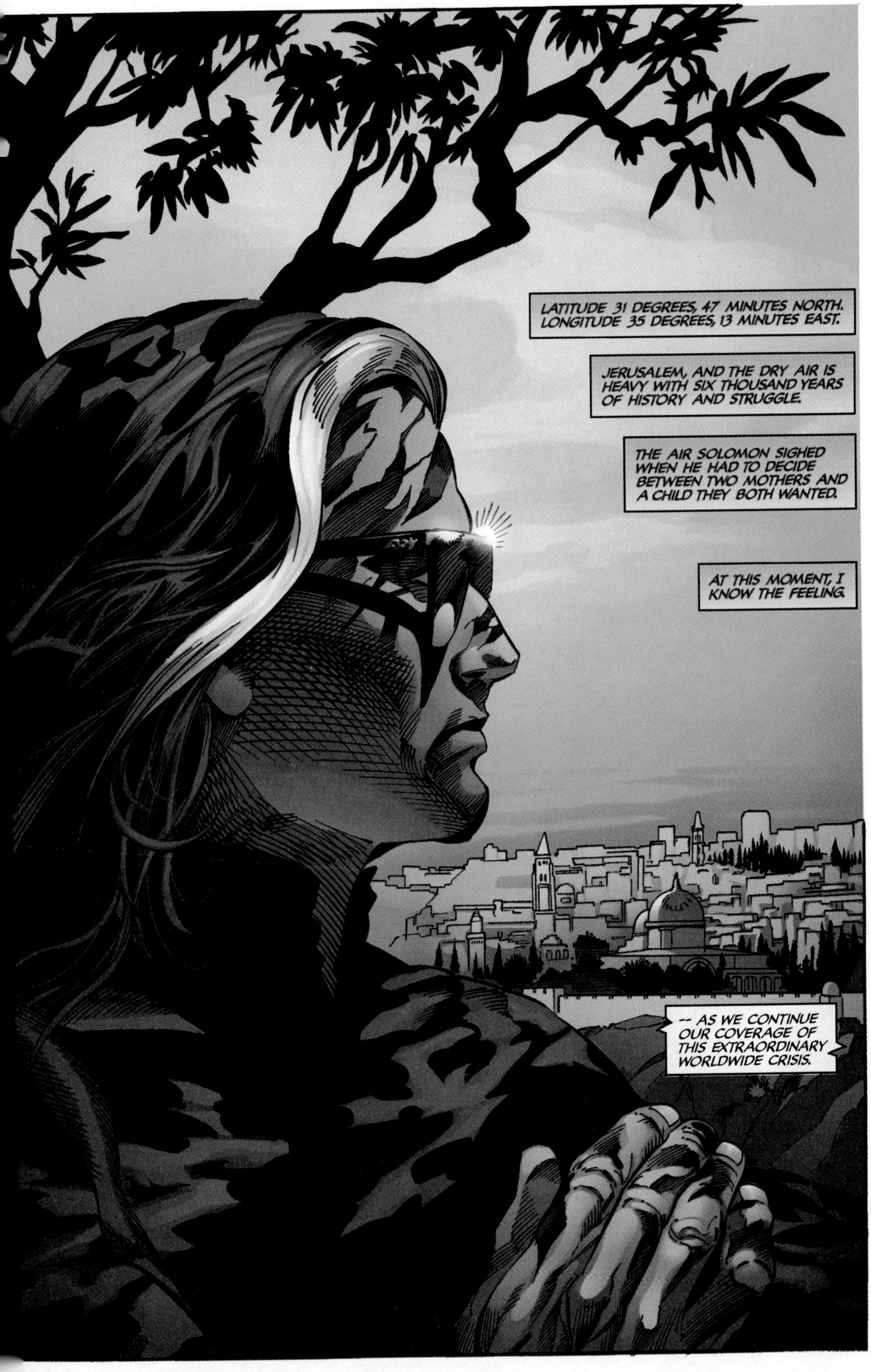
LATITUDE 31 DEGREES, 47 MINUTES NORTH. LONGITUDE 35 DEGREES, 13 MINUTES EAST.
JERUSALEM, AND THE DRY AIR IS HEAVY WITH SIX THOUSAND YEARS OF HISTORY AND STRUGGLE.
THE AIR SOLOMON SIGHED WHEN HE HAD TO DECIDE BETWEEN TWO MOTHERS AND A CHILD THEY BOTH WANTED.
AT THIS MOMENT, I KNOW THE FEELING.
-- AS WE CONTINUE OUR COVERAGE OF THIS EXTRAORDINARY WORLDWIDE CRISIS.

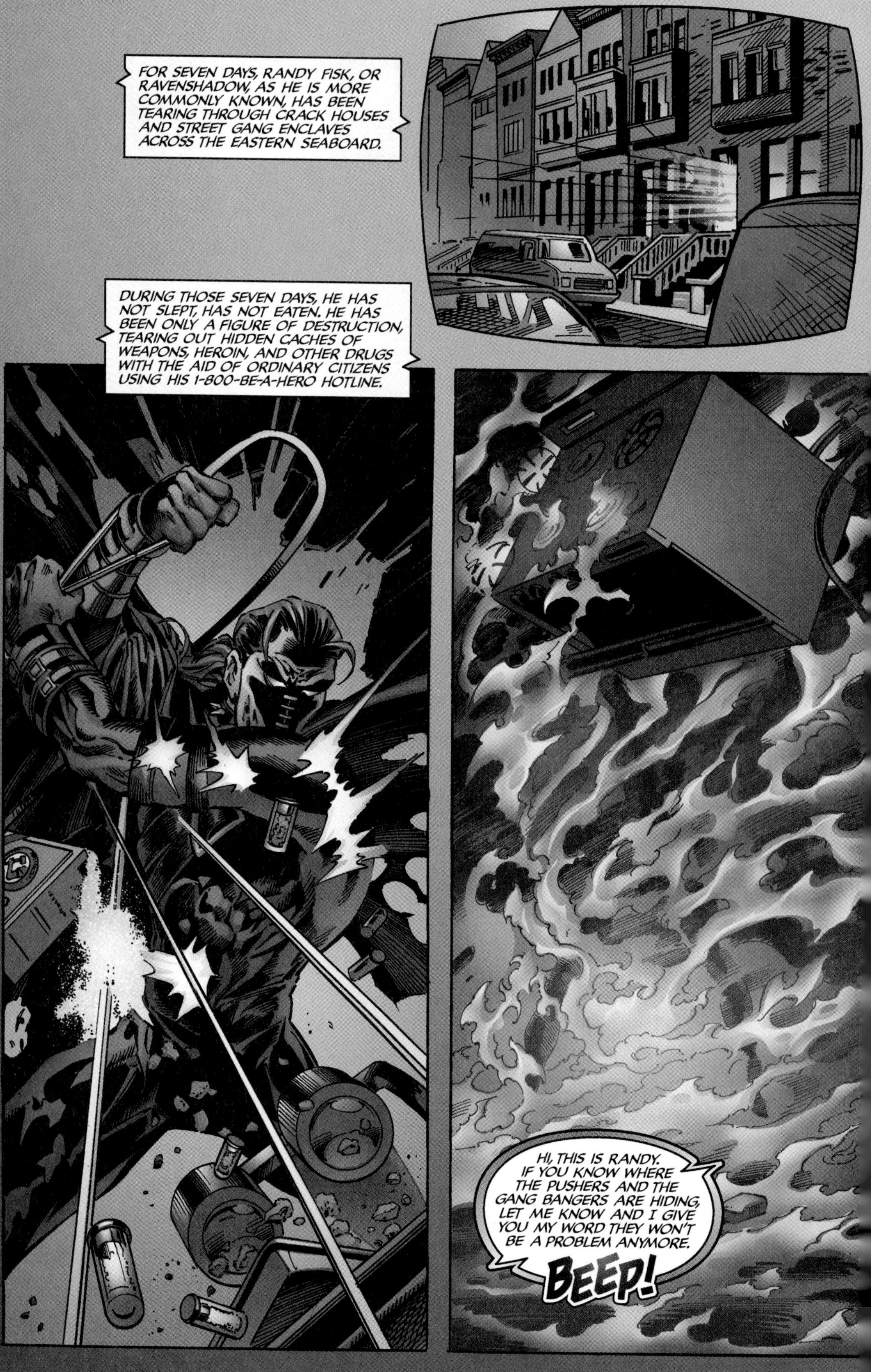
FOR SEVEN DAYS, RANDY FISK, OR RAVENSHADOW, AS HE IS MORE COMMONLY KNOWN, HAS BEEN TEARING THROUGH CRACK HOUSES AND STREET GANG ENCLAVES ACROSS THE EASTERN SEABOARD.
DURING THOSE SEVEN DAYS, HE HAS NOT SLEPT, HAS NOT EATEN. HE HAS BEEN ONLY A FIGURE OF DESTRUCTION, TEARING OUT HIDDEN CACHES OF WEAPONS, HEROIN, AND OTHER DRUGS WITH THE AID OF ORDINARY CITIZENS USING HIS 1-800-BE-A-HERO HOTLINE.
HI, THIS IS RANDY. IF YOU KNOW WHERE THE PUSHERS AND THE GANG BANGERS ARE HIDING, LET ME KNOW AND I GIVE YOU MY WORD THEY WON'T BE A PROBLEM ANYMORE.
BEEP!

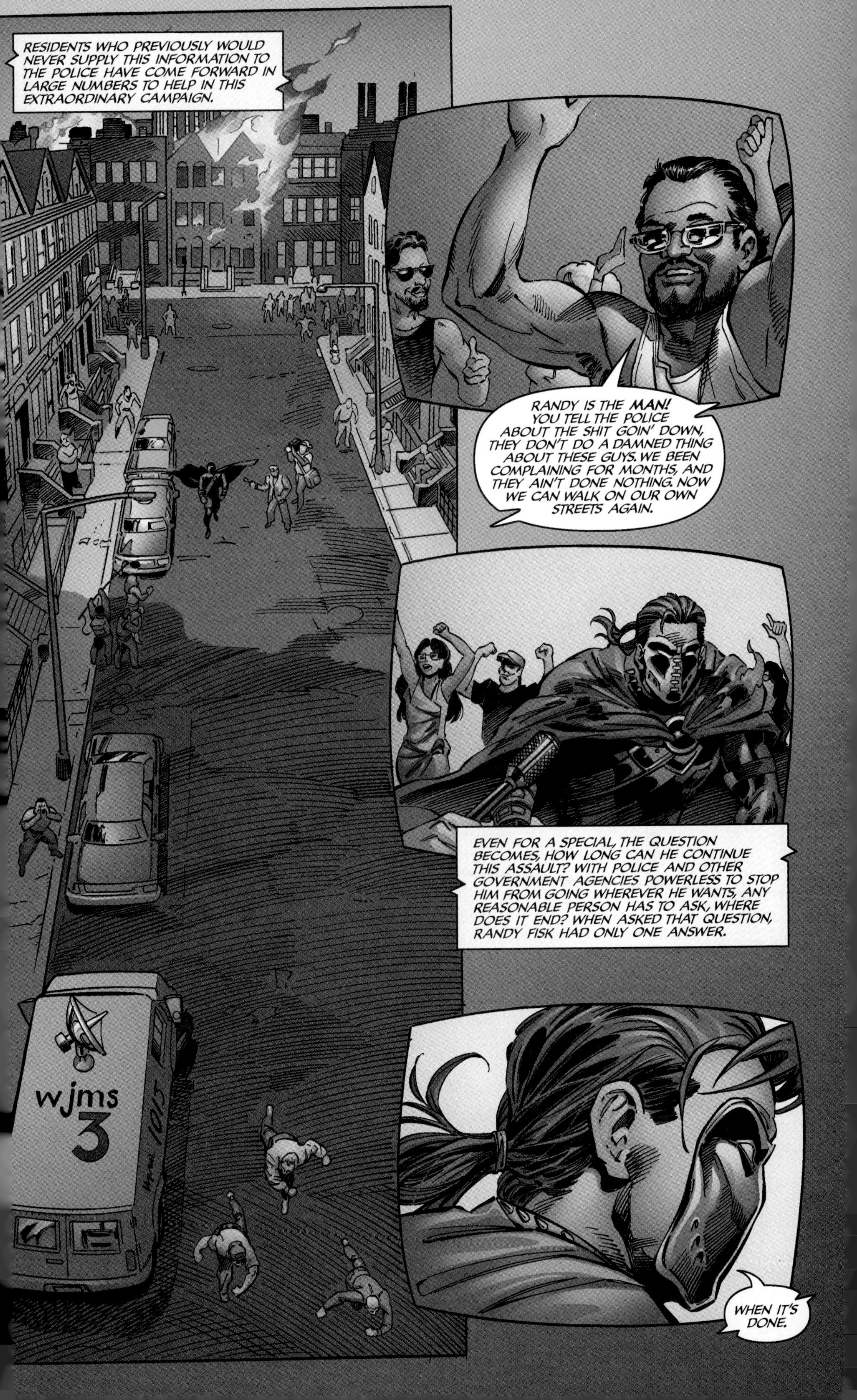
RESIDENTS WHO PREVIOUSLY WOULD NEVER SUPPLY THIS INFORMATION TO THE POLICE HAVE COME FORWARD IN LARGE NUMBERS TO HELP IN THIS EXTRAORDINARY CAMPAIGN.
RANDY IS THE MAN! YOU TELL THE POLICE ABOUT THE SHIT GOIN' DOWN, THEY DON'T DO A DAMNED THING ABOUT THESE GUYS. WE BEEN COMPLAINING FOR MONTHS, AND THEY AIN'T DONE NOTHING. NOW WE CAN WALK ON OUR OWN STREETS AGAIN.
EVEN FOR A SPECIAL, THE QUESTION BECOMES, HOW LONG CAN HE CONTINUE THIS ASSAULT? WITH POLICE AND OTHER GOVERNMENT AGENCIES POWERLESS TO STOP HIM FROM GOING WHEREVER HE WANTS, ANY REASONABLE PERSON HAS TO ASK, WHERE DOES IT END? WHEN ASKED THAT QUESTION, RANDY FISK HAD ONLY ONE ANSWER.
WHEN IT'S DONE.
wjms
3

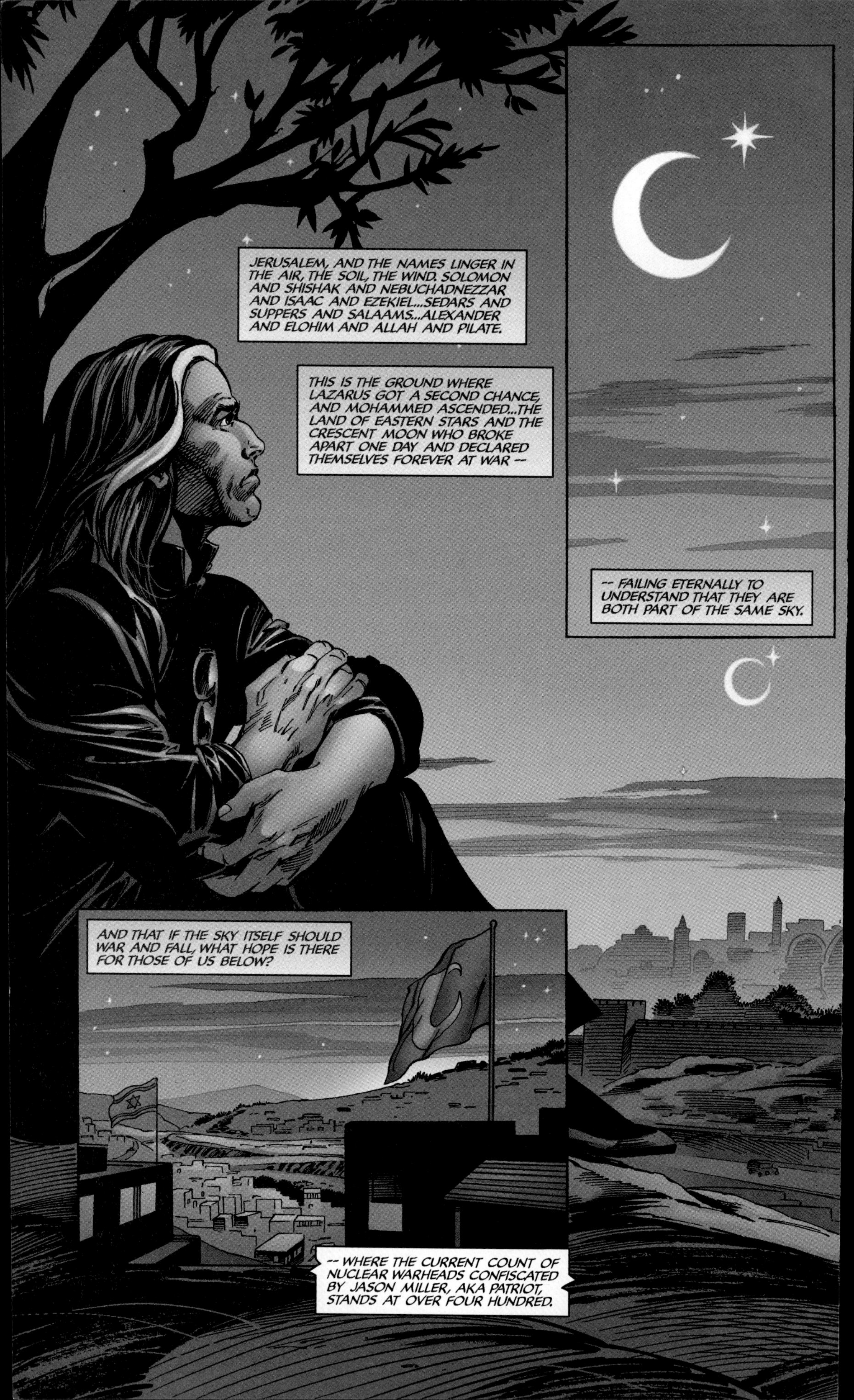
JERUSALEM, AND THE NAMES LINGER IN THE AIR, THE SOIL, THE WIND. SOLOMON AND SHISHAK AND NEBUCHADNEZZAR AND ISAAC AND EZEKIEL...SEDARS AND SUPPERS AND SALAAMS...ALEXANDER AND ELOHIM AND ALLAH AND PILATE.
THIS IS THE GROUND WHERE LAZARUS GOT A SECOND CHANCE, AND MOHAMMED ASCENDED...THE LAND OF EASTERN STARS AND THE CRESCENT MOON WHO BROKE APART ONE DAY AND DECLARED THEMSELVES FOREVER AT WAR --
-- FAILING ETERNALLY TO UNDERSTAND THAT THEY ARE BOTH PART OF THE SAME SKY.
AND THAT IF THE SKY ITSELF SHOULD WAR AND FALL, WHAT HOPE IS THERE FOR THOSE OF US BELOW?
-- WHERE THE CURRENT COUNT OF NUCLEAR WARHEADS CONFISCATED BY JASON MILLER, AKA PATRIOT, STANDS AT OVER FOUR HUNDRED.

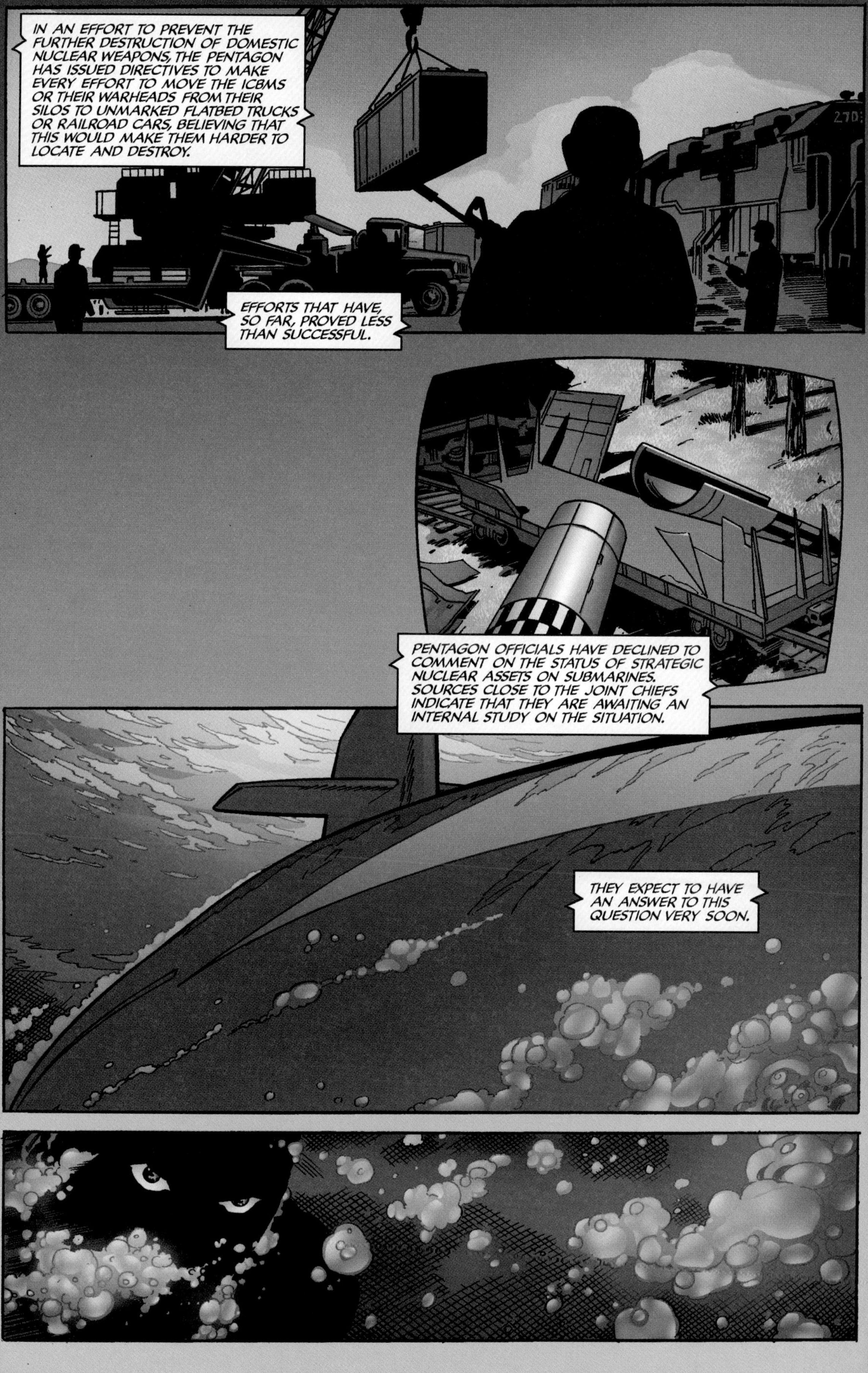
IN AN EFFORT TO PREVENT THE FURTHER DESTRUCTION OF DOMESTIC NUCLEAR WEAPONS, THE PENTAGON HAS ISSUED DIRECTIVES TO MAKE EVERY EFFORT TO MOVE THE ICBMS OR THEIR WARHEADS FROM THEIR SILOS TO UNMARKED FLATBED TRUCKS OR RAILROAD CARS, BELIEVING THAT THIS WOULD MAKE THEM HARDER TO LOCATE AND DESTROY.
EFFORTS THAT HAVE, SO FAR, PROVED LESS THAN SUCCESSFUL.
PENTAGON OFFICIALS HAVE DECLINED TO COMMENT ON THE STATUS OF STRATEGIC NUCLEAR ASSETS ON SUBMARINES. SOURCES CLOSE TO THE JOINT CHIEFS INDICATE THAT THEY ARE AWAITING AN INTERNAL STUDY ON THE SITUATION.
THEY EXPECT TO HAVE AN ANSWER TO THIS QUESTION VERY SOON.

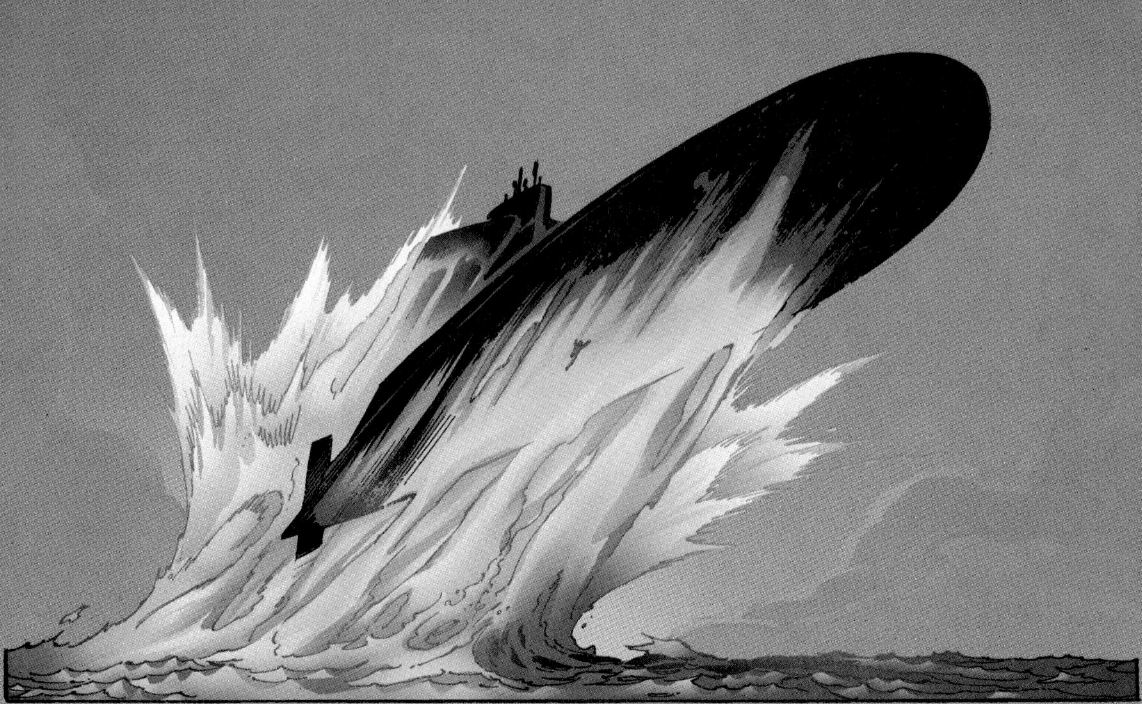

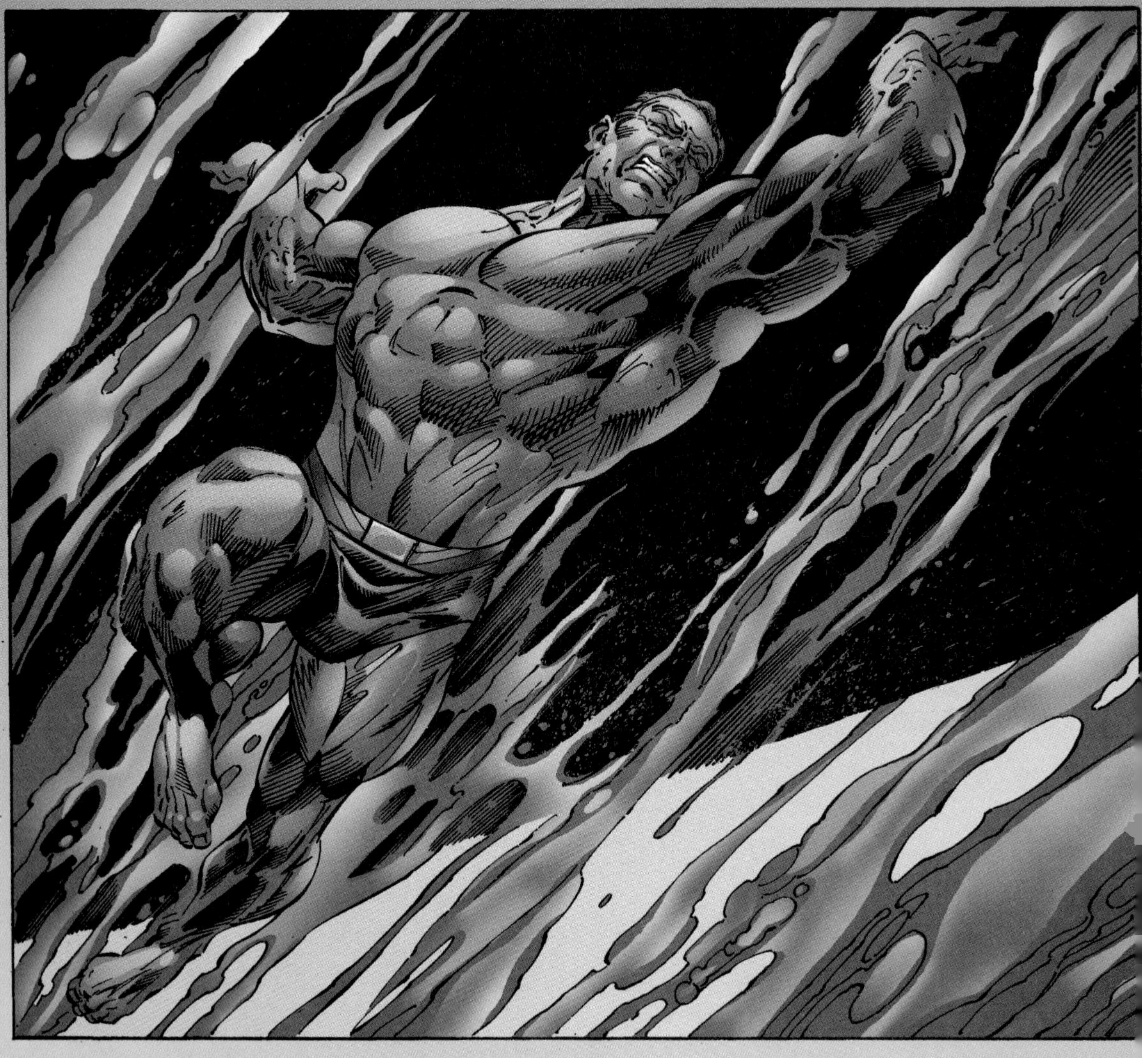

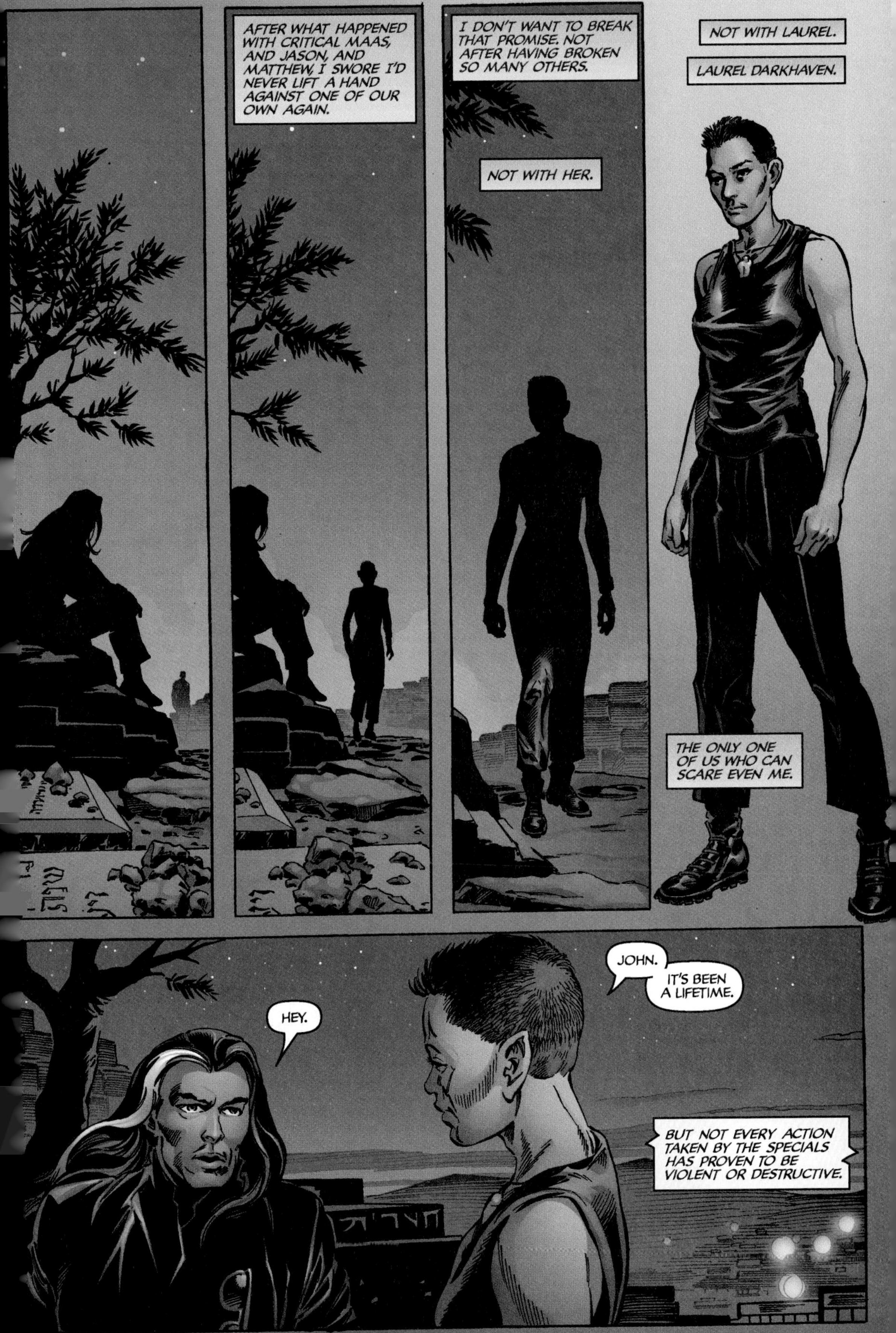
AFTER WHAT HAPPENED WITH CRITICAL MAAS, AND JASON, AND MATTHEW, I SWORE I'D NEVER LIFT A HAND AGAINST ONE OF OUR OWN AGAIN.
I DON'T WANT TO BREAK THAT PROMISE. NOT AFTER HAVING BROKEN SO MANY OTHERS.
NOT WITH HER.
NOT WITH LAUREL.
LAUREL DARKHAVEN.
THE ONLY ONE OF US WHO CAN SCARE EVEN ME.
HEY.
JOHN.
IT'S BEEN A LIFETIME.
BUT NOT EVERY ACTION TAKEN BY THE SPECIALS HAS PROVEN TO BE VIOLENT OR DESTRUCTIVE.

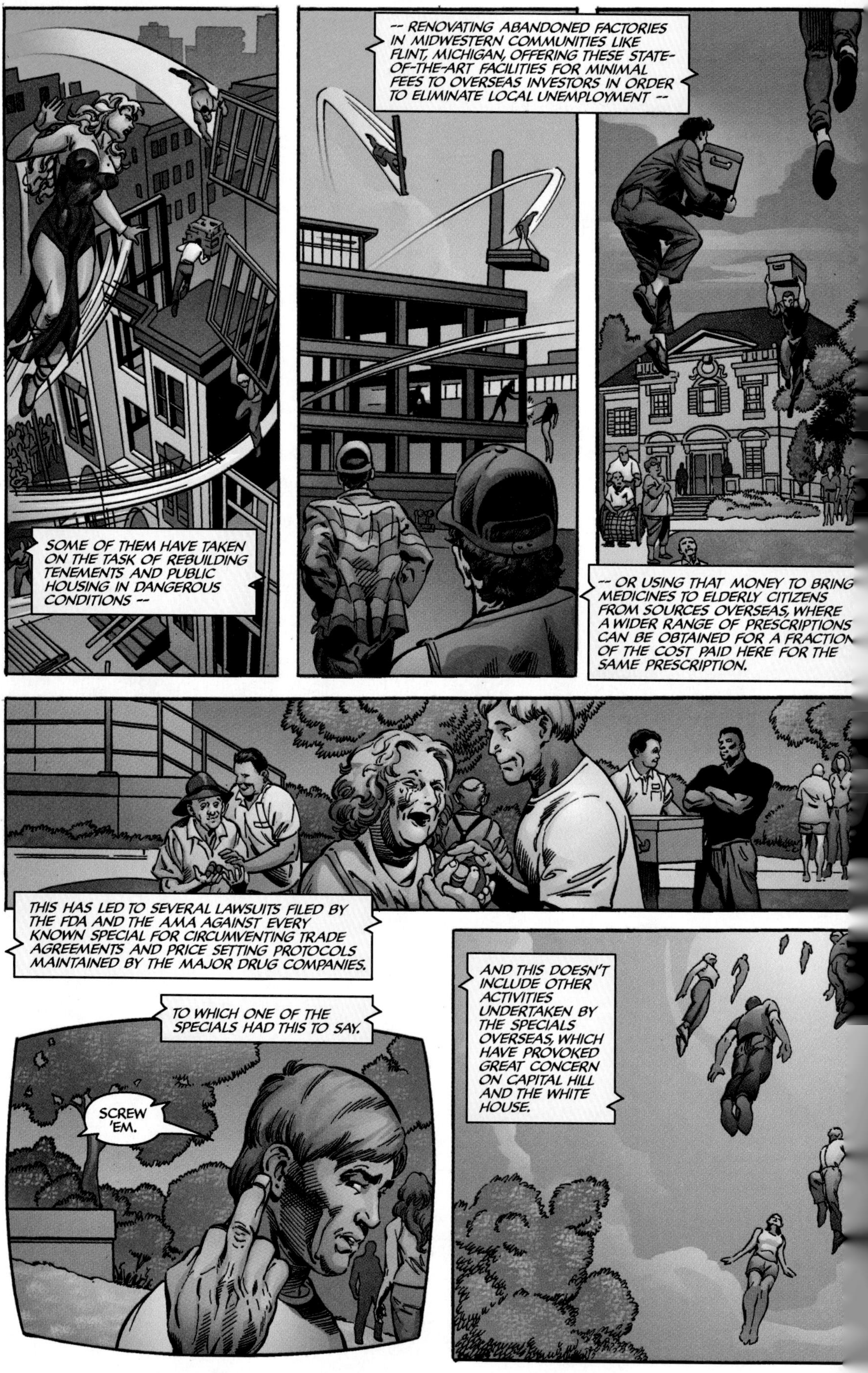
-- RENOVATING ABANDONED FACTORIES IN MIDWESTERN COMMUNITIES LIKE FLINT, MICHIGAN, OFFERING THESE STATE-OF-THE-ART FACILITIES FOR MINIMAL FEES TO OVERSEAS INVESTORS IN ORDER TO ELIMINATE LOCAL UNEMPLOYMENT --
SOME OF THEM HAVE TAKEN ON THE TASK OF REBUILDING TENEMENTS AND PUBLIC HOUSING IN DANGEROUS CONDITIONS --
-- OR USING THAT MONEY TO BRING MEDICINES TO ELDERLY CITIZENS FROM SOURCES OVERSEAS, WHERE A WIDER RANGE OF PRESCRIPTIONS CAN BE OBTAINED FOR A FRACTION OF THE COST PAID HERE FOR THE SAME PRESCRIPTION.
THIS HAS LED TO SEVERAL LAWSUITS FILED BY THE FDA AND THE AMA AGAINST EVERY KNOWN SPECIAL FOR CIRCUMVENTING TRADE AGREEMENTS AND PRICE SETTING PROTOCOLS MAINTAINED BY THE MAJOR DRUG COMPANIES.
TO WHICH ONE OF THE SPECIALS HAD THIS TO SAY.
SCREW 'EM.
AND THIS DOESN'T INCLUDE OTHER ACTIVITIES UNDERTAKEN BY THE SPECIALS OVERSEAS, WHICH HAVE PROVOKED GREAT CONCERN ON CAPITAL HILL AND THE WHITE HOUSE.

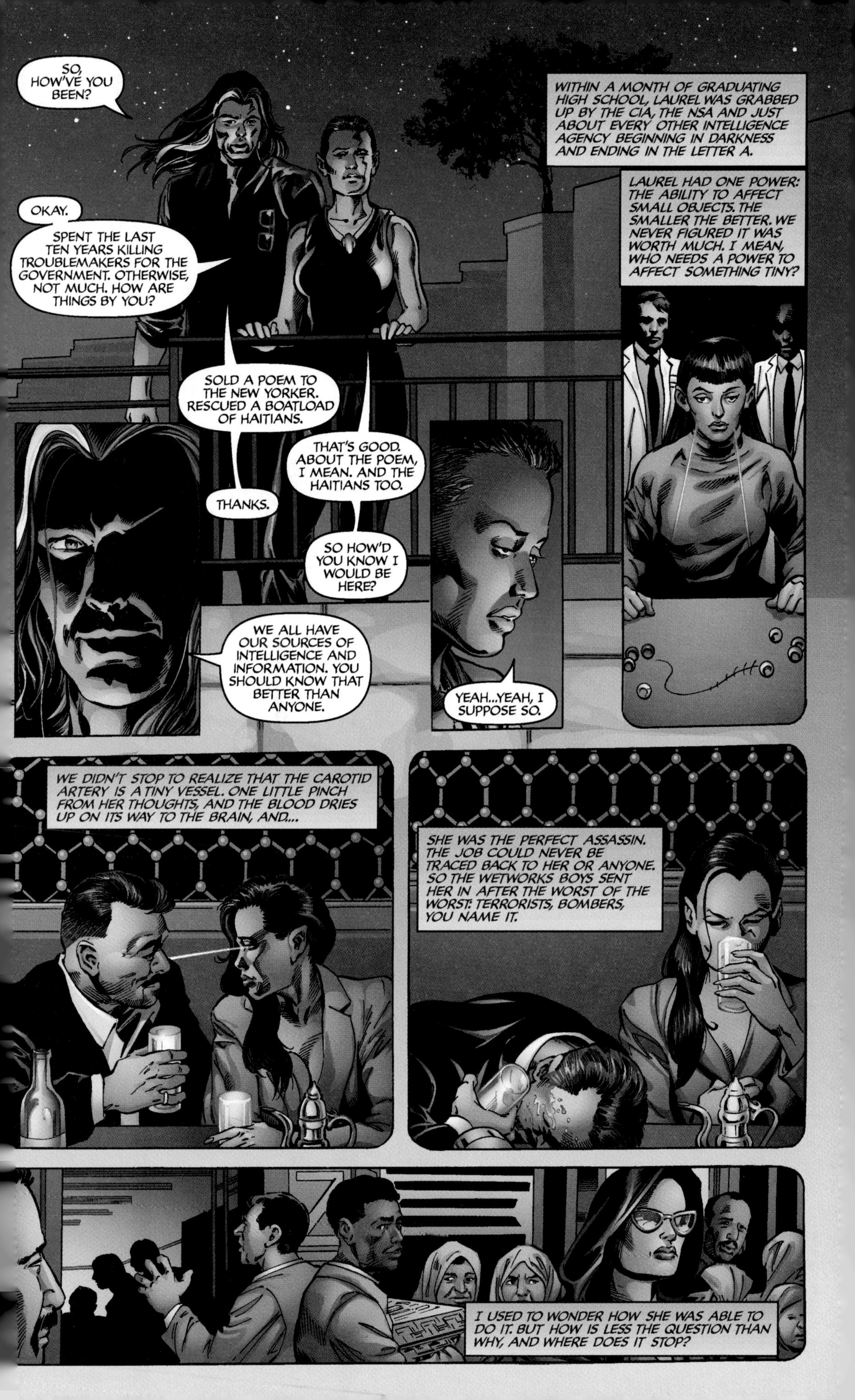
SO, HOW'VE YOU BEEN?
WITHIN A MONTH OF GRADUATING HIGH SCHOOL, LAUREL WAS GRABBED UP BY THE CIA, THE NSA AND JUST ABOUT EVERY OTHER INTELLIGENCE AGENCY BEGINNING IN DARKNESS AND ENDING IN THE LETTER A.
OKAY.
SPENT THE LAST TEN YEARS KILLING TROUBLEMAKERS FOR THE GOVERNMENT. OTHERWISE, NOT MUCH. HOW ARE THINGS BY YOU?
LAUREL HAD ONE POWER: THE ABILITY TO AFFECT SMALL OBJECTS. THE SMALLER THE BETTER. WE NEVER FIGURED IT WAS WORTH MUCH. I MEAN, WHO NEEDS A POWER TO AFFECT SOMETHING TINY?
SOLD A POEM TO THE NEW YORKER. RESCUED A BOATLOAD OF HAITIANS.
THAT'S GOOD. ABOUT THE POEM, I MEAN. AND THE HAITIANS TOO.
THANKS.
SO HOW'D YOU KNOW I WOULD BE HERE?
WE ALL HAVE OUR SOURCES OF INTELLIGENCE AND INFORMATION. YOU SHOULD KNOW THAT BETTER THAN ANYONE.
YEAH...YEAH, I SUPPOSE SO.
WE DIDN'T STOP TO REALIZE THAT THE CAROTID ARTERY IS A TINY VESSEL. ONE LITTLE PINCH FROM HER THOUGHTS, AND THE BLOOD DRIES UP ON ITS WAY TO THE BRAIN, AND...
SHE WAS THE PERFECT ASSASSIN. THE JOB COULD NEVER BE TRACED BACK TO HER OR ANYONE. SO THE WETWORKS BOYS SENT HER IN AFTER THE WORST OF THE WORST: TERRORISTS, BOMBERS, YOU NAME IT.
I USED TO WONDER HOW SHE WAS ABLE TO DO IT. BUT HOW IS LESS THE QUESTION THAN WHY, AND WHERE DOES IT STOP?

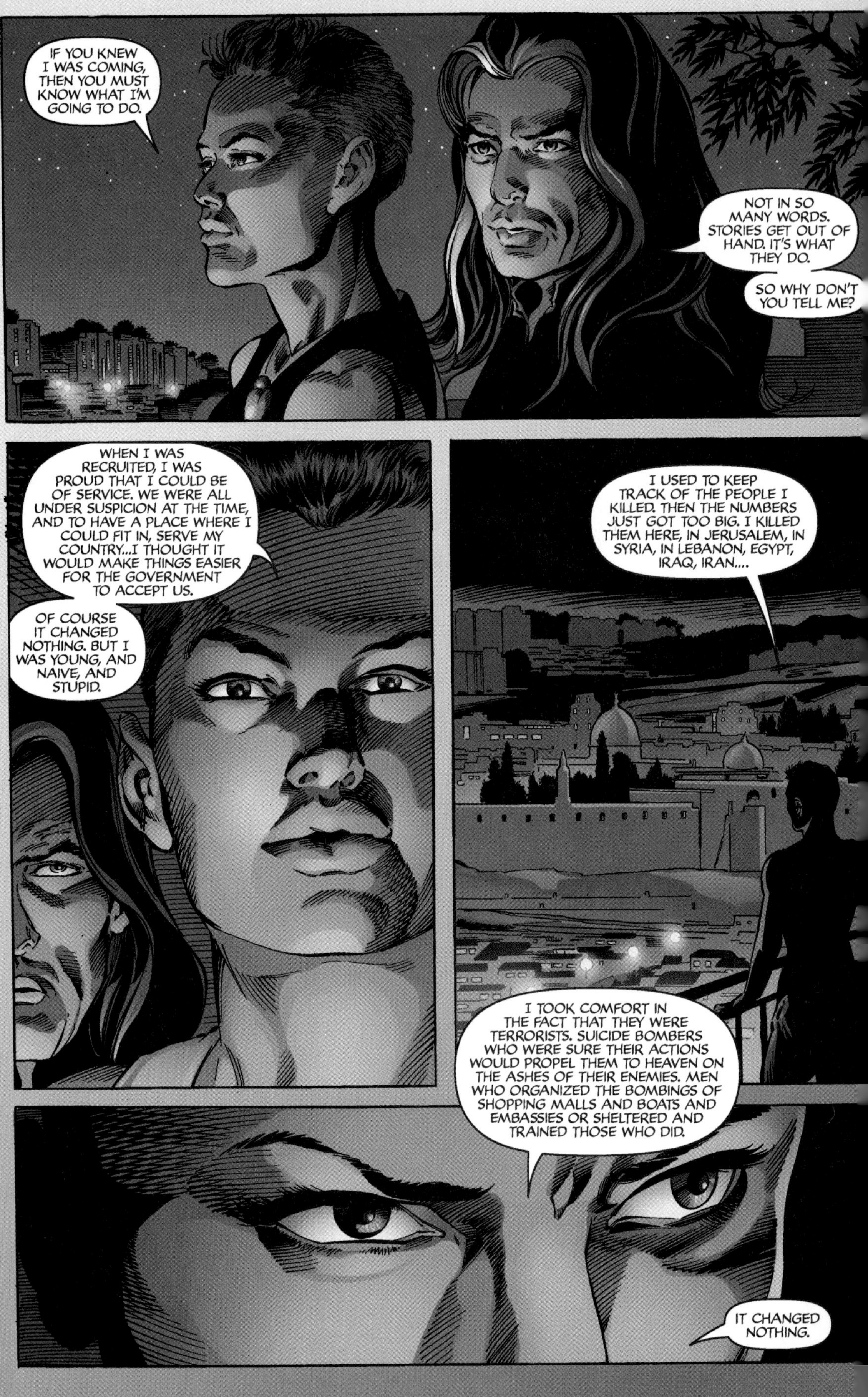
IF YOU KNEW I WAS COMING, THEN YOU MUST KNOW WHAT I'M GOING TO DO.
NOT IN SO MANY WORDS. STORIES GET OUT OF HAND. IT'S WHAT THEY DO.
SO WHY DON'T YOU TELL ME?
WHEN I WAS RECRUITED, I WAS PROUD THAT I COULD BE OF SERVICE. WE WERE ALL UNDER SUSPICION AT THE TIME, AND TO HAVE A PLACE WHERE I COULD FIT IN, SERVE MY COUNTRY...I THOUGHT IT WOULD MAKE THINGS EASIER FOR THE GOVERNMENT TO ACCEPT US.
OF COURSE IT CHANGED NOTHING. BUT I WAS YOUNG, AND NAIVE, AND STUPID.
I USED TO KEEP TRACK OF THE PEOPLE I KILLED. THEN THE NUMBERS JUST GOT TOO BIG. I KILLED THEM HERE, IN JERUSALEM, IN SYRIA, IN LEBANON, EGYPT, IRAQ, IRAN....
I TOOK COMFORT IN THE FACT THAT THEY WERE TERRORISTS. SUICIDE BOMBERS WHO WERE SURE THEIR ACTIONS WOULD PROPEL THEM TO HEAVEN ON THE ASHES OF THEIR ENEMIES. MEN WHO ORGANIZED THE BOMBINGS OF SHOPPING MALLS AND BOATS AND EMBASSIES OR SHELTERED AND TRAINED THOSE WHO DID.
IT CHANGED NOTHING.

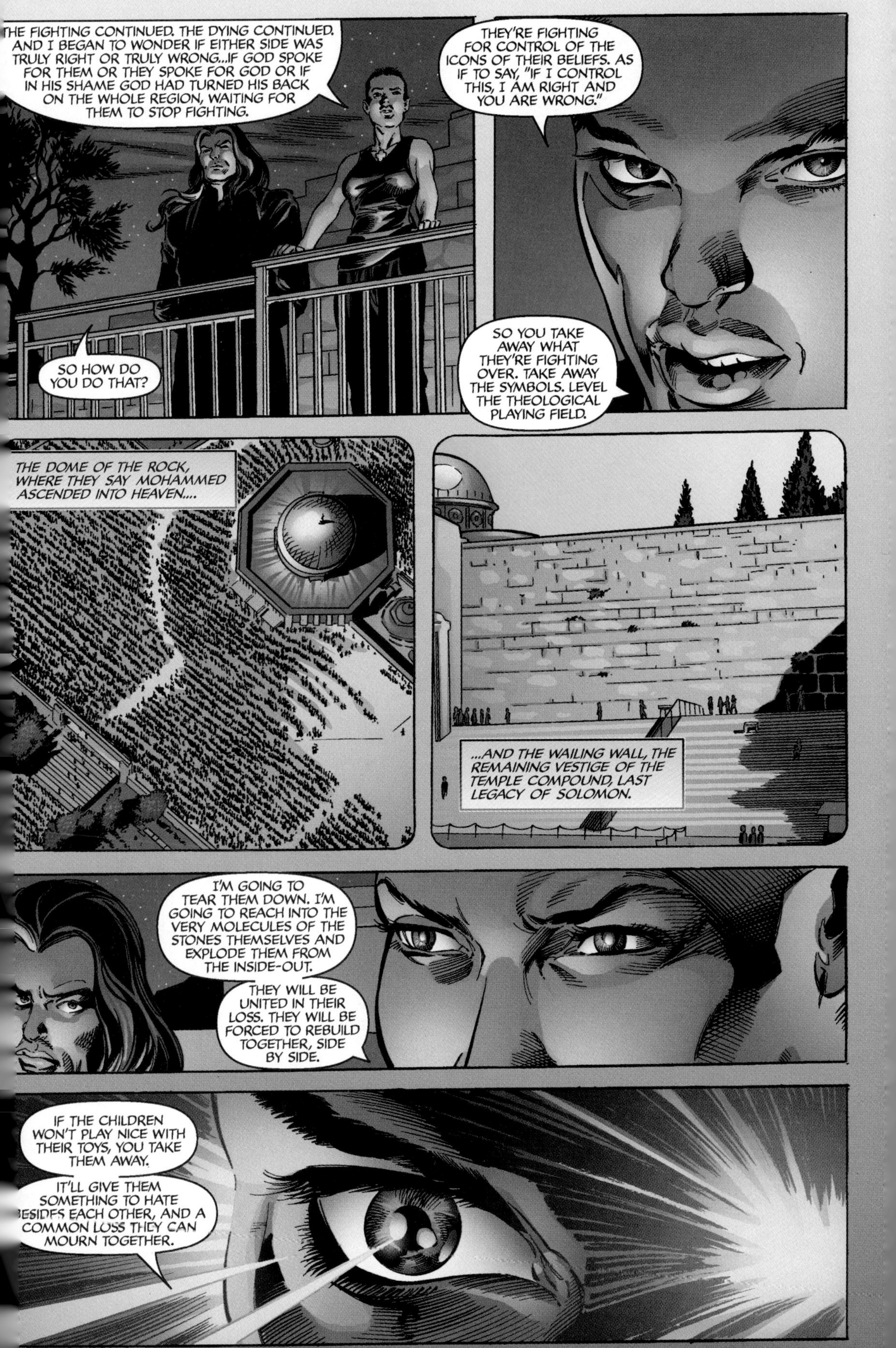
THE FIGHTING CONTINUED. THE DYING CONTINUED. AND I BEGAN TO WONDER IF EITHER SIDE WAS TRULY RIGHT OR TRULY WRONG...IF GOD SPOKE FOR THEM OR THEY SPOKE FOR GOD OR IF IN HIS SHAME GOD HAD TURNED HIS BACK ON THE WHOLE REGION, WAITING FOR THEM TO STOP FIGHTING.
THEY'RE FIGHTING FOR CONTROL OF THE ICONS OF THEIR BELIEFS. AS IF TO SAY, "IF I CONTROL THIS, I AM RIGHT AND YOU ARE WRONG."
SO HOW DO YOU DO THAT?
SO YOU TAKE AWAY WHAT THEY'RE FIGHTING OVER. TAKE AWAY THE SYMBOLS. LEVEL THE THEOLOGICAL PLAYING FIELD.
THE DOME OF THE ROCK, WHERE THEY SAY MOHAMMED ASCENDED INTO HEAVEN....
...AND THE WAILING WALL, THE REMAINING VESTIGE OF THE TEMPLE COMPOUND, LAST LEGACY OF SOLOMON.
I'M GOING TO TEAR THEM DOWN. I'M GOING TO REACH INTO THE VERY MOLECULES OF THE STONES THEMSELVES AND EXPLODE THEM FROM THE INSIDE-OUT.
THEY WILL BE UNITED IN THEIR LOSS. THEY WILL BE FORCED TO REBUILD TOGETHER, SIDE BY SIDE.
IF THE CHILDREN WON'T PLAY NICE WITH THEIR TOYS, YOU TAKE THEM AWAY.
IT'LL GIVE THEM SOMETHING TO HATE BESIDES EACH OTHER, AND A COMMON LOSS THEY CAN MOURN TOGETHER.

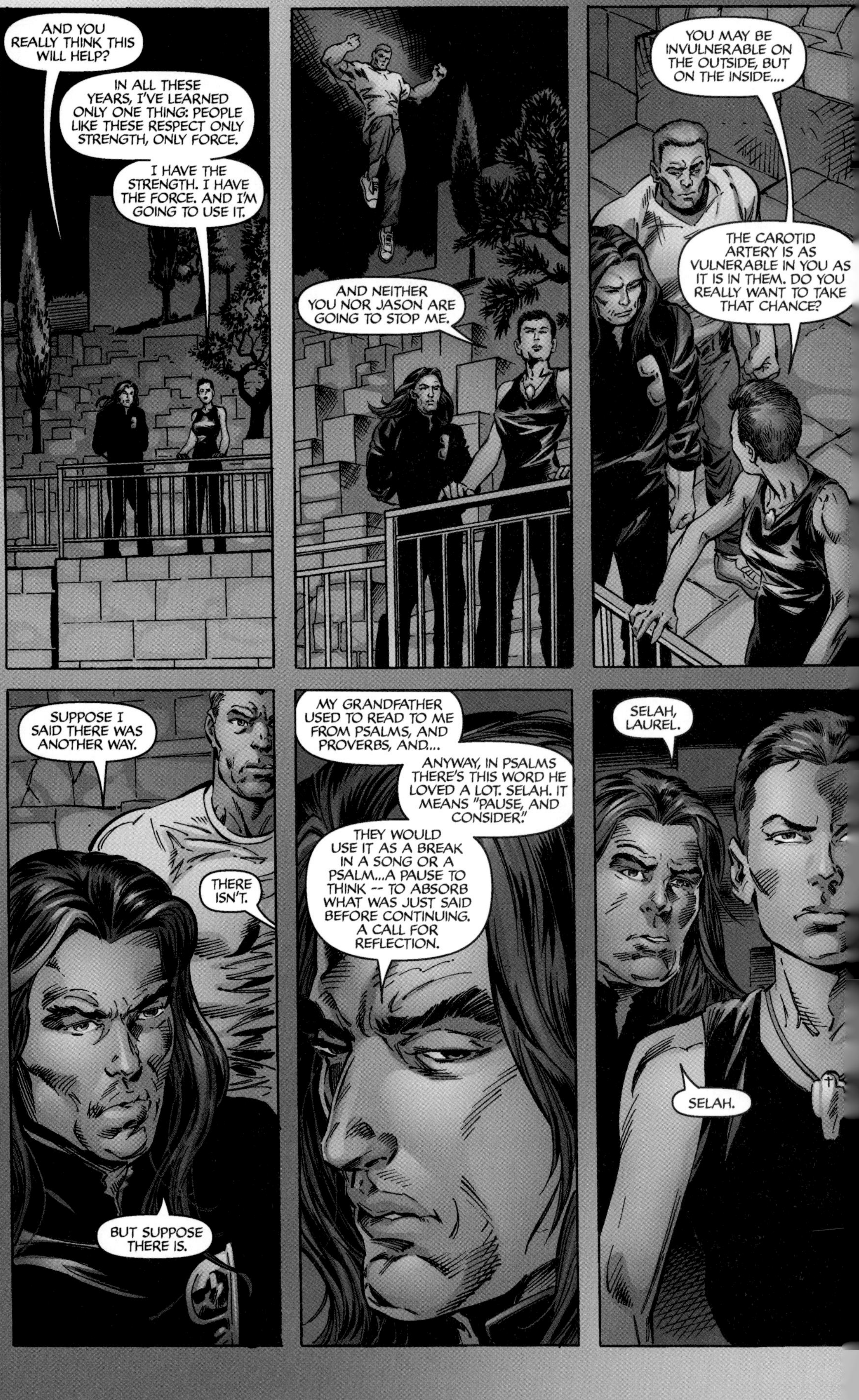
AND YOU REALLY THINK THIS WILL HELP?
IN ALL THESE YEARS, I'VE LEARNED ONLY ONE THING: PEOPLE LIKE THESE RESPECT ONLY STRENGTH, ONLY FORCE.
I HAVE THE STRENGTH. I HAVE THE FORCE. AND I'M GOING TO USE IT.
AND NEITHER YOU NOR JASON ARE GOING TO STOP ME.
YOU MAY BE INVULNERABLE ON THE OUTSIDE, BUT ON THE INSIDE....
THE CAROTID ARTERY IS AS VULNERABLE IN YOU AS IT IS IN THEM. DO YOU REALLY WANT TO TAKE THAT CHANCE?
SUPPOSE I SAID THERE WAS ANOTHER WAY.
THERE ISN'T.
BUT SUPPOSE THERE IS.
MY GRANDFATHER USED TO READ TO ME FROM PSALMS, AND PROVERBS, AND...
ANYWAY, IN PSALMS THERE'S THIS WORD HE LOVED A LOT. SELAH. IT MEANS "PAUSE, AND CONSIDER."
THEY WOULD USE IT AS A BREAK IN A SONG OR A PSALM...A PAUSE TO THINK -- TO ABSORB WHAT WAS JUST SAID BEFORE CONTINUING. A CALL FOR REFLECTION.
SELAH, LAUREL.
SELAH.

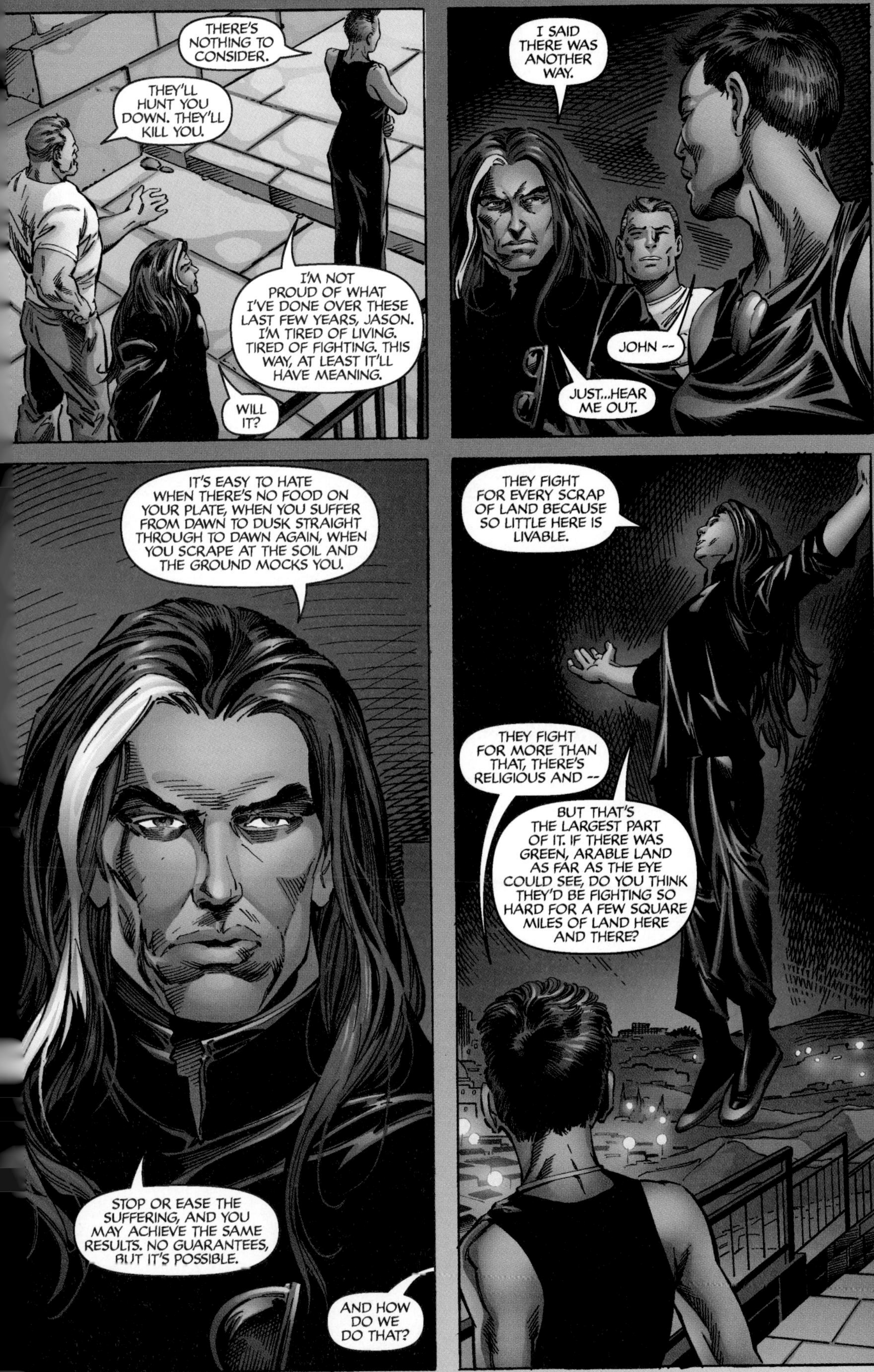
THERE'S NOTHING TO CONSIDER.
THEY'LL HUNT YOU DOWN. THEY'LL KILL YOU.
I'M NOT PROUD OF WHAT I'VE DONE OVER THESE LAST FEW YEARS, JASON. I'M TIRED OF LIVING. TIRED OF FIGHTING. THIS WAY, AT LEAST IT'LL HAVE MEANING.
WILL IT?
I SAID THERE WAS ANOTHER WAY.
JOHN --
JUST...HEAR ME OUT.
IT'S EASY TO HATE WHEN THERE'S NO FOOD ON YOUR PLATE, WHEN YOU SUFFER FROM DAWN TO DUSK STRAIGHT THROUGH TO DAWN AGAIN, WHEN YOU SCRAPE AT THE SOIL AND THE GROUND MOCKS YOU.
STOP OR EASE THE SUFFERING, AND YOU MAY ACHIEVE THE SAME RESULTS. NO GUARANTEES, BUT IT'S POSSIBLE.
AND HOW DO WE DO THAT?
THEY FIGHT FOR EVERY SCRAP OF LAND BECAUSE SO LITTLE HERE IS LIVABLE.
THEY FIGHT FOR MORE THAN THAT, THERE'S RELIGIOUS AND --
BUT THAT'S THE LARGEST PART OF IT. IF THERE WAS GREEN, ARABLE LAND AS FAR AS THE EYE COULD SEE, DO YOU THINK THEY'D BE FIGHTING SO HARD FOR A FEW SQUARE MILES OF LAND HERE AND THERE?

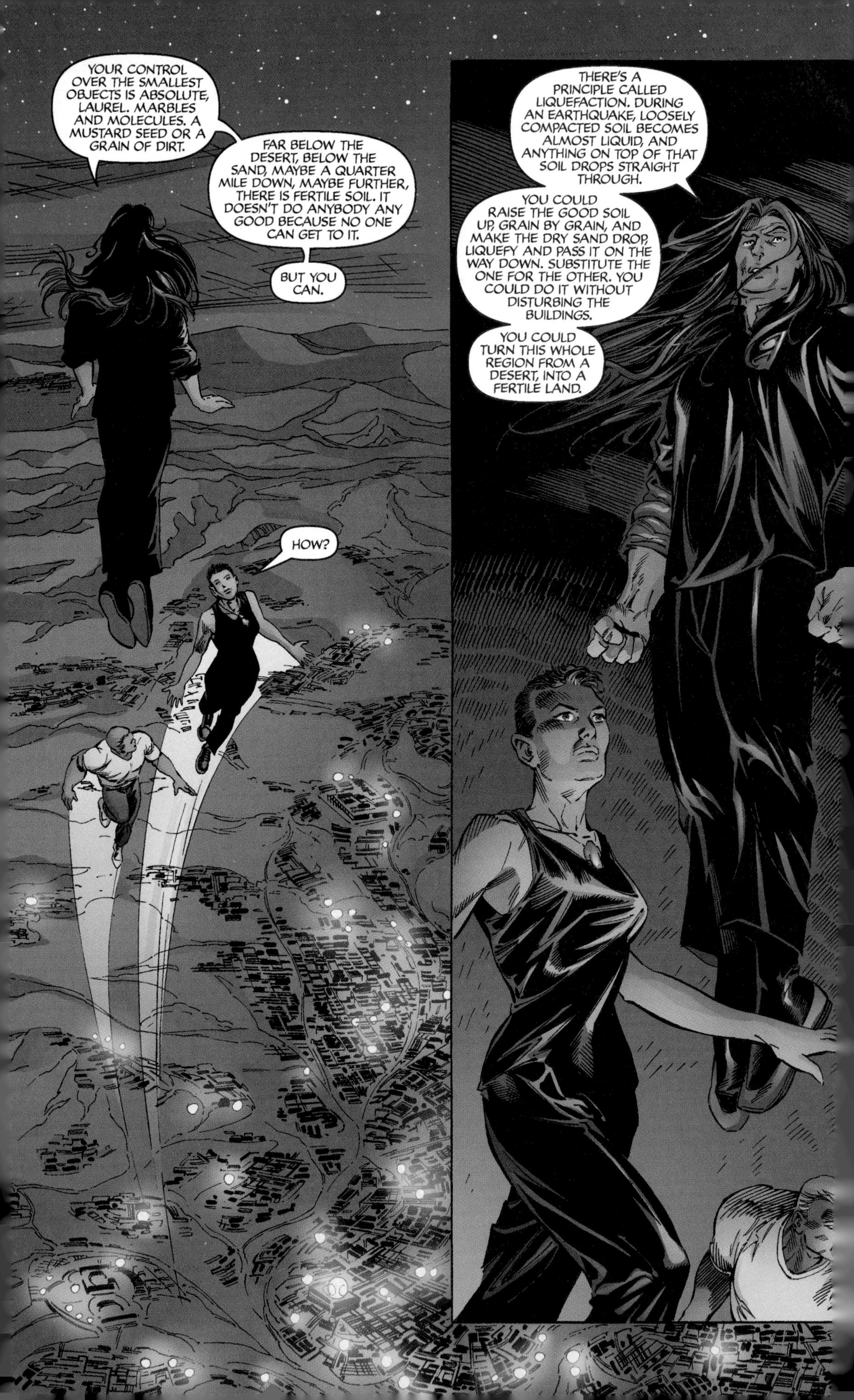
YOUR CONTROL OVER THE SMALLEST OBJECTS IS ABSOLUTE, LAUREL. MARBLES AND MOLECULES. A MUSTARD SEED OR A GRAIN OF DIRT.
FAR BELOW THE DESERT, BELOW THE SAND, MAYBE A QUARTER MILE DOWN, MAYBE FURTHER, THERE IS FERTILE SOIL. IT DOESN'T DO ANYBODY ANY GOOD BECAUSE NO ONE CAN GET TO IT.
BUT YOU CAN.
HOW?
THERE'S A PRINCIPLE CALLED LIQUEFACTION. DURING AN EARTHQUAKE, LOOSELY COMPACTED SOIL BECOMES ALMOST LIQUID, AND ANYTHING ON TOP OF THAT SOIL DROPS STRAIGHT THROUGH.
YOU COULD RAISE THE GOOD SOIL UP, GRAIN BY GRAIN, AND MAKE THE DRY SAND DROP, LIQUEFY AND PASS IT ON THE WAY DOWN. SUBSTITUTE THE ONE FOR THE OTHER. YOU COULD DO IT WITHOUT DISTURBING THE BUILDINGS.
YOU COULD TURN THIS WHOLE REGION FROM A DESERT, INTO A FERTILE LAND.

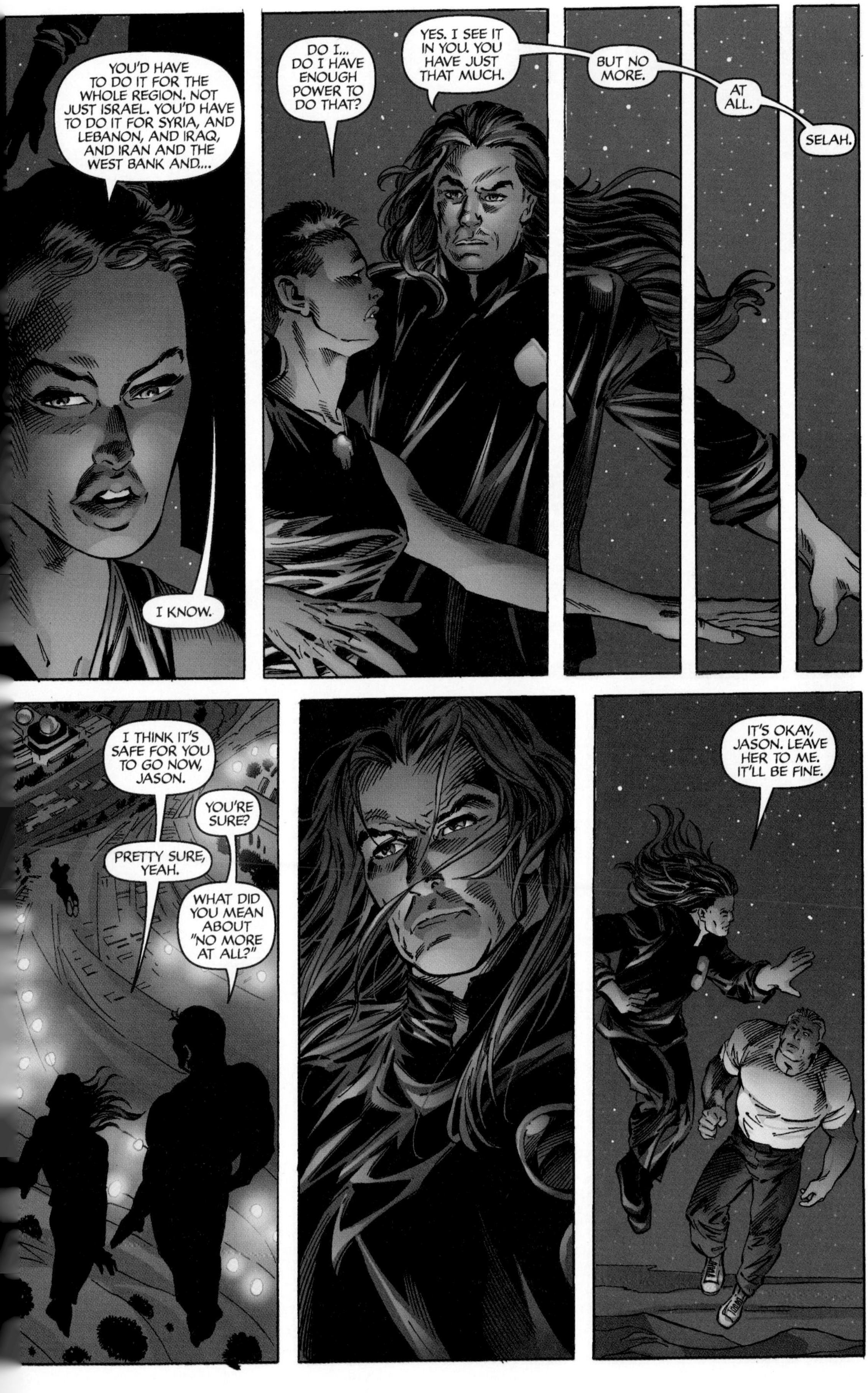
YOU'D HAVE TO DO IT FOR THE WHOLE REGION. NOT JUST ISRAEL. YOU'D HAVE TO DO IT FOR SYRIA, AND LEBANON, AND IRAQ, AND IRAN AND THE WEST BANK AND...
I KNOW.
DO I... DO I HAVE ENOUGH POWER TO DO THAT?
YES. I SEE IT IN YOU. YOU HAVE JUST THAT MUCH.
BUT NO MORE.
AT ALL.
SELAH.
I THINK IT'S SAFE FOR YOU TO GO NOW, JASON.
YOU'RE SURE?
PRETTY SURE, YEAH.
WHAT DID YOU MEAN ABOUT "NO MORE AT ALL?"
IT'S OKAY, JASON. LEAVE HER TO ME. IT'LL BE FINE.

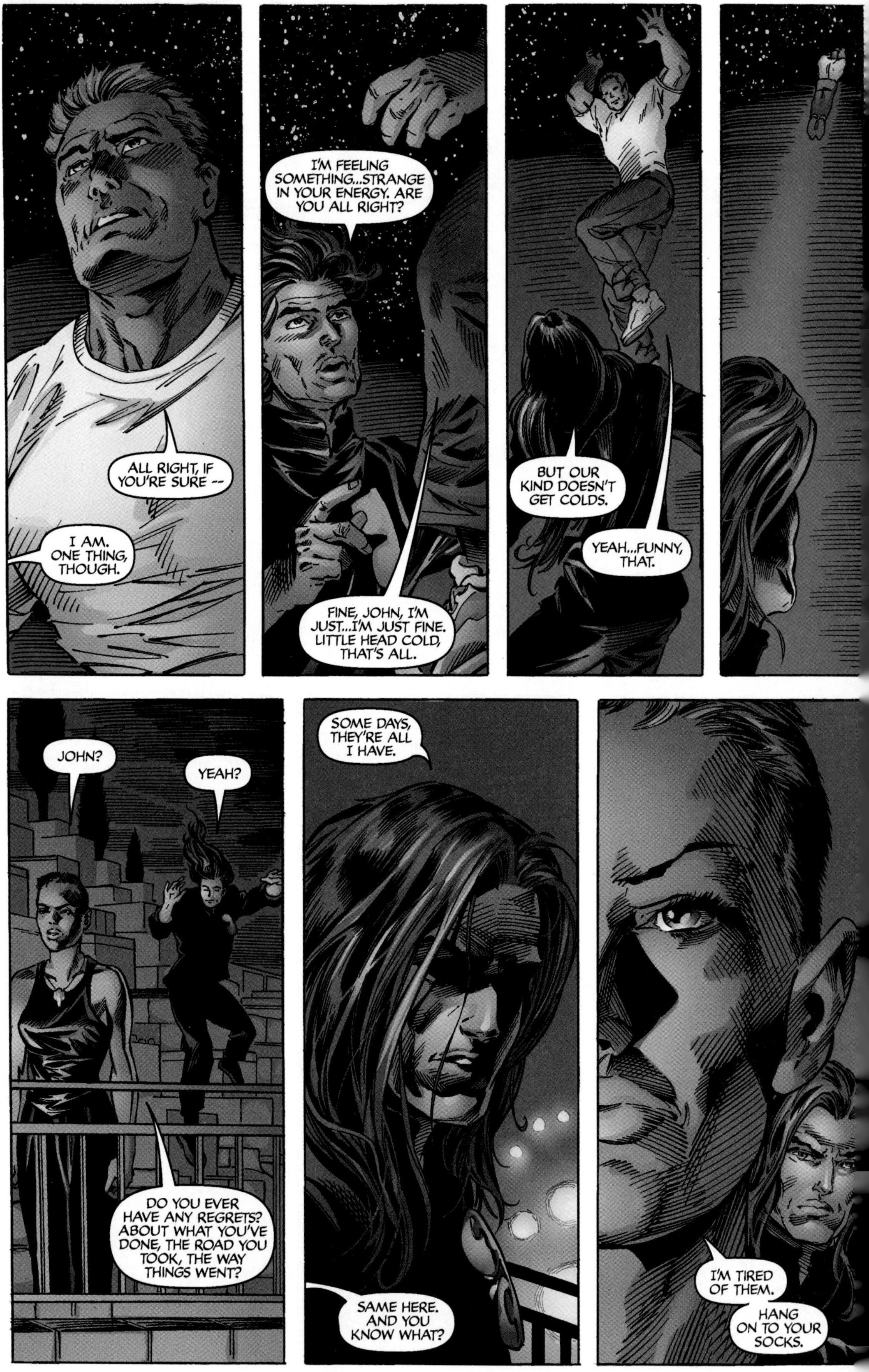
I'M FEELING SOMETHING...STRANGE IN YOUR ENERGY. ARE YOU ALL RIGHT?
FINE, JOHN, I'M JUST...I'M JUST FINE. LITTLE HEAD COLD, THAT'S ALL.
BUT OUR KIND DOESN'T GET COLDS.
YEAH...FUNNY, THAT.
ALL RIGHT, IF YOU'RE SURE --
I AM. ONE THING, THOUGH.
JOHN?
YEAH?
DO YOU EVER HAVE ANY REGRETS? ABOUT WHAT YOU'VE DONE, THE ROAD YOU TOOK, THE WAY THINGS WENT?
SOME DAYS, THEY'RE ALL I HAVE.
SAME HERE. AND YOU KNOW WHAT?
I'M TIRED OF THEM.
HANG ON TO YOUR SOCKS.

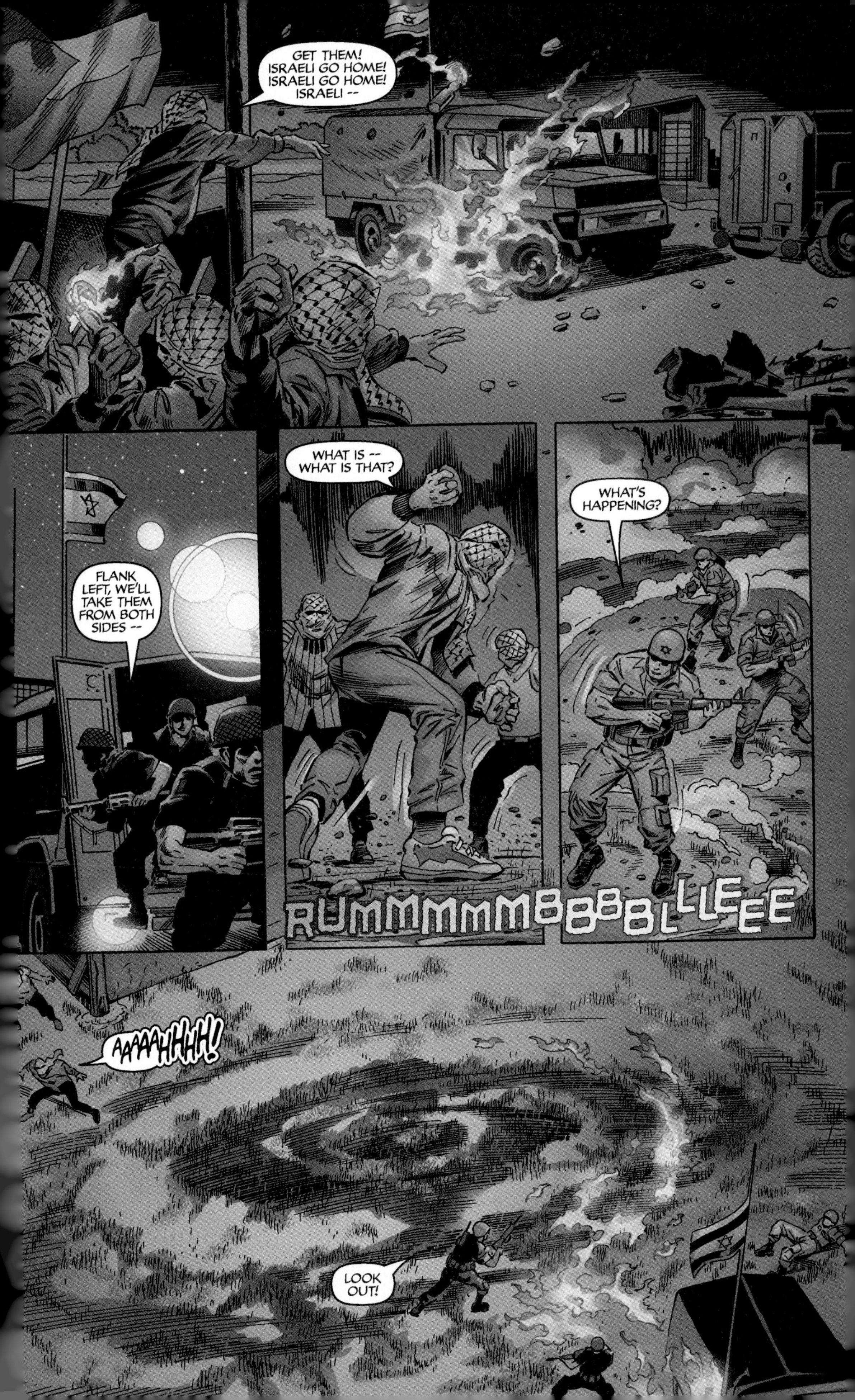
GET THEM! ISRAELI GO HOME! ISRAELI GO HOME! ISRAELI --
FLANK LEFT, WE'LL TAKE THEM FROM BOTH SIDES --
WHAT IS -- WHAT IS THAT?
WHAT'S HAPPENING?
RUMMMMMMBBBBLLLEEE
AAAAAHHHH!
LOOK OUT!

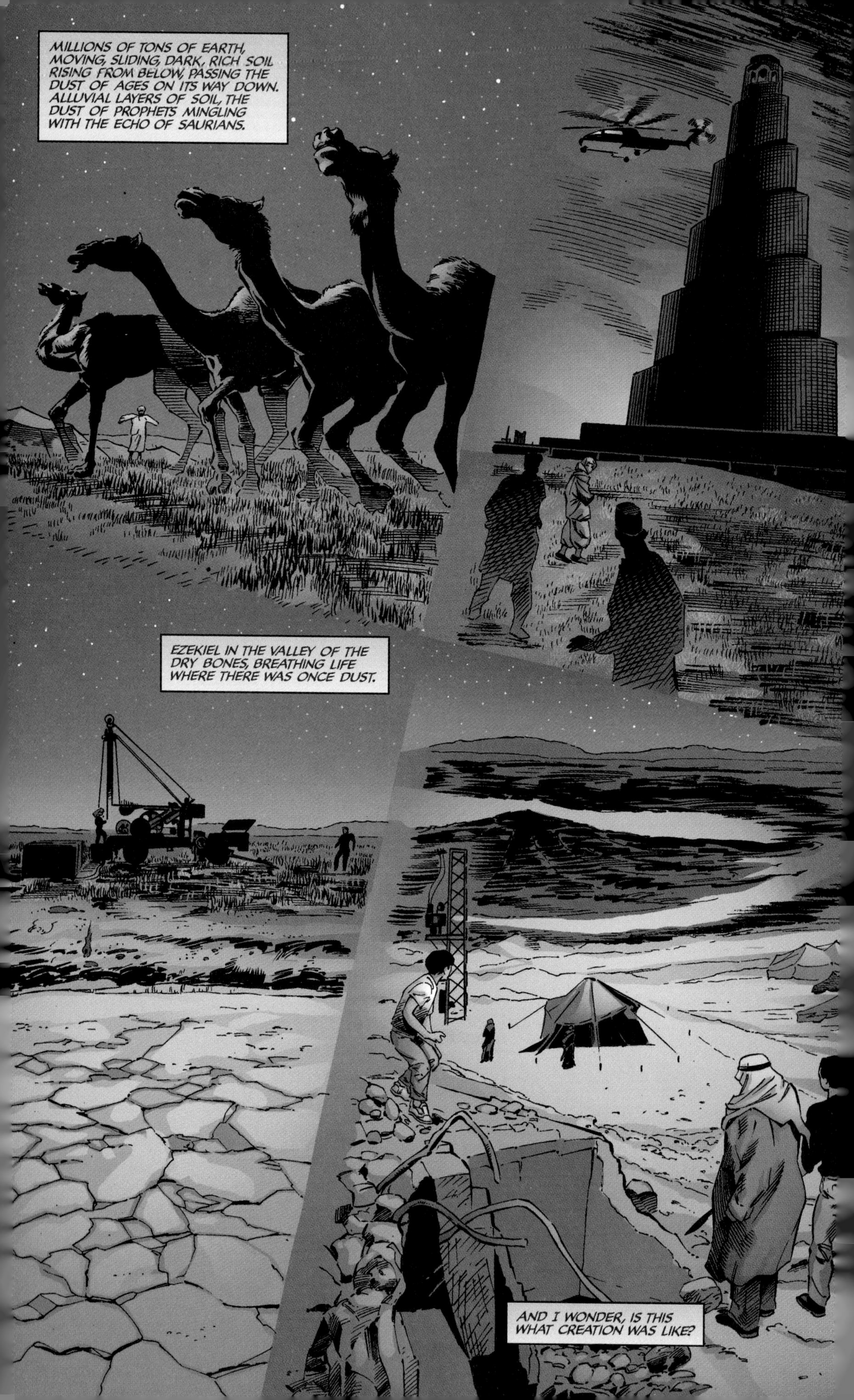
MILLIONS OF TONS OF EARTH, MOVING, SLIDING, DARK, RICH SOIL RISING FROM BELOW, PASSING THE DUST OF AGES ON ITS WAY DOWN. ALLUVIAL LAYERS OF SOIL, THE DUST OF PROPHETS MINGLING WITH THE ECHO OF SAURIANS.
EZEKIEL IN THE VALLEY OF THE DRY BONES, BREATHING LIFE WHERE THERE WAS ONCE DUST.
AND I WONDER, IS THIS WHAT CREATION WAS LIKE?

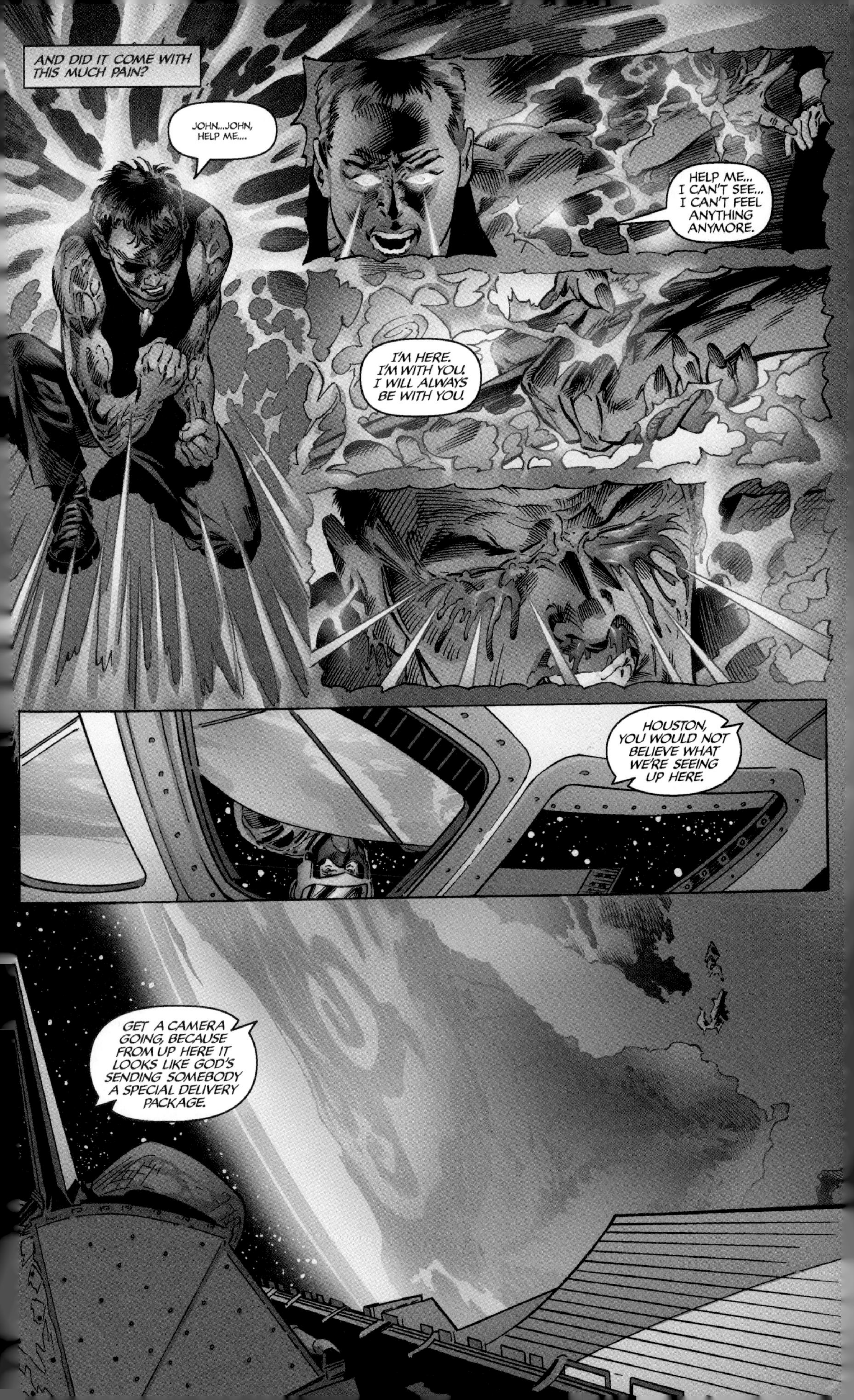
AND DID IT COME WITH THIS MUCH PAIN?
JOHN...JOHN, HELP ME....
HELP ME... I CAN'T SEE... I CAN'T FEEL ANYTHING ANYMORE.
I'M HERE. I'M WITH YOU. I WILL ALWAYS BE WITH YOU.
HOUSTON, YOU WOULD NOT BELIEVE WHAT WE'RE SEEING UP HERE.
GET A CAMERA GOING, BECAUSE FROM UP HERE IT LOOKS LIKE GOD'S SENDING SOMEBODY A SPECIAL DELIVERY PACKAGE.

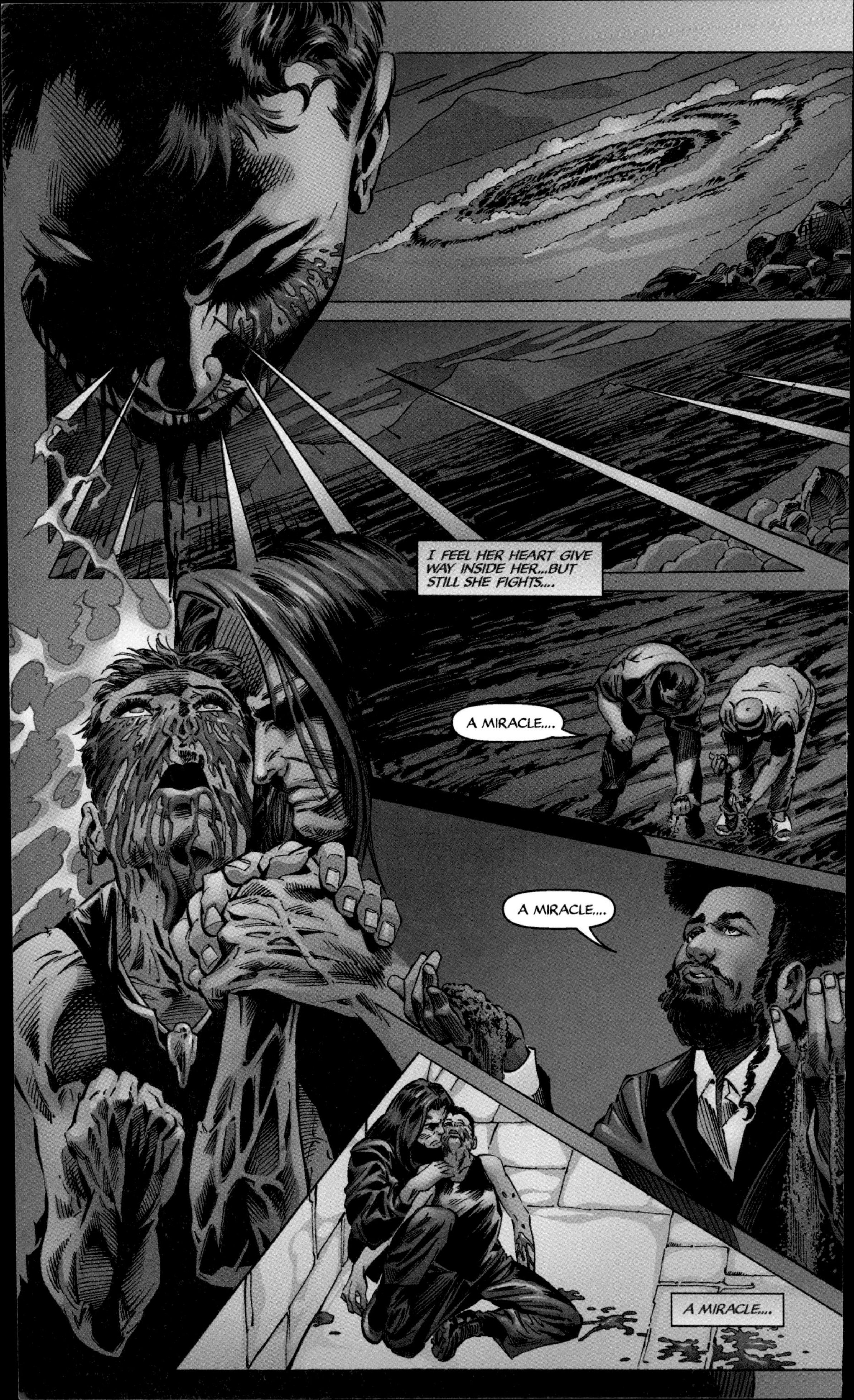
I FEEL HER HEART GIVE WAY INSIDE HER...BUT STILL SHE FIGHTS....
A MIRACLE....
A MIRACLE....
A MIRACLE....

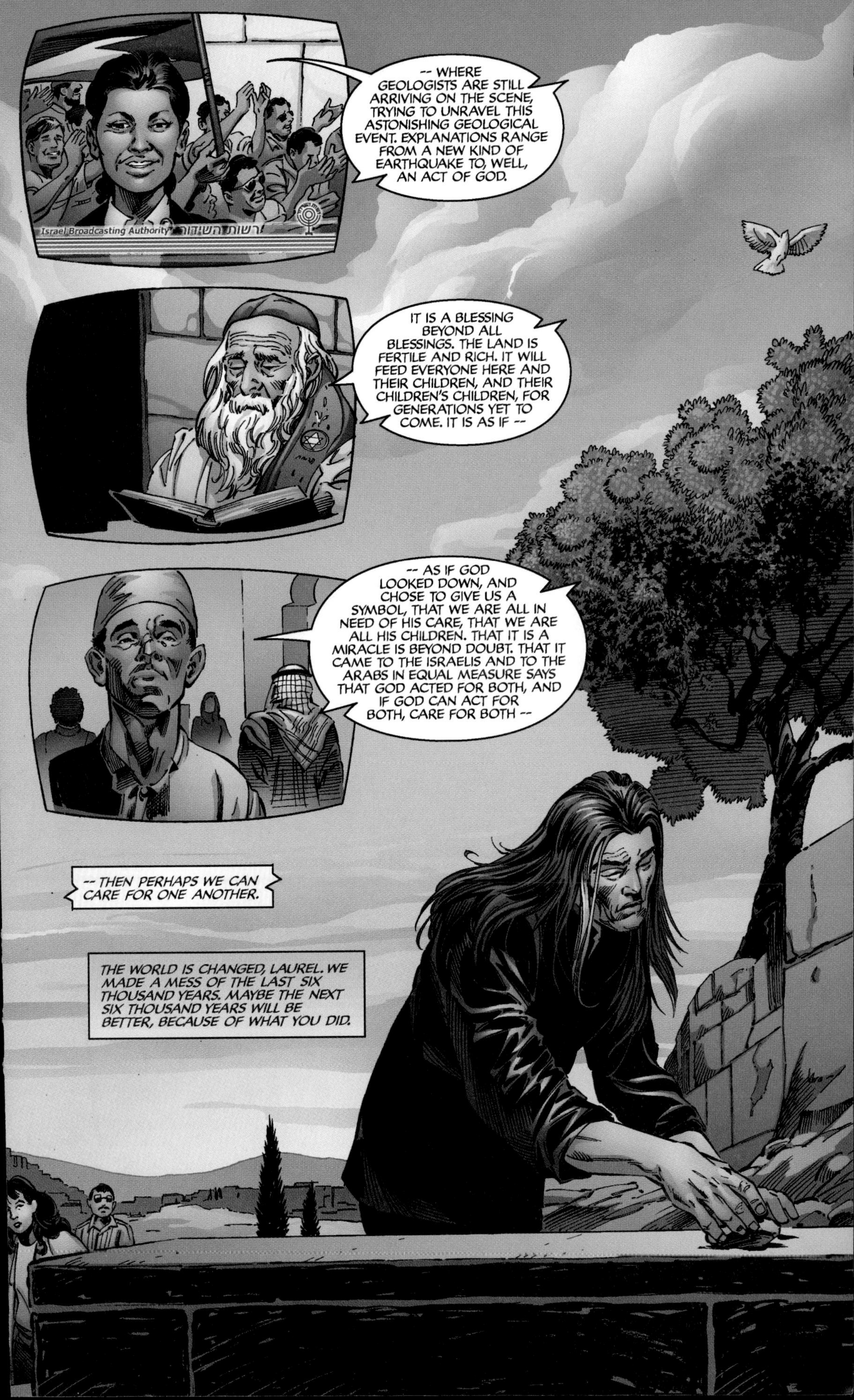
-- WHERE GEOLOGISTS ARE STILL ARRIVING ON THE SCENE, TRYING TO UNRAVEL THIS ASTONISHING GEOLOGICAL EVENT. EXPLANATIONS RANGE FROM A NEW KIND OF EARTHQUAKE TO, WELL, AN ACT OF GOD.
Israel Broadcasting Authority רשות השידור
IT IS A BLESSING BEYOND ALL BLESSINGS. THE LAND IS FERTILE AND RICH. IT WILL FEED EVERYONE HERE AND THEIR CHILDREN, AND THEIR CHILDREN'S CHILDREN, FOR GENERATIONS YET TO COME. IT IS AS IF --
-- AS IF GOD LOOKED DOWN, AND CHOSE TO GIVE US A SYMBOL, THAT WE ARE ALL IN NEED OF HIS CARE, THAT WE ARE ALL HIS CHILDREN. THAT IT IS A MIRACLE IS BEYOND DOUBT. THAT IT CAME TO THE ISRAELIS AND TO THE ARABS IN EQUAL MEASURE SAYS THAT GOD ACTED FOR BOTH, AND IF GOD CAN ACT FOR BOTH, CARE FOR BOTH --
-- THEN PERHAPS WE CAN CARE FOR ONE ANOTHER.
THE WORLD IS CHANGED, LAUREL. WE MADE A MESS OF THE LAST SIX THOUSAND YEARS. MAYBE THE NEXT SIX THOUSAND YEARS WILL BE BETTER, BECAUSE OF WHAT YOU DID.

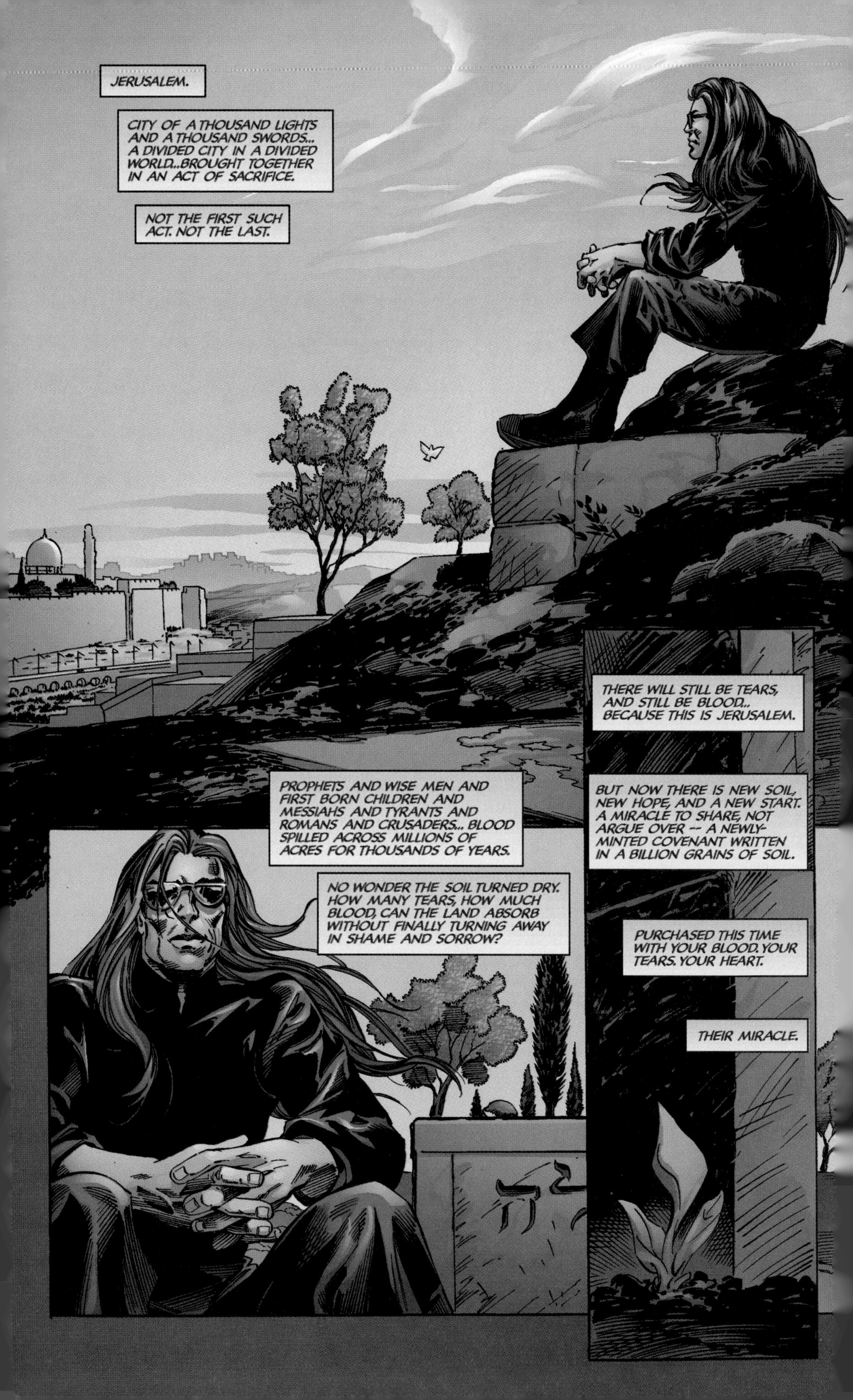
JERUSALEM.
CITY OF A THOUSAND LIGHTS AND A THOUSAND SWORDS... A DIVIDED CITY IN A DIVIDED WORLD...BROUGHT TOGETHER IN AN ACT OF SACRIFICE.
NOT THE FIRST SUCH ACT. NOT THE LAST.
THERE WILL STILL BE TEARS, AND STILL BE BLOOD... BECAUSE THIS IS JERUSALEM.
PROPHETS AND WISE MEN AND FIRST BORN CHILDREN AND MESSIAHS AND TYRANTS AND ROMANS AND CRUSADERS... BLOOD SPILLED ACROSS MILLIONS OF ACRES FOR THOUSANDS OF YEARS.
NO WONDER THE SOIL TURNED DRY. HOW MANY TEARS, HOW MUCH BLOOD, CAN THE LAND ABSORB WITHOUT FINALLY TURNING AWAY IN SHAME AND SORROW?
BUT NOW THERE IS NEW SOIL, NEW HOPE, AND A NEW START. A MIRACLE TO SHARE, NOT ARGUE OVER -- A NEWLY-MINTED COVENANT WRITTEN IN A BILLION GRAINS OF SOIL.
PURCHASED THIS TIME WITH YOUR BLOOD. YOUR TEARS. YOUR HEART.
THEIR MIRACLE.

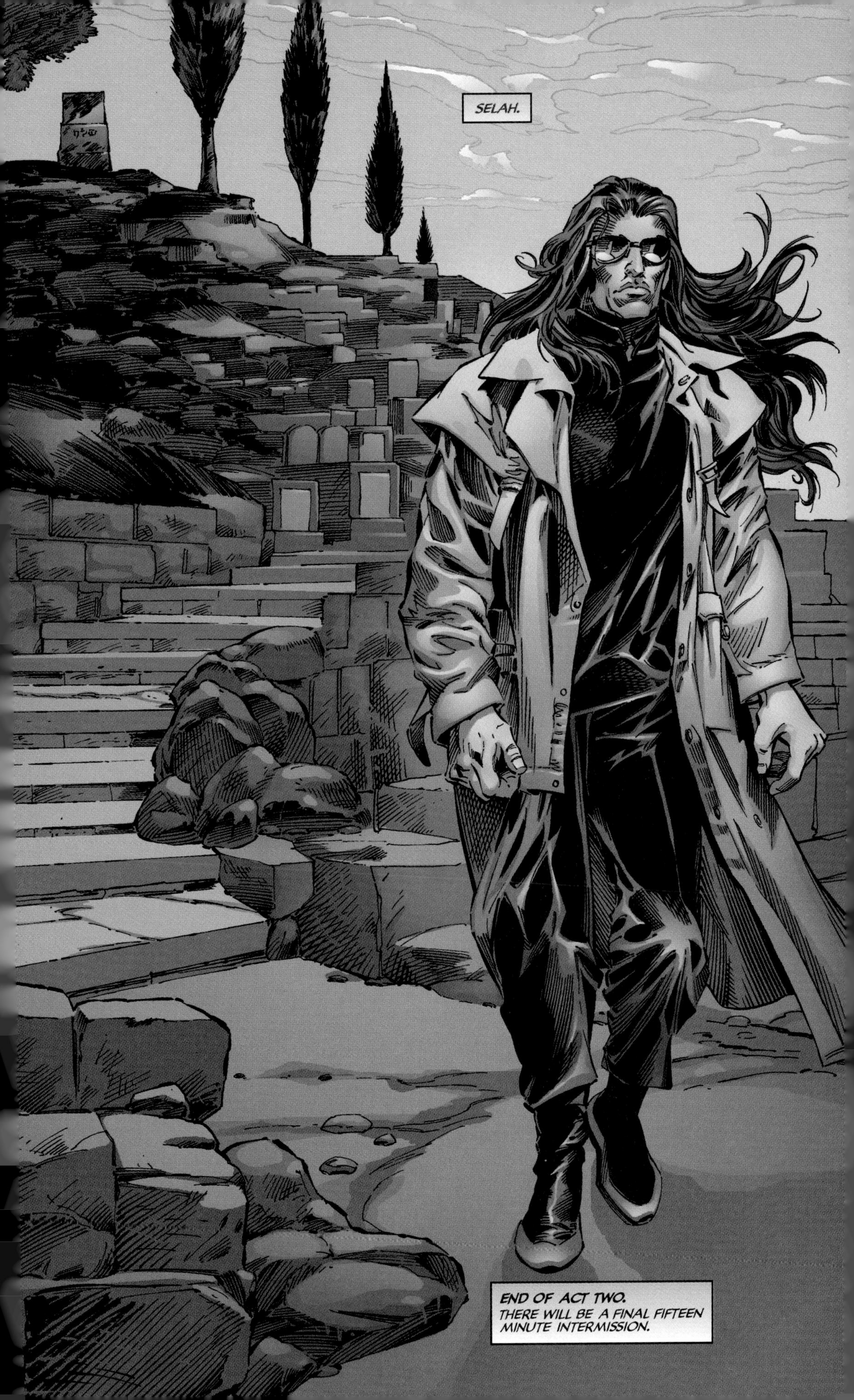
SELAH.
END OF ACT TWO.
THERE WILL BE A FINAL FIFTEEN MINUTE INTERMISSION.

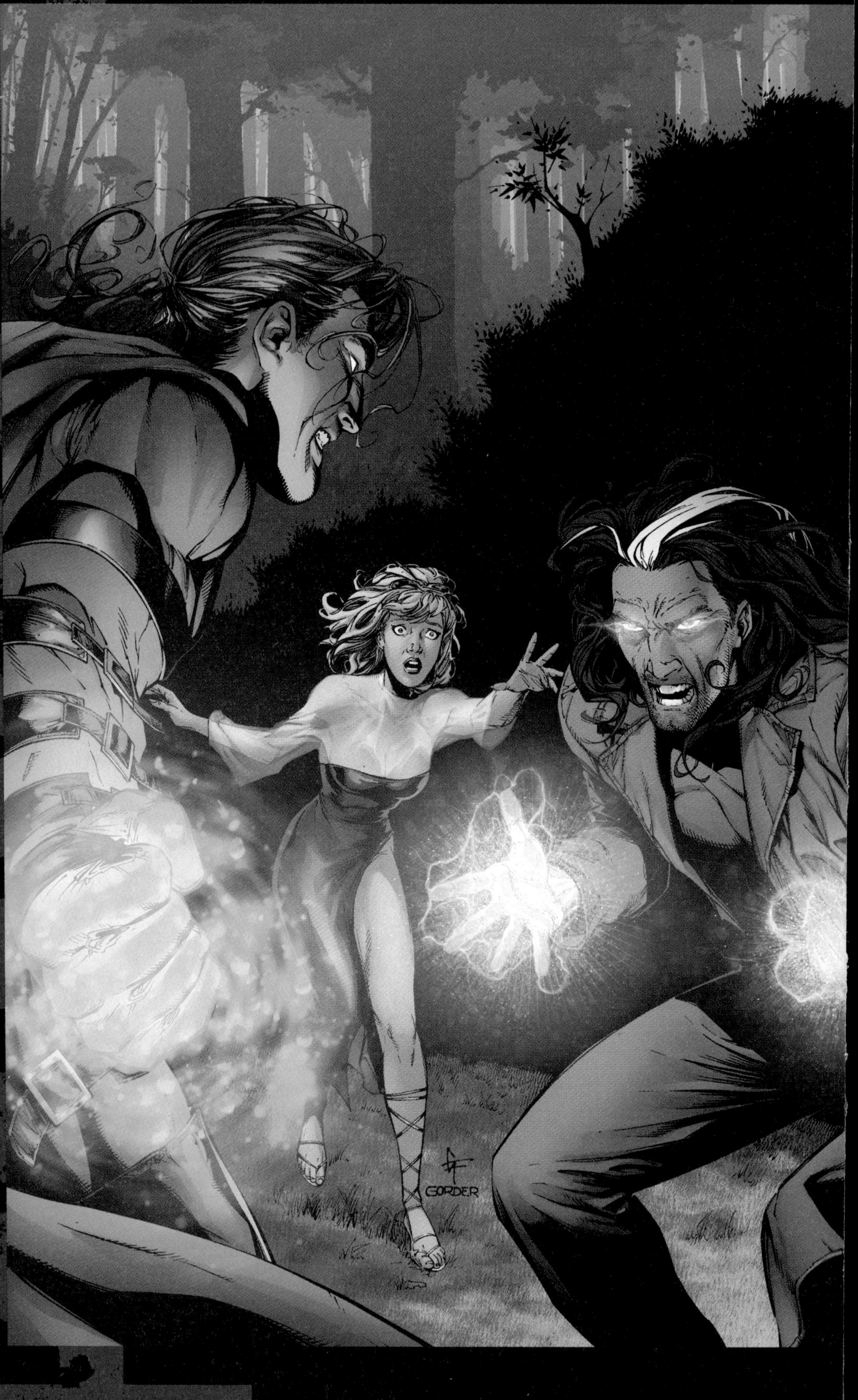
GORDER

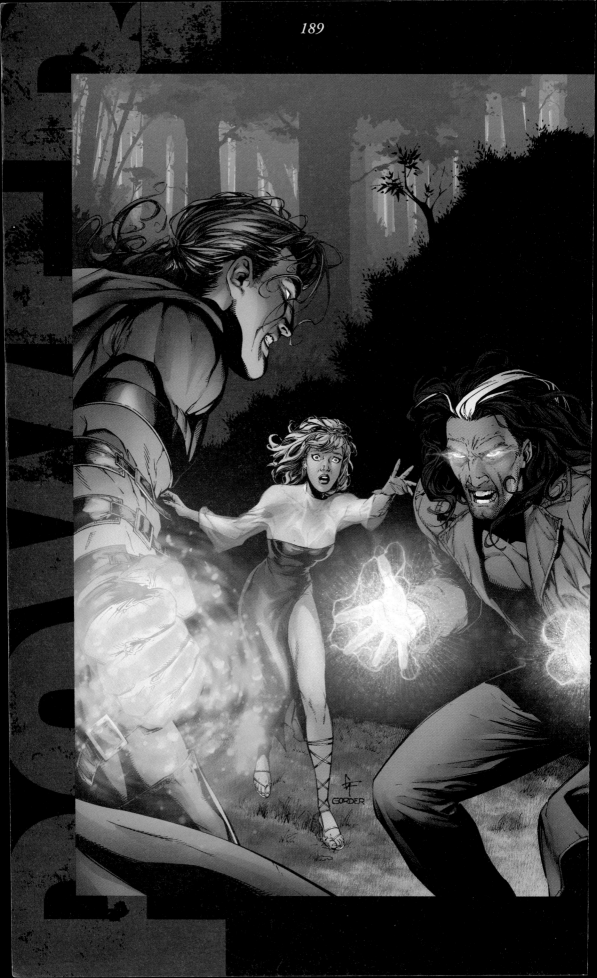